SEAMUS HEANEY
A BIBLIOGRAPHY

SEAMUS HEANEY
A BIBLIOGRAPHY
1959–2003

Rand Brandes
and
Michael J. Durkan

faber and faber

First published in 2008
by Faber and Faber Limited
3 Queen Square London WC1N 3AU

Photoset by RefineCatch Limited, Bungay, Suffolk
Printed and bound in the UK by CPI Mackays, Chatham ME5 8TD

A CIP record for this book
is available from the British Library

ISBN 978–0–571–23439–4

2 4 6 8 10 9 7 5 3 1

for
Beth and Blake

i.m.
Michael J. Durkan

CONTENTS

A GRACE NOTE FOR MICHAEL

What stays with me is the rich braid of his voice
As deeply laid as the North Atlantic cable.
When he said 'Seamus' I could hear a wash
Of ocean over me and his person-to-person call
Coming in on the life-line like *sean-nós*.

Seamus Heaney (1996)

INTRODUCTION

Michael J. Durkan published the first comprehensive bibliographical listing of the works of Seamus Heaney in 1986 in the *Irish Literary Review*: 'Seamus Heaney: A Checklist for a Bibliography'. His work as a bibliographer, however, had begun earlier when he, in collaboration with Ronald Ayling, published *Sean O'Casey: A Bibliography*, University of Washington Press, 1978. Michael continued to work on the Heaney bibliographical materials following his initial 'Checklist', which included a list of scholarly studies and reviews of Heaney's publications. Then in 1992, Michael and I joined together to produce *Seamus Heaney: A Reference Guide* (G. K. Hall, 1996). The *Reference Guide* is an annotated bibliography of over 1,500 works about Seamus Heaney published between 1965 and 1993; it lists and describes books, doctoral dissertations, essays in books, journal articles and reviews, newspaper articles and reviews and interviews. It was therefore sad that Michael died in 1996; he never saw the book nor did he complete his bibliography of the primary works. As a result, in 1997 I assumed responsibility for the completion of the project. I was anxious to carry on the work of such an esteemed scholar and bibliographer and attracted also by the work of the subject, Seamus Heaney, by then a Nobel Laureate in Literature.

I have attempted to remain true to Michael Durkan's original vision of the work. The bibliographical conventions and principles that informed Michael's manuscript also inform this book. As stated in the 'Preface' to the O'Casey bibliography, 'The descriptive method used . . . is intended to provide the information ordinarily needed about twentieth-century books, in a form simple and brief enough to be clearly understood . . . The book's overall structure and internal ordering . . . follow basically . . . what may now be called . . . "the Soho formula" ' (xii). This formula calls for the separation of items into individual sections based upon the type of publication; each section is then organised chronologically.

The Soho formula has been adopted and adapted by many recent literary bibliographies. Michael obviously believed that this formula would produce a 'reader-friendly' bibliography that would be of use to students and scholars of Heaney's writings as well as to librarians and collectors.

We have concentrated on Seamus Heaney's printed work. However, we have included commercial vinyl recordings, cassette tapes and CDs, dedicated to Heaney and readily available on the retail market in section G. Given the vast amount of non-print, non-trade materials accessible today, we anticipate others will document the analog and digital Heaney, the bootleg and the official. Here on the other hand, we have included a representative sample of ephemera in section H. For instance, while Heaney has been generous in his praise of fellow writers, we have not listed every 'blurb' that appears on the works of others. Also, many well-intentioned and enterprising folk have made use of Heaney's poetry, both with and without his consent, and we have only listed the more notable items, such as the Poetry in Motion posters and 'Signatory'. Finally, if one 'Googles' Seamus Heaney the odds are that one will be given over one million possible sites to visit. The 'virtual' Heaney will surely grow exponentially; tangentially, access to much of this material will complement our work. For instance, many of the covers and dust-jackets described here can be seen on the internet. With so much virtual Heaney available, it is crucial that the record of his publications be rooted in the non-virtual world of bibliography.

This bibliography presents a comprehensive view of Seamus Heaney's publications in all of their distinctive permutations and variations. The great scholar of bibliography, G. Thomas Tanselle, argues that there is no definitive format for the modern bibliography, no one-size-fits-all paradigm, and that a bibliography should be constructed in such a way as to truly represent the unique qualities of the subject as well as the objectives of the author. Seamus Heaney's creativity and energy extend far beyond the poetry and prose collected since the 1960s. He has been an advocate for the arts, for art's potential to centre the individual, to connect communities and perhaps even to guide public policy and inform international relations. Consequently, in addition to working with individual artists, educators and local organisations, he has contributed to the wider cultural and political discourse through his involvement with organisations like the Field Day Theatre Company and Amnesty International. Often this involvement takes the form of contributing a poem or prose piece to a publication in support of a specific event or general cause.

With this in mind, it is important to note two sections in the bibliography that are in response to Heaney's complex publishing history: section A is divided into two sub-sections: items listed as 'A' items, 'Books and Pamphlets' and those listed as 'AA' items, 'Broadsides and Cards'. This division allowed us to maintain the prominence of the trade publications conventionally listed in 'A' sections, while acknowledging the unique importance of the privately printed 'AA' items in Heaney's publishing life. In sub-section 'AA' the many Christmas cards, occasional cards, poster poems and those broadsides that were the result of collaboration with a particular artist, publisher or non-profit organisation document the vast range of the poet's publishing interests and outlets. Also, as the many beautifully produced limited editions listed in both sections 'A' and 'AA' demonstrate, the poet's work has been served by many of the finest people in the world of printing and book production. One can feel in these works, the creative give and take between font and leaf, word and image. Finally, as with section D, section AA not only reveals Heaney's interest in the visual and performing arts, it also documents his readiness to help worthy causes and to acknowledge the accomplishments of others.

As with section AA, section D is designed to highlight Heaney's commitment to and participation in a broad range of cultural endeavours. Seamus Heaney is very much a public poet who has added his creative weight to many individual and organisational artistic projects. Section D lists the poet's 'Contributions to Exhibition Catalogues and Programmes'. Many of the items in this section make their first and only appearance here. In addition to the substantial *Personal Selection*, there are several important prose works that appear in these publications only. Cases in point are Heaney's comments on *The Cure at Troy* for a Fringe Theatre production of the play (D36) and his illuminating note on 'Squarings' that appears in a programme for the West Cork Music Festival (D47). In addition, many of the poems that appear here are later collected with significant revisions, such as 'Shifting

Angles' which appeared first in an exhibition catalogue for Carolyn Mulholland (D37) and was subsequently collected as 'The Poet's Chair' dedicated to Mulholland. Section D records the poet in dialogue with the visual and performing arts as well as with cultural and political organisations like the Field Day Theatre Company, the Linen Hall Library, and even the Seamus Heaney Centre for Poetry at Queen's University Belfast.

In section B and section C we have documented Heaney's contributions to books and periodicals respectively. In order to capture the full range of the poet's publishing history in these sections, we have documented his contributions to books and periodicals in his three main audience areas: Ireland, England and the United States. Heaney's publishing practices are worth commenting on here. He rarely publishes the same poem twice in the same country. When he does so, the poem usually accompanies an unpublished poem or poems or is a different version. However, the poet does see the three countries as possessing distinct audiences, and thus often publishes the same poem in each country. Sections B and C reflect this practice. We have also included a small sampling of publications in English from a few other countries mainly to illustrate Heaney's reach and influence.

In section E, 'Translations of the Works of Seamus Heaney', we have documented only book-length translations of Heaney's work. Consequently, we do not include translations that appear as contributions to periodicals or anthologies. It is obvious, nevertheless, that Seamus Heaney has found a substantial audience in non-English-speaking countries. Section F records the many interviews with Seamus Heaney whether they were published in periodical or book form. These interviews constitute an ongoing and parallel discourse with Heaney's other publications. They function as a meta-critical layer over the poems in much the same way as do many of Heaney's autobiographical and self-reflexive essays. The interviews give us access and insights into the inner working of the poet's vision and external forces shaping it.

It is hoped that this bibliography will help to foster a new generation of Heaney scholars, and enable teachers to engage their students more fully as they chart newly discovered territories in Heaney's work. In addition, we hope that librarians and collectors, upon whom scholars, teachers, and students alike depend, will find this book useful in their own pursuits. There will certainly be future editions of this bibliography; so, we encourage those interested to identify missing items, provide additional information, or, heaven forbid, point out errors. Even though Michael Durkan's original work underpins this book, I accept full responsibility for its contents.

GUIDELINES

SECTION A: BOOKS AND PAMPHLETS; AA: BROADSIDES AND CARDS

Section A documents the first collected appearance in English of a poem or prose piece as well as the first separate appearance of a poem, even if it has been previously collected, as in 'Whinlands' or 'Digging'. Only Irish, British and American first editions have been included. Numbers of copies printed for any first or limited edition are listed only if verified by the publisher. Seamus Heaney's two main publishers, Faber and Faber and Farrar, Straus, and Giroux have provided those figures which they can verify. We have avoided citing number of copies printed based upon speculation. Only significant variations between editions are described in detail and are assigned a separate designation as in 'a. trade edition' and 'b. limited edition'. In the descriptions, unless noted, the details are as follows: all edges are trimmed; all endpapers are white; measurements are rounded to the nearest 0.5 cm. In the descriptions of the title-page only when the font varies within a single line is the font size noted, as in [small caps]. The titles of poems and prose pieces are as they appear in the table of contents.

Pagination

For wholly unpaginated books, pamphlets, and cards we used Arabic numbers in square brackets (e.g. [1], [2], [3], etc.). For items where some pages are numbered but the preliminary pages are not, we use lower-case Roman numerals in square brackets (e.g. [i], [ii], [iii], etc.). For extra or tipped-in pages before the preliminaries, we use lower-case letters (e.g. [a], [b], [c], etc.). All other pagination is as printed.

SECTION B: CONTRIBUTIONS TO BOOKS

Guidelines as above in section A with the following exceptions. Section B includes the first appearance of a poem or prose piece between covers prior to collection. There are a few exceptions to this rule mentioned above. Publication may be simultaneous in Ireland, England and the United States. Only when the poem/essay is revised or otherwise differs from other appearances is it noted in the description of the book. Previously collected items are not listed. The book's total number of pages includes everything between the endpapers.

SECTION C: CONTRIBUTIONS TO PERIODICALS

Section C includes a first appearance before collection in Ireland, England and the United States. Multiple publications of the same poem within the same country are listed when revisions occur. In rare instances, some works appear in periodicals after collection. These are noted. 'Collected with revisions' indicates any change between versions from line breaks, to punctuation, to individual words, to entire stanzas. More significant variations are noted, such as the work listed appears later as a demonstrably different or retitled poem/essay. It is not the scale of the revision that affects its importance, but its relationship to the entire poem. Re-printed poems are listed if they appear with new information. The designation of 'Essay' to an item refers to any prose piece, whether a few sentences, paragraphs or pages. Given the current access to information and materials, only those periodicals that do not have a specific publication date, academic term or season are listed at the end of the appropriate year. Poems are only cross-referenced within the section with versions that have been revised prior to collection.

SECTION D: CONTRIBUTIONS TO EXHIBITION CATALOGUES AND PROGRAMMES

The logic of section D has been discussed above. Items listed in this section often document specific events. However, their listing here does not imply that Seamus Heaney took part in the event. Only items that have been collected with revisions have been noted.

SECTION E: TRANSLATIONS OF THE WORKS OF SEAMUS HEANEY

Information provided on the publications listed here is taken from the book's title-page. Only book-length translations of Heaney's publications are included. Those items not seen have been verified by WorldCat.

SECTION F: INTERVIEWS WITH SEAMUS HEANEY

This section includes interviews published in periodicals and books as 'Interviews' and substantial interview material that appears as part of an article or chapter.

SECTION G: COMMERCIAL AUDIO RECORDINGS

The recordings listed here are those that are or have been available on the retail market.

SECTION H: EPHEMERA

Listed here is a sampling of miscellaneous items by Seamus Heaney including 'blurbs'.

ACKNOWLEDGEMENTS

I would not have accepted the challenge of completing Michael Durkan's work if it had not been for the encouragement and faith of the poet himself. Seamus Heaney's admiration of Michael's contributions and their long friendship were always a sustaining element during the ongoing project. While writers in general, and perhaps poets in particular, are typically wary of bibliographers, Seamus Heaney has cooperated with this project with the same largesse that has guided all of his life and work. The absence of certain libraries from the listings in these 'Acknowledgements' is the direct result of the access given to me by the poet to his personal library and records. While conducting this work since the 1990s, I have also enjoyed the hospitality and guidance of Seamus Heaney's wife Marie. Her presence was always a steadying force when things got crazy. The Heaneys graciously opened their home and allowed me to share their family space. I thank their children, now adults, Michael, Christopher and Catherine Ann for the many times they went out of their way to make me feel welcome and for their friendship and good humour.

All bibliographies require two sets of eyes to inspect and ratify each other's observations. The inspecting eyes for this bibliography are those of Jim O'Halloran of Wilton, CT. Jim is an independent scholar of Irish Literature, a collector of Seamus Heaney's work and a friend of Michael Durkan. I have spent time with Jim's collection in Wilton, and he has travelled to Hickory to work with me. His attention to detail, understanding of the publishing trade and bibliographical scholarship have been invaluable resources. I am not exaggerating when I say that I could not have completed this bibliography without Jim's expertise and commitment to the work. He is a great friend and a deft scholar.

Two sets of eyes may be required for a project like this, but I was lucky to acquire a third set. Patrick Brennan, a native of Heaney's home parish in Bellaghy, Northern Ireland, joined us shortly before he began his second career as the curator at Bellaghy Bawn. Like Jim O'Halloran, he has been a collector as well as a student/scholar of Heaney's work. In particular, Pat helped us track down and verify a covey of fugitive items that had eluded us heretofore. He also has an amazing eye for detail. Jim, Pat and I worked together in Ireland for a brief time in the summer of 2003 as we made a final push to complete the project – a moment I shall never forget and for which I shall always be grateful. Peter Fallon of the Gallery Press acted as shepherd on the earlier drafts of the bibliography. As a publisher and an editor, his instinct and eye contributed greatly to the tightness and accuracy of the entries and, as a well-known poet himself, his appreciation and knowledge of Seamus Heaney's work proved invaluable. Finally, on the research front and always ready in the wings was Philip Murray of Sligo. Philip too opened his home and Heaney collection to this project. He was our last-chance go-to man. Philip has worn out his fax machine while contributing to this project over the years.

Since I was conducting much of the research 3,000 miles from home, I have often been the grateful recipient of wonderful assistance and hospitality. Joan and Joe McBreen provided friendship, guidance and resources that kept me going at all stages. Declan and Beth Kiberd helped and hosted me at their home and at UCD. Also in Ireland Colm Larkin and Orlagh O'Farrell provided sustenance and sagacious advice. Others in Ireland and England who provided significant assistance along the way are: Des Lally; Michael A. Kinsella; Andrew Carpenter; Joe McCann; John and Hilary Dunne; Terry Gifford. Marco Sonzogni, along with many members of ITIA, provided invaluable help with the translations in section E.

In the United States, my good friend and mentor, Dr Ronald Schuchard of Emory University in Atlanta, Georgia, was an invaluable guide. In addition, Steve Enniss of Emory's Special Collections provided much help as did Charles McNamara of UNC Chapel Hill, home of Henry Pearson's comprehensive collection of Heaney material. Many scholars have kindly alerted me to new Heaney publications during the course of this project, and I appreciate their contributions greatly. Of those scholars, Dr Jonathan Allison of the University of Kentucky has been a notably steadfast supplier. In

Hickory, I want to thank the Honorable Forest Ferrell for his judicious advice and my resident Belfast scholar, Adrian Rice.

Several of my students have contributed to this book: Kate Cartwright; Amanda Sperry; Amy Greensfelder; Thackston Lundy; and my hip hoppin, rappin son and Marshall Scholar, Blake Brandes.

My home institution, Lenoir–Rhyne College, in Hickory, NC, has provided generous support for this project. The Fulbright Commission made much of my research in Ireland possible. I also want to thank the English Department at University College Dublin for supporting my 2003 Fulbright residency.

I have been honoured by Michael Durkan's family's faith in this project. They have been supportive from beginning to end.

At the heart of this book is my wife, Beth. Her good spirit and fortitude are in every letter and the spaces in between.

PERIODICALS CITED IN SECTION C

Age (Melbourne, Australia)
Agenda (London, England)
Agni (Boston University, Boston, MA)
Airthrey Journal (Stirling, Scotland)
Almanac (University of Pennsylvania, Philadelphia, PA)
Alpha (Trinity College, Oxford, England)
American Irish Foundation Report (New York, NY)
American Poet: bi-annual journal of the Academy of American Poets (New York, NY)
American Poetry Review (Philadelphia, PA)
American Scholar: the quarterly magazine of Phi Beta Kappa (Washington, DC)
An Múinteoir: Irish teachers journal (Dublin, Ireland)
Antaeus (Hopewell, NJ)
Aquarius (Benburb, Co. Tyrone, Northern Ireland)
Aquarius (London, England)
Ardboe (Ardboe, Northern Ireland)
Arion: a journal of humanities and the classics (Boston University, Boston, MA)
Armadillo 3 (New York, NY)
Around the Globe (London, England)
Art Matters (Dublin, Ireland)
Arts in Ireland (Dublin, Ireland)
Atlanta Review (Atlanta, GA)
Atlantic Monthly (Boston, MA)
Atlantis (Dublin, Ireland)
Ballyscullion Parish Bulletin (Bellaghy, Co. Derry, Northern Ireland)
Bananas (London, England)
Belfast Review (Belfast, Northern Ireland)
Belfast Telegraph (Belfast, Northern Ireland)
Big Issues (Dublin, Ireland)

Blue Moon News (University of Arizona, Tucson, AZ)
Books Ireland (Dublin, Ireland)
Boston Globe (Boston, MA)
Boston Review (Boston, MA)
Boston Sunday Globe (Boston, MA)
Brangle: new writing from the School of English (Queen's University Belfast, Northern Ireland)
Broadsheet (Hayden Murphy, ed., Dublin, Ireland)
Broadsheet 2 (Richard Ryan, ed., University College Dublin, Ireland)
Bullán (St John's College, Oxford, England)
Cambridge Review (Cambridge, England)
Capella 4 (Dublin, Ireland)
Cara: the inflight magazine of Aer Lingus (Dublin, Ireland)
Céide (Co. Mayo, Ireland)
Chapel-Hill Herald (Chapel-Hill, NC)
Chapman (Edinburgh, Scotland)
College Green (Trinity College Dublin, Ireland)
Cork Literary Review (Cork, Ireland)
Cork Review (Cork, Ireland)
Crab Orchard Review (Southern Illinois University, Carbondale, IL)
The Crane Bag (Dublin, Ireland)
The Criterion (University College Galway, Ireland)
Critical Inquiry (University of Chicago, Chicago, IL)
Critical Quarterly (Manchester, England)
Cumberland Poetry Review (Nashville, TN)
CutBank 42 (University of Montana, Missoula, MT)
Cyphers (Dublin, Ireland)
DAM: Poetry International documents (Rotterdam, The Netherlands)
Derry Journal (Derry, Northern Ireland)
Digraphe (Paris, France)
Drumragh Parish Magazine (Drumragh, Ireland)
Dublin Magazine (Dublin, Ireland)
Dublin Review (Dublin, Ireland)
Dubliner (Dublin, Ireland)
Dutch Quarterly Review of Anglo-American Letters (Amsterdam, The Netherlands)
Edge (Tokyo, Japan)

Education Times (Dublin, Ireland)
Education Today (University of London, College of Teachers, England)
Éire–Ireland (Irish American Cultural Institute, Morristown, NJ)
Encounter (London, England)
End: journal of European Nuclear Disarmament (London, England)
England Review (n. p.)
English (The English Association, London, England)
Envoi (Cheltenham, Newport, Stoke-on-Trent, England)
Envoy (Academy of American Poets, New York, NY)
Epoch (Cornell University, Ithaca, NY)
ERATO (Harvard University, Cambridge, MA)
Eureka Street (Richmond, VIC, Australia)
European English Messenger (Coimbra, Portugal)
European Poetry Festival Special Issue: A Poet's Europe (Louvain, Belgium)
Evening Press (Dublin, Ireland)
Everyman (Benburb, Co. Tyrone, Northern Ireland)
Exile (Toronto, Ontario, Canada)
Fiction Magazine (London, England)
Field (Oberlin College, Oberlin, OH)
Forbes (New York, NY)
Force 10 (Sligo, Ireland)
Fordham (Fordham University, New York, NY)
Fortnight (Belfast, Northern Ireland)
Four Quarters (La Salle University, Philadelphia, PA)
Furrow (St Patrick's College, Maynooth, Ireland)
Fuse (St John's College, Oxford, England)
Garm Lu: a Canadian Celtic arts journal (Toronto, Ontario, Canada)
Gazette of the Grolier Club (New York, NY)
Georgetown Review (Washington, DC)
Georgia Review (University of Georgia, Athens, GA)
Gorgon (Queen's University Belfast, Northern Ireland)
Gown (Queen's University Belfast, Northern Ireland)
Graham House Review (Colgate College, Hamilton, NY)
Graph: Irish cultural review (Dublin, Ireland)
Graph (University of Cork, Ireland)

Grilled Flowers (University of Arizona, Tucson, AZ)
Guardian (London, England)
Guardian Review (London, England)
Harp: International Association for the Study of Irish Literatures (Tokyo, Japan)
Harper's Magazine (New York, NY)
Harvard Advocate (Harvard University, Cambridge, MA)
Harvard Magazine (Harvard University, Cambridge, MA)
Harvard Review (Harvard University, Cambridge, MA)
Hermathena (Trinity College Dublin, Ireland)
Hibernia (Dublin, Ireland)
Honest Ulsterman (Belfast, Northern Ireland)
Horizon (Montgomery, LA)
Hudson Review (New York, NY)
Illuminations (University of South Carolina, Columbia, SC)
In Other Words: journal of the Translators Association (London, England)
In Touch 2 (n. p.)
Independent (Dublin, Ireland)
Independent (London, England)
Independent on Sunday (London, England)
Index on Censorship (London, England)
Inscape '95 (Pasadena City College, Pasadena, CA)
Inside Tribune (Dublin, Ireland)
Interest (Belfast, Northern Ireland)
Ireland at Home and Abroad (n. p.)
Ireland Fund (New York, NY)
Ireland of the Welcomes (Dublin, Ireland)
Irish Digest (Dublin, Ireland)
Irish Independent (Dublin, Ireland)
Irish Literary Supplement (Boston College, Boston, MA)
Irish News (Belfast, Northern Ireland)
Irish Pages (Belfast, Northern Ireland)
Irish Press (Dublin, Ireland)
Irish Review (Dublin, Ireland)
Irish Times (Dublin, Ireland)
Irish University Review (University College Dublin, Ireland)
Island (Sandy Bay, Tasmania, Australia)
James Joyce Quarterly (University of Tulsa, Tulsa, OK)

John Clare Society Journal (Nottingham Trent University, Nottingham, England)
Kairos (Co. Kildare, Ireland)
Kenyon Review (Kenyon College, Gambier, OH)
Kestrel (Fairmont State College, Fairmont, WV)
Kilkenny Magazine (Kilkenny, Ireland)
Lapis (New York Open Center, New York, NY)
Lift Magazine (Somerville, MA)
Link-up (Dublin, Ireland)
Listener (London, England)
Literary and Historical Magazine (University College Dublin, Ireland)
Literary Review (London, England)
Literary Review (Madison, NJ)
Little Word Machine (Birmingham, England)
London Magazine (London, England)
London Review of Books (London, England)
Los Angeles Times (Los Angeles, CA)
lower stumpf lake review (St John's University/Benedict College, Collegeville, MN)
Lynx (Amherst, MA)
Magill (Dublin, Ireland)
Malahat Review (University of Victoria, Victoria, BC, Canada)
Manchester Guardian (Manchester, England)
Mars (London, England)
Massachusetts Review (Amherst, MA)
Merton Journal (Birmingham, England)
Metre (Trinity College Dublin, Ireland)
Mica (Aberdeen University, Aberdeen, Scotland)
Michigan Quarterly Review (University of Michigan, Ann Arbor, MI)
Modern Painter (London, England)
Modern Poetry in Translation (Oxford, England)
Mondogreco (Boston, MA)
Múinteoir Náisúnta: journal of the Irish National Teachers Organization (Dublin, Ireland)
New Blackfriars (Oxford, England)
New Departures (Bisley, England)
New England Review (Middlebury College, Hanover, NH)

New England Review and Bread Loaf Quarterly (Middlebury College, Hanover, NH)
New Ireland (Queen's University Belfast, Northern Ireland)
New Nation (Dublin, Ireland)
New Poetry: Critical Quarterly Poetry Supplement (London, England)
New Republic (Washington, DC)
New Review (London, England)
New Statesman (London, England)
New Welsh Review (University of Wales, Cardiff, Wales)
New York Review of Books (New York, NY)
New York Times (New York, NY)
New Yorker (New York, NY)
Newman (Cardinal Newman Society, Queen's University Belfast, Northern Ireland)
News Letter (Belfast, Northern Ireland)
Northern Review (Belfast, Northern Ireland)
Notre Dame Review (University of Notre Dame, Southbend, IN)
Numbers (Cambridge, England)
O *Write* (Birmingham, England)
Oar 8 (Orkney, Scotland)
Observer (London, England)
Observer Review (London, England)
Occident (University of California, Berkeley, CA)
Orbis (Nuneaton, Warwickshire, England)
Outposts (Walton on Thames, Surrey, England)
Owl (Oxford, England)
Oxford Magazine (Oxford University, England)
Oxford Poetry (Oxford University, England)
Oxford Today (Oxford University, England)
Oxford University Gazette (Oxford University, England)
Pages: postgraduate research in progress (University College Dublin, Ireland)
Paris Review (Paris, France)
Paris/Atlantic (Paris, France)
Parnassus (New York, NY)
Partisan Review (New York, NY)
Pequod (San Francisco, CA)
Persephone (Harvard University, Cambridge, MA)

Phoenix (Belfast, Northern Ireland)
Phoenix (Manchester, England)
Planet: the Welsh Internationalist (Dyfed, Wales)
Ploughshares (Cambridge, MA)
PN Review (Manchester, England)
Poetry (Chicago, IL)
Poetry and Audience (Leeds, England)
Poetry Australia (Five Dock, NSW, Australia)
Poetry Book Society Bulletin (London, England)
Poetry Ireland (Dublin, Ireland)
Poetry Ireland Review (Dublin, Ireland)
Poetry Kanto (Kanto Gakuin University, Yokohama, Japan)
Poetry Pilot: the Academy of American Poets (New York, NY)
Poetry Review (London, England)
Poetry Supplement (London, England)
Poetry Wales (Swansea, Wales)
Poet's House Member's Magazine (Donegal, Ireland)
Portal: published monthly for the period June–October 2000 by the Irish Pavillion at Expo2000 (Hanover, Germany)
Princeton Library Chronicle (Princeton University, Princeton, NJ)
Printer's Devil (Hove, England)
Prometheus (Harvard University, Cambridge, MA)
Prospice 5 (Isle of Skye, Scotland)
Q (Queen's University Belfast, Northern Ireland)
Quarryman (University College Cork, Ireland)
Quarto (London, England)
Quarto (University of Colraine, Northern Ireland)
Quest (Pasadena, CA)
Reader (Liverpool, England)
Recorder: the American Irish Historical Society (New York, NY)
Reflections: journal of the Society of Writers, UN Recreation Council (New York, NY)
Religious Life Review (Dublin, Ireland)
Review (London, England)
RIAI Bulletin: Royal Institute of the Architects of Ireland (Dublin, Ireland)
River City (University of Memphis, Memphis, TN)
Roscrea Review (Cistercian College, Roscrea, Union, Ireland)
Rosebud (Cambridge, MA)

RTE Guide (Dublin, Ireland)
Runway: the staff magazine of Aer Rianta–Irish Airports (Dublin, Ireland)
Salmagundi (Skidmore College, Saratoga, NY)
Scotland on Sunday (Edinburgh, Scotland)
Scotsman (Edinburgh, Scotland)
Seneca Review (Hobart and Williams Colleges, Geneva, NY)
Sequoia (Stanford University, Stanford, CA)
Sewanee Review (University of the South, Sewanee, TN)
Shenandoah (Washington and Lee University, Lexington, VA)
Shop (Skeagh, Schull, Co. Cork, Ireland)
Slate on Paper (Redmond, WA)
Southern Review (Louisiana State University, Baton Rouge, LA)
Spectator (London, England)
Spirituality (Dublin, Ireland)
Square Times (Belfast, Northern Ireland)
St Stephen's (University College Dublin, Ireland)
Stand (Newcastle upon Tyne, England)
Stet (Belfast, Northern Ireland)
Stone Ferry Review (Hull, England)
Straight Lines (Birmingham, England)
Strawberry Fare (St Mary's College, Strawberry Hill, London, England)
Studies in Medievalism (Cambridge, England/Rochester, NY)
Studies in the Literary Imagination (Georgia State University, Atlanta, GA)
Sunday Business Post (Dublin, Ireland)
Sunday Independent (Dublin, Ireland)
Sunday Telegraph (London, England)
Sunday Times (London, England)
Sunday Tribune (Dublin, Ireland)
Sunday Tribune Magazine (Dublin, Ireland)
Sunday Tribune Review (Dublin, Ireland)
Tabla (Aylesbury, England)
Tandem (Worcester, England)
Thames Poetry (Harrow, Middlesex, England)
Thinker Review (Louisville, KY)
Three (n. p.)
Threepenny Review (Berkeley, CA)

Threshold (Belfast, Northern Ireland)
Thumbscrew (Oxford, England)
Tikkun (Oakland, CA)
Times (London, England)
Times Educational Supplement (London, England)
Times Literary Supplement (London, England)
Tomorrow (Dublin, Ireland)
Tracks (Dublin, Ireland)
Translation (Columbia University, New York, NY)
Translation Ireland (Dublin, Ireland)
Trench (Belfast, Northern Ireland)
Ulster Local Studies (Downpatrick, Co. Down, Northern Ireland)
University of Toronto Review (Toronto, Canada)
University Review (National University of Ireland, Cork, Ireland)
University Review (National University of Ireland, Dublin, Ireland)
Use of English (London, England)
Verse (Oxford University, Oxford, England)
Verso (Oxford, England)
VIA (University of California, Berkley)
Vogue (London, England)
Washington Post (Washington, DC)
Weekend Telegraph (London, England)
Worcester Review (Worcester, MA)
Word & Image, Poems on Pictures (London, England)
Words (Belfast, Northern Ireland)
Wordsworth Circle (New York University, New York, NY)
Working Papers in Irish Studies (Northeastern University, Boston, MA)
Workshop 11 (London, England)
Y (Derwent College, University of York, England)
Yale Review (Yale University, New Haven, CT)

A

BOOKS AND PAMPHLETS

a. *first edition, first issue*

Eleven poems | by | Seamus | Heaney | [9-point sun symbol in purple] | FESTIVAL PUBLICATIONS | QUEEN'S UNIVERSITY OF BELFAST
20.5 × 13 cm.

[1], cover, as above, serves as title-page; [2], blank; [3]–[16], text; [17], biographical note, acknowledgments; [18]–[19], blank; [20], back cover with publisher's advertisement, price and publisher's name and address.

Stapled pamphlet, printed on cream laid paper watermarked: 'POLTON | PATENT LEDGER | PAPER'; front cover as above; the back cover states: 'This pamphlet is one in a series to be published | monthly and to include | Michael Longley | Seamus Heaney | Derek Mahon | Arthur Terry | Joan Watton | Philip Hobsbaum | Stewart Parker | James Simmons | Seamus Deane', followed by the price and publisher's name and address.

Published November 1965 at 'Two shillings and sixpence each; subscription for series one pound (including postage)'.

Contents: Personal Helicon—Mid-Term Break—Follower—The Diviner—Peter Street at Bankside—Waterfall—Docker—For the Commander of 'The Eliza'—Lovers on Aran—Scaffolding—Death of a Naturalist.

Notes: 1. A misprint occurs in the fifth line of 'Docker': the word 'fist' is printed 'first'. The misprint persists in A1b and A1c.
2. *Eleven Poems* is Seamus Heaney's first separately published work. Four of the poems – 'Follower', 'The Diviner', 'Peter Street at Bankside' and 'For the Commander of "The Eliza" ' – had not been previously published. With the exception of 'Peter Street at Bankside' all the poems were collected in *Death of a Naturalist* A2.

b. *first edition, second issue*

Eleven poems | by | Seamus | Heaney | [10-point sun symbol in blackish purple] | FESTIVAL PUBLICATIONS | QUEEN'S UNIVERSITY OF BELFAST
20 × 12.5 cm.

Pagination as in A1a.

Stapled pamphlet, printed on white wove paper; front cover, which serves as the title-page, has a 10-point sun symbol, redrawn and slightly larger than that in A1a, printed in blackish purple; back cover as in A1a.

Published 1966 at 'Two shillings and sixpence each; subscription for the series one pound (including postage)'.

Contents: As in A1a.

Note: While it is certain that the second issue of *Eleven Poems* was published in 1966 the exact date is unknown.

c. *first edition, third issue*

ELEVEN POEMS | by | SEAMUS HEANEY | [design of herald with drum and trumpet] | Festival Publications | Queen's University Belfast
21 × 14.5 cm.

Pagination as in A1a. The publisher's advertisement on the back cover has been expanded to include the availability of reprints and the 6 titles of a new series of poetry pamphlets.

Stapled pamphlet in green card covers; text printed on heavy grey laid paper watermarked: '[image of a crown] | Glastonbury' (see note 2 below); the front cover, which serves as the title-page, carries the design of a herald with drum and trumpet; the back cover announces: 'Our first series of poetry pamphlets are still | available containg [sic] the works of the following | poets. | (Reprints – 3s. od.) each. | Michael Longley | Seamus Heaney | Derek Mahon | Philip Hobsbaum |

(Original editions – 2s. 6d. each) | Arthur Terry | Joan Newmann | Stewart Parker | James Simmons | Seamus Dean | Our second series of 6 poetry pamphlets is now | available containing the work of the following | poets. | Laurence Lerner | John Montague | Norman Buller | John Hewitt | Arthur Terry | Norman Dugdale | (3s. od. each) | Festival Publications | 40 Fitzwilliam Street | BELFAST. 9. | BOTANIC HOUSE PRINTERS LTD, | 48 BOTANIC AVE., | BELFAST 7 | PHONE BELFAST 21193.

Published 1966/1967 at 3s. od.; printed by Botanic House Printers (see note 2 below).

Contents: As in A1a.

Notes: 1. Unlike the first and second issues, which carry on their covers the sun-symbol device used as the logo of the 1965 Belfast Festival, the third issue of *Eleven Poems* bears the herald with drum and trumpet device of the 1966 Festival. The pamphlet was published in late 1966 or early 1967.
2. The following variations have been noted in copies of the third issue: the dimensions of the pamphlet vary considerably; the sequence of poems varies; a printer may or may not be listed on the back cover; the paper on which the text is printed may be laid paper (with a watermark) or wove paper; we have even seen copies of *Eleven Poems* bound in the covers of Derek Mahon's *Twelve Poems*. No priority has been determined for any of these states.
3. On the back cover, the poet listed as Joan Watton in A1a and A1b is listed as Joan Newmann and Seamus Deane's surname is misspelled 'Dean'.

A2 DEATH OF A NATURALIST 1966

a. *first edition in boards*

[title in outline letters] DEATH | OF A | NATURALIST | *by Seamus Heaney* | FABER AND FABER LTD | 24 Russell Square London
21.5 × 14 cm.

[1]–[2], blank; [3], half-title: DEATH OF A NATURALIST; [4], blank; [5], title-page as above; [6], publishing information, printing information, rights, copyright; [7], dedication: *FOR MARIE*; [8], blank; 9–10, Contents; 11, Acknowledgements; [12], blank; 13–57, text; [58]–[62], blank.

Blue-green cloth-covered boards; front and back covers blank; spine lettered lengthwise, top to bottom, in gold: DEATH OF A NATURALIST [ornamental design] SEAMUS HEANEY FABER; dust-jacket in olive, salmon and white, lettered in black.

Published 19 May 1966 at 18 shillings; printed by Latimer Trend & Co. Ltd, Plymouth.

Contents: Digging—Death of a Naturalist—The Barn—An Advancement of Learning—Blackberry-Picking—Churning Day—The Early Purges—Follower—Ancestral Photograph—Mid-Term Break—Dawn Shoot—At a Potato Digging—For the Commander of the 'Eliza'—The Diviner—Turkeys Observed—Cow in Calf—Trout—Waterfall—Docker—Poor Women in a City Church—Gravities—Twice Shy—Valediction—Lovers on Aran—Poem—Honeymoon Flight—Scaffolding—Storm on the Island—Synge on Aran—Saint Francis and the Birds—In Small Townlands—The Folk Singers—The Play Way—Personal Helicon.

Note: The Faber and Faber archives do not list the number of copies printed of this edition.

b. *first American edition in boards*

[title in outline letters] DEATH | OF A | NATURALIST | *by Seamus Heaney* | New York | OXFORD UNIVERSITY PRESS | 1966
21.5 × 14 cm.

[1]–[2], blank; [3], half-title: DEATH OF A NATURALIST; [4], blank; [5], title-page as above; [6], copyright and printing information; [7], dedication: *FOR MARIE*; [8], blank; 9–10, Contents; 11, Acknowledgements; [12], blank; 13–57, text; [58]–[62], blank.

Blue-green cloth-covered boards; front and back covers blank; spine lettered lengthwise, top to bottom, in gold: DEATH OF A NATURALIST [ornamental design] SEAMUS HEANEY OXFORD; dust-jacket in olive, salmon and white, lettered in black.

1,000 copies published 2 June 1966 at $3.75; no printer specified.

Contents: As in A2a.

Notes: 1. Oxford University Press purchased 1,000 sheets from Faber and Faber on 12 April 1966.
2. Oxford University Press did not issue a paperback edition.

c. *first edition in wrappers*

[title in outline letters] DEATH | OF A | NATURALIST | *by Seamus Heaney* | FABER AND FABER LTD | 24 Russell Square London
18 × 12 cm.

Pagination as in A2a with [63]–[64], blank.

Perfect bound in stiff white glossy paper covers, printed in black, salmon and olive.

Published July 1969 at 7s / £0.35; printed by Latimer Trend & Co. Ltd, Whitstable.

Contents: As in A2a.

Note: Copyright page states '*First published in this edition 1969*'.

A3 THE ISLAND PEOPLE 1968

first edition

The | island | people [the preceding in blue at bottom left of cover with black and blue illustration of cottages, stone walls and a boy leading a donkey] | [the following in black across the bottom] MUSIC WORKSHOP STAGE I BBC RADIO FOR SCHOOLS SUMMER 1968
23.5 × 17.5 cm.

[1], cover-title as above; 2, information on times of broadcasts, series producer, illustrator; fly-title: 'The island people | An Irish sequence of music and poetry by Seamus Heaney. | Music by Gerard Victory.' | illustration | The evening land | text; 3–28, text, musical notation, illustrations; 29, full page illustration; 30–31, text and musical notation; [32], back cover with continuation of the illustration on front cover, and at bottom left: 'MUSIC WORKSHOP | STAGE I | SUMMER 1968 P56'; at bottom right: copyright and publishing information, price.

Stapled pamphlet printed in black, blue and brown with illustrations by Doreen Roberts throughout.

Published by The British Broadcasting Corporation, London 1968; price ninepence; printed by Hollen St Press Ltd, Slough.

The programmes were first broadcast on BBC Home Service, Radio 4, 1 May–27 June, 1968. They were rebroadcast 30 April–26 June, 1969 and the pamphlet was re-issued at that time.

Contents: The evening land—Ceili on the deck—Inisheer—The oarsmen's song—The basket-maker—The basket-maker's song—Michael—Neddy—The dealing man—The dealer—The cargo—Lullaby.

Note: With the exception of 'Inisheer' and 'The dealing man', all the poems are set to music and appear as lyrics within the text.

A4 A LOUGH NEAGH SEQUENCE 1969

a. *first edition in boards*

A LOUGH NEAGH SEQUENCE
20 × 12.5 cm.

[i], title-page as above; [ii], publication information, limitation statement, editors, copyright, printer; [iii], dedication: 'FOR | THE FISHERMEN'; 1, Acknowledgements; 2, quotes from *The Fishes of Great Britain and Ireland* by Francis Day; 3, blank; 4, fly-title: '*A | Lough Neagh | Sequence* | design'; 5–11, text; [12], design; [13], Faber & Faber advertisement showing photograph of poet above blurbs for *Death of a Naturalist* and *Door into the Dark*.

The first 50 copies of an edition of 1,000 were signed by the author on the title-page and bound in dark green cloth; glossy white dust-jacket with '*A | Lough Neagh | Sequence* | SEAMUS HEANEY | design | Phoenix Pamphlet Poets Press' on front panel; price £1–1–0 on inside flap; photograph and biographical sketch of poet on back panel.

Published by Phoenix Pamphlet Poets Press in January 1969 in an edition of 50 copies, hand-numbered 1 to 50, signed by the author, priced at £1–1–0; printed by Peter C. Woolley.

Contents: A Lough Neagh Sequence consists of seven poems: Up The Shore—Beyond Sargasso—Bait—Setting—Lifting—Return—Vision.

Note: The sequence of poems first appeared in *University Review*, Winter 1967 (C83) and is collected with revisions in *Door into the Dark*.

b. *first edition in wrappers*

A LOUGH NEAGH SEQUENCE
20 × 12.5 cm.

[i], title-page as above; [ii], publication information, limitation statement, editors, copyright, printer; [iii], dedication: 'FOR | THE FISHERMEN'; 1, Acknowledgements; 2, quotes from *The Fishes of Great Britain and Ireland* by Francis Day; 3, blank; 4, fly-title: '*A | Lough Neagh | Sequence* | design'; 5–11, text; [12], design; [13], Faber & Faber advertisement showing photograph of poet above blurbs for *Death of a Naturalist* and *Door into the Dark*.

Of a limited edition of 1,000 copies, 950 were stapled in glossy white card covers; front cover title: '*A | Lough Neagh | Sequence* | SEAMUS HEANEY | design | Phoenix Pamphlet Poets Press | 3/-'; photograph and biographical sketch of the poet on back cover.

Published by Phoenix Pamphlets Poets Press in January 1969; priced at 3/-; printed by Peter C. Woolley.

Contents: Same as A4a.

A5 DOOR INTO THE DARK 1969

a. *first edition in boards*

[title in outline letters] DOOR INTO | THE DARK | *by Seamus Heaney* | FABER AND FABER LTD | 24 Russell Square London
21.5 × 14 cm.

[1]–[2], blank; [3], half-title: DOOR INTO THE DARK; [4], *by the same author*; [5], title-page as above; [6], publishing information, printing information, rights, SBN, copyright; [7], dedication: For my father and mother; [8], blank; 9–10, Contents; 11, Acknowledgements; [12], blank; 13–56, text.

Black cloth-covered boards; front and back covers blank; spine lettered lengthwise, top to bottom: DOOR INTO THE DARK [within heavily ruled box] Seamus Heaney Faber; lettered and decorated in gold; cream dust-jacket lettered and decorated in red and dark green.

Published 16 June 1969 at 15 shillings; printed by Latimer Trend & Co. Ltd, Plymouth.

Contents: Night-Piece—Gone—Dream—The Outlaw—The Salmon Fisher to the Salmon—The Forge—Thatcher—The Peninsula—In Gallarus Oratory—Girls Bathing, Galway 1965—Requiem for the Croppies—Rite of Spring—Undine—The Wife's Tale—Mother—Cana Revisited—Elegy for a Still-born Child—Victorian Guitar—Night Drive—At Ardboe Point—Relic of Memory—A Lough Neagh Sequence: 1. Up the Shore; 2. Beyond Sargasso; 3. Bait; 4. Setting; 5. Lifting; 6. The Return; 7. Vision—The Given Note—Whinlands—The Plantation—Shoreline—Bann Clay—Bogland.

Note: The Faber and Faber archives do not list the number of copies printed of this edition.

b. *first American edition in boards*

[title in outline letters] DOOR INTO | THE DARK | *by Seamus Heaney* | New York | OXFORD UNIVERSITY PRESS | 1969
21.5 × 13.5 cm.

[1]–[2], blank; [3], half-title: DOOR INTO THE DARK; [4], *by the same author*; [5], title-page as above; [6], printing information, copyright; [7], dedication: For my father and mother; [8], blank; 9–10, Contents; 11, Acknowledgements; [12], blank; 13–56, text.

Black cloth-covered boards, front and back covers blank; spine lettered lengthwise, top to bottom: DOOR INTO THE DARK [as above] Seamus Heaney OXFORD; lettered and decorated in gold; cream dust-jacket lettered and decorated in red and dark green.

1,000 copies published 1969 at $3.75; no printer specified.

Contents: As in A5a.

Notes: 1. Oxford University Press purchased 1,000 copies from Faber and Faber on 18 February 1969.
2. Oxford University Press did not issue a paperback edition.

c. *first edition in wrappers*

[title in outline letters] DOOR INTO | THE DARK | *by Seamus Heaney* | FABER AND FABER LTD | 3 Queen Square London
18.5 × 12 cm.

Pagination as in A5a.

Perfect bound in stiff white glossy paper covers printed in black, red and dark green.

500 copies published September 1972 at 50p; printed by Latimer Trend & Co. Ltd, Whitstable.

Contents: As in A5a.

Note: Copyright page states '*First published in this edition 1972*'.

A6 NIGHT DRIVE 1970

first edition

NIGHT DRIVE | by | SEAMUS HEANEY
25.5 × 19 cm.

[1]–[2], blank; [3], title-page as above; [4], holograph poem; [5]–[16], text; [17], colophon; [18], series, textual note; [19]–[20], blank.

An edition of 100 copies, all numbered, signed and dated by the author, published by Richard Gilbertson, Bow, Crediton, Devon. Copies 1–3 are unbound and have each poem in author's manuscript facing the printed text. Copies 4–100 were sewn in bluish green simulated pony-skin covers with 'NIGHT DRIVE | by | SEAMUS HEANEY' stamped in gold on the front cover. Copies 4–20 were issued with the poem 'Wedding Day' in the author's manuscript although the printed colophon calls for 'The Dream' but Heaney has crossed this out and written in 'Wedding Day'; copies 21–30 have the poem 'Night Drive' in the author's manuscript; copies 31–55 have one of the other poems in the book in the author's manuscript; copies 56–100 were issued without a manuscript poem.

Published July 1970 as No. 9 in *The Manuscript Series*; printed by Suttons, Paignton.

Contents: [holograph poem where present]—Night Drive—Twice Shy—Lovers on Aran—Honeymoon Flight—Scaffolding—Girls Bathing, Galway 1965—Undine—The Wife's Tale—Victorian Guitar—Mother—Elegy for a Still-Born Child—Wedding Day.

Notes: 1. In copies 4–55, the placement of the manuscript poem may vary.
2. All of the poems were previously collected except 'Wedding Day', which was later revised for *Wintering Out*.

A7 A BOY DRIVING HIS FATHER TO CONFESSION 1970

first separate edition

A BOY DRIVING HIS FATHER TO | CONFESSION | SEAMUS HEANEY
20.5 × 12.5 cm.

[1], cover-title as above; [2], blank; [3], ornament, publisher's name and address; [4], limitation statement, copyright; [5]–[6], blank; [7], fly-title: 'Boy Driving His Father To Confession'; [8], blank; [9], text; [10]–[13], blank; [14], note on author; [15], printer's name and address; [16], back cover, blank.

Stapled white card covers; front cover serves as title-page; pages [5], [6], [11] and [12], are tan laid paper, watermarked '[crown] | Abbey Mills | Greenfield'; pages [3], [4], [7], [8], [9], [10], [13], [14], are white laid paper, watermarked 'Glastonbury'.

Published December 1970 by the Sceptre Press, Farnham, Surrey in an edition of 150 numbered copies; copies numbered 1–50 are signed by the poet on the limitation page. The unsigned copies were priced at £0.25. Printed by the Haslemere Printing Co., Surrey.

In addition, five copies numbered I–V were bound in dark red leather and signed by the publisher, Martin Booth, and by the poet. These copies sold at £2.10. [not seen].

Note: This poem was written in 1965. It was first published in *Phoenix*, March 1967 and is reprinted here with revisions. It was collected in *Poems and a Memoir*.

A8 WINTERING OUT 1972

a. *first edition in wrappers*

[title in outline letters] WINTERING | OUT | *by Seamus Heaney* | FABER AND FABER LTD | 3 Queen Square London
19.5 × 13 cm.

[1], half-title: WINTERING OUT; [2], *by the same author*; [3], title-page as above; [4], publishing information, printing information, rights, ISBN, conditions of sale, copyright; [5], dedication: For David Hammond and Michael Longley; poem of three quatrains: *This morning from a dewy motorway*; [6], blank; 7–8, Contents; 9, Acknowledgements and Notes; [10], blank; [11]–80, text.

White paper wrappers; front cover lettered and decorated in light greenish-blue, black and grey: WINTERING | OUT [on white panel] | SEAMUS | HEANEY [on grey panel]; spine lettered lengthwise, top to bottom, in black: WINTERING OUT [ornamental design] SEAMUS HEANEY [ornamental design] FABER; back cover has publisher's list of poets, lettered and decorated in black.

2,500 copies published 20 November 1972 at £1.00; printed by Latimer Trend & Co. Ltd, Plymouth.

Contents: [Dedicatory Poem:] For David Hammond and Michael Longley.

Part One: Fodder—Bog Oak—Anahorish—Servant Boy—The Last Mummer—Land—Gifts of Rain—Toome—Broagh—Oracle—The Backward Look—Traditions—A New Song—The Other Side—The Wool Trade—Linen Town—A Northern Hoard: 1. Roots; 2. No Man's Land; 3. Stump; 4. No Sanctuary; 5. Tinder—Midnight—The Tollund Man—Nerthus—Cairn-maker—Navvy—Veteran's Dream—Augury.

Part Two: Wedding Day—Mother of the Groom—Summer Home—Serenades—Somnambulist—A Winter's Tale—Shore Woman—Maighdean Mara—Limbo—Bye-Child—Good-night—First Calf—May—Fireside—Dawn—Travel—Westering.

b. ***first American edition in boards***

[title in outline letters] WINTERING | OUT | *by Seamus Heaney* | New York | OXFORD UNIVERSITY PRESS | 1973
19.5 × 13 cm.

[1], half-title: WINTERING OUT; [2], *by the same author*; [3], title-page as above; [4], printing information, copyright; [5], dedication: For David Hammond and Michael Longley; poem of three quatrains: *This morning from a dewy motorway*; [6], blank; 7–8, Contents; 9, Acknowledgements and Notes; [10], blank; [11]–80, text.

Light greenish-blue cloth-covered boards; front and back covers blank; spine lettered lengthwise, top to bottom, in gold: Seamus Heaney WINTERING OUT Oxford; dust-jacket front cover has black lettering on grey, white and light greenish-blue panels; back cover is white with black lettering; spine is white lettered in black.

500 copies published 26 April 1973 at $4.00; no printer specified.

Contents: As in A8a.

Notes: 1. Oxford University Press purchased 500 copies from Faber and Faber on 6 June 1972.
2. Oxford University Press did not issue a paperback edition.

c. ***first English edition in boards***

[title in outline letters] WINTERING | OUT | *by Seamus Heaney* | FABER AND FABER LTD | 3 Queen Square London
19.5 × 12.5 cm.

Pagination as in A8a.

Light greenish-blue cloth-covered boards; front and back covers blank; spine lettered lengthwise, top to bottom, in gold: Seamus Heaney WINTERING OUT Faber; dust-jacket as the covers on A8a except price on front flap – £1.75.

500 copies published 1973 at £1.75; printed by Whitstable Litho Straker Brothers Ltd.

Contents: As in A8a.

Note: Copyright page states '*First published in this edition 1973*'.

A9 EXPLORATIONS 1974

first edition

Teacher's notes SPRING 1974 | BBC | Radio 4 VHF | Explorations | A series provided for the BBC at the request of the | School Broadcasting Council for the United Kingdom | Age 14–15 Thursday 9.55–10.15 a.m. | Series produced by David Hammond | [rule] | [description of programme]
21 × 30 cm.

[1], cover, as above, serves as title-page; 2–22, text; [back cover], 'EXPLORATIONS | 130T | Spring 1974 | © British Broadcasting Corporation 1973 | First Published 1973 | Published at the request of the School Broadcasting | Council for the United Kingdom | by the British Broadcasting Corporation, | 35 Marylebone High Street, London W1M 4AA | Printed in England by John Brown (Printers) Ltd Nottm. | ISBN 0 563 193921 price 10p.'

Note: Although not named, Seamus Heaney is the author of this issue of *Explorations*. He makes brief observations about the text under discussion, then suggests questions, and concludes by offering possible writing assignments. The literary texts discussed are drawn from the Certificate of Secondary Education syllabus for 1973 and 1974, which included Joyce, Friel, McLaverty, Golding, Lawrence, Hughes and Synge. Seamus Heaney also produced a Student's Pamphlet to accompany the teacher's notes (not seen).

A10 STATIONS 1975

first edition

STATIONS | by | SEAMUS HEANEY | – ULSTERMAN PUBLICATIONS –
22 × 15.5 cm.

[1], title-page as above; [2], publishing information; copyright; 3, foreword; 4–24, text.

Yellow paper covers; front cover has drop-out of poet's face printed in orange and 'SEAMUS HEANEY / Stations' [printed lengthwise from bottom to top along the fore-edge] | Ulsterman Publications; inside front cover has 'PRICE 10p'; back cover has printing information at bottom left; inside back cover has 'SEAMUS HEANEY: Born Co. Derry' [sic] 1939' followed by a 4-line note on his publications.

Published March 1975 at 10p. Printed by Regency Press, Belfast.

Contents: Cauled—Branded—Hedge-school—Nesting-ground—Sinking the shaft—Waterbabies—Patrick and Oisin—Sweet William—The discharged soldier—The Sabbath-breakers—Kernes—July—England's difficulty—Visitant—Trial runs—The wanderer—Cloistered—Ballad—The stations of the west—Inquisition—Incertus.

Note: A typographical error appears in the author's foreword, page 3, line 10: for 'lodes of nodes' read 'lodes or nodes'.

A11 BOG POEMS 1975

first edition

[title printed in ornate gold script] BOG | poems | [illustration] | Seamus Heaney | Illustrated by Barrie Cooke | THE RAINBOW PRESS | 1975
25.5 × 20 cm. (top edges gilt).

[i]–[ii], blank; [iii], half-title: BOG POEMS; [iv], blank; [1], title-page as above; [2], copyrights; [3], contents; [4], blank; [5], introductory note by Seamus Heaney; [6], blank; [7], illustration; [8], blank; 9–36, text (illustrations on pp. [17], [25], [33] and pp. [18], [24], [26], [34], blank); [37], colophon; [38]–[40], blank.

Morocco spine and fore-edge strip over marbled boards (some copies have papyrus-covered boards); front cover has 'BOG poems' in ornate script stamped in gold; spine stamped lengthwise, top to bottom, in gold: 'BOG POEMS [star] SEAMUS HEANEY'; back cover blank; top edges trimmed and gilded; issued in tan linen-covered slipcase.

Published May 1975 in an edition of 150 hand-numbered copies signed by the author, priced at £40.00 or $102.00. Printed by the John Roberts Press, London on Italian paper watermarked 'L'AMATRUDA | AMALFI'; bound by Sangorski and Sutcliffe.

Contents: Bone Dreams—Come to the Bower—Bog Queen—Punishment—The Grauballe Man—Tête Coupée—Kinship—Belderg.

Notes: 1. In the table of contents (p. [3]) and in the title of the poems themselves, pp. 21–22 and pp. 35–36, the words 'Grauballe' and 'Belderg' are misprinted as 'Graubulle' and 'Beldberg'.
2. The pagination may differ in the papyrus-covered copies and the title on the front cover of some copies bound in marbled boards is blind stamped rather than stamped in gold. No priority has been determined for the different bindings.
3. The eight poems in *Bog Poems* were subsequently collected in *North*, where 'Tête Coupée' is entitled 'Strange Fruit'.

A12 NORTH 1975

a. *first edition in boards*

[title in outline letters] NORTH | *by Seamus Heaney* | FABER AND FABER LTD | 3 Queen Square London
21.5 × 13.5 cm.

[i]–[ii], blank; [1], half-title: NORTH; [2], blank; [3], title-page as above; [4], publishing information, printing information, rights, ISBNs, copyright; 5–6, Contents; 7, Acknowledgements; 8–73, text; [74]–[76], blank.

Light blue cloth-covered boards; front and back covers blank; spine lettered lengthwise, top to bottom, in gold: NORTH *Seamus Heaney Faber*; pale-blue dust-jacket, lettered in black with illustration of Viking ship in blue on white panel on front; portrait of Seamus Heaney by Edward McGuire reproduced in black and white on back.

Published 9 June 1975 at £2.95; printed by W. & J. Mackay Ltd, Chatham.

Contents: Mossbawn: Two Poems in Dedication *For Mary Heaney*: 1. Sunlight; 2. The Seed Cutters.

Part I: Antaeus—Belderg—Funeral Rites—North—Viking Dublin: Trial Pieces—The Digging Skeleton—Bone Dreams—Come to the Bower—Bog Queen—The Grauballe Man—Punishment—Strange Fruit—Kinship—Ocean's Love to Ireland—Aisling—Act of Union—The Betrothal of Cavehill—Hercules and Antaeus.

Part II: The Unacknowledged Legislator's Dream—Whatever You Say Say Nothing—Freedman—Singing School: 1. The Ministry of Fear; 2. A Constable Calls; 3. Orange Drums, Tyrone, 1966; 4. Summer 1969; 5. Fosterage; 6. Exposure.

Notes: 1. The Faber and Faber archives do not list the number of copies printed for this edition.
2. In 1981 the sheets for 25 copies of this first edition were discovered in the Faber & Faber warehouse. These copies, numbered 1 to 25, were issued, specially bound in three point green canvas, by Brian Dickson. In addition, *North* was reissued in a Faber Library edition in 1996 at £8.95.

b. *first edition in wrappers*

[title in outline letters] NORTH | *by Seamus Heaney* | FABER AND FABER LTD | 3 Queen Square London
19.5 × 13 cm.

Pagination as in A12a with [77]–[78], blank.

Perfect bound in stiff white glossy paper covers, lettered and decorated in black and light blue.

6,750 copies published 9 June 1975 at £1.25; printed by W. & J. Mackay Ltd, Chatham.

Contents: As in A12a.

Note: Published at the same time as A12a.

c. *first American edition in boards*

[title in outline letters] NORTH | *by Seamus Heaney* | New York | Oxford University Press | 1976

21.5 × 13.5 cm.

[i]–[ii], blank; [1], half-title: NORTH; [2], blank; [3], title-page as above; [4], printing information, rights, copyright, Library of Congress card number; 5–6, Contents; 7, Acknowledgements; 8–73, text; [74]–[76], blank.

Light blue cloth-covered boards; front and back covers blank; spine lettered lengthwise, top to bottom, in gold: NORTH *Seamus Heaney Oxford University Press | New York*; pale-blue dust-jacket lettered and decorated in black and white; front has illustration of Viking ship; portrait of Seamus Heaney by Edward McGuire reproduced in black and white on back.

1,250 copies published 1976 at $5.95; no printer specified.

Contents: As in A12a.

Note: Oxford University Press purchased 1,250 unbound copies from Faber and Faber on 7 March 1975.

d. *first American edition in wrappers*

[title in outline letters] NORTH | *by Seamus Heaney* | Oxford University Press | New York
20.5 × 13.5 cm.

Pagination as in A12c with [77]–[78], blank.

Perfect bound in stiff glossy white paper covers, lettered and decorated in black and light blue.

Published 1977 by Oxford University Press as a Galaxy Book at $3.95; printed in the United States of America.

Contents: As in A12a.

Note: Copyright page states '*First issued as an Oxford University Press paperback, 1977*'.

A13 THE FIRE I' THE FLINT 1975

first separate edition

The Fire i' the Flint: | REFLECTIONS ON | THE POETRY OF | GERARD MANLEY HOPKINS | BY | SEAMUS HEANEY | CHATTERTON

LECTURE | ON AN | ENGLISH POET | BRITISH ACADEMY | 1974 | FROM THE PROCEEDINGS OF THE | BRITISH ACADEMY, LONDON, VOLUME LX (1974) | OXFORD UNIVERSITY PRESS
25 × 15.5 cm.

[1], title-page as above; [2], publishing information, copyright, ISBN, printing information; [3]–19, text; [20], blank.

Stapled in yellowish green paper covers lettered in brown; front cover: 'THE FIRE I' THE FLINT: | *Reflections on the Poetry of* | *Gerard Manley Hopkins* | SEAMUS HEANEY | *Published for* THE BRITISH ACADEMY, LONDON | *by* OXFORD UNIVERSITY PRESS | *Price* 75p *net*'; back cover has listing of the Chatterton Lectures.

Published August 1975 at 75p; printed at the University Press, Oxford by Vivian Ridler, Printer to the University.

A14 FOUR POEMS [1976]

first edition

FOUR POEMS | BY | SEAMUS HEANEY | With Illustrations by Margaret McCord | Crannog Press [title-page protected by bound-in tissue sheet]
23 × 15 cm.

[1]–[2], blank; [3], half-title: 'FOUR POEMS'; [4], blank; [5], title-page as above; [6], blank; [7]; permissions; [8], blank; [9], poem; [10], blank; [11]–[13], poem; [14], blank; [15], poem; [16], blank; [17]–[18], poem; [19], blank; [20], colophon: 'CRANNOG PRESS | 205 Sandown Road Belfast 5 | 1975 | Limited to 12 copies only | of which this is number: (*written in*) | [publisher's logo]'; [21], acknowledgements and small drawing; [22]–[24], blank. Illustrations on bound-in tissue precede each of the four poems.

Quarter bound in black leather and beige silk-covered boards; spine blind stamped, 'FOUR POEMS'; French and Japanese endpapers; handset and printed in black with illustrations in grey or grey-lilac on white Basingwerk Parchment paper.

Published Spring 1976, although dated 1975, in an edition of 12 copies, signed and numbered by the artist.

Contents: Rite of Spring—Death of a Naturalist—The Barn—Shoreline.

Note: The poems are reprinted from *Death of a Naturalist* and *Door into the Dark*.

A15 GLANMORE SONNETS 1977

first edition

GLANMORE SONNETS | von | SEAMUS HEANEY | mit Pastellen von | CECIL KING | [publisher's logo] | EDITION MONIKA BECK
35 × 35 cm.

Ten unbound sheets printed on recto only; [1], title as above; one sonnet each on [2], [4], [6] and [8]; abstract oil paintings by Cecil King on [3], [5], [7] and [9]; [10], colophon.

Printed in an edition of 50 hand-numbered copies: 25 copies in a blue cloth-covered portfolio for distribution in Ireland and 25 copies (10 in a blue cloth-covered portfolio, 15 in black wrappers) for distribution in Germany. All copies are signed by the poet and the artist.

Published 10 October 1977 at DM 400.00; printed by Conrad & Bothner, Zweibrücken.

Contents: Thunderlight on the split logs—This evening the cuckoo and the corncrake—Dogger, Rockall, Malin, Irish Sea—Vowels ploughed into other: opened ground.

A16 ROBERT LOWELL 1978

first edition

ROBERT LOWELL | [ornament] | *a memorial address* | *and an elegy* | [ornament, inverted] | by | SEAMUS HEANEY | Privately printed by | FABER AND FABER | London and Boston
21.5 × 13.5 cm.

[1]–[2], blank; [3], title-page as above; [4], printing information, rights, copyright; 5–13, text; [14]–[16], blank.

Sewn in bluish grey wrappers with flaps; title-page reproduced in black on front wrapper; back wrapper blank.

Published 1978; [250 copies] printed by the John Roberts Press, London.

Note: A memorial service with readings from Lowell's poetry and with an address by Seamus Heaney was held at St Luke's Church, Redcliffe Square, London on Wednesday 5 October 1977 at 6.00 p.m. This is the text of that address followed by Seamus Heaney's 52-line poem, 'Elegy'. The thirteenth line of the poem was replaced by five lines in the version printed in *After Summer*. The revised version was collected in *Field Work*.

A17 AFTER SUMMER 1978

first edition

Seamus Heaney | [title printed in outline letters] AFTER SUMMER | [publisher's logo] | Illustrations by Timothy Engelland | THE DEERFIELD PRESS | THE GALLERY PRESS
22 × 15 cm.

[1]–[2], blank; [3], title-page as above; [4], copyright; [5]–[6], blank; [7], portrait of Robert Lowell; [8]–[10], text; [11], illustration; [12], blank; [13], colophon; [14]–[16], blank.

Bound in dark brown cloth-covered boards; front and back covers blank; spine lettered lengthwise, top to bottom, in gold: 'AFTER SUMMER: Seamus Heaney Deerfield / Gallery'; light-grey endpapers; light-grey dust-jacket, lettered and decorated in brown.

Published May 1978 simultaneously in Old Deerfield, Massachusetts (Deerfield Press) at $6.50 and in Dublin (Gallery Press) at £3.60, in an edition of 250 copies. Printed by Harold McGrath at the Hampshire Typothetae, Massachusetts, and bound by Museum Bookbindings, Dublin; all copies signed by the author.

Contents: Elegy—Leavings.

Note: See *Robert Lowell* (A16) for a note on the text of 'Elegy'.

A18 HEDGE SCHOOL 1979

first edition

[coloured woodcut] | Seamus Heaney Hedge School Sonnets from | Glanmore with colour woodcuts by Claire Van Vliet | & printed for Charles Seluzicki, Fine Books in Salem | Oregon at the Janus Press, Newark Vermont in 1979
28 × 18 cm. (bottom edges untrimmed).

[1], title-page as above; [2], copyright; [3], coloured woodcut, dedicatory note; [4]–[13], text, with half-page coloured woodcuts on [5], [7], [9], [11], [13]; [14], blank; [15], colophon; [16], blank.

Printed on rough paper and handsewn in folded brown card covers; front cover blind stamped: 'Seamus Heaney – Hedge School'; back cover and spine blank; brown endpapers; title, dedication and colophon pages printed in brown with title and name of dedicatee, Ann Saddlemeyer, in black; text printed in black with numerals in brown; woodcuts printed in green, blue, tan, brown, violet and white.

Published September 1979 in an edition of 285 copies, designed, set and printed on Barcham Green DeWint paper by Claire Van Vliet; each copy numbered and signed by the author and the artist; priced $50.00.

Contents: I. Vowels ploughed into other: opened ground—II. Sensings, mountings from the hiding places—III. This evening the cuckoo and the corncrake—IV. I used to lie with an ear to the line—V. Soft corrugations in the boortree's trunk—VI. He lived there in the unsayable lights—VII. Dogger, Rockall, Malin, Irish Sea—VIII. Thunderlight on the split logs: big raindrops—IX. Outside the kitchen window a black rat—X. I dreamt we slept in a moss in Donegal.

Note: Six copies were specially bound in various coloured cloths with central panels of pine green Momi and an impression of one of the woodcuts on front cover.

A19 UGOLINO 1979

first edition

SEAMUS HEANEY | UGOLINO | *with two lithographs by* | Louis Le Brocquy | ANDREW CARPENTER | DUBLIN MCMLXXIX
29.5 × 20.5 cm. (front and bottom edges untrimmed).

[1]–[2], blank; [3], half-title: UGOLINO; [4], blank; [5], title-page as above; [6], copyrights; publishing information; printing information; [7], note on the poem, quoting Seamus Heaney on why he was drawn to the story; [8]–[9], blank; [10], illustration; [11]–[14], text; [15], illustration; [16], blank; [17], signatures; [18], blank; [19], colophon; [20]–[24], blank.

Printed on Penshurst wove paper and bound in black flexible leather covers, title blind-stamped on front cover and spine; orange endpapers; issued in black paper-covered slipcase with orange label.

Published September 1979 by Andrew Carpenter in an edition of 125 hand-numbered copies of which 30, numbered 96 to 125, were for sale. Designed by Liam Millar and printed at the Dolmen Press. Each copy signed by author, artist, designer and publisher.

Note: According to the publisher, of the 125 copies: 70 were bound in black goat skin and issued in a paper-covered slipcase; 25 were bound in black paper covers and issued without a slipcase and 30 were bound in black textured morocco and issued in a paper-covered slipcase.

A20 FIELD WORK 1979

a. ***first edition in boards***

Field Work | [swelled rule] | *Seamus Heaney* | FABER AND FABER | London · Boston
21.5 × 14 cm.

[1], half-title: Field Work; [2], blank; [3], title-page as above; [4], publishing information, printing information, copyright, British

Library Cataloguing in Publication Data, ISBNS; [5], dedication: for Karl and Jane Miller; [6], blank; [7], Contents; [8], blank; 9, Acknowledgements; [10], blank; 11–64, text.

Dark-brown paper-covered boards; front and back covers blank; spine lettered lengthwise, top to bottom, in gold: Field Work [rule] *Seamus Heaney* FABER; brown dust-jacket with map on orange panel on front; lettered in white and black; ivory endpapers.

3,000 copies published 15 October 1979 at £3.00; printed by Ebenezer Baylis & Son Limited, The Trinity Press, Worcester and London.

Contents: Oysters—Triptych: I. After a Killing; II. Sibyl; III. At the Water's Edge—The Toome Road—A Drink of Water—The Strand at Lough Beg—A Postcard from North Antrim—Casualty—The Badgers—The Singer's House—The Guttural Muse—In Memoriam Sean O'Riada—Elegy—Glanmore Sonnets—September Song—An Afterwards—High Summer—The Otter—The Skunk—Homecomings—A Dream of Jealousy—Polder—Field Work—Song—Leavings—The Harvest Bow—In Memoriam Francis Ledwidge—Ugolino.

b. *first edition in wrappers*

Field Work | [swelled rule] | *Seamus Heaney* | FABER AND FABER | London · Boston
21.5 × 14 cm.

Pagination as in A20a.

Perfect bound in stiff white glossy paper covers, printed in brown, with map on orange panel on front, lettered in white and black.

12,000 copies published 15 October 1979 at £1.65; printed by Ebenezer Baylis & Son Limited, The Trinity Press, Worcester, and London.

Contents: As in A20a.

Note: Published at the same time as A20a.

c. *first American edition in boards*

Field Work | [swelled rule] | *Seamus Heaney* | FARRAR · STRAUS · GIROUX | New York
21 × 14 cm.

[3], half-title: Field Work; [4], blank; [5], title-page as above; [6], dedication, copyright, rights, publishing information, printing information, Library of Congress Cataloging in Publication Data; [7], Contents; [8], blank; 9, Acknowledgements; [10], blank; 11–64, text; 65–[66], Notes.

Dark-brown cloth-covered boards; front cover stamped in gold: [ornamental design] *SH* [ornamental design] | [short rule]; back cover blank; spine lettered lengthwise, top to bottom, in gold: *Seamus Heaney* [ornamental design] FIELD WORK [ornamental design] *Farrar · Straus · Giroux*; cream dust-jacket with map on front and with photograph of the poet on back; lettered and decorated in black and tan; flecked light tan endpapers.

Published 1979 at $8.95; printed in the United States of America.

Contents: As A20a, except for the addition of 'Notes', pp. 65–[66].

d. *first American edition in wrappers*

Field Work | [swelled rule] | *Seamus Heaney* | FARRAR · STRAUS · GIROUX | New York
21 × 14 cm.

Pagination as in A20c.

Perfect bound in stiff glossy cream paper covers with map on front, lettered and decorated in black and tan.

6,000 copies published 1 April 1981 at $4.95; printed in the United States of America.

Contents: As A20a, except for the addition of 'Notes', pp. 65–[66].

Note: Copyright page states '*Second printing, 1981*'.

A21 GRAVITIES 1979

first edition

GRAVITIES | *A COLLECTION OF POEMS AND DRAWINGS* | SEAMUS HEANEY · NOEL CONNOR | [publisher's logo] | CHARLOTTE PRESS PUBLICATIONS | NEWCASTLE UPON TYNE | 1979
18 × 24 cm.

[i], half-title: '[drawing] | GRAVITIES'; [ii], blank; [iii], title-page as above; [iv], publisher's logo, copyrights, edition and publishing information, ISBN, design and printing information, rights; [1], Contents; 2–3, Introduction by Roger Garfitt; 4–[19], text (drawings on pp. [5], [7], [9], [11], [13], [15], [17], [19]); 20–21, biographies and portraits of Heaney and Connor; 22, Acknowledgements; [23], drawing or blank in some signed copies; [24], blank.

Black card covers; front and back covers lettered and decorated in white. 40 copies were numbered and dated and signed on the half-title by the author and artist.

Published November 1979 at £1.75; printed at the Tyneside Free Press Workshop.

Contents: Introduction—Gravities—Oracle—Personal Helicon—Digging—Freedman—Follower—Westering—Exposure.

Note: The eight poems in this collection had previously been published and collected in *Death of a Naturalist, Wintering Out* and *North*.

A22 A FAMILY ALBUM 1979

first edition

A FAMILY ALBUM | [rule] | *Seamus Heaney* | [ornament] | *BYRON PRESS*
24 × 16 cm.

[1], title-page as above; [2], blank; [3]–[7], text ([4] and [6] blank); [8], colophon.

Sewn in grey paper wrappers; tan paper label on front cover: '*Seamus Heaney* | [rule] | *A FAMILY ALBUM* | [ornament] | *BYRON PRESS*'; [all within single rules]; back cover blank.

Published December 1979 in an edition of 50 hand-numbered copies, printed by Peter Woolfenden at the Byron Press.

Contents: A Villanelle for Marie—A Kite for Michael & Christopher—A Toy for Catherine.

Notes: 1. 'A Villanelle for Marie' had been published in *Quatro*, Summer 1980 (C318), the other three had not been published.
2. There is a typographical error in line 6 of 'A Kite for Michael & Christopher': for 'rows' read 'bows.'

A23 TOOME 1980

first edition

TOOME | Seamus Heaney | Illustrated by Jane Proctor | National College of Art and Design 1980
28 × 18 cm.

[i]–[ii], blank; [1], half-title: TOOME; [2], blank; [3], title-page as above; [4], blank; [5], contents; [6]–23, text, with illustrations on pages [6], [8], [10], [12]–13, [14], [16], [18], [20], [22]; [24], colophon; [25]–[26], blank.

Bound in paper-covered boards printed with silver, orange and red patterns and a brown cloth spine, stamped in silver: 'TOOME Seamus Heaney'. The illustrations and cover design are serigraphs by Jane Proctor.

Published October 1980 in an edition of 15 hand-numbered copies, dated and signed by author and illustrator. Printed letterpress and silkscreen at the National College of Art and Design, Dublin.

Contents: Broagh—Augury—Toome—Song—Strange Fruit—Nerthus—Anahorish—First Calf—Come to the Bower.

Note: All of the poems had previously been collected.

A24 THE MAKINGS OF A MUSIC 1980

first edition

THE KENNETH ALLOTT LECTURES | NO. 1. | THE MAKINGS OF A MUSIC: | REFLECTIONS ON THE POETRY | OF WORDSWORTH AND YEATS | DELIVERED ON | 9 February, 1978 | By | SEAMUS HEANEY
21 × 15 cm.

[i], Details of the Kenneth Allott Lectureship in Poetry; [ii], publishing information, ISBN, copyright; [iii], title-page as above; [iv], blank; 1–18, text; [19]–[20], blank.

Stapled in green card covers; the front cover is lettered in white: 'THE KENNETH ALLOTT LECTURES | 1 | The Makings of a Music: | Reflections on the Poetry | of Wordsworth and Yeats | by | Seamus Heaney'; back cover blank.

Published by the University of Liverpool in December 1980 at 75p.; 2,000 copies printed.

Note: A list of The Kenneth Allott Lectures is printed on the inside of the front cover.

A25 PREOCCUPATIONS 1980

a. *first edition in boards*

SEAMUS HEANEY | *Preoccupations* | SELECTED PROSE | 1968–1978 | FABER & FABER | London · Boston
21.5 × 13.5 cm.

[1], half-title: PREOCCUPATIONS; [2], *Also by Seamus Heaney*; [3], title-page as above; [4], publishing information, printing information, rights, copyright, British Library Cataloguing in Publication Data, ISBN; [5], dedication: *for Seamus Deane and Thomas Flanagan*; [6], blank; [7], quotation from Yeats, 'Samhain: 1905'; [8], blank; 9–10, Contents; 11, Acknowledgements; [12], blank; 13–14, Foreword; [15]–224, text.

Blue paper-covered boards; front and back covers blank; spine lettered in gold lengthwise, top to bottom, in three groups of words on two lines: SEAMUS | HEANEY | [rule] | PREOCCUPATIONS | Selected Prose 1968–1978 | FABER & | FABER; white endpapers; grey dust-jacket printed black and blue.

Published 20 October 1980 at £7.95; printed by Fakenham Press Ltd, Fakenham, Norfolk.

Contents: [divided into three sections]: [I], Mossbawn—Belfast; [II], Feeling into Words—The Makings of a Music: Reflections on Wordsworth and Yeats—The Fire i' the Flint: Reflections on the Poetry of Gerard Manley Hopkins—Yeats as an Example?—From Monaghan to the Grand Canal: The Poetry of Patrick Kavanagh—The Sense of Place—Englands of the Mind; [III], In the Country of Convention: English Pastoral Verse—The God in the Tree: Early Irish Nature Poetry—Canticles to the Earth: Theodore Roethke—Tradition and an Individual Talent: Hugh MacDiarmid—A Memorable Voice: Stevie Smith—The Labourer and the Lord: Francis Ledwidge and Lord Dunsany—The Poetry of John Hewitt—The Mixed Marriage: Paul Muldoon—Digging Deeper: Brian Friel's 'Volunteers'—Faith, Hope and Poetry: Osip Mandelstam—Full Face: Robert Lowell.

b. *first American edition in boards*

SEAMUS HEANEY | *Preoccupations* | SELECTED PROSE | 1968–1978 | [publisher's logo] | Farrar · Straus · Giroux | New York
21 × 14 cm.

[1]–[2], blank; [3], half-title: PREOCCUPATIONS; [4], *By Seamus Heaney*; [5], title-page as above; [6], copyright, rights, publishing information, printing information; Library of Congress Cataloguing in Publication Data; [7], dedication: *for Seamus Deane and Thomas Flanagan*; [8], blank; [9], Acknowledgements; [10], blank; [11]–[12], Foreword; [13], Contents; [14], quotation from Yeats's 'Samhain: 1905'; [15], I; [16], blank; [17]–[224], text; [225]–[226], Selected Bibliography.

Brown paper-covered boards; front cover: [ornamental design] *SH* [ornamental design] | [short rule]; back cover blank; spine has all following within black panel at top, lettered and decorated in gold:

[double rule, one heavy, one light] | *Seamus* | *Heaney* | [ornamental designs] | PREOCCU– | PATIONS: | SELECTED | PROSE | 1968–1978 | [ornamental designs] | F · S · G | [double rule, one light, one heavy]; light tan dust-jacket lettered and decorated in black, and in dark and light brown; photograph of Seamus Heaney on back.

Published 1980 at $15.00; printed in the United States of America.

Contents: As in A25a, except for the addition of 'Selected Bibliography', pp. [225]–[226].

c. *first American edition in wrappers*

SEAMUS HEANEY | *Preoccupations* | SELECTED PROSE | 1968–1978 | [publisher's logo] | Farrar · Straus · Giroux | New York
21 × 14 cm.

Pagination as in A25b.

Perfect bound in stiff glossy light tan covers and decorated in black, and in dark and light brown.

3,000 copies published 1 September 1981 at $7.95; printed in the United States of America.

Contents: As in A25a.

Note: Copyright page states 'Second printing, 1981'.

d. *first English edition in wrappers*

SEAMUS HEANEY | *Preoccupations* | SELECTED PROSE | 1968–1978 | ff | *faber and faber* | LONDON · BOSTON
19.5 × 12.5 cm.

Pagination as in A25a.

Perfect bound in stiff white paper covers with matte finish, printed in black, light grey and pale green, with a portrait of the author on the front cover.

Published 1984 at £2.95; printed by Whitstable Litho Ltd, Whitstable, Kent.

Contents: As in A25a.

Note: Copyright page states 'This edition first published in 1984'.

A26 SELECTED POEMS 1965–1975 1980

a. *first edition in boards*

SELECTED | POEMS [all preceding in outline letters] | 1965–1975 | SEAMUS HEANEY | FABER & FABER | LONDON AND BOSTON
20 × 12.5 cm.

[1], half-title: SELECTED POEMS [all preceding in outline letters] | 1965–1975; [2], *by the same author*; [3], title-page as above; [4], publishing information, printing information, rights, copyright, British Library Cataloguing in Publication Data, ISBNS; [5], dedication: For Marie | and Michael and Christopher | and Catherine Ann; [6]–[8], Contents; [9]–136, text.

Blue paper-covered boards; front and back covers blank; spine lettered lengthwise, top to bottom, in gold: SEAMUS HEANEY SELECTED POEMS FABER [title in outline letters]; dust-jacket printed in black and blue with photograph of the poet on front.

Published 20 October 1980 at £3.95; printed by Whitstable Litho, Whitstable, Kent.

Contents: from *Death of a Naturalist*: Digging—Death of a Naturalist—The Barn—Blackberry-Picking—Churning Day—Follower—Mid-Term Break—At a Potato Digging—The Diviner—Lovers on Aran—Poem—Personal Helicon.

from *Door into the Dark*: The Forge—Thatcher—The Peninsula—Requiem for the Croppies—Undine—The Wife's Tale—Night Drive—At Ardboe Point—A Lough Neagh Sequence: 1. Up the Shore; 2. Beyond Sargasso; 3. Bait; 4. *from* Setting; 5. Lifting; 6. The Return; 7. Vision—The Given Note—The Plantation—Shoreline—Bogland.

from *Wintering Out*: Bog Oak—Anahorish—Servant Boy—The Last Mummer—Gifts of Rain—Broagh—Oracle—Traditions—A New Song—The Other Side—*from* A Northern Hoard: 1. Roots; 3. Stump; 5. Tinder—The Tollund Man—Nerthus—Wedding Day—Summer Home—Serenades—Shore Woman—Maighdean Mara—Limbo—Bye-Child—Good-Night—Westering.

from *North*: Mossbawn: Two Poems in Dedication: 1. Sunlight; 2. The Seed Cutters—Funeral Rites—North—Viking Dublin: Trial Pieces—Bog Queen—The Grauballe Man—Punishment—Strange Fruit—Kinship—Act of Union—Hercules and Antaeus—*from* Singing School: 1. The Ministry of Fear; 2. A Constable Calls; 5. Fosterage; 6. Exposure.

b. ***first edition in wrappers***

SELECTED | POEMS [all preceding in outline letters] | 1965–1975 | SEAMUS HEANEY | FABER & FABER | LONDON AND BOSTON
19.5 × 12.5 cm.

Pagination as in A26a.

Perfect bound in stiff white paper covers with matte finish, printed in black and blue, with a photograph of the poet on the front cover.

Published 20 October 1980 at £1.95; printed by Whitstable Litho, Whitstable, Kent.

Contents: As in A26a.

Note: Published at the same time as A26a.

A27 POEMS 1965–1975 1980

a. ***first edition in boards***

Seamus Heaney | [swelled rule] | [printed in outline letters] POEMS | 1965–1975 | [swelled rule] | [all of the following titles printed in outline letters] Death of a Naturalist | Door into the Dark | Wintering Out | North | [swelled rule] | *Farrar, Straus and Giroux* | NEW YORK
21 × 14 cm.

[i], half-title: *Seamus Heaney* | [swelled rule] | [printed in outline letters] POEMS | 1965–1975; [ii], *By Seamus Heaney*; [iii], title-page as above; [iv], copyright, rights, printing information, Library of Congress catalog card number, note on contents; v–ix, Contents; [x], blank; [1]–[228], text; [229]–[230], blank.

Green paper-covered boards; front cover: [ornamental design] SH [ornamental design] | [short rule]; back cover blank; spine lettered and decorated in gold on a black panel at top as follows: [double rule, top rule heavy] | *Seamus* | *Heaney* | [ornamental designs] | POEMS | 1965–1975 | [ornamental designs] | F · S · G | [double rule, top rule light]. Cream dust-jacket printed in black, green and slate with photograph of Seamus Heaney on back cover.

Published 1980 at $12.95; printed in the United States of America.

Contents: *Death of a Naturalist*: Digging—Death of a Naturalist—The Barn—An Advancement of Learning—Blackberry-Picking—Churning Day—The Early Purges—Follower—Ancestral Photograph—Mid-Term Break—Dawn Shoot—At a Potato Digging—For the Commander of the 'Eliza'—The Diviner—Turkeys Observed—Cow in Calf—Trout—Docker—Gravities—Twice Shy—Valediction—Lovers on Aran—Poem—Honeymoon Flight—Scaffolding—In Small Townlands—Personal Helicon.

Door into the Dark: Night-Piece—Gone—Dream—The Outlaw—The Salmon Fisher to the Salmon—The Forge—Thatcher—The Peninsula—In Gallarus Oratory—Girls Bathing, Galway, 1965—Requiem for the Croppies—Rite of Spring—Undine—The Wife's Tale—Mother—Cana Revisited—Elegy for a Still-born Child—Victorian Guitar—Night Drive—At Ardboe Point—Relic of Memory—A Lough Neagh Sequence: 1. Up the Shore; 2. Beyond Sargasso; 3. Bait; 4. Setting; 5. Lifting; 6. The Return; 7. Vision—The Given Note—Whinlands—The Plantation—Shoreline—Bann Clay—Bogland.

Wintering Out: Part One: Fodder—Bog Oak—Anahorish—Servant Boy—The Last Mummer—Land—Gifts of Rain—Toome—Broagh—Oracle—The Backward Look—Traditions—A New Song—The Other Side—The Wool Trade—Linen Town—A Northern Hoard: 1. Roots; 2. No Man's Land; 3. Stump; 4. No Sanctuary; 5. Tinder—Midnight—The Tollund Man—Nerthus—Cairn-maker—Navvy—Veteran's Dream—Augury.

Part Two: Wedding Day—Mother of the Groom—Summer Home—Serenades—Somnambulist—A Winter's Tale—Shore Woman—Maighdean Mara—Limbo—Bye-Child—Good-night—First Calf—May—Fireside—Dawn—Travel—Westering.

North: Mossbawn: Two Poems in Dedication for Mary Heaney; 1. Sunlight; 2. The Seed Cutters.

Part One: Antaeus—Belderg—Funeral Rites—North—Viking Dublin: Trial Pieces—The Digging Skeleton—Bone Dreams—Come to the Bower—Bog Queen—The Grauballe Man—Punishment—Strange Fruit—Kinship—Ocean's Love to Ireland—Aisling—Act of Union—The Betrothal of Cavehill—Hercules and Antaeus.

Part Two: The Unacknowledged Legislator's Dream—Whatever You Say Say Nothing—Freedman—Singing School: 1. The Ministry of Fear; 2. A Constable Calls; 3. Orange Drums, Tyrone, 1966; 4. Summer 1969; 5. Fosterage; 6. Exposure.

b. *first edition in wrappers*

Seamus Heaney | [swelled rule] | POEMS [in outline letters] | 1965–1975 | [swelled rule] | [the following titles in outline letters] Death of a Naturalist | Door into the Dark | Wintering Out | North | [swelled rule] | *Farrar, Straus and Giroux* | NEW YORK
21 × 14 cm.

Pagination as in A27a.

Perfect bound in stiff glossy cream paper covers printed in black, green and slate.

1,500 copies published 1 October 1981 at $6.95; printed in the United States of America.

Contents: As in A27a.

Note: Copyright page states '*Second printing, 1981*'.

A28 A SENSE OF IRELAND 1981

first edition

A SENSE | TROCAIRE '81 | OF | IRELAND [all above incorporated in a Celtic design]
30 × 21 cm.

[1], Foreword by Members of the Working Party, Trocaire '81 National Programme (Ireland); [2], blank; [3], Preface; [4]–[12], text.

Green paper covers, stapled; front cover serves as title-page; back cover blank; reproduced from typewritten copy.

No publishing or printing information.

Note: A meditation (meant to promote discussion at a retreat) privately presented to and circulated by the Sisters of Mercy, Carysfort College, Dublin, January 1981.

A29 SWEENEY PRAISES THE TREES 1981

first edition

SEAMUS HEANEY | SWEENEY PRAISES THE TREES | ILLUSTRATION BY | HENRY PEARSON | NEW YORK 1981
19 × 12.5 cm. (bottom edges untrimmed)

[1]–[2], blank; [3], half-title: 'Sweeney Praises The Trees'; [4], frontispiece illustration by Henry Pearson printed in brown; [5], title-page as above; [6], blank; [7]–[13], text, (pp. [8], [10], [12], blank); [14], blank; [15], colophon; [16], blank.

Sewn tan card covers; illustration blind stamped on front cover; back cover blank.

Published by Henry Pearson in July 1981 in an edition of 110 hand-numbered copies; printed at the Kelly/Winterton Press.

Note: The verses printed here are slightly revised versions of section 40, verses 3–13, of *Sweeney Astray* in which Sweeney, having arrived at Gleann na n-Eachtach, makes his poem praising the trees of Ireland.

A30 VERSES FOR A FORDHAM COMMENCEMENT 1982

a. *first edition*

VERSES FOR A FORDHAM COMMENCEMENT | by | Seamus Heaney | FORDHAM UNIVERSITY | MAY 23, 1982
24 × 18.5 cm. (four-page leaflet)

[1]–[4], Title as above followed by a poem of 46 stanzas of 7 lines each.

Printed in black on light-tan paper.

Published 23 May 1982.

Note: This poem was read by the author and distributed to attendees at the Fordham University Commencement on 23 May 1982 at which he was awarded the honorary degree of Doctor of Letters. A sudden downpour of rain and the general rush for cover resulted in most of these leaflets being ruined or abandoned.

b. *limited edition in boards*

[title in purple] VERSES | FOR | A | FORDHAM | COMMENCEMENT | [author in blue] SEAMUS | HEANEY | [publisher in black] NADJA
28 × 19.5 cm. (front edges untrimmed)

[1]–[4], blank; [5]–[6], blank (conjugate with front paste-down); [7], title-page as above; [8], copyright; [9], note on original appearance: 'Verses For A Fordham Commencement | Fordham University | May 23, 1982'; [10], blank; [11]–[17], text; [18], blank; [19], colophon; [20], blank; [21], publisher's name and address; [22], blank; [23]–[24], blank (conjugate with rear paste-down); [25]–[28], blank.

Printed on Whatman watermarked paper in an edition of 26 copies, lettered A–Z and signed in pencil by the poet; hand sewn and bound in blue linen-covered boards, with the title printed in black on a purple triangular inset on the bottom left of the front cover; back cover blank.

c. *limited edition in wrappers*

[title in purple] VERSES | FOR | A | FORDHAM | COMMENCEMENT | [author in blue] SEAMUS | HEANEY | [publisher in black] NADJA
28 × 19.5 cm. (front edges untrimmed)

[1]–[2], blank; [3], title-page as above; [4], copyright; [5], note on original appearance: 'Verses For A Fordham Commencement | Fordham University | May 23, 1982'; [6], blank; [7]–[13], text; [14], blank; [15], colophon; [16], blank; [17], publisher's name and address; [18]–[20], blank.

Printed on Whatman watermarked paper and sewn in greenish-blue double wrappers; the title is printed in black on the bottom left of the front cover: 'VERSES | FOR | A | FORDHAM | COMMENCEMENT'; back cover blank.

Published 1984. 200 copies sewn in double wrappers, hand numbered, and signed in pencil by the poet.

Note: The Nadja editions, A30b and A30c, omit stanzas 2, 10, 11, 21, 22, 23, 24, 25, 38 and 43 of the first edition and have revisions in the remaining text.

A31 CHEKHOV ON SAKHALIN 1982

first separate edition

[thick-thin rules] | THE BENNETT AWARD, 1982 | *The Hudson Review* is honored to announce that the Bennett Award for | 1982 is presented to | SEAMUS HEANEY | in recognition of his distinguished achievement in the art of lyric poetry. He | has gone to the roots of his language and his landscape, and recreated what | seems, in its uncanny immediacy, the surge and grip of reality itself. | Celebrant of nature's splendid impurities, fathomer of abysmal losses, seeker | of the internal rhyme of things, Heaney has in a few decades created a body | of poetry unsurpassed in its beautiful authenticity. | Award Ceremony Tuesday, November 16, 1982 | 684 Park Avenue New York City | [thin-thick rules]

Sheet folded to: 23 × 20.5 cm.

[1], title-page as above; [2]–[3], brief note on Seamus Heaney, list of his works, photograph, text of poem is printed in the poet's holograph; [4], details of Bennett Award, 1982 Selection Committee members and previous recipients.

Folded leaflet printed in black and white.

Published 16 November 1982 and distributed at the Award Ceremony.

Note: The poem had first appeared in the Field Day Theatre programme for Brian Friel's adaptation of Anton Chekhov's *Three Sisters*, September 1981 (D13).

A32 POEMS AND A MEMOIR 1982

first edition

[the author's name and the swelled rules are printed in brown; all other printing in black] SEAMUS | HEANEY | POEMS AND A MEMOIR | [swelled rule] | Selected and Illustrated | by Henry Pearson with | an Introduction by | Thomas Flanagan and a | Preface by Seamus Heaney | [swelled rule] | THE LIMITED EDITIONS CLUB

30.5 × 18 cm.

[i], half-title: 'SEAMUS HEANEY'; [ii], blank; [iii], title-page as above; [iv], copyright notices and edition statement; [v]–[vii], contents; [viii], blank; ix–xvi, 'The Poetry of Seamus Heaney' by Thomas Flanagan; xvii–xviii, 'Preface' by Seamus Heaney; [1], illustration, divisional title: 'Early Uncollected Poems'; [2], blank; 3–10, text; [11], illustration, divisional title: 'Death of a Naturalist'; [12], blank; 13–25, text; [26], blank; [27], illustration, divisional title: 'Door into the Dark'; [28], blank; 29–46, text; [47], illustration, divisional title; 'Wintering Out'; [48], blank; 49–68, text; [69], illustration, divisional title: 'North'; [70], blank; 71–114, text; [115], illustration, divisional title: 'Field Work'; [116], blank; 117–144, text; [145], illustration, divisional title: 'Memoir'; [146], blank; 147–150, text: 'Secret Nests of Derry'; [151]–[152], blank; 153, 'Artist's Note' by Henry Pearson;

[154], blank; [155], colophon with signatures of Seamus Heaney, Thomas Flanagan and Henry Pearson, within double hand-drawn rules; [156]–[158], blank.

Printed on Mohawk Mills letterpress paper with a laid finish and bound in vat-dyed dark-brown leather by Robert Burlen & Son, Hingham, Massachusetts; engraving by Henry Pearson blind-stamped on front cover; spine stamped in gold: 'SEAMUS | HEANEY'; back cover blank; top edges gilded.

Published 17 November 1982 in an edition of 2,000 hand-numbered copies, signed by Seamus Heaney, Thomas Flanagan and Henry Pearson, and issued in a slipcase. Printed for members of the Limited Editions Club by Daniel Keleher at The Wild Carrot Letterpress.

Contents: Introduction: The Poetry of Seamus Heaney. Preface. *Early Uncollected Poems*: Fisher—Pastoral—Thaw—Rookery—Corncrake—May Day—Expectant—Boy Driving His Father to Confession.

Death of a Naturalist: Digging—Death of a Naturalist—Blackberry-Picking—Churning Day—Follower—Mid-Term Break—At a Potato Digging—The Diviner—Docker—Poem—Scaffolding—Personal Helicon.

Door into the Dark: The Forge—Thatcher—The Peninsula—Requiem for the Croppies—The Wife's Tale—At Ardboe Point—A Lough Neagh Sequence: 1. Up the Shore; 2. Beyond Sargasso; 3. Bait; 4. Setting; 5. Lifting; 6. The Return; 7. Vision—The Plantation—Shoreline—Bogland.

Wintering Out: Bog Oak—Anahorish—Servant Boy—Gifts of Rain—Oracle—A Northern Hoard: 1. Roots; 2. No Man's Land; 3. Stump; 4. No Sanctuary; 5. Tinder—The Tollund Man—Wedding Day—Summer Home—Serenades—Shore Woman.

North: Mossbawn: Two Poems in Dedication: 1. Sunlight; 2. The Seed Cutters—Antaeus—Belderg—Funeral Rites—North—Viking Dublin: Trial Pieces—Bone Dreams—Bog Queen—The Grauballe Man—Punishment—Kinship—Hercules and Antaeus—Whatever You Say Say Nothing—Singing School: 1. The Ministry of Fear; 2. A Constable Calls; 3. Orange Drums, Tyrone, 1966; 4. Summer 1969; 5. Fosterage; 6. Exposure.

Field Work: Oysters—Triptych: 1. After a Killing; 2. Sibyl; 3. At the Water's Edge—The Strand at Lough Beg—Casualty—The Singer's House—The Guttural Muse—Elegy—Glanmore Sonnets—The Otter—The Skunk—Field Work.

Memoir: Secret Nests of Derry.

Artist's Note.

Note: The poems were selected by Henry Pearson from Seamus Heaney's published work. 'Secret Nests of Derry' had already appeared as part of 'Mossbawn' in *Preoccupations*. The introduction 'The Poetry of Seamus Heaney' is by Heaney's friend, the novelist and critic Thomas Flanagan.

A33 AN OPEN LETTER 1983

first edition

An Open Letter | *by Seamus Heaney*
22 × 14 cm.

[1], half-title: '*An Open Letter*'; [2], publishing information, printing information, copyright, conditions of sale, British Library Cataloguing in Publication Data, ISBN; [3], title-page as above; [4], blank; [5], quotation from Gaston Bachelard; [6], blank; 7–13, text; 14, Notes; [15]–[16], blank.

Printed in brown and stapled in cream card covers within tan wrappers; front wrapper: 'An Open Letter | by Seamus Heaney | A FIELD DAY PAMPHLET | Number 2', front flap has the names of the Field Day directors; back wrapper blank, back flap has the titles of the first three Field Day Pamphlets.

Published September 1983 at £2.25 by the Field Day Theatre Company, Derry; printed by Dorman & Sons Limited, Belfast.

A34 SWEENEY ASTRAY 1983

a. *first edition in boards*

Seamus Heaney | SWEENEY ASTRAY [in burnt orange] | A version from the Irish | [publisher's logo in burnt orange] | A Field Day Publication | Derry 1983
23 × 14 cm.

[i], half-title: Sweeney Astray; [ii], *By the same author*; [iii], title-page as above; [iv], publishing information, printing information, rights, copyright, illustration details, permissions, British Library Cataloguing in Publication Data, ISBNS; [v]–[vi], blank; vii–ix, introduction; x, notes and acknowledgements; [xi], illustration by Colin Middleton; [xii], blank; 13–77, text; [78]–[80], blank.

Greyish white rexine-covered boards; front cover has reproduction of a drawing by Colin Middleton; back cover blank; spine lettered lengthwise, top to bottom, in black: Seamus Heaney SWEENEY ASTRAY Field Day; black endpapers; olive-green dust-jacket, lettered and decorated in black and white.

1,000 copies published November 1983 at £10.00; printed by Mount Salus Press Limited.

b. *first edition in wrappers*

Seamus Heaney | SWEENEY ASTRAY [in burnt orange] | A version from the Irish | [publisher's logo in burnt orange] | A Field Day Publication | Derry 1983
23 × 14 cm.

Pagination as in A34a.

Perfect bound in stiff glossy olive-green paper covers, lettered and decorated in black and white.

3,000 copies published November 1983 at £4.50; printed by Mount Salus Press Limited.

Note: Published at the same time as A34a.

c. *first American edition in boards*

Sweeney Astray | *A Version from the Irish by Seamus Heaney* | *Farrar Straus Giroux · New York* | [celtic design]
23.5 × 14.5 cm.

[i], half-title: Sweeney Astray; [ii], blank; [iii], title-page as above; [iv], BY SEAMUS HEANEY, copyright, rights, publishing information, printing information, Library of Congress Cataloging in Publication Data; [v]–[viii], Introduction; [ix], Notes and Acknowledgements; [x], blank; [1], text title; [2], blank; 3–85, text; [86], blank.

Quarter bound in brown cloth over flecked green paper-covered boards; spine lettered lengthwise, top to bottom, in silver: SWEENEY ASTRAY [rule] SEAMUS HEANEY [rule] FSG; green dust-jacket lettered and decorated in red, white and black, photograph of Seamus Heaney on back.

5,500 copies published 1 May 1984 at $13.95; printed in the United States of America.

d. *first English edition in boards*

[the following, down to and including the illustration, within double box with thin outer, thick inner rules] SEAMUS | HEANEY | [short rule] | *Sweeney Astray* | [illustration] | ff | *faber and faber* | LONDON · BOSTON
19.5 × 12.5 cm.

[i], half-title: Sweeney Astray; [ii], *Also by Seamus Heaney*; [iii], title-page as above; [iv], publishing information, printing information, rights, copyright, British Library Cataloguing in Publication Data, ISBNS; [v]–[viii], Introduction; [ix], Notes and Acknowledgements; [x], blank; [1], text title; [2], blank; 3–85, text; [86], blank.

Black paper-covered boards; front and back covers blank; spine lettered and decorated in silver: [double rule] | SEAMUS HEANEY *Sweeney Astray* [preceding lettered lengthwise, top to bottom] | ff [horizontal] | [double rule]; dust-jacket has publisher's logo, ff, repeated in red on black background with white panels on front, back, spine and both flaps, lettered and decorated in black and red.

Published 15 October 1984 at £6.95; printed by Whitstable Litho, Whitstable, Kent.

e. ***first English edition in wrappers***

[the following, down to and including the illustration, within double box with thin outer, thick inner rules] SEAMUS | HEANEY | [short rule] | *Sweeney Astray* | [illustration] | ff | *faber and faber* | LONDON · BOSTON
19.5 × 12.5 cm.

Pagination as in A34d.

Perfect bound in stiff white paper covers with matte finish, lettered and decorated in black and red with a pattern of the publisher's logo, ff, repeated in red on a black background with white panel on front.

Published 15 October 1984 at £2.95; printed by Whitstable Litho, Whitstable, Kent.

Note: Published at the same time as A34d.

f. ***limited edition***

Sweeney Astray | *A Version from the Irish by Seamus Heaney* | *Farrar Straus Giroux · New York* | [celtic design]
23.5 × 14.5 cm.

[a], tipped in limitation statement with number and author's signature; [b], blank; pagination continues as in A34c with the exception of eight monotype illustrations by Barrie Cooke inserted between pp. 8–9, 26–27, 36–37, 46–47, 56–57, 70–71, 74–75, 82–83.

Green cloth-covered boards; back cover blank; celtic design blind stamped on front cover; spine lettered lengthwise, top to bottom, in gold: SWEENEY ASTRAY [rule] SEAMUS HEANEY [rule] FSG; cream endpapers; issued in a lime marbled slipcase.

Published December 1984; 350 numbered copies signed by the author; printed in the United States of America.

g. *first American edition in wrappers*

Sweeney Astray | *A Version from the Irish by Seamus Heaney* | *Farrar Straus Giroux · New York* | [celtic design]
23.5 × 15 cm.

Pagination as in A34c.

Perfect bound in stiff glossy green paper covers, lettered and decorated in red, white and black.

Published April 1985 at $7.95; printed in the United States of America.

Note: Copyright page states '*Second American printing, 1985*'.

h. *revised English edition with photographs*

SWEENEY'S FLIGHT | BASED ON THE REVISED TEXT OF | 'SWEENEY ASTRAY' | SEAMUS HEANEY | PHOTOGRAPHS BY | RACHEL GIESE | [short rule] | WITH THE COMPLETE | REVISED TEXT OF | 'SWEENEY ASTRAY' | [short rule] | ff | *faber and faber*
27.5 × 21.5 cm.

[i], photograph, Mist near Muckish; [ii], *also by Seamus Heaney; also by Rachel Giese*; [iii], title-page as above; [iv], publishing information, printing information, rights, copyright, CIP, ISBN, note on 'The King of the Ditchbacks'; [v], Contents; [vi], blank; vii–viii, Preface; ix, Photographer's Acknowledgements; [x], blank; [1], text-title: SWEENEY'S FLIGHT; [2], blank; [3], photograph; 4–6, The King of the Ditchbacks; 7, photograph; 8, Irish text; 9–79, 'Sweeney's Flight' text with photographs; 80, blank; 81, photograph; 82, THE PHOTOGRAPHS; 83, photograph; [84], blank; [85], half-title: SWEENEY ASTRAY | *revised 1992*; [86], blank; 87–88, Introduction; 89, Notes and Acknowledgements; [90], blank; 91–117, Sweeney Astray text; [118], blank.

Green cloth-covered boards; front and back cover blank; spine lettered in gold: SWEENEY'S FLIGHT SEAMUS HEANEY / RACHEL GIESE [preceding lettered lengthwise, top to bottom] ff [horizontal]; tan endpapers, glossy white dust-jacket lettered in black with black and white photographs by Rachel Giese on front and back covers.

Published 1992 at £20.00; printed by Jolly and Barber, Rugby, Warks.

Note: This edition includes a new two-page preface by the author.

i. *revised American edition with photographs*

SWEENEY'S FLIGHT | BASED ON THE REVISED TEXT OF | 'SWEENEY ASTRAY' | SEAMUS HEANEY | PHOTOGRAPHS BY | RACHEL GIESE | [short rule] | WITH THE COMPLETE | REVISED TEXT OF | 'SWEENEY ASTRAY' | [short rule] | FARRAR STRAUS GIROUX | NEW YORK
27.5 × 21.5 cm.

Pagination as in A34h.

Bindings as in A34h, except spine lettering of 'ff' changed to 'FSG'; dust-jacket redesigned slightly.

Published 1992 at $35.00; printed by Jolly and Barber, Rugby, Warks.

A35 AMONG SCHOOLCHILDREN 1984

a. *first edition*

THE QUEEN'S UNIVERSITY OF BELFAST | *In Memory of John M. Malone* | Among Schoolchildren | *A Public Lecture given by* | SEAMUS HEANEY | *on 9 June, 1983* | [University Arms] | Department of Further Professional Studies in Education | The Queen's University of Belfast
21 × 14.5 cm.

[1], title-page, as above; [2], copyright, series, printing information; [3], note on the lecture; [4], blank; 5–17, text; [18]–[20], blank.

Stapled in stiff green textured covers; title-page reproduced in gold on front cover; back cover blank.

Published in 1984; printed by GPS Colour Graphics.

Note: The first issue was withdrawn by the John Malone Memorial Committee after approximately 70 copies had been distributed.

b. ***second edition***

[rule] | *Among Schoolchildren* | [rule] | *A lecture dedicated to the memory of* | JOHN MALONE | *given by* | SEAMUS HEANEY | *on Thursday 9th June 1983* | *at The Queen's University, Belfast* | *and published by the* | JOHN MALONE MEMORIAL COMMITTEE
21 × 15 cm.

[1], title-page as above; [2], list of John Malone Memorial Committee members, copyright; 3–16, text [all of the foregoing printed in black on light-blue paper].

Stapled in dark-blue card covers; front cover: '*Among* | *Schoolchildren* | *Seamus Heaney* | A JOHN MALONE MEMORIAL LECTURE', lettered in white and light blue; back cover blank.

Published 1984; no printer specified.

Note: The second issue contains an erratum slip acknowledging permission to print lines from W. B. Yeats's 'Among Schoolchildren'. The copyright date of 1983 on p. [2] of the second issue is incorrect; the correct date is 1984.

A36 STATION ISLAND 1984

a. ***first edition in boards***

[the following, down to and including the illustration, within double box with thin outer, thick inner rules] SEAMUS | HEANEY | [short rule] | *Station Island* | [illustration] | ff | *faber and faber* | LONDON · BOSTON
19.5 × 12.5 cm.

[3], half-title: Station Island; [4], Also by Seamus Heaney; [5], title-page as above; [6], publishing information, printing information, rights, copyright, British Library Cataloguing in Publication Data, ISBNs; [7], dedication: For Brian Friel; [8], blank; 9–10, Contents; [11]–121, text; 122–123, Notes; [124]–[126], blank.

Black cloth-covered boards; front and back covers blank; spine lettered and decorated in gold: [double rule] | SEAMUS HEANEY *Station Island* [preceding lettered lengthwise, top to bottom] | ff [horizontal] | [double rule]; dust-jacket has publisher's logo, ff, repeated in black on grey background with white panels on front, back, spine and both flaps, lettered and decorated in black and red.

3,000 copies published 15 October 1984 at £5.95; printed by Whitstable Litho Limited, Whitstable, Kent.

Contents: *Part One*: The Underground—La Toilette—Sloe Gin—Away from it All—Chekhov on Sakhalin—Sandstone Keepsake—Shelf Life: 1. *Granite Chip*; 2. *Old Smoothing Iron*; 3. *Old Pewter*; 4. *Iron Spike*; 5. *Stone from Delphi*; 6. *A Snowshoe*—A Migration—Last Look—Remembering Malibu—Making Strange—The Birthplace—Changes—An Ulster Twilight—A Bat on the Road—A Hazel Stick for Catherine Ann—A Kite for Michael and Christopher—The Railway Children—Sweetpea—An Aisling in the Burren—Widgeon—Sheelagh na Gig—The Loaning—The Sandpit: 1. *1946*; 2. *The Demobbed Bricklayer*; 3. *The Sand Boom*; 4. *What the Brick Keeps*—The King of the Ditchbacks.

Part Two: Station Island: Station Island.

Part Three: Sweeney Redivivus: The First Gloss—Sweeney Redivivus—Unwinding—In the Beech—The First Kingdom—The First Flight—Drifting Off—Alerted—The Cleric—The Hermit—The Master—The Scribes—A Waking Dream—In the Chestnut Tree—Sweeney's Returns—Holly—An Artist—The Old Icons—In Illo Tempore—On the Road.

b. *first edition in wrappers*

[the following, down to and including the illustration, within double box with thin outer, thick inner rules] SEAMUS | HEANEY | [short rule] | *Station Island* | [illustration] | ff | *faber and faber* | LONDON · BOSTON
19.5 × 13 cm.

[1]–[2], blank; [3], half-title . . . pagination continues as in A36a with [127]–[128], blank.

Perfect bound in stiff white paper covers with matte finish with publisher's logo, ff, repeated in black on grey background with white panel on front, lettered and decorated in black and red.

10,000 copies published 15 October 1984 at £2.95; printed by Whitstable Litho Ltd, Whitstable, Kent.

Contents: As in A36a.

Note: Published at the same time as A36a.

c. *first American edition in boards*

[all the following within borders of double – thin outer, thick inner – rules] SEAMUS | HEANEY | [short rule] | *Station Island* | [publisher's logo] | FARRAR · STRAUS · GIROUX | NEW YORK |
21 × 14 cm.

[1]–[2], blank; [3], half-title: Station Island; [4], BY SEAMUS HEANEY; [5], title-page as above; [6], copyright, rights, publishing information, printing information, Library of Congress Cataloging in Publication Data; [7], dedication: For Brian Friel; [8], blank; 9–10, Contents; [11]–121, text; 122–123, Notes; [124]–[128], blank.

Buff paper-covered boards with green linen spine; front and back covers blank; spine lettered and decorated lengthwise, top to bottom, in gold: HEANEY · *Station Island* · FSG; tan dust-jacket lettered and decorated in black, white and red, has reproduction in colour of painting 'St. Patrick's Purgatory' by Sir John Lavery on front; photograph of Seamus Heaney on back flap.

6,000 published 1 January 1985 at $11.95; printed in the United States of America.

Contents: As in A36a.

d. *first American edition in wrappers*

[all the following within double box with thin outer, thick inner rules] SEAMUS | HEANEY | [short rule] | *Station Island* | [publisher's logo] | FARRAR · STRAUS · GIROUX | NEW YORK
21 × 14 cm.

Pagination as in A36c.

Perfect bound in stiff glossy tan paper covers lettered and decorated in black, white and red, has reproduction in colour of painting 'St. Patrick's Purgatory' by Sir John Lavery on front.

Published 1 January 1986 at $6.95; printed in the United States of America.

Contents: As in A36a.

Note: Copyright page states '*Second printing, 1985*'.

A37 HAILSTONES 1984

a. *first edition in boards*

Seamus Heaney | HAILSTONES | [publisher's logo] Gallery Books
21.5 × 13.5 cm.

[1]–[2], blank; [3], half-title: 'Gallery Books | *Editor*: Peter Fallon | [rule] | HAILSTONES'; [4], blank; [5], title-page as above; [6], publishing information, copyright, rights, ISBNs, permissions; [7], contents; [8], dedication: *for Helen Vendler*; 9–24, text; [25]–[28], blank.

Bound in black cloth with gold lettering on the spine, black end-papers; blue dust-jacket lettered in black with quotation from the poem 'Hailstones' on the inside flap of the front panel; all copies were signed by the author.

Published 12 December 1984 by the Gallery Press, Dublin in an edition of 750 copies, of which these 250 were bound in cloth, price £10.00.

Contents: Tremor—Alphabets—The Spoonbait—Terminus—Hailstones—The Riddle—The Stone Verdict—Grotus and Coventina—The Milk Factory—The Mud Vision.

Note: All of the poems except 'Tremor' were collected in *The Haw Lantern*.

b. *first edition in wrappers*

Title-page as in A37a.
21.5 × 14 cm.

Pagination as in A37a.

Published 12 December 1984 by The Gallery Press in an edition of 750 copies of which these 500 copies were bound in plain white card covers and issued in a blue dust-jacket identical to that in A37a, price £3.00.

Contents: As in A37a.

A38 PLACE AND DISPLACEMENT 1985

first edition

Place and Displacement | [rule] | Recent Poetry of Northern Ireland | Seamus Heaney | Pete Laver Memorial Lecture | delivered at Grasmere 2nd August 1984 | Published by the Trustees of Dove Cottage
21 × 15 cm.

[i], cover, as above, serves as title-page; [ii], blank; [iii], subtitle: 'Recent Poetry of Northern Ireland | [rule]'; [iv], blank; 1–22, text; [23], blank; [24], printing information at bottom.

Stapled in cream covers; front cover serves as title-page, back cover has printer's name and address at bottom; grey dust-jacket with the title, sub-title, author's name and publisher's name on the front panel; back panel has ISBN and copyright.

3,000 copies published August 1985; price £2.95; printed by Frank Peters Printers Ltd, Kendal, Cumbria.

A39 FROM THE REPUBLIC OF CONSCIENCE 1985

first edition

Seamus Heaney | FROM THE REPUBLIC | OF CONSCIENCE | Illustrated by | John Behan | [publisher's logo] | Amnesty International
21 × 14.5 cm.

[1], title-page as above; [2], blank; [3]–[6], text with illustration by John Behan on [4]; [7], blank; [8], colophon.

Stapled in grey card covers; front cover has the names of the author and the publisher printed in black and the title in blue:

SEAMUS HEANEY FROM | THE REPUBLIC OF | CONSCIENCE AMNESTY'; back cover has the publisher's logo in black and the price in blue. Printed on grey laid paper watermarked 'conqueror'.

Published 10 December 1985; 2,000 copies, produced by Peter Fallon for Amnesty International, Irish Section, 8 Shaw Street, Dublin, price £1.80.

Notes: 1. The poem was written in response to a request from Amnesty International to commemorate its 25th anniversary.
2. In February 1987, Parts I and II of the poem were printed in a pamphlet issued by University College Galway Amnesty International Group.
3. Reprinted as a broadside (AA24a) and card (AA24b).

A40 CLEARANCES 1986

first edition

SEAMUS HEANEY | [ornament] | CLEARANCES | Cornamona Press | 1986
24 × 16 cm. (front and bottom edges untrimmed)

[i]–[ii], blank; [1], half-title: CLEARANCES; [2], blank; [3], title-page as above; [4], copyright, ISBN; [5], dedication: IN MEMORIAM M.K.H. / 1911–1984; [6], blank; 7–14, text; [15], colophon; [16]–[18], blank.

Sewn in grey wrappers folded over the first and last leaves; front wrapper: 'SEAMUS HEANEY | [ornament] | CLEARANCES'; back wrapper blank.

Published by the Cornamona Press in December 1986 in an edition of 80 copies, printed by the Sunday Printers, Amstelveen, The Netherlands. 'Twenty copies, unnumbered, are meant for the kin and kith of the poet and the printers. Sixty copies, numbered from 1 to 60, comprise the edition proper of the Cornamona Press. This copy is number (*written in*)'.

Contents: I. A cobble thrown a hundred years ago—II. Polished linoleum shone there. Brass taps shone.—III. When the other woman was away at Mass—IV. In the first flush of the Easter holidays—V. Fear of affectation made her affect—VI. When Cezanne died watching the empty door—VII. In the last minutes he said more to her—VIII. I thought of walking round and round a space.

Note: With the exception of 'When Cezanne died watching the empty door . . .', all of the poems were collected (some with revisions) in the 'Clearances' sequence in *The Haw Lantern*.

A41 THE HAW LANTERN 1987

a. *first edition in boards*

SEAMUS | HEANEY | [short rule] | *The Haw* | *Lantern* [all the preceding within double box with inner thick, outer thin rules] | ff | *faber and faber* | LONDON · BOSTON
19.5 × 12.5 cm.

[i]–[ii], blank; [iii], half-title: The Haw Lantern; [iv], Also by Seamus Heaney; [v], title-page as above; [vi], publishing information, printing information, rights, copyright, condition of sale; British Library Cataloguing in Publication Data, ISBNs; [vii], dedication: *For Bernard and Jane McCabe* | The riverbed, dried-up, half-full of leaves. | Us, listening to a river in the trees.; [viii], blank; [ix], Acknowledgements; [x], blank; [xi], Contents; [xii], blank; 1–51, text; [52], blank.

Red paper-covered boards; front and back covers blank; spine stamped in silver: [double rule] | SEAMUS HEANEY *The Haw Lantern* [preceding lettered lengthwise, top to bottom] | ff [horizontal] | [double rule]; dust-jacket has publisher's logo, ff, repeated in black on grey background with white panels on front, back, spine and both flaps lettered and decorated in black and red.

Published June 1987; price £7.95; printed by Richard Clay Ltd, Bungay, Suffolk.

Contents: Alphabets—Terminus—From the Frontier of Writing—The Haw Lantern—The Stone Grinder—A Daylight Art—Parable Island—From the Republic of Conscience—Hailstones—Two Quick Notes—The Stone Verdict—From the Land of the

Unspoken—A Ship of Death—The Spoonbait—In Memoriam: Robert Fitzgerald—The Old Team—Clearances—The Milk Factory—The Summer of Lost Rachel—The Wishing Tree—A Postcard from Iceland—A Peacock's Feather—Grotus and Coventina—Holding Course—The Song of the Bullets—Wolfe Tone—A Shooting Script—From the Canton of Expectation—The Mud Vision—The Disappearing Island—The Riddle.

b. ***first edition in wrappers***

SEAMUS | HEANEY | [short rule] | *The Haw* | *Lantern* [all the preceding within double box with thin outer, thick inner rules] | ff | *faber and faber* | LONDON · BOSTON
19.5 × 12.5 cm.

Pagination as in A41a.

Perfect bound in stiff white paper covers with matte finish, with publisher's logo, ff, repeated in black on grey background with white panel on front, lettered and decorated in black and red.

Published June 1987 at £3.95; printed by Richard Clay Ltd, Bungay, Suffolk.

Contents: As in A41a.

Note: Published at the same time as A41a.

c. ***first American edition in boards***

The Haw Lantern | *Seamus Heaney* | [illustration] | *Farrar Straus Giroux* | *New York*
20.5 × 13.5 cm.

[i], blank; [ii], *By Seamus Heaney*; [iii], half-title: *The Haw Lantern*; [iv], blank; [v], title-page as above; [vi], copyright, rights, publishing information, printing information, Library of Congress Cataloging-in-Publication Data, acknowledgements; [vii], dedication as in A41a; [viii], blank; [ix], *Contents*; [x], blank; [xi], text-title: *The Haw Lantern*; [xii], blank; 1–51, text; [52], *Notes*.

Red cloth-covered boards; front and back covers blank; spine lettered lengthwise, top to bottom, in gold: *The Haw Lantern* /

Seamus Heaney Farrar Straus Giroux; tan dust-jacket lettered and decorated in grey, black and red.

7,250 copies published 1 October 1987 at $12.95; printed in the United States of America.

Contents: As in A41a.

d. *first American edition in wrappers*

The Haw Lantern | *Seamus Heaney* | [illustration] | *The Noonday Press* | *Farrar Straus Giroux* | *New York*
21 × 14 cm.

Pagination as in A41c.

Perfect bound in stiff glossy tan covers, lettered and decorated in grey, black and red.

Published 1 February 1989 at $7.95; printed in The United States of America.

Contents: As in A41a.

Note: The copyright page states '*Noonday Press edition, 1989*'.

e. *limited edition*

The Haw Lantern | *Seamus Heaney* | [illustration] | *Farrar Straus Giroux* | *New York*
20.5 × 13.5 cm.

[a], tipped in limitation statement with number and author's signature; [b], blank; pagination continues as in A41c.

Dark-red cloth-covered boards; stamped design of branch and fruit on front cover; back cover blank; spine has black panel stamped lengthwise, top to bottom, in gold: [rule] THE HAW LANTERN · SEAMUS HEANEY · FSG [rule]; issued in a wine paper-covered slipcase.

Published 1987 at $70; 250 numbered copies signed by the author; printed in the United States of America.

Contents: As in A41a.

A42 SEAMUS HEANEY 1988

first edition

READINGS IN CONTEMPORARY POETRY | NUMBER 4 | SEAMUS HEANEY | THE REED FOUNDATION POETRY | CHAPBOOK SERIES | DIA ART FOUNDATION · NEW YORK · 1988
18 × 13.5 cm.

[1], half title: SEAMUS HEANEY; [2], blank; [3], title-page as above; [4], publishing information, copyrights, rights, Library of Congress Catalogue Card Number, ISBN, permissions, acknowledgements, printing information; [5], contents; [6], blank; 7–43, text; [44], permissions; [45]–[48], blank.

Card covers decorated overall with a design in grey, black and white; front cover has: 'DIA ART FOUNDATION · NEW YORK | SEAMUS HEANEY' printed in a cream panel within heavy single rules; reverse of covers in blue.

Published 23 March 1988 at $5.00; 350 copies printed by Conrad Gleber Printing and Publishing.

Contents: Death of a Naturalist—Bogland—The Tollund Man—Anahorish—*from* Mossbawn—Funeral Rites—*from* Singing School—Casualty—The Singer's House—An Afterwards—The Skunk—*from* Station Island—The Scribes—From the Frontier of Writing—*from* Clearances—The Mud Vision.

Note: The book was issued on the occasion of a reading of the poems by the poet at the Dia Art Foundation, New York, on 23 March 1988.

A43 THE SOUNDS OF RAIN 1988

a. *first edition*

SEAMUS HEANEY [printed in black] | [ornament printed in grey] | THE SOUNDS | OF RAIN [printed in black] | EMORY UNIVERSITY [printed in blue]
19 × 12.5 cm.

[1]–[2], blank; [3], note on the poem having been printed to inaugurate the Richard Ellmann Lectures at Emory University; [4], blank; [5], title-page as above; [6], copyright notice printed in grey; [7], fly-title printed in blue; [8]–[9], text; [10]–[12], blank; [13], colophon; [14]–[16], blank.

Printed on wove paper and sewn in blue wrappers with a white label: 'SEAMUS HEANEY | [ornament] | THE SOUNDS | OF RAIN' printed in blue within grey rules; issued in a white envelope with: 'SEAMUS HEANEY | ornament | THE SOUNDS | OF RAIN' printed in blue on the top left.

Published 11 April 1988 in an edition of 300 copies; printed at the Shadowy Waters Press.

b. *limited edition*

Title-page as in A43a.
19.5 × 12.5 cm.

Pagination as in A43a.

Printed on hand-made paper and sewn in marbled wrappers over plain cream card covers; front wrapper label, as in A43a, except all printing in blue; issued in an envelope as in A43a.

Published 14 April 1988 in an edition of 25 hand-lettered copies signed and dated by the author.

Notes: 1. The unfolded proof sheets of the poem, printed on hand-made paper, numbered 1–15 and signed by the author, were also issued.
2. The poem was written in memory of Richard Ellmann and published to mark the inauguration of the Richard Ellmann Lectures in Modern Literature, 11–15 April 1988 at Emory University, Atlanta, Georgia, where he had served as Woodruff Professor of English.

A44 THE GOVERNMENT OF THE TONGUE 1988

a. *first edition in boards*

ff | [rule] | THE | GOVERNMENT | OF THE | TONGUE | [rule] | *The 1986 T. S. Eliot* | *Memorial Lectures and* | *Other Critical Writings*

| [rule] | Seamus Heaney | [all above within ruled border] | *faber and faber* | LONDON · BOSTON
21.5 × 13.5 cm.

[i], half-title: *The Government of the Tongue*; [ii], *by the same author*; [iii], title-page as above; [iv], publishing information, printing information, rights, copyrights, British Library Cataloguing in Publication Data; ISBN; [v], dedication: For Charles Monteith; [vi], blank; vii, *Contents*; [viii], blank; ix–x, *Acknowledgements*; xi–xxiii, *The Interesting Case of Nero, Chekhov's Cognac and a Knocker*; [xxiv], blank; [1]–170, text; 171–172, *Publishers' Acknowledgements*; [173]–[174], blank.

Red cloth-covered boards; front and back covers blank; spine lettered and decorated in white: [rule] | ff | [rule] | [the following lettering lengthwise, top to bottom] THE GOVERNMENT OF THE TONGUE | *The 1986 T. S. Eliot Memorial Lectures and Other Critical Writings* | Seamus Heaney | [rule]; dust-jacket has publisher's logo, ff, repeated in white on red background, lettered and decorated in red, black and white with white panels front, back, spine and flaps printed in black.

Published June 1988 at £12.95; printed by Mackays of Chatham, Kent.

Contents: The Interesting Case of Nero, Chekhov's Cognac and a Knocker.

Part I: The Placeless Heaven: Another Look at Kavanagh—The Main of Light—The Murmur of Malvern—The Poems of the Dispossessed Repossessed—The Impact of Translation—The Fully Exposed Poem—Atlas of Civilization—Osip and Nadezhda Mandelstam.

Part II: The Government of the Tongue—Sounding Auden—Lowell's Command—The Indefatigable Hoof-taps: Sylvia Plath.

b. *first American edition in boards*

[rule] | SEAMUS HEANEY | *The Government of the Tongue* | SELECTED PROSE | 1978–1987 | *Farrar, Straus and Giroux* | New York | [publisher's logo]
21 × 13.5 cm.

[a], blank; [b], BY SEAMUS HEANEY; [i], half-title: [rule] | *The Government of the Tongue*; [ii], blank; [iii], title-page as above; [iv], copyright, rights, Library of Congress catalog card number, publishing information, printing information; [v], dedication: [rule] | For Charles Monteith; [vi], blank; vii, *Contents*; [viii], blank; ix–x, *Acknowledgements*; xi–xxiii, *The Interesting Case of Nero, Chekhov's Cognac and a Knocker*; [xxiv], blank; [1]–[170], text; [171]–[174], blank.

Grey paper-covered boards; black cloth spine lettered in gold: SEAMUS HEANEY · *The Government of the Tongue* [preceding lettered lengthwise, top to bottom] FSG [horizontal]; ivory end-papers; dust-jacket in grey printed in black, designed by Cynthia Krupat, has twelve illustrations on front showing the position of the tongue in producing certain sounds; photograph of Seamus Heaney on back.

4,000 copies published 1 February 1989 at $17.95; printed in the United States of America.

Contents: As in A44a.

c. ***first edition in wrappers***

ff | [rule] | THE | GOVERNMENT | OF THE | TONGUE | [rule] | *The 1968 T. S. Eliot* | *Memorial Lectures and* | *Other Critical Writings* | [rule] | Seamus Heaney [all the preceding within single rule borders] | *faber and faber* | LONDON · BOSTON
19.5 × 12.5 cm.

[a]–[b], blank; [i], half-title . . . pagination continues as in A44a with [175]–[182], blank.

Perfect bound in stiff white glossy paper covers, with publisher's logo, ff, repeated in dark green on orange background, lettered and decorated in black, dark green and orange with white panel on front.

Published 1989 at £4.99; printed by Richard Clay Ltd, Bungay, Suffolk.

Contents: As in A44a.

Note: The copyright page states 'This paperback edition first published in 1989'.

d. ***first American edition in wrappers***

[rule] | SEAMUS HEANEY | *The Government of the Tongue* | SELECTED PROSE | 1978–1987 | *The Noonday Press* | *Farrar, Straus and Giroux* | *New York*
21 × 14 cm.

Pagination as in A44b with [171], acknowledgements.

Perfect bound in grey stiff glossy paper covers printed in black, designed by Cynthia Krupat, has twelve illustrations on front showing the position of the tongue in producing certain sounds.

Published 1 June 1990 at $8.95; printed in the United States of America.

Contents: As in A44a except for the addition of 'acknowledgements' to p. [171].

Note: Copyright page states '*Noonday Press edition, 1990*'.

A45 THE PLACE OF WRITING 1989

first edition

[all the following within single rule borders] THE PLACE OF WRITING | by | SEAMUS HEANEY | INTRODUCTION | by | RONALD SCHUCHARD | SCHOLARS PRESS | Atlanta, Georgia
21.5 × 14 cm.

[i]–[ii], blank; [iii], half title: THE PLACE OF WRITING; [iv], frontispiece photograph of Seamus Heaney and Richard Ellmann on the Hill of Howth, Summer 1982; [v], title-page as above; [vi], information on series, author/title, copyright, Library of Congress Cataloging in Publication, publishing information, ISBN; [vii], dedication: *For Mary Ellmann*; [viii], blank; [1], contents; [2]–16, Introduction by Ronald Schuchard; 17, *Author's Note*; 18–72, text; [73], photograph of Seamus Heaney and Richard Ellmann walking away from the camera; [74]–[80], blank.

Dark-blue cloth-covered boards; the front cover is lettered in gold: 'THE PLACE | OF WRITING | BY SEAMUS HEANEY'; the spine is lettered in gold lengthwise from top to bottom: 'THE PLACE OF

WRITING SEAMUS HEANEY'; back cover blank; light-green dust-jacket, lettered in black with a photograph of the Wicklow Gap spread across the front, spine and back; photograph of the author on the back flap.

Published by Scholars Press for Emory University in June 1989 at $19.95 in an edition of 3,000 copies. Sixty copies were numbered and signed by the author on a special leaf inserted following the front free endpaper: 'This edition of 3,000 copies is the first in the series, | The Richard Ellmann Lectures | in Modern Literature. | Of 60 copies numbered and signed by the author, numbers 1 to 30 are not for sale. | This is number [number written in] | [author's signature].'

Contents: The Place of Writing: W. B. Yeats and Thoor Ballylee—The Pre-Natal Mountain: Vision and Irony in Recent Irish Poetry—Cornucopia and Empty Shell: Variations on a Theme from Ellmann.

Notes: 1. In addition to the 3,000 copies there were 15 'author's copies', so marked, numbered and signed by Seamus Heaney, and 10 'out-of-series' copies, so marked, numbered and signed by Seamus Heaney. 2. The essays that comprise *The Place of Writing* were written to inaugurate the Richard Ellmann Lectures in Modern Literature at Emory University, Atlanta, Georgia, in 1988. Revised versions of 'W. B. Yeats and Thoor Ballylee' and the Thomas Kinsella section of 'Cornucopia and Empty Shell: Variations on a Theme from Ellmann' are collected in *Finders, Keepers: Selected Prose 1971–2001*.

A46 NEW SELECTED POEMS 1966–1987 1990

a. *first edition in boards*

SEAMUS HEANEY | New Selected Poems | 1966–1987 | [short rule] | ff | *faber and faber* | LONDON · BOSTON
21.5 × 13.5 cm.

[i], half-title: NEW SELECTED POEMS; [ii], *by the same author*; [iii], title-page as above; [iv], publishing information, printing information, rights, copyright, conditions of sale, ISBNS; [v],

dedication: For Marie and Michael and | Christopher and Catherine Ann; [vi], blank; vii–x, Contents; 1–240, text; 241, Notes; [242], blank; 243–245, Index; [246], blank.

Dark-tan cloth-covered boards; front and back covers blank; spine lettered and decorated in gold: [double rule, one thin, one thick] | [the following two lines lettered lengthwise, top to bottom] SEAMUS HEANEY | *New Selected Poems 1966–1987* | ff [horizontal] | [double rule, one thick, one thin]; cream endpapers; dust-jacket has publisher's logo, ff, repeated in black on grey background with white panels on front, back, spine and flaps lettered in black with a reproduction of a collotype lithograph of the poet by Louis le Brocquy on front panel.

Published March 1990 at £11.99; printed by Richard Clay Ltd, Bungay, Suffolk.

Contents: from *Death of A Naturalist*: Digging—Death of a Naturalist—Blackberry-Picking—Follower—Mid-Term Break—Poem—Personal Helicon.

from *Door into the Dark*: Thatcher—The Peninsula—Requiem for the Croppies—The Wife's Tale—Night Drive—Relic of Memory—Bogland.

from *Wintering Out*: Bog Oak—Anahorish—Gifts of Rain—Broagh—Oracle—A New Song—The Other Side—The Tollund Man—Wedding Day—Summer Home—Limbo—Bye-Child—Westering.

from *Stations*: Nesting-Ground—England's Difficulty—Visitant—Trial Runs—Cloistered—The Stations of the West—Incertus.

from *North*: Mossbawn: Two Poems in Dedication; 1. Sunlight; 2. The Seed Cutters—Funeral Rites—North—Viking Dublin: Trial Pieces—Bone Dreams—Bog Queen—The Grauballe Man—Punishment—Strange Fruit—Act of Union—Hercules and Antaeus—*from* Whatever You Say Say Nothing—*from* Singing School: 1. The Ministry of Fear; 2. A Constable Calls; 4. Summer 1969; 5. Fosterage; 6. Exposure.

from *Field Work*: Oysters—Triptych: I. After a Killing; II. Sibyl; III. At the Water's Edge—The Toome Road—A Drink of Water—The Strand at Lough Beg—Casualty—The Badgers—The Singer's House—The Guttural Muse—Glanmore Sonnets—An

Afterwards—The Otter—The Skunk—A Dream of Jealousy—*from* Field Work—Song—The Harvest Bow—In Memoriam Francis Ledwidge.

from *Sweeney Astray*: Sweeney Praises the Trees—Sweeney Astray—Sweeney's Lament on Ailsa Craig—Sweeney in Connacht—Sweeney's Last Poem.

from *Station Island*: The Underground—Sloe Gin—Chekhov on Sakhalin—Sandstone Keepsake—*from* Shelf Life: Granite Chip; Old Smoothing Iron; Stone from Delphi—Making Strange—A Hazel Stick for Catherine Ann—A Kite for Michael and Christopher —The Railway Children—The King of the Ditchbacks—Station Island—*from* Sweeney Redivivus: In the Beech—The First Kingdom—The First Flight—Drifting Off—The Cleric—The Master—The Scribes—Holly—An Artist—In Illo Tempore—On the Road.

from *The Haw Lantern*: For Bernard and Jane McCabe—Alphabets—Terminus—From the Frontier of Writing—The Haw Lantern—From the Republic of Conscience—Hailstones—The Stone Verdict—The Spoonbait—Clearances—The Milk Factory—The Wishing Tree—Wolfe Tone—From the Canton of Expectation—The Mud Vision—The Disappearing Island.

b. *first edition in wrappers*

SEAMUS HEANEY | New Selected Poems | 1966–1987 | [short rule] | ff | *faber and faber* | LONDON · BOSTON
19.5 × 13 cm.

[i], half-title: NEW SELECTED POEMS followed by a 14-line biographical sketch of the author; [ii] pagination continues as in A46a.

Perfect bound in stiff white paper covers with a matte finish, publisher's logo, ff, repeated in black on grey background with white panel on front with a reproduction of a collotype lithograph of the poet by Louis le Brocquy.

Published March 1990 at £4.99; printed by Richard Clay Ltd, Bungay, Suffolk.

Contents: As in A46a with the addition of the biographical sketch to the half-title.

Note: Published at the same time as A46a.

c. *English limited edition*

SEAMUS HEANEY | New Selected Poems | 1966–1987 | [short rule] | ff | *faber and faber* | LONDON · BOSTON
21.5 × 13.5 cm.

[i], half-title: NEW SELECTED POEMS; [ii], *by the same author*; [iii], title-page as above; [iv], publishing information, printing information, rights, copyright, conditions of sale, ISBNs; [v], dedication: For Marie and Michael and | Christopher and Catherine Ann; [vi], blank; vii–x, Contents; 1–240, text; 241, Notes; [242], blank; 243–245, Index; [246], blank; [247], limitation statement with number and author's signature; [248], blank.

Bound in tan paper-covered boards with black cloth quarter spine; white pasted-on label on spine, lettered in burnt orange: SEAMUS | HEANEY | New | Selected | Poems | 1966–1987; issued in a tan paper slipcase with black cloth top and bottom.

Published 1990; 125 numbered copies signed by the author, 100 copies numbered 1–100 for sale, 25 copies numbered I–XXV reserved for author; printed by Richard Clay Ltd, Bungay, Suffolk.

Contents: As in A46a.

d. *first American edition in boards*

Seamus Heaney | *Selected Poems* | *1966–1987* | [rule] | [ornamental design] | *Farrar, Straus and Giroux* | *New York*
22.5 × 15 cm.

[i], blank; [ii], BOOKS BY SEAMUS HEANEY; [iii], half-title: *Selected Poems 1966–1987*; [iv], blank; [v], title-page as above; [vi], copyright, rights, Library of Congress catalog card number, printing information, publishing information; [vii]; dedication: *For Marie and Michael* | *and Christopher and Catherine Ann*; [viii], blank; [ix]-[xiii], *Contents*; [xiv], blank; [1]–261, text; [262], blank; 263, *Notes*; [264], blank; 265–267, *Index of Titles*; [268], blank; 269–273, *Index of First Lines*; [274], blank.

Black cloth-covered boards; front cover blind-stamped: SH | [ornamental design]; spine lettered in gold: [rule] | *Seamus* | *Heaney* | [short rule] | *Selected* | *Poems* | *1966–1987* | [short rule] | *Farrar* | *Straus* | *Giroux* | [rule] | [ornamental design]; dust-jacket front cover and spine has background photograph of stone carving at Newgrange; back cover has photo of Seamus Heaney; front cover printed in white and tan; black spine panel printed in white and tan.

7,500 copies published 22 August 1990 at $20.00; printed in the United States of America.

Contents: As in A46a, except for the addition 'Index of First Lines'.

Note: This is the American edition of *New Selected Poems 1966–1987*.

e. *American limited edition*

Seamus Heaney | *Selected Poems* | *1966–1987* | [rule] | [ornamental design] | *Farrar, Straus and Giroux* | *New York*
23 × 15 cm.

[a], tipped in limitation statement with number and author's signature; [b], blank; pagination continues as in A46d.

Grey-brown cloth-covered boards; front cover blind-stamped: SH | [ornamental design]; spine lettered and decorated in gold on black panel: [rule] | *Seamus* | *Heaney* | [short rule] | *Selected* | *Poems* | *1966–1987* | [short rule] | *Farrar* | *Straus* | *Giroux* | [rule] | [ornamental design]; issued in a black paper-covered slipcase.

Published 1990; 200 numbered copies signed by the author; printed in the United States of America.

Contents: As in A46a, except for the addition 'Index of First Lines'.

f. *first American edition in wrappers*

Seamus Heaney | *Selected Poems* | *1966–1987* | [rule] | [ornamental design] | *The Noonday Press* | *Farrar, Straus and Giroux* | *New York*
23 × 15 cm.

Pagination as in A46d.

Perfect bound in stiff white glossy paper covers, printed in black, tan and grey, with a photograph of stone carving at Newgrange in various tones of grey over the front cover and spine.

Published 4 December 1991 at $15.00; printed in the United States of America.

Contents: As in A46a, except for the addition 'Index of First Lines'.

Note: Copyright page states '*This edition first published in 1991 by The Noonday Press*'.

A47 THE REDRESS OF POETRY 1990

first edition

THE REDRESS | OF POETRY | [swelled rule] | An Inaugural Lecture | delivered before | the University of Oxford | on 24 October 1989 | by | SEAMUS HEANEY | Professor of Poetry | CLARENDON PRESS · OXFORD | 1990
21.5 × 14 cm.

[i], title-page as above; [ii], publishing information, copyright, rights, condition of sale, British Library Cataloguing data; ISBN; Library of Congress Cataloging data, printing information; [1]–20, text; [21]–[22], blank.

Stapled in light-blue card covers with the title-page reproduced in black on the front cover and the ISBN printed on the bottom right of the back cover.

Published 1990 at £2.95; printed by Oxuniprint, Oxford University Press, Walton Street, Oxford.

Note: This is the text of Seamus Heaney's inaugural lecture as Professor of Poetry, delivered on 24 October 1989 before the University of Oxford. The lecture first appeared in an abridged version in the *Times Literary Supplement*, 22–28 December 1989 (C538).

A48 THE TREE CLOCK 1990

a. *first edition*

[title in gold decorative script] THE | TREE | CLOCK | Seamus Heaney | [publisher's seal] | THE LINEN HALL LIBRARY | BELFAST
21 × 14.5 cm.

[1], half-title: 'The Tree Clock'; [2], blank; [3], title-page as above; [4], publishing information; copyright; ISBN; permissions; acknowledgements; printing information; [5], dedication: '*For Tom Paulin*'; [6], blank; [7], contents; [8], blank; 9–28, text; [29]–[32], [blank].

Bound in tan linen-covered boards; front cover blind-stamped: 'THE | TREE | CLOCK'; back cover and spine blank; endpapers decorated with a pattern of celtic designs in tan; textured tan-coloured dust-jacket with the title in gold and the author's name in black on front panel; note by Seamus Heaney, blurb and price on front flap; back flap contains a note on the Linen Hall Library, ISBN and publisher's seal and address.

Published in September 1990 by the Linen Hall Library in an edition of 870 copies, of which 750 copies are bound in cloth and priced £12.95 (as A48a above); 'the remaining 120 are hand-bound, numbered and signed by the author; of these, twenty also contain a manuscript poem' (see A48b and A48c following). Printed in Northern Ireland by Nicholson & Bass Ltd.

Contents: The Point—Among the Whins—The Pitchfork—The Butter-print—The Ash Plant—The Journey Back—The Schoolbag—Glanmore Revisited: 1. Scrabble; 2. 1973; 3. The Skylight; 4. Lustral Sonnet—The First Words—Proper Names—The Crossing—A Royal Prospect—The Sounds of Rain—Fosterling.

b. *limited manuscript edition*

Title-page as in A48a.
25.5 × 16 cm.

[i]–[ii], blank; [iii], half-title: 'The Tree Clock'; [iv], copyright; [1], title-page as in A48a; [2], blank; [3], dedication; '*For Tom Paulin*'; [4], blank; [5], contents; [6], blank; [7], poem: 'The Point' in the author's manuscript; [8], blank; 9–28, text; [29]–[30], blank; [31], colophon; [32]–[34], blank.

Marbled paper-covered boards with linen spine and fore-edges; title foil-blocked in gold on the front cover; back cover and spine blank, marbled endpapers. Issued in a marbled-paper-covered slipcase with linen fore-edges.

Published in an edition of 20 copies, printed on hand-made paper with deckled edges, numbered I–XX and signed by the author, priced £400.00.

Note: The proceeds from A48b & A48c were donated to the Linen Hall Library (Belfast) development fund. The Library celebrated its bicentenary in 1988. The celebrations featured a poetry reading by Seamus Heaney and Michael Longley, the proceeds of which were also donated to the Library.

c. ***limited signed edition***

Title-page as in A48a.
21 × 14 cm.

[i]–[ii], blank; [1], half-title: The Tree Clock; [2], copyright; [3], title-page as A48a; [4], blank; [5], dedication: '*For Tom Paulin*'; [6], blank; [7], contents; [8], blank; 9–28, text; [29]–[30], blank; [31], colophon, signature; [32]–[34], blank.

Marbled paper-covered boards with linen spine and fore-edges; title foil-blocked in gold on front cover; back cover and spine blank; marbled endpapers; issued in marbled-paper covered slipcase with linen fore-edges.

Published by the Linen Hall Library in September 1990 in an edition of 100 copies, numbered 21 to 120 and signed by the author. Printed on frost-white paper, hand-bound by Sydney Aiken and priced at £90.00. (For the first 20 copies see A48b above.)

Contents: As in A48a.

A49 THE CURE AT TROY 1990

a. ***first edition***

SEAMUS | HEANEY | The Cure at Troy | *A Version of* | *Sophocles' Philoctetes* | Field Day [all above within single-ruled box]
19.5 × 12.5 cm.

[i], half title: The Cure at Troy; [ii], *by the same author* [13 titles]; [iii], title-page as above; [iv], publishing information, printing information, rights, copyright, permissions; performance rights,

ISBN; [v], dedication: In memory of Robert Fitzgerald | poet and translator | 1910–1985; [vi], blank; [vii], quotation from poem by W. H. Auden; [viii], list of characters; [ix], first production cast, production crew; [x], blank; 1–81, text; [82], blank; [83], limitation statement with number and author's signature; [84]–[86], blank.

Bluish-grey cloth-covered boards; front and back covers blank; spine lettered lengthwise, top to bottom, in gold: SEAMUS HEANEY THE CURE AT TROY [publisher's logo]; light-brown dust-jacket lettered and decorated in black and white, colour reproduction of painting by Basil Blackshaw on the front panel, blurb and information on Field Day on front flap, back panel blank, back flap has a short biographical note and a photograph of Seamus Heaney.

Published October 1990 at £25; 500 numbered copies signed by the author; printed by Clays Ltd, St Ives.

Note: A loose erratum slip states: The part of Philoctetes was played by Des McAleer. The third member of the Chorus was played by Zara Turner.

b. *first English edition*

SEAMUS | HEANEY | The Cure at Troy | *A Version of* | *Sophocles' Philoctetes* | Faber and Faber | in association | with Field Day [all above within ruled box]
19.5 × 13 cm.

[i], half-title: The Cure at Troy; biographical note; [ii], *by the same author*; [iii], title-page as above; [iv], publishing information, printing information, rights, copyright, note on Auden quotation, performance rights, conditions of sale, ISBN; [v], dedication: In memory of Robert Fitzgerald | poet and translator | 1910–1985; [vi], blank; [vii], quotation from poem by W. H. Auden; [viii], list of characters; [ix], first production cast, production crew; [x], blank; 1–81, text; [82]–[86], blank.

Stiff paper covers in light blue with Faber logo, ff, repeated in darker blue; front cover, on white panel within border of double rules: SEAMUS | HEANEY | [short rule] | *The Cure* | *at Troy* | [illustration, two arrows and bow] | A version of | Sophocles's *Philoctetes*; back cover has similar panel with description of the play, price, ISBN and barcode within border of double rules; white panel on spine lettered and decorated in black: [double rule] SEAMUS HEANEY *The Cure at Troy* [preceding lettered lengthwise, top to bottom] | ff [horizontal] | [double rule].

Published October 1990 at £4.99; printed by Clays Ltd, St Ives plc.

c. *first American edition in boards*

THE CURE | AT TROY | A VERSION OF | SOPHOCLES' | Philoctetes | [ornamental design] | SEAMUS HEANEY | Farrar, Straus and Giroux | New York
21 × 13 cm.

[i], blank; [ii], BOOKS BY SEAMUS HEANEY; [iii], half-title: THE CURE AT TROY A Version of Sophocles' Philoctetes; [iv], blank; [v], title-page as above; [vi], copyright, rights, printing information, publishing information, permission to quote from W. H. Auden's poem 'As I Walked Out One Evening', Library of Congress Catalog Card Number; [vii], dedication: In memory of Robert Fitzgerald | poet and translator | 1910–1985; [viii], blank; [ix], quotation from poem by W. H. Auden; [x], blank; [xi], list of characters and first performance cast; [xii], blank; [xiii], text-title, THE CURE AT TROY | A Version of Sophocles' Philoctetes; [xiv], blank; 1–81, text; [82], blank.

Brown cloth-covered boards; front and back covers blank; spine lettered and decorated lengthwise, top to bottom, in gold: THE CURE AT TROY [ornamental design] SEAMUS HEANEY [ornamental design] FSG; antique yellow dust-jacket lettered in black with an image of Philoctetes by James Barry on front and photograph of Seamus Heaney on back.

1,009 copies published 4 December 1991 at $20.00; printed in the United States of America.

d. *first American edition in wrappers*

THE CURE | AT TROY | A VERSION OF | SOPHOCLES' | *Philoctetes* | [ornamental design] | SEAMUS HEANEY | *The Noonday Press* | *Farrar, Straus and Giroux* | *New York*
21 × 14 cm.

Pagination as in A49c.

Perfect bound in stiff glossy antique yellow paper covers, lettered in black, with James Barry's painting, *Philoctetes*, on front cover.

Published 4 December 1991 at $9.00; printed in the United States of America.

Note: Copyright page states '*This edition first published in 1991 by The Noonday Press*'.

A50 SEEING THINGS 1991

a. *first edition in boards*

Seeing Things | SEAMUS HEANEY | [short rule] | ff | *faber and faber* | LONDON · BOSTON
21.5 × 13.5 cm.

[i], half-title: SEEING THINGS; [ii], *by the same author*; [iii], title-page as above; [iv], publishing information, printing information, rights, copyright, ISBNS; [v], dedication: for Derek Mahon; [vi], blank; [vii]–[viii], Contents; [ix], Acknowledgements; [x], blank; 1–113, text; [114]–[118], blank.

Grey cloth-covered boards; front and back covers blank; spine lettered and decorated in gold: [double rule] | SEAMUS HEANEY *Seeing Things* [all preceding lettered lengthwise, top to bottom] | ff [horizontal] | [double rule]; fawn endpapers; dust-jacket has publisher's logo, ff, repeated in rust on grey background; white panels on front and back and on spine and flaps, lettered and decorated in black; front jacket illustration shows a detail from the Gundestrup cauldron.

Published June 1991 at £12.99; printed by Clays Ltd, St. Ives plc.

Contents: The Golden Bough

Part I: The Journey Back—Markings—Three Drawings: 1, *The Point*; 2, *The Pulse*; 3, *A Haul*—Casting and Gathering—Man and Boy—Seeing Things—The Ash Plant—I.I.87—An August Night—Field of Vision—The Pitchfork—A Basket of Chestnuts—The Biretta—The Settle Bed—The Schoolbag—Glanmore Revisited: 1, *Scrabble*; 2, *The Cot*; 3, *Scene Shifts*; 4, *1973*; 5, *Lustral Sonnet*; 6,

Bedside Reading; 7, *The Skylight*—A Pillowed Head—A Royal Prospect—A Retrospect—The Rescue—Wheels within Wheels—The Sounds of Rain—Fosterling.

Part II: Squarings: 1, Lightenings; 2, Settings; 3, Crossings; 4, Squarings—The Crossing

Note: The poems in Part II are what the poet has referred to as 'twelve-liners'. These poems are comprised of 4 tercets and do not have individual titles. Each section suggests a certain 'mood'.

b. *first edition in wrappers*

Seeing Things | SEAMUS HEANEY | [short rule] | ff | *faber and faber* | LONDON · BOSTON
19.5 × 13 cm.

[i], half title: SEEING THINGS followed by a 13-line biographical sketch of the author; [ii] . . . pagination continues as in A50a.

Perfect bound in stiff white paper covers with a matte finish, publisher's logo, ff, repeated in rust on grey background, lettered and decorated in black with illustration from the Gundestrup cauldron on white front panel.

Published June 1991 at £4.99; printed by Clays Ltd, St Ives plc.

Contents: As in A50a with the addition of the biographical sketch to the half-title.

c. *limited edition*

Seeing Things | SEAMUS HEANEY | [short rule] | ff | *faber and faber* | LONDON · BOSTON
21.5 × 13.5 cm.

[i], half-title: SEEING THINGS; [ii], *by the same author*; [iii], title-page as above; [iv], publishing information, printing information, rights, copyright, ISBNs; [v], dedication: for Derek Mahon; [vi], blank; [vii]–[viii], Contents; [ix], Acknowledgements; [x], blank; 1–113, text; [114], blank; [115], limitation statement with number and author's signature; [116]–[120], blank.

Rust paper-covered boards with black cloth spine; front and back covers blank; white pasted-on paper label on spine, lettered in rust: SEAMUS | HEANEY | [short rule] | Seeing | Things; issued in a rust slipcase with black cloth top and bottom.

Published 1991; 250 numbered copies signed by the author; printed by Clays Ltd, St Ives plc.

Contents: As in A50a.

d. *first American edition in boards*

SEEING | THINGS | [ornamental design] | SEAMUS | HEANEY | *Farrar Straus Giroux: New York*
21 × 13.5 cm.

[i]–[iii], blank; [iv], BOOKS BY SEAMUS HEANEY; [v], half title: *Seeing Things*; [vi], blank; [vii], title-page as above; [viii], copyright, rights, printing information, publishing information, Library of Congress Cataloging-in-Publication Data; [ix], dedication: *for Derek Mahon*; [x], blank; [xi], Acknowledgements; [xii], blank; [xiii], Contents; [xiv], blank; [xv], [Contents cont.]; [xvi], blank; [1], text-title; [2], blank; 3–107, text; [108]–[112], blank.

Black cloth-covered boards; front cover blind-stamped: S [ornamental design] H; back cover blank; spine lettered and decorated lengthwise, top to bottom, in gold: SEAMUS HEANEY · SEEING THINGS · FSG; dust-jacket lettered and decorated in yellow, black and gold; front has illustration of Broigher gold boat on black background; back cover has photograph of Seamus Heaney.

6,577 copies published 1 December 1991 at $19.00; printed in the United States of America.

Contents: As in A50a.

e. *first American edition in wrappers*

SEEING | THINGS | [ornamental design] | SEAMUS | HEANEY | *The Noonday Press* | *Farrar, Straus and Giroux* | *New York*
21 × 14 cm.

Pagination as in A50d.

Perfect bound in stiff black glossy paper covers, lettered and decorated in black, white and light yellow, with an illustration of the Broigher gold boat on the front cover.

Published 1 April 1993 at $8.00; printed in the United States of America.

Contents: As in A50d.

Note: Copyright page states '*This edition first published in 1993 by The Noonday Press*'.

A51 SQUARINGS 1991

a. *first edition, ordinary copies*

SQUARINGS
29 × 29 cm. (all edges untrimmed).

[1]–[4], blank; [5], title-page: 'SQUARINGS' [within embossed square]; [6], blank; [7], 'SEAMUS HEANEY | Twelve Poems | FELIM EGAN | Four Lithographs | Dublin 1991'; [8], blank; [9]; divisional title in pink: 'LIGHTENINGS'; [10], blank; [11]–[13], text; [14], blank; [15], lithograph; [16], blank; [17], divisional title in yellow: 'SETTINGS'; [18], blank; [19]–[21], text; [22], blank; [23], lithograph; [24], blank; [25], divisional title in blue: 'CROSSINGS'; [26], blank; [27]–[29], text; [30], blank; [31], lithograph; [32], blank; [33], divisional title in green: 'SQUARINGS'; [34], blank; [35]–[37], text; [38], blank; [39], lithograph; [40]–[42], blank; [43], author's note; [44], blank; [45], limitation and signatures of Felim Egan and Seamus Heaney; [46], colophon; [47], embossed square; [48], blank.

Printed on Velin Arches Blanc paper and bound in natural calf; the front cover is blind stamped: 'SQUARINGS' within a square emboss; the spine and back cover are blank; slate blue Fabriano Roma laid paper endpapers. Issued in a blue solander box. The lid of the box is stamped in silver: 'SQUARINGS' within an embossed square; the spine of the box is stamped in silver: 'SEAMUS HEANEY FELIM EGAN'.

Published in Dublin, October 1991 by Hieroglyph Editions Ltd in an edition of 100 numbered copies, of which, copies 41–100 were for sale. The edition was designed by Felim Egan and signed by him and by Seamus Heaney. 'The text, composed in 14 point Futura Light, was printed on an Albion press at Graphic Studio Dublin.

The lithographs were printed from stone by James McCreary at Graphic Studio Dublin. The printing was coordinated by Mary Farl Powers . . . The binding in natural calf and the solander box cover were executed by Museum Bookbindings, Dublin'.

Note: In the order of their appearance here, these poems are collected in *Seeing Things* as 'Squarings' numbers i, vi, viii, xiv, xv, xxii, xxvi, xxxi, xxxvi, xl, xli, xlviii.

b. *first edition, special copies*

SQUARINGS
29 × 29 cm. (all edges untrimmed).

[1], blank; [2], [original coloured lithograph signed in pencil by Felim Egan]; [3], [quotation in ink in the author's hand and signed by him] [4], blank; collation continues as in A51a.

The binding and contents as in A51a except for having green Fabriano Roma laid endpapers, an original lithograph signed by Felim Egan, a hand-written quotation signed by Seamus Heaney, and six bound-in tissue paper protectors. Issued in a heavily constructed dark blue solander box.

Published in Dublin, October 1991, by Hieroglyph Editions Ltd, in a 'special edition' of 12 numbered copies signed by Seamus Heaney and Felim Egan.

Note: The author's note on p. [43] states: 'In 1986, when Felim Egan and I worked together on a small exhibition entitled "Towards a Collaboration", we had no exact sense of how the collaboration would be fulfilled. Yet the paintings on the walls and the writing in the catalogue had this much in common: they were about natural landmarks that had become marked absences. Two years later, therefore, when I got going on these twelve-line poems (the whole sequence was published in *Seeing Things*), I realized it was time for our next move. What I was doing seemed to have real connection with Felim's approach, since the writing was usually an attempt to catch at something fleet and promising, and the lines I liked best had a quality which recalled my earlier characterization of certain Egan paintings as "brightness air-brushed on the air." This book is intended to provide a setting for some of those commonly intuited "lightenings." '

c. *first complete separate edition*

SQUARINGS | a sequence of forty-eight poems | by | SEAMUS HEANEY | with forty-eight drawings | by | SOL LEWITT | and with an introduction | by | HELEN VENDLER | published at San Francisco in 2003 | by | THE ARION PRESS
27.5 × 25.5 cm. (front and bottom edges untrimmed)

[1]–[6], blank; [7], title-page as above; [8], copyright, rights, publishing information; [9]–[25], Introduction by Helen Vendler; [26], blank; [27], fly-title: 'SQUARINGS'; [28], blank; [29], divisional title: '1. LIGHTENINGS'; [30]–[53], drawings nos. 1–12 and poems nos. I–XII [with drawings on versos and poems on rectos]; [54], blank; [55], divisional title: '2. SETTINGS'; [56]–[79], drawings nos. 13–24 and poems nos. XIII–XXIV [with drawings on versos and poems on rectos]; [80], blank; [81], divisional title: '3. CROSSINGS'; [82]–[105], drawings nos. 25–36 and poems nos. XXV–XXXVI [with drawings on versos and poems on rectos]; [106], blank; [107], divisional title: '4. SQUARINGS'; [108]–[131], drawings nos. 37–48 and poems nos. XXXVII–XXXXVIII [with drawings on versos and poems on rectos]; [132], blank; [133], colophon; [134]–[140], blank.

Printed in black on Pescia mould-made paper and bound in grey cloth over boards; the front and back covers are each divided into four squares, containing straight and not straight horizontal and vertical lines, overprinted at their intersection with a smaller square containing the title and author's name; the spine designs are continued from the front cover at the top and the back cover at the bottom, with the title 'SQUARINGS in the centre. The slipcase is in dark grey cloth with the smaller square of the book's covers repeated on the front and back.

Published November 2003, at $950 in an edition of 400 numbered copies for sale and 26 lettered copies for complimentary distribution, all are signed by the poet and the artist.

Contents: 'Squarings' i–xlviii.

Note: The 48 poems were first collected as 'SQUARINGS' in *Seeing Things* (1991).

A52 THE GRAVEL WALKS 1992

a. *limited numbered edition*

SEAMUS HEANEY | THE GRAVEL WALKS | LENOIR RHYNE COLLEGE | HICKORY, NORTH CAROLINA | 1992
14.5 × 13.5 cm.

[1]–[2], blank; [3], title-page as above; [4]–[5], blank; [6]–[7], poem of thirty-two lines; [8]–[9], blank; [10], decoration, colophon; [11]–[12], blank.

Printed on wove paper and sewn in grey wrappers; front wrapper lettered: SEAMUS HEANEY | THE GRAVEL WALKS.

Published on 14 March 1992 by Lenoir Rhyne College in an edition of 175 hand-numbered copies on the occasion of the annual meeting of the American Conference for Irish Studies Southern Region at Lenoir-Rhyne College, Hickory, North Carolina; printed at the Shadowy Waters Press.

b. *limited lettered edition*

Title-page as in A52a.
14.5 × 13.5 cm. (some front and bottom edges untrimmed).

[1]–[2], blank; [3], half-title: 'THE GRAVEL WALKS'; [4], blank; [5], title-page as in A52a..[6]–[7], blank; [8]–[9], poem of thirty-two lines; [10]–[11], blank; [12], colophon; [13]–[16], blank

A special edition of 26 copies printed on hand-made paper, lettered A–Z and signed by the author; sewn in marbled wrappers over black card inner covers; cream rectangular label on front wrapper with: '*THE GRAVEL WALKS* | BY SEAMUS HEANEY' printed in grey.

Published on 14 March 1992 by Lenoir Rhyne College; printed at the Shadowy Waters Press.

Note: 10 copies, identical to A52b above, marked 'Artists Copies', and 10 copies of the unfolded, unbound sheets, all numbered and signed by the author were also issued.

A53 DYLAN THE DURABLE? ON DYLAN THOMAS 1992

first edition

THE BENNINGTON | CHAPBOOKS IN | LITERATURE | [square illustration] | *Published* | *in memory of* | *William Troy* | [circle filled in black] Dylan the Durable? | On Dylan Thomas | [rule] | SEAMUS HEANEY | [rule] | Originally delivered | at Bennington College | as Lecture Fourteen | in the Ben Belitt | Lectureship Series | MAY FOURTEENTH, 1992
23 × 15 cm.

[1], title-page as above; 2, list of previous participants in the lectureship series; 3, note on lectureship; 4, photograph of Seamus Heaney; 5–10, introduction by Stephen Sandy; 11, blank; 12, sketch of Dylan Thomas; 13–32 text; 33, list of selected works by Seamus Heaney and his signature in facsimile; [34]–[35], blank; 36, colophon.

Printed in black on laid paper and stapled in flecked grey card covers; front cover has the series name printed in blue, the title and author's name printed in green and a sketch of Dylan Thomas in black; the covers are green on the insides.

Published in 1992 by Bennington College. Printed by offset lithography at A–B Graphics & Printing, Inc., Hoosick Falls, New York, in an edition of 1,000 copies, numbered by hand.

A54 THE GOLDEN BOUGH 1992

first edition

SEAMUS HEANEY | *The Golden Bough* | [double-page black and gold-leaf screenprint] | *With Screenprints by Jan Hendrix* | BANHOLT · MEXICO D.F. | MCMXCII
37 × 24.5 cm. (top edges gilt).

[i–ii], blank; [1], half-title: 'THE GOLDEN BOUGH'; [2], left part of double-page screenprint; [3], title-page as above; [4], blank; [5], dedication: *In memory of Jack and Máire Sweeney* | *Aeneid*, Book

VI, | lines 98–211; [6], blank; 7–8, text: English above Latin; [9], blank; [10]–[11], double-page screenprint; [12], blank; 13–16, text: English above Latin; [17], blank; [18]–[19], double-page screenprint; [20], blank; 21–[24], text: English above Latin; [25], blank; [26]–[27], double-page screenprint; [28], blank; [29], *Postscript*; [30], blank; 31–[32], text [of *Postscript*]; [33], blank; [34]–[35], double-page screenprint; [36], blank; [37], colophon; [38], blank.

Printed on Lanaquarelle paper. The text was hand-set in Bembo, narrow italic for the English and roman for the Latin, and printed by Hans van Eijk at the Bonnefant Press of Banholt. The illustrations, five double-page screenprints on a background of gold-leaf, are by Jan Hendrix and were printed by him at his studio in Mexico City.

Published in May 1992 by Imprenta de los Tropicos in Mexico D. F., and In de Bonnefant, Banholt, The Netherlands, in an edition of 50 copies numbered 1–50 in the press, and 3 copies printed 'ad personam'. All copies are signed by the artist and the author at the colophon. The edition binding was by Hans van der Horst of Eenhoorn Binderij, in Amsterdam, with 8 copies being bound in full leather and 45 in paper boards. Both bindings are blocked with a design based on one of the prints.

Issued in a flimsy black paper slipcase.

Note: In the postscript, pages 31–[32], Seamus Heaney discusses his reasons for choosing to translate this particular passage of Virgil, Book vi.

A55 THE MIDNIGHT VERDICT 1993

a. *first edition in boards*

Seamus Heaney | THE MIDNIGHT | VERDICT | [publisher's logo] | Gallery Books
21 × 13.5 cm.

[1]–[2], blank; [3], half-title: Gallery Books | *Editor*: Peter Fallon | [rule] | THE MIDNIGHT VERDICT; [4], blank; [5], title-page as above; [6], publishing information, copyright, rights, ISBN; [7],

fly-title, 'THE MIDNIGHT VERDICT'; [8], blank; [9], dedication: '*for Jean and Peter*'; [10], blank; 11, *Translator's Note* by Seamus Heaney; [12], blank; [13], divisional title: 'ORPHEUS AND | EURYDICE' [14], '*Ovid,* Metamorphoses, *Book X*'; 15–19, text; [20], blank; [21], divisional title: THE MIDNIGHT | VERDICT; [22], '*Excerpted from Brian Merriman's Cúirt an Mheán Oíche; | lines 1–194 and an abridged version of lines 855–1026.*'; 23–34, text; [35]–[36], blank; [37], divisional title: 'THE DEATH OF | ORPHEUS'; [38], '*Ovid*, Metamorphoses, *Book* XI'; 39–42, text; [43]–[48], blank.

Printed on wove paper and bound in black cloth-covered boards; front and back covers blank; spine lettered lengthwise, top to bottom, in gold: 'Seamus Heaney THE MIDNIGHT VERDICT Gallery Books'; black endpapers. Light bluish-grey dust-jacket lettered in blue and white with Tony O'Malley's wood-collage 'Winter' on the front panel, the spine has 'Seamus Heaney THE MIDNIGHT VERDICT Gallery Books', the back panel is blank.

Published 14 December 1993 by the Gallery Press in a limited edition of 1,000 copies of which 75 copies are numbered and signed by the author on the fly-title and reserved for Patrons of The Gallery Press; price £15.00.

Contents: *The Midnight Verdict* is composed of three translations by Seamus Heaney: Ovid's *Metamorphoses*, Book X, which the poet titles 'Orpheus and Eurydice'; Brian Merriman's *Cuirt an Mhean Oiche*, lines 1–194, and an abridged version of lines 855–1026, which the poet titles, 'The Midnight Verdict'; and Ovid's *Metamorphoses*, Book XI, which the poet titles, 'The Death of Orpheus'.

Note: There were also 40 author's copies, marked A.C., numbered and signed by Seamus Heaney on the fly-title of the patrons' issue.

b. ***first edition in wrappers***

Seamus Heaney | THE MIDNIGHT | VERDICT | [publisher's logo] | Gallery Books
21.5 × 14 cm.

Pagination as in A55a.

Bound in card covers printed inblack, with stiff blue fly-leaves; front cover and spine are as the front panel and spine of the dust-jacket in A92a; back cover has photograph and brief biographical sketch of the author, blurb, credits, ISBN, price, publisher's details.

Published by in November 2000 by The Gallery Press at £6.95.

Contents: Same as A55a with slight revisions.

A56 KEEPING GOING 1993

a. *first edition in boards*

[illustration] | Keeping Going | *Poems by Seamus Heaney* | *Illustrations by Dimitri Hadzi* | The Bow & Arrow Press · Adams House, Harvard University | for William B. Ewert, Publisher · Concord, New Hampshire | MXMIII
30 × 22.5 cm.

[1]–[6], blank; [7], half-title: KEEPING GOING; [8], blank; [9], title-page as above; [10], copyrights and note on poems; [11], contents; [12], blank; [13], illustration; [14]–[17], text; [18]–[19], double-page illustration; [20]–[23], text; [24]–[25], double-page illustration; [26]–[29], text; [30]–[31], double-page illustration; [32]–[34], text; [35], illustration; [36], blank; [37], note by Seamus Heaney with illustration on bottom; [38], blank; [39], colophon; [40]–[48], blank.

An edition of 200 numbered copies (of a total edition of 250 copies designed and printed by Gino Lee) signed in pencil by the author, the artist and the printer. Copies numbered 1–50 are cased in linen-covered boards with red leather label on the front cover stamped in gold: 'KEEPING GOING | *Seamus Heaney*'; grey endpapers.

Published in spring 1993 by William B. Ewert, Concord, New Hampshire, in an edition of 250 copies, designed by Gino Lee, and printed by hand by the Bow & Arrow Press, Adams House, Harvard University. Two hundred copies are printed on Mohawk Superfine paper with copies numbered 1–50 specially cased in boards (A56a) and copies 51–200 bound in wrappers (A56b). Fifty roman-numeral unbound copies, printed on Arches Cover and numbered I–L, contain original etchings by Dimitri Hadzi and are laid into a cloth-covered box (A56c). All copies are signed by the author, the artist and the printer.

Contents: To a Dutch Potter in Ireland—Mint—A Sofa in the Forties—Keeping Going—Diptych—Poet's Chair—An Invocation—At Banagher.

Note: The note on page [10] states: '*Earlier versions of some of these poems have appeared in various periodicals or as broadsides. "Keeping Going" was first published in The New Yorker*' (C592).

b. ***first edition in wrappers***

[illustration] | Keeping Going | *Poems by Seamus Heaney* | *Illustrations by Dimitri Hadzi* | The Bow & Arrow Press · Adams House, Harvard University | for William B. Ewert, Publisher · Concord, New Hampshire | MXMIII
30 × 22.5 cm.

Pagination as in A56a.

Copies numbered 51–200 are printed on Mohawk Superfine paper, signed in pencil by the author, the artist and the printer, and bound in grey paper wrappers with 'KEEPING GOING' stamped in gold on the front wrapper; cream endpapers.

Contents: As in A56a.

c. ***first portfolio edition***

[illustration] | Keeping Going | *Poems by Seamus Heaney* | *Illustrations by Dimitri Hadzi* | The Bow & Arrow Press · Adams House, Harvard University | for William B. Ewert, Publisher · Concord, New Hampshire | MXMIII
Unbound: 30 × 22.5 cm.

In the following pagination pp.[1]–[2], pp.[3]–[4], and pp.[57]–[58], are loose single leaves; pp.[5]–[8], pp.[9]–[12], pp.[13]–[16], pp.[17]–[20], pp.[21]–[24], pp.[25]–[28], pp.[29]–[32], pp.[33]–[36], pp.[37]–[40], pp.[41]–[44], pp.[45]–[48], pp.[49]–[52], and pp.[53]–[56] are loose 4-page bifolia:

[1], title-page as above; [2], copyright and note on poems; [3], CONTENTS; [4], blank; [5]–[6], blank; [7], etching; [8], blank; [9], poem title: 'To a Dutch Potter in Ireland'; [10]–[12], poem; [13], poem title: 'Mint'; [14], blank; [15], poem; [16], blank; [17], blank; [18]–[19], double-page etching; [20], blank; [21], poem title: 'A Sofa in the Forties'; [22]–[23], poem; [24], blank; [25], poem title: 'Keeping Going'; [26]–[28], poem; [29], blank; [30]–[31], double-page etching; [32], blank; [33], poem title: 'Diptych'; [34], blank; [35], poem; [36], blank; [37], poem title 'Poet's Chair'; [38]–[39], poem; [40], blank; [41], blank; [42]–[43], double-page etching; [44], blank; [45], poem title: 'An Invocation'; [46]–[47], poem; [48], blank; [49], poem title: 'At Banagher'; [50], blank; [51], poem; [52], blank; [53]–[54], blank; [55], etching; [56], blank; [57], author's note; colophon, signatures, illustration; [58], blank.

Fifty roman-numeral copies, numbered I–L, containing original etchings by Dimitri Hadzi, are printed on Arches Cover paper and signed in pencil by the author, the artist, and the printer. The title-page, etchings, and colophon are protected by loose tissue papers. The unbound sheets, consisting of 3 single leaves and 13 bifolia, are wrapped in overlapping cream covers with 'Keeping Going' printed in black on the front and laid in a linen-covered solander box with leather label stamped in gold: KEEPING GOING, on spine.

Contents: Same as A56a.

A57 JOY OR NIGHT 1993

first edition

JOY OR NIGHT: LAST THINGS IN | THE POETRY OF | W B YEATS AND PHILIP LARKIN | W D Thomas Memorial Lecture | Delivered at the College | on 18 January 1993 | by | Seamus Heaney | [5 asterisks] | UNIVERSITY COLLEGE OF SWANSEA
21 × 15 cm.

[i], title-page as above; [ii], publishing information, copyright, rights, ISBN; [1]–22, text.

Printed in black on white wove paper and stapled in red paper covers; front cover: 'SEAMUS HEANEY | JOY OR NIGHT: LAST

THINGS IN | THE POETRY OF | W B YEATS AND PHILIP LARKIN | [arms of the university] | University College of Swansea'; back cover has ISBN at bottom left.

Published 1993.

A58 EXTENDING THE ALPHABET: ON CHRISTOPHER MARLOWE'S 'HERO AND LEANDER' 1994

first edition

Extending the Alphabet: | On Christopher Marlowe's | 'Hero and Leander' | The Pratt Lecture, 1993 | by | Seamus Heaney | Harvard University | Department of English | MEMORIAL UNIVERSITY OF NEWFOUNDLAND | 1994
21.5 × 13.5 cm.

[1], title-page as above; [2], blank; [3], fly-title: Extending the Alphabet: | On Christopher Marlowe's | 'Hero and Leander'; [4], photograph of Seamus Heaney; [5]–18, text; [19]–[20], list of previous Pratt Lectures.

Printed on white wove paper and stapled in red card covers; the front cover is lettered in white and has a black and white woodcut of Leander swimming in the Hellespont; the back is lettered in white with the publisher's name and university arms.

Published by the Department of English, Memorial University of Newfoundland.

Note: This lecture is collected with revisions in *Finders Keepers: Selected Prose 1971–2001.*

A59 SPERANZA IN READING: ON 'THE BALLAD OF READING GAOL' 1994

first edition

SPERANZA IN READING | ON 'THE BALLAD OF | READING GAOL' | Seamus Heaney | Boylston Professor of Rhetoric and

Oratory | Harvard University | The James McAuley Memorial Lecture, 1994 | University of Tasmania
21 × 14.5 cm.

[1], title-page as above; [2], note on the lectures series, brief biographical sketch of Seamus Heaney, copyright, ISBN, publishing information, printing information; 3–27, text; [28], blank.

Printed in black on wove paper and stapled in light-blue card covers; the front cover repeats the information on the title-page with the addition of the University of Tasmania coat-of-arms; the back cover is blank.

Published 1994 by The University of Tasmania; printed by University of Tasmania Printing.

Note: Seamus Heaney gave this lecture at the University of Tasmania, Hobart, on 6 October 1994, and at University of Tasmania, Launceston, on 7 October 1994.

A60 OSCAR WILDE DEDICATION 1995

first edition

WESTMINSTER ABBEY | [green rule] | Oscar Wilde Dedication | *by* Seamus Heaney | Poets' Corner | Tuesday 14 February 1995 | [coat of arms] | [green rule]
24.5 × 15 cm.

[1], front cover as above serves as title-page; [2], blank; [3]–[7], text; [8], back cover: 'OSCAR WILDE | [rule in green] | [quotes from *Lady Windermere's Fan* (1892) and The *Ballad of Reading Gaol* (1898)] | [green rule] | THE MERRION PRESS, LONDON'.

Printed in black and green on two loose sheets of cream wove paper folded one inside the other to make an eight page gathering; first and last pages as above; there is a green rule at the top and bottom of each text page.

Published February 1995 by Westminster Abbey; printed by The Merrion Press, London.

A61 THE REDRESS OF POETRY 1995

a. *first edition in boards*

The Redress of Poetry | *Oxford Lectures* | SEAMUS HEANEY | ff | *faber and faber* | LONDON · BOSTON
21.5 × 13.5 cm.

[a]–[b], blank; [i], half-title: THE REDRESS OF POETRY; [ii], *by the same author*; [iii], title-page as above; [iv], publishing information, printing information, copyright, ISBN; [v], dedication: for Bernard and Heather O'Donoghue; [vi], blank; [vii], Contents; [viii], blank; ix–xi, 'Preface'; [xii], blank; xiii–xviii, 'Introduction'; 1–203, text; 204–212, 'Notes'; 213, 'Acknowledgements'; [214]–[220], blank.

Black cloth-covered boards; front and back covers blank; spine lettered in white; ff [horizontal] | [the following printed lengthwise, top to bottom, in two lines] Seamus Heaney | The Redress of Poetry; cream endpapers; black dust-jacket, lettered in white with a reproduction in gold of woodcut from '*Opusculum*' on the front cover; back cover has photo of Seamus Heaney, blurbs, and ISBN.

Published September 1995 at £15.99; printed by Clays Ltd, St Ives plc.

Contents: Preface—Introduction—The Redress of Poetry—Extending the Alphabet: On Christopher Marlowe's 'Hero and Leander'—Orpheus in Ireland: On Brian Merriman's *The Midnight Court*—John Clare's Prog—Speranza in Reading: On 'The Ballad of Reading Gaol'—A Torchlight Procession of One: On Hugh MacDiarmid—Dylan the Durable? On Dylan Thomas—Joy or Night: Last Things in the Poetry of W. B. Yeats and Philip Larkin—Counting to a Hundred: On Elizabeth Bishop—Frontiers of Writing—*Notes—Publisher's Acknowledgements*.

b. *first American edition in boards*

THE | REDRESS | OF | POETRY | [harp and shamrock design] | SEAMUS | HEANEY | *Farrar, Straus and Giroux* | *New York*
21 × 13.5 cm.

[a]–[c], blank; [d], BOOKS BY SEAMUS HEANEY; [i], half-title: *The Redress of Poetry*; [ii], blank; [iii], title-page as above; [iv], copyright, rights, publishing information, printing information, Library of Congress Cataloging-in-Publication Data, acknowledgements; [v], dedication, '*for Bernard and Heather O'Donoghue*'; [vi], blank; [vii], Contents; [viii], blank; ix–xi, 'Preface'; [xii], blank; xiii–xviii, 'Introduction'; [xix], text title; [xx], blank; 1–203, text; 204–[212], 'Notes'; [213]–[216], blank.

White paper-covered boards with black cloth spine; SH blind stamped on front cover; back cover blank; spine lettered in gold: *The* | *Redress* | *of* | *Poetry* | [rule] | *Seamus* | *Heaney* | [ornamental design] | *Farrar* | *Straus* | *Giroux*; cream endpapers; tan dust-jacket with oatmeal panel on front and spine, lettered and designed in black; back cover has photograph of Seamus Heaney.

12,689 copies published 30 November 1995 at $22; printed in the United States of America.

Contents: As in A61a except for the exclusion of *Publisher's Acknowledgements*.

c. *first edition in wrappers*

The Redress of Poetry | *Oxford Lectures* | SEAMUS HEANEY | ff | *faber and faber* | LONDON · BOSTON
19.5 × 12.5 cm.

[a]–[b], blank; [i], half-title: THE REDRESS OF POETRY followed by an 8-line biographical sketch of the author; [ii] . . . pagination continues as in A61a.

Perfect bound in stiff black glossy paper covers, lettered in white with a reproduction in gold of a woodcut from *Opuscalum* in a yellow panel on the front cover.

Published 1996 at £8.99; printed by Clays Ltd, St Ives plc.

Contents: As in A61a except for the addition of the biographical sketch to the half-title.

Note: Copyright page states 'This Paperback edition first published in 1996'.

d. ***first American edition in wrappers***

THE | REDRESS | OF | POETRY | [harp and shamrock design] | SEAMUS | HEANEY | *The Noonday Press* | *Farrar, Straus and Giroux* | *New York*
21 × 14 cm.

[a]–[b], blank; [c], publisher's logo; [d], ALSO BY SEAMUS HEANEY; [i], half-title . . . pagination continues as in A61b.

Perfect bound in stiff tan paper covers with a matte finish, with oatmeal panel on front lettered and designed in black.

Published 30 October 1996 at $12.00; printed in the United States of America.

Contents: As in A61a with the addition of the publisher's logo to p. [c].

Note: Copyright page states '*First Noonday Press paperback edition, 1996*'.

A62 CHARLES MONTGOMERY MONTEITH 1995

first edition

ALL SOULS COLLEGE | CHARLES MONTGOMERY MONTEITH | MA, BCL | 9 February 1921–9 May 1995 | *Magdalen College Demy 1939–49, 1945–47; Senior Demy 1948* | *Fellow of All Souls College 1948–88, Emeritus Fellow 1988* | Address delivered at the | Memorial Service at St. George's Church, | Bloomsbury | on Thursday, 21 September 1995 | by | Professor Seamus Heaney
18.5 × 12 cm.

[1], front cover as above serves as title-page; [2], blank; [3]–[10], text; [11]–[12], blank.

Printed in black on white wove paper; stapled with the first page serving title-page and front cover.

No publishing information.

Note: Charles Monteith succeeded T. S. Eliot as editor of Faber and Faber.

A63 JAN KOCHANOWSKI: LAMENTS 1995

a. *first edition in boards*

Laments JAN KOCHANOWSKI | 1530–1584 | translated by Seamus Heaney and Stanisław Barańczak | ff | faber and faber | LONDON · BOSTON.

19.5 × 12.5 cm.

[a]–[b], blank; [i], half-title: Laments; [ii], *also by Seamus Heaney*; [iii], title-page as above; [iv], publishing information, printing information, rights, copyright, ISBNs; [v], Contents; [vi], blank; vii–xvii, Introduction by Stanislaw Barańczak; [xviii], blank; [1], text-title: *Treny* [vertical short rule] Laments; 2–53, bilingual text with Polish on left and English translation on right; [54]–[60], blank.

Black cloth-covered boards; front and back covers blank; spine lettered in white: ff [horizontal] | [the following lettered lengthwise, top to bottom] Kochanowski Laments; white dust-jacket with front cover lettered in black with Giovanni-Battista Moroni's *Portrait of a Young Girl* in colour; back cover has Czesław Miłosz statement on the translation.

Published 1995 at £12.99; printed by Clays Ltd, St. Ives plc.

Contents: Lament 1. All Heraclitus' tears . . .; 2. If my vocation had been children's rhymes . . .; 3. You've scorned me . . .; 4. Ungodly Death . . .; 5. Just as an olive seedling, . . .; 6. My Slavic Sappho, . . .; 7. Pathetic garments that my girl once wore . . .; 8. The void that fills my house is so immense . . .; 9. I'd buy you, Wisdom. . . .; 10. Ursula, my sweet girl . . .; 11. 'Virtue's a trifle!' . . .; 12. I think no father ever doted more . . .; 13. Sweet girl, I wish . . .; 14. Where is that gate for grief . . .; 15. Golden-haired Erato . . .; 16. No end to misery . . .; 17. That the Lord's hand could destroy . . .; 18. My Lord, each of us is your willful child . . .; 19. Through the long night, grief kept me wide awake . . .

b. *first edition in wrappers*

Laments JAN KOCHANOWSKI | 1530–1584 | translated by Seamus Heaney and Stanisław Barańczak | ff | *faber and faber* | LONDON · BOSTON

20 × 12.5 cm.

[a]–[b], blank; [i], half-title: Laments followed by a 7-line biographical sketch of Seamus Heaney and an 8-line biographical sketch of Stanisław Barańczak; [ii] . . . pagination continues as in A63a.

Perfect bound in stiff white paper covers with a matte finish, lettered in black, with Giovanni-Battista Moroni's *Portrait of a Young Girl* on the front cover.

Published 1995 at £6.99; printed by Clays Ltd, St Ives plc.

Contents: As in A63a.

Note: Published at the same time as A63a.

c. *first American edition in boards*

LAMENTS | [ornamental design] | *Jan Kochanowski* | TRANSLATED BY | STANISLAW BARANCZAK | AND SEAMUS HEANEY | *Farrar, Straus and Giroux* | NEW YORK
21 × 14 cm.

[i], half-title: *Treny / Laments*; [ii], *Books by the translators*; [iii], title-page as above; [iv], copyright, rights, publishing information, printing information, Library of Congress Cataloguing-in-Publication Data; v–xx, Introduction by Stanislaw Baranczak; [1], text-title: *Treny/Laments*, 2–59, bilingual text with Polish on the left and English on the right; [60], blank.

Oatmeal paper-covered boards; front cover stamped with ornamental design in black; spine lettered lengthwise, top to bottom, in black: *Jan Kochanowski* LAMENTS *Farrar, Straus and Giroux*; oatmeal dust-jacket, front cover lettered in black with ornamental design in black; back cover contains a note by Czeslaw Milosz.

Published 1995 at $17.50; printed in the United States of America.

Contents: As in A63a.

d. *first American edition in wrappers*

LAMENTS | [ornamental design] | *Jan Kochanowski* | TRANSLATED BY | STANISLAW BARANCZAK | AND SEAMUS HEANEY | *The Noonday Press* | *Farrar, Straus and Giroux* | New York
21 × 14 cm.

[i], half-title: *Treny/Laments* with publisher's logo at bottom of page; [ii], *Books by the translators* . . . pagination continues as in A63c.

Perfect bound in stiff oatmeal paper covers with a matte finish, lettered and decorated in black.

Published 1996 at $9.00; printed in the United States of America.

Contents: As in A63a except for the addition of the publisher's logo to the half-title.

Note: Copyright page states '*First Noonday Press paperback edition, 1996*'.

A64 CREDITING POETRY 1995

a. *first edition*

Seamus Heaney | CREDITING | POETRY | [publisher's logo] | Gallery Books
21.5 × 14 cm.

[1]–[2], blank; [3], half-title: Gallery Books | *Editor*: Peter Fallon | [rule] | CREDITING POETRY; [4], blank; [5], title-page as above; [6], publishing information, rights, copyright, ISBN, acknowledgements; [7], fly-title: CREDITING | POETRY; [8], blank; 9–29, text [page numbers in words]; [30]–[32], blank.

Printed in black on white wove paper and bound in yellow card covers over brown inner wrappers; front cover: CREDITING | POETRY | Seamus Heaney | [image of Greek stone relief] | THE NOBEL LECTURE | 1995; back cover has price, ISBN, and publisher's address.

Published 12 December 1995 at £5.00.

Notes: 1. The text of Seamus Heaney's lecture was printed and circulated in unbound sheets in Stockholm by the Nobel Foundation/Swedish Academy on the day of the awards ceremonies. 2. The Nobel Foundation retains the copyright to *Crediting Poetry*; thus it may be reprinted universally according to their copyright provisions.

b. *first English edition*

CREDITING POETRY | The Nobel Lecture SEAMUS HEANEY | *Privately printed for Faber and Faber*
21.5 × 13.5 cm.

[1], half-title: CREDITING POETRY; [2], blank; [3], title-page as above; [4], blank; 5–29, text; [30]–[31], blank; [32], colophon.

Printed in black on white wove paper and sewn in blue paper wrappers; olive-green dust-jacket, front has: CREDITING POETRY [in black] | The Nobel Lecture SEAMUS HEANEY [in white], back has publisher's logo in black.

Published 1996 in an edition of 500 copies for private circulation; printed by Smith Settle, Ótley, West Yorkshire.

c. *first American edition*

CREDITING | POETRY | THE NOBEL LECTURE | SEAMUS | HEANEY | FARRAR STRAUS GIROUX | NEW YORK
19 × 12 cm.

[i]–[ii], blank; [iii], publisher's logo; [iv], blank; [v], half-title: CREDITING POETRY; [vi], blank; [vii], title-page as above; [viii], copyright, rights, publishing information, printing information, Library of Congress Cataloging-in-Publication Data; [1], text title: CREDITING POETRY; [2], blank; 3–[54], text; [55]–[56], blank.

Cream paper-covered boards; front cover stamped in black: SH; back cover blank; spine lettered lengthwise, top to bottom, in black: CREDITING POETRY · SEAMUS HEANEY · FSG; antique white endpapers; dust-jacket lettered in black and red and contains an image from the Ashmole Bestiary on front and back.

Published 1996 at $12.00; printed in the United States of America.

A65 THE SPIRIT LEVEL 1996

a. *first edition in boards*

SEAMUS HEANEY | The Spirit Level | [short rule] | ff | *faber and faber* | LONDON · BOSTON
21.5 × 13.5 cm.

[i], half-title: THE SPIRIT LEVEL; [ii], *by the same author*; [iii], title-page as above; [iv], publishing information, printing information, rights, copyright, ISBNs; [v], dedication: For Helen Vendler; [vi], blank; [vii]–[viii], Contents; [ix], Notes and Acknowledgements; [ix], blank; 1–70, text.

Green cloth-covered boards; front and back covers blank; spine stamped in gold: ff [horizontal] | [following lettered lengthwise top to bottom] Seamus Heaney The Spirit Level; glossy green dust-jacket; front cover lettered in white and block colour illustration from Ashmole Bestiary; back cover lettered in white with photograph of Seamus Heaney top-left corner, excerpts from reviews of other books by Seamus Heaney, and ISBN.

Published 1996 at £14.99; printed by Clays Ltd, St Ives plc.

Contents: The Rain Stick—To a Dutch Potter in Ireland—A Brigid's Girdle—Mint—A Sofa in the Forties—Keeping Going—Two Lorries—Damson—Weighing In—St Kevin and the Blackbird—The Flight Path—An Invocation—Mycenae Lookout: 1. The Watchman's War; 2. Cassandra; 3. His Dawn Vision; 4. The Nights; 5. His Reverie of Water—The First Words—The Gravel Walks—Whitby-sur-Moyola—The Thimble—The Butter-Print—Remembered Columns—Poet's Chair—The Swing—The Poplar—Two Stick Drawings—A Call—The Errand—A Dog Was Crying Tonight in Wicklow Also—M.—An Architect—The Sharping Stone—The Strand—The Walk—At the Wellhead—At Banagher—Tollund—Postscript.

b. *first edition in wrappers*

SEAMUS HEANEY | The Spirit Level | [short rule] | ff | *faber and faber* | LONDON · BOSTON

19.5 × 12.5 cm.

[i], half-title: THE SPIRIT LEVEL followed by a 9-line biographical sketch; [ii], *by the same author* . . . pagination continues as in A65a.

Perfect bound in stiff very dark green glossy paper covers, lettered in white, with a sixteenth-century coloured illustration of bees returning to their hives from the Ashmole Bestiary on the front cover.

Published 1996 at £7.99; printed by Clays Ltd, St Ives plc.

Contents: As in A65a with the addition of the biographical sketch to the half-title.

c. *English limited edition*

SEAMUS HEANEY | The Spirit Level | [short rule] | ff | *faber and faber* | LONDON · BOSTON
21.5 × 13.5 cm.

[i], half-title: THE SPIRIT LEVEL; [ii], *by the same author*; [iii], title-page as above; [iv], publishing information, printing information, rights, copyright, ISBNs; [v], dedication: For Helen Vendler; [vi], blank; [vii]–[viii], Contents; [ix], Notes and Acknowledgements; [ix], blank; 1–70, text; [71], blank; [72], limitation statement with number and author's signature; [73]–[74], blank.

Slate-blue paper-covered boards with black cloth spine; front and back covers blank; white pasted-on paper label on spine, lettered lengthwise, top to bottom, in blue: SEAMUS HEANEY The Spirit Level; issued in a slate-blue paper-covered slipcase with black cloth top and bottom.

Published 1996; 350 numbered copies signed by the author; printed by Clays Ltd, St Ives plc.

Contents: As in A65a.

d. *first American edition in boards*

THE | SPIRIT | LEVEL | [ornamental design] | SEAMUS | HEANEY | *Farrar Straus Giroux: New York*
21 × 13.5 cm.

[i], publisher's logo; [ii], BY SEAMUS HEANEY; [iii], half-title: *The Spirit Level*; [iv], blank; [v], title-page as above; [vi], copyright, rights, publishing information, Library of Congress Cataloging-in-Publication Data; [vii], dedication: *For Helen Vendler*; [viii], blank; [ix], *Notes and Acknowledgements*; [x], blank; [xi]–[xii], *Contents*; [1], text-title: *The Spirit Level*; [2], blank; 3–[82], text; [83]–[84], blank.

Black cloth-covered boards, front cover blind stamped: S [ornamental design] H; back cover blank; spine stamped lengthwise, top to bottom, in silver: SEAMUS HEANEY · THE SPIRIT LEVEL ·

FSG; black dust-jacket, lettered in white with colour photograph of a spirit level bubble on front and black and white photograph of Seamus Heaney on back.

Published 30 June 1996 at $18.00; printed in the United States of America.

Contents: As in A65a.

Note: This edition was also issued in a box-set that included an audiocassette recording of Seamus Heaney reading all of the poems in *The Spirit Level* at $30.

e. *American limited edition*

THE | SPIRIT | LEVEL | [ornamental design] | SEAMUS | HEANEY | *Farrar Straus Giroux: New York*
21 × 13.5 cm.

[a], tipped in limitation statement with number and author's signature; [b], blank; pagination continues as in A65d.

Green cloth-covered boards; front cover stamped in black: S [ornamental design] H; back cover blank; spine lettered lengthwise, top to bottom, in silver on black panel: [rule] | SEAMUS HEANEY · THE SPIRIT LEVEL FSG [rule]; issued in a black cloth-covered slipcase together with audio cassette of Seamus Heaney reading all of the poems.

Published 1996; 200 numbered copies signed by the author; printed in the United States of America.

Contents: As in A65a.

f. *first American edition in wrappers*

THE | SPIRIT | LEVEL | [ornamental design] | SEAMUS | HEANEY | THE NOONDAY PRESS | FARRAR, STRAUS AND GIROUX | NEW YORK
21 × 14 cm.

[i], blank; [ii], BY SEAMUS HEANEY . . . pagination continues as in A65d.

Perfect bound in stiff black paper covers with a matte finish, lettered in white, with a close-up photograph of a spirit level bubble on the front cover.

Published 10 April 1997 at $11.00; printed in the United States of America.

Contents: As in A65a except p. [i], blank.

Note: Copyright page states '*First Noonday paperback edition, 1997*'.

A66 COMMENCEMENT ADDRESS 1996

first edition

Dr. Seamus Heaney | Commencement Address | The University of North Carolina | at Chapel Hill | May 12, 1996 | [design] | 1 | [rule]
18.5 × 13.5 cm.

1, title-page as above; 2–3, preface; 4–5, citation for honorary degree; 6–16, photograph and text [page 16 also includes: copyright, printing and limitation information].

Printed in black on wove paper and sewn in white card covers; grey-green laid paper dust-jacket with the front panel lettered in black: 'S*eamus* H*eaney* [swelled rule] M*ay 12, 1996*'; back panel blank.

Published in 1996 by the University of North Carolina at Chapel Hill in an edition of 500 hand-numbered copies, the first 100 of which are signed by Seamus Heaney; printed by Stinehour Press, Lunenburg, Vermont.

A67 POET TO BLACKSMITH 1997

first edition

EOGHAN RUA O'SUILLEABHAIN | Poet To Blacksmith | TRANSLATED BY | SEAMUS HEANEY
24 × 15 cm. (bottom and fore edges untrimmed).

[1], blank; [2], drawing of coal-scoop between four small red squares; [3], title-page as above; [4], blank; [5], poem in three 4-line verses; [6], blank; [7], colophon; [8], blank.

Printed in black, red and blue on cream wove paper and sewn in slate-blue laid paper wrappers. The poem is printed in black with its initial letter in blue and the title '*Eoghan Rua O'Suilleabhain's instructions to Seamus MacGearailt*' printed in red. The front wrapper is printed in black: 'EOGHAN RUA O'SUILLEABHAIN | Poet To Blacksmith'.

Printed in 1997 in an edition of 43 copies by Pim Witteveen, Hoogeveen, the Netherlands to celebrate the first twenty years of Hans van Eijk's private press, In DE BONNEFANT.

A68 AN AFTER DINNER SPEECH 1997

first edition

[colour illustration] | *On the occasion of The Atlantic Foundation's Irish Odyssey: October 1997* [all in gold] | AN AFTER DINNER SPEECH BY SEAMUS HEANEY, NOBEL LAUREATE [all in black]
24 × 15 cm.

The speech is printed in black on pp. 'ONE' to 'SEVEN' of a 23.5 × 14.5 cm. stapled paper insert pasted to the centre panel of trifold overlapping card covers. The overlapping covers are as follows:

[outer fold recto], title-page as above; [verso], quote from speech, illustration credit; [centre panel recto], speech pasted on; [verso], 'TARA | CONSULTANTS LIMITED'; [inner fold recto], 'Chorus from '*The Cure at Troy*' in calligraphic facsimile; [verso], introduction recounting the occasion, place and date of Seamus Heaney's speech.

The speech is printed in black on white wove paper. The cream overlapping card covers are lettered in black, brown and gold; the colour illustration is by Desmond Kinney and was 'inspired by Seamus Heaney's version of *Sweeney Astray*'; the calligraphy for the Chorus from *The Cure at Troy* is also by Desmond Kinney. The covers are held closed by a thin green ribbon threaded through the back panel.

Published 1997 for private circulation within and by the Atlantic Foundation.

Note: The speech was delivered after a dinner in Dublin on Tuesday, 21 October 1997.

A69 AUDENESQUE 1998

first separate edition

Seamus Heaney | Audenesque | Max Neumann | Maeght Éditeur
10 × 7.5 cm. (front and bottom edges untrimmed).

[1], title-page as above; [2], [illustration in black]; [3], *In memory of Joseph Brodsky*; [4]–[5], text; [6]–[7], [double page illustration in black]; [8]–[9], text; [10]–[11], [double page illustration in black]; [12]–[13], text; [14], [illustration in red and the word 'GILGAMESH' in black]; [15], Exemplaire No. [copy number and signatures, both in pencil]; [16], colophon.

Printed in black and red on four loose bifolia of vélin d'Arches paper and placed inside cream hand-made covers; the front cover and spine have the title 'Audenesque', in black; the back cover has a black and white image of Joseph Brodsky; issued in a greyish-green paper-covered slipcase. The illustrations are original lithographs by Max Neumann.

Published by Adrien Maeght on 25 May 1998 in an edition of 120 hand-numbered copies: 100 copies numbered 1–100 and 20 *hors commerce* copies numbered in roman numerals, I–XX. All copies were signed by the artist and author. Printed in Paris 'sur les presses de l'Imprimerie nationale pour la typographie et sur le presses d'Imprimerie Arte Adrien Maeght le 25 mai 1998'.

Note: The poem first appeared in *The Times Literary Supplement*, 9 February 1996 (C675).

A70 OPENED GROUND 1998

a. *first edition in boards*

SEAMUS HEANEY | [short rule] | Opened Ground | POEMS 1966–1996 | ff | *faber and faber*

[a]–[b], blank; [i], half-title: OPENED GROUND | POEMS 1966–1996; [ii], *by the same author*; [iii], title-page as above; [iv], publishing information, printing information, rights, copyright,

ISBN; [v], dedication: for Marie; [vi], Author's Note; vii–xiii, Contents; [xiv], blank; [1], text-title: Poems 1966–1996; [2], blank; 3–467, text; [468], blank; 469–471, Index of Titles; [472], blank; 473–478, Index of First Lines; [479]–[480], blank.

Green paper-covered boards; front and back covers blank; spine lettered in rust: ff | Seamus | Heaney | Opened | Ground | Poems | 1966–1996; dark green dust-jacket; front cover lettered in white with colour design from *Christ Carrying the Cross* by Hieronymus Bosch; back cover contains publisher's note, excerpts from reviews of previous books, and ISBN lettered in white; spine lettered in white.

Published August 1998 at £20; printed by Clays Ltd, St Ives plc.

Contents: from *Death Of A Naturalist* (1966): Digging—Death of a Naturalist—The Barn—Blackberry-Picking—Churning Day—Follower—Mid-Term Break—The Diviner—Poem—Personal Helicon.

Antaeus (1966).

from *Door Into The Dark* (1969): The Outlaw—The Forge—Thatcher—The Peninsula—Requiem for the Croppies—Undine—The Wife's Tale—Night Drive—Relic of Memory—A Lough Neagh Sequence—The Given Note—Whinlands—The Plantation—Bann Clay—Bogland.

from *Wintering Out* (1972): Fodder—Bog Oak—Anahorish—Servant Boy—Land—Gifts of Rain—Toome—Broagh—Oracle—The Backward Look—A New Song—The Other Side—Tinder (*from* A Northern Hoard)—The Tollund Man—Nerthus—Wedding Day—Mother of the Groom—Summer Home—Serenades—Shore Woman—Limbo—Bye-Child—Good-night— Fireside—Westering.

from *Stations* (1975): Nesting-Ground—July—England's Difficulty—Visitant—Trial Runs—The Wanderer—Cloistered—The Stations of the West—Incertus.

from *North* (1975): Mossbawn: Two Poems in Dedication; 1. Sunlight; 2. The Seed Cutters—Funeral Rites—North—Viking Dublin: Trial Pieces—Bone Dreams—Bog Queen—The Grauballe Man—Punishment—Strange Fruit—Kinship—Act of Union—Hercules and Antaeus—*from* Whatever You Say Say Nothing—

Singing School, 1. The Ministry of Fear; 2. A Constable Calls; 3. Orange Drums, Tyrone, 1966; 4. Summer 1969; 5. Fosterage; 6. Exposure.

from *Field Work* (1979): Oysters—Triptych: After a Killing; Sibyl; At the Water's Edge—The Toome Road—A Drink of Water—The Strand at Lough Beg—Casualty—Badgers—The Singer's House—The Guttural Muse—Glanmore Sonnets—An Afterwards—The Otter—The Skunk—A Dream of Jealousy—Field Work—Song—Leavings—The Harvest Bow—In Memoriam Francis Ledwidge—Ugolino.

from *Sweeney Astray* (1983): Sweeney in Flight.

The Names Of The Hare (1981).

from *Station Island* (1984): The Underground—Sloe Gin—Chekhov on Sakhalin—*from* Shelf Life: Granite Chip; Old Smoothing Iron; Stone from Delphi—Making Strange—The Birthplace—Changes—A Bat on the Road—A Hazel Stick for Catherine Ann—A Kite for Michael and Christopher—The Railway Children—Widgeon—Sheelagh na Gig—Aye (from *The Loaning*)—The King of the Ditchbacks—Station Island—*from* Sweeney Redivivus: The First Gloss; Sweeney Redivivus; In the Beech; The First Kingdom; The First Flight; Drifting Off; The Cleric; The Hermit; The Master; The Scribes; Holly; An Artist; The Old Icons; In Illo Tempore; On the Road.

Villanelle For An Anniversary (1986).

from *The Haw Lantern* (1987): For Bernard and Jane McCabe—Alphabets—Terminus—From the Frontier of Writing—The Haw Lantern—From the Republic of Conscience—Hailstones—The Stone Verdict—The Spoonbait—Clearances—The Milk Factory—The Wishing Tree—Grotus and Coventina—Wolfe Tone—From the Canton of Expectation—The Mud Vision—The Disappearing Island—The Riddle.

from *The Cure At Troy* (1990): Voices from Lemnos.

from *Seeing Things* (1991): The Golden Bough—Markings—Man and Boy—Seeing Things—An August Night—Field of Vision—The Pitchfork—The Settle Bed—*from* Glanmore Revisited—A Pillowed Head—A Royal Prospect—Wheels within Wheels—

Fosterling—*from* Squarings: Lightenings; Settings; Crossings; Squarings.

A Transgression (1994).

from *The Spirit Level* (1996): The Rain Stick—Mint—A Sofa in the Forties—Keeping Going—Two Lorries—Damson—Weighing In—St Kevin and the Blackbird—*from* The Flight Path—Mycenae Lookout—The Gravel Walks—Whitby-sur-Moyola—'Poet's Chair'—The Swing—Two Stick Drawings—A Call—The Errand—A Dog Was Crying Tonight in Wicklow Also—The Strand—The Walk—At the Wellhead—At Banagher—Tollund—Postscript.

Crediting Poetry (1995).

b. *first edition in wrappers*

SEAMUS HEANEY | [short rule] | Opened Ground | POEMS 1966–1996 | ff | *faber and faber*
19.5 × 12.5 cm.

[i], half-title: OPENED GROUND | POEMS 1966–1996; [ii], *by the same author* . . . pagination continues as in A70a with 473–479, Index of First Lines; [480]–[482], blank.

Perfect bound in stiff dark-green glossy covers, lettered in white, with a colour painting from *Christ Carrying the Cross* by Hieronymus Bosch on the front cover.

Published August 1998 at £12.99; printed by Mackays of Chatham plc, Chatham, Kent.

Contents: As in A70a except for the 'Index of First Lines' extending to p. [479].

c. *limited edition*

SEAMUS HEANEY | [short rule] | Opened Ground | POEMS 1966–1996 | ff | *faber and faber*

[a]–[b], blank; [i], half-title: OPENED GROUND | POEMS 1966–1996; [ii], *by the same author*; [iii], title-page as above; [iv], publishing information, printing information, rights, copyright, ISBN; [v], dedication: for Marie; [vi], Author's Note; vii–xiii, Contents; [xiv], blank; [1], text-title: Poems 1966–1996; [2],

blank; 3–467, text; [468], blank; 469–471, Index of Titles; [472], blank; 473–478, Index of First Lines; [479], blank; [480], limitation statement with number and author's signature; [481]–[482], blank.

Tan paper-covered boards with black cloth spine; front and back covers blank; white pasted-on paper label on spine, lettered in tan: SEAMUS HEANEY | Opened Ground | *Poems 1966–1996*; issued in a tan paper-covered slipcase with black cloth top and bottom.

Published 1998; 325 numbered copies signed by the author, 300 copies numbered 1–300 for sale, 25 copies numbered I–XXV reserved for the author; printed by Clays Ltd, St Ives plc.

Contents: As in A70a.

d. *first American edition in boards*

Seamus Heaney | *Opened Ground* | *Selected Poems* | *1966–1996* | [ornamental design] | *Farrar, Straus and Giroux* | *New York*

[i], blank; [ii], ALSO BY SEAMUS HEANEY; [iii], half-title: *Opened Ground* | *Selected Poems* | *1966–1996*; [iv], blank; [v], title-page as above; [vi], publishing information, copyright, rights, printing information, Library of Congress Cataloging-in-Publication Data; [vii], dedication: *for Marie*; [viii], blank; [ix], *Author's Note*; [x], blank; [xi]–[xviii], *Contents*; [1]–430, text; [431], *Index of Titles* | *Index of First Lines*; [432], blank; 433–436, *Index of Titles*; 437–[444], *Index of First Lines*; [445]–[446], blank.

Rust paper-covered boards with black cloth spine; front cover stamped, lettered and decorated in black: SH | [ornamental design]; back cover blank; spine lettered and decorated in gold: [rule] | *Seamus* | *Heaney* | [short rule] | *Opened* | *Ground* | [short rule] | *Selected* | *Poems* | *1966–1996* | [rule] | [ornamental design] | F S G; dust-jacket lettered in black and yellow; front cover illustrated with the painting *Field* by Sean Scully; photograph of Seamus Heaney on back.

11,000 copies published 9 November 1998 at $25.00; printed in the United States of America.

Contents: As in A70a.

e. *first American edition in wrappers*

Seamus Heaney | *Opened Ground* | *Selected Poems* | *1966–1996* | [ornamental design] | *Farrar, Straus and Giroux* | *New York*
21 × 14 cm.

Pagination as in A70d.

Perfect bound in stiff white paper covers with a matte finish, lettered in black and light orange, with Sean Scully's painting, *Field*, on the front cover.

Published 25 October 1999 at $15.00; printed in the United States of America.

Contents: As in A70a.

Note: Copyright page states '*First Farrar, Straus and Giroux paperback edition, 1999*'.

A71 THE LIGHT OF THE LEAVES 1999

first edition

SEAMUS HEANEY | THE | [oversize 'L' in green] LIGHT | OF THE | [oversize 'L' in green] LEAVES | WITH SCREENPRINTS BY JAN HENDRIX | BANHOLT · MCMXCIX · MEXICO D.F.
36.5 × 24.5 cm.

[1]–[2], blank; [3], half-title: THE LIGHT OF THE LEAVES; [4]–[5], blank; [6], blank; [7], title-page as above; [8], blank; [9], fly-title: THE LIGHT OF THE LEAVES, contents in English; [10], blank; [11]–[25], text in English; [26–[27], blank; [28]–[29], blank; [30]–[31], blank; [32], blank; [33],'LA LUZ DE LAS HOJAS | Traducción de PURA LÓPEZ COLOMÉ'; [34], blank; [35]–[49], text in Spanish; [50]–[51], blank; [52]–[53], blank; [54]–[55], blank; [56], blank; [57], 'HET LICHT VAN DE BLADEREN | Vertaling van JAN EIJKELBOOM'; [58], blank; [59]–[72], text in Dutch; [73], blank; [74]–[75], [76]–[77], blank; [78]–[79], blank; [80], blank; [81], colophon; [82]–[88], blank. Four double-page illustrations between [4]–[5]; one double-page illustration between: [26]–[27]; [28]–[29]; [30]–[31]; [50]–[51]; [52]–[53]; [54]–[55]; [74]–[75]; [76]–[77]; [78]–[79].

Printed on heavy Hahnemühle paper and bound in off-white Japanese paper boards and black oasis-leather spine with a 10 × 10 cm. print let into the front board; the spine is lettered, top to bottom, in gold: 'SEAMUS HEANEY · THE LIGHT OF THE LEAVES'. The screenprint images are printed on very thin Nepalese paper. Each copy is signed by the author and the artist. The book is accompanied by a separate set of ten of the prints on a silver background in 11 × 7 cm. format, signed by the artist and bound in black paper wrappers. Issued in a paper-covered slipcase.

Published in February 1999; price (NL) *f*1600, (GB) £525 (US) $850.

Colophon: 'The text of *Light of the Leaves*, with translations into Spanish by Pura López Colomé and into Dutch by Jan Eijkelboom, has been set in 14 pt Bembo by Jan Keijser and Harrie Saveur, and printed by Hans van Eijk. The prints have been made by Jan Hendrix in his studio in Mexico City. The edition consists of 70 copies, numbered 1–63 and seven copies printed "ad personam", and bound by Philipp Janssen of Binderij Phoenix. Published by Imprenta de los Tropicos · Mexico D. F., [and] In de Bonnefant ·Banholt · Holland February MCMXCIX.'

Contents: On a New Work in the English Tongue—A Norman Simile—Would They Had Stayed—The Stick—W.H. Auden (1907–1973)—Audenesque—Our Lady of Guadeloupe—The Little Canticles of Asturias—Willow, Ophelia, Moyola—Hyperborean.

A72 BEOWULF 1999

a. *first edition in boards*

Beowulf | *Translated by* SEAMUS HEANEY | ff | *faber and faber*
21.5 × 13.5 cm.

[a]–[b], blank; [i], half-title: BEOWULF; [ii], *also by Seamus Heaney*; [iii], title-page as above; [iv], publishing information, printing information, rights, copyright, ISBNS; [v], dedication: In memory of Ted Hughes; [vi], blank; [vii], CONTENTS; [viii], blank; ix–xxx, INTRODUCTION; [1], text-title; [2], opening lines of poem in Anglo-Saxon; 3–99, text; [100], blank; 101, FAMILY TREES;

[102], blank; 103, A NOTE ON NAMES; [104], blank; 105–106, ACKNOWLEDGEMENTS; [107]–[112], blank.

Dark-blue paper-covered boards, front and back covers blank, spine lettered in gold: BEOWULF [the following in two lines] TRANSLATED BY | SEAMUS HEANEY [the preceding lettered lengthwise, top to bottom] ff [horizontal]; rust endpapers; dust-jacket lettered in white and grey over detail from the painting, *Then Rain*, by Barrie Cooke.

Published October 1999 at £14.99; printed by Clays Ltd, St. Ives plc.

b. *limited edition*

Beowulf | *Translated by* SEAMUS HEANEY | ff | *faber and faber*
21.5 × 13.5 cm.

[a]–[b], blank; [c], limitation statement with number and author's signature; [d], blank; [i], note on the only surviving Beowulf manuscript; [ii], [colour reproduction of the opening page of the Beowulf manuscript]; [iii], title-page as above; [iv], publishing information, printing information, rights, copyright, ISBNS; [v], dedication: In memory of Ted Hughes; [vi], blank; [vii], CONTENTS; [viii], blank; ix–xxx, INTRODUCTION; [1], text-title; [2], opening lines of poem in Anglo-Saxon; 3–99, text; [100], blank; 101, FAMILY TREES; [102], blank; 103, A NOTE ON NAMES; [104], blank; 105–106, ACKNOWLEDGEMENTS; [107]–[112], blank.

Cream paper-covered boards, front and back covers blank, red cloth spine lettered lengthwise, top to bottom, in gold on black label: [rule] | BEOWULF [the following in two lines] TRANSLATED BY | SEAMUS HEANEY | [rule]; issued in a green paper covered slipcase with red cloth top and bottom.

Published 1999; 325 numbered copies signed by the author, 300 copies numbered 1–300 for sale, 25 copies numbered I–XXV reserved for the author; printed by Clays Ltd, St Ives plc, specially bound by Smith Settle, Otley, West Yorkshire.

c. *first American edition in boards*

BEOWULF [in red] | A NEW VERSE TRANSLATION | SEAMUS HEANEY | *Farrar, Straus and Giroux* | *New York* [all of the preceding within a light-grey border]

22.5 × 15 cm.

[a], blank; [b], ALSO BY SEAMUS HEANEY; [i], half-title: BEOWULF; [ii], blank; [iii], title-page as above; [iv], publishing information, copyright, rights, printing information, Library of Congress Cataloguing-in-Publication Data, note on the Old English Text; [v], dedication: *In memory of Ted Hughes*; [vi], blank; [vii], *Contents*; [viii], blank; [ix]–xxx, *Introduction*; [xxxi], *A Note on Names* by Alfred David; [xxxii], blank; [1], text title: BEOWULF; 2–213 bilingual text [Old English on left, Translation on right]; [214], blank; [215], *Family Trees* | *Acknowledgements*; [216], blank; [217], *Family Trees* text; [218], blank; [219]–[220], *Acknowledgements* text; [221]–[222], blank.

Black flecked paper-covered boards; front and back covers blank; black cloth spine lettered in silver: [rule] | BEOWULF | [short rule] | SEAMUS | HEANEY | [rule] | FSG; dust-jacket lettered in silver and white with photograph of chainmail-covered torso on front.

17,000 copies published 15 February 2000 at $25; printed in the United States of America.

d. *first edition in wrappers*

Beowulf | *Translated by* SEAMUS HEANEY | ff | *faber and faber*
19.5 × 13 cm.

[i], half-title: BEOWULF; [ii], *also by Seamus Heaney* . . . pagination continues as in A72a with the addition of [113]–[114], blank.

Perfect bound in stiff black paper covers with matte finish, printed in bluish grey, lettered in white, with a detail from Barrie Cooke's painting, *Then Rain*, on the front.

Published 2000 at £7.99; printed by MPG Books Ltd, Bodmin, Cornwall.

Note: Copyright page states 'This paperback edition first published in 2000'.

e. *first American edition in wrappers*

BEOWULF | A NEW VERSE TRANSLATION | SEAMUS HEANEY | [publisher's logo] | W. W. NORTON & COMPANY | *New York · London* [all of the preceding within a light-grey border]
21 × 15.5 cm.

[a]–[c], More Praise for Seamus Heaney's *Beowulf*; [d], blank; [i], half-title: BEOWULF; [ii], ALSO BY SEAMUS HEANEY; [iii], title-page as above; [iv], copyright, rights, printing information, publishing information, Library of Congress Cataloging-in-Publication Data, ISBN, note on the Old English Text; [v], dedication: *In memory of Ted Hughes*; [vi], blank; [vii], *Contents*; [viii], blank; [ix]–xxx, *Introduction*; [xxxi], *A Note on Names* by Alfred David; [xxxii], blank; [1], text title: BEOWULF; 2–213, bilingual text [Old English on left, Translation on right]; [214], blank; [215], *Family Trees* | *Acknowledgements*; [216], blank; [217], *Family Trees* text; [218], blank; [219]–[220], *Acknowledgements* text.

Black paper wrappers; front cover lettered in black and white with an embossed silver image of a chainmail torso; back covers lettered in silver; spine lettered lengthwise, top to bottom, in white: BEOWULF | [label lettered horizontally: WINNER OF THE WHITBREAD AWARD] | A NEW VERSE TRANSLATION BY | [the following printed under the previous line] SEAMUS HEANEY | [all the following printed horizontally] [publisher's logo] | NORTON.

Published 2001 at $13.95; printed in the United States of America.

f. *large print edition*

SEAMUS HEANEY | BEOWULF | A NEW VERSE TRANSLATION | [publisher's logo to the left of the following in three lines] WHEELER | PUBLISHING, INC. | ROCKLAND, MA | [rule] | * AN AMERICAN COMPANY*
23 × 14.5 cm.

[i], half-title: BEOWULF; [ii], blank; [iii], title-page as above; [iv], copyright, rights, publishing information, note on the Old English Text, Library of Congress Cataloging-in-Publication Data; [v], dedication: *In memory of Ted Hughes*; [vi], blank; [vii], *Contents*;

[viii], blank; [ix]–xl, *Introduction*; xli–xlii, *A Note on Names* by Alfred David; [1], text title: BEOWULF; 2–243 bilingual text [Old English on left, Translation on right]; [244], blank; [245], *Family Trees | Acknowledgements*; [246], blank; [247], *Family Trees* text; [248], blank; [249]–[251], *Acknowledgements* text; [252]–[254], blank.

Dark-blue paper-covered boards, front and back covers blank, spine lettered in gold: [publisher's logo] | [the following title and author lettered lengthwise, top to bottom] BEOWULF | [the following in two lines] SEAMUS | HEANEY | [the following printed horizontally within gold border] Large | Print; dust-jacket lettered in white, grey, and red with photo of knight's armour on front.

Published 2000, at $25.95; no printer specified.

A73 DIARY OF ONE WHO VANISHED 1999

a. *first edition*

DIARY OF | ONE WHO VANISHED | [short rule] | a song cycle by Leoš Janáček | in a new version by | SEAMUS HEANEY | ff | *faber and faber*
21.5 × 13.5 cm.

[i], half-title: DIARY OF ONE WHO VANISHED; [ii], blank; [iii], title-page as above; [iv], publishing information, printing, information, rights, copyright, ISBN; [v]–[vi], Introduction; [vii], text-title, performers, production information, Irish premiere information, British premiere information; [viii], blank; [ix]–[xxxi], text; [xxxii], blank.

Stapled dark-green plain papers wrappers; front and back covers blank; bright-yellow dust-jacket, printed in black and red.

Published October 1999 at £3.99; printed by Character Print and Design Ltd, England.

b. *first American edition*

DIARY OF ONE | WHO VANISHED | [single-leaf design] | A SONG CYCLE BY Leoš Janáček | OF POEMS BY Ozef Kalda | IN A NEW

VERSION BY | Seamus Heaney | FARRAR, STRAUS AND GIROUX | NEW YORK
15 × 13.5 cm.

[i], half-title: DIARY OF ONE | WHO VANISHED; [ii], ALSO BY Seamus Heaney; [iii], title-page as above; [iv], copyright, rights, printing information, publishing information, Library of Congress Cataloging-in-Publication data, ISBN; v–ix, Introduction; [x], blank; [xi], text-title; [xii], blank; [xiii], performers, production information, Irish premier information, British premier information; [xiv], blank; [xv]–[xlvi], text; [xlvii]–[xlviii], blank.

Paper covers; front and back covers decorated in black, green, and white forest motif; front cover contains title, composer and poets' names within white rule rectangle; back cover contains price, bar-code, and ISBN; spine lettered lengthwise, top to bottom, in white: DIARY OF ONE WHO VANISHED [leaf design] SEAMUS HEANEY FSG.

11,000 copies published 27 October 2000 at $9.00; printed in the United States of America.

A74 BALLYNAHINCH LAKE 1999

a. *first edition*

Seamus Heaney | BALLYNAHINCH LAKE | traduzione Marco Sonzogni | foto Nicola Pellegrini
16.5 × 12 cm. (unpaginated).

[1]–[2], blank; [3], title-page as above; [4], blank; [5], colour photograph pasted in; [6], blank; [7], text; [8], blank; [9], text; [10], blank; [11], text in Italian; [12], blank; [13], text in Italian; [14], blank; [15], NOTA AL TESTO by Marco Sonzogni; [16], blank.

Grey paper-covered boards; front cover with author and title printed in black; back cover blank; grey endpapers; printed in black on grey paper; verso of back cover: *en plein* officina | Milano, dicembre 1999 | 70 copie; inserted leaf: UN CARPE DIEM IRLANDESE (a note by Marco Sonzogni).

70 copies published by Marco Sonzogni to mark the 60th birthday of Seamus Heaney; hand printed by Meri Gorni.

b. ***first separate edition***

[within a ruled frame with celtic designs at the corners] Ballynahinch | Lake [title in Aladdin type] | by | Seamus Heaney | December 31st 1999

Card: folded 21 × 15 cm.

[1], cover-title as above; [2], 'Ballynahinch Castle [in Aladdin type] | *Turning the Millennium* | Limited Edition of 500 Copies'; [3], 'Seamus Heaney | *Ballynahinch Lake* | poem of twenty-six line printed in italics | [copy number stamped in red] of 500' [contents of [2]–[3] within a double-page ruled frame with celtic designs at the corners]; [4], [following within a ruled frame with a celtic designs at the corners] '© Seamus Heaney 1999 | Privately Printed for Ballynahinch Castle | with the kind permission of the author | Limited Edition of 500 copies'.

Note: Printed privately for Ballynahinch Castle Hotel, Co. Galway, in a limited edition of 500 numbered copies and read by Des Lally to the assembled guests of the castle at midnight on 31 December 1999.

A75 ELECTRIC LIGHT 2001

a. ***first edition in boards***

SEAMUS HEANEY | Electric Light | [short rule] | ff | *faber and faber*
21.5 × 14 cm.

[i], half-title: ELECTRIC LIGHT; [ii], *also by Seamus Heaney*; [iii], title-page as above; [iv], publishing information, printing information, rights, copyright, ISBNs; [v], dedication: for Matthew and Caroline; [vi], blank; [vii]–[viii], Contents; [1]–81, text; [82]–[88], blank.

Black cloth-covered boards; front and back covers blank; spine stamped in white: SEAMUS HEANEY Electric Light [preceding lettered lengthwise, top to bottom] | ff [horizontal]; bright orange dust-jacket; front cover lettered in white and grey; back cover lettered in white with ISBN; inside flaps lettered in white with review information.

Published 2001 at £14.99; printed in Italy.

Contents: [*Part I*] At Toomebridge—Perch—Lupins—Out of the Bag—Bann Valley Eclogue—Montana—The Loose Box—Turpin Song—The Border Campaign—Known World—The Little Canticles of Asturias—Ballynahinch Lake—The Clothes Shrine—Red, White and Blue—Virgil: Eclogue IX—Glanmore Eclogue—Sonnets from Hellas: 1. Into Arcadia; 2. Conkers; 3. Pylos; 4. The Augean Stables; 5. Castalian Spring; 6. Desfina—The Gaeltacht—The Real Names—The Bookcase—Vitruviana—Ten Glosses—The Fragment

[*Part II*] On His Work in the English Tongue—Audenesque—To the Shade of Zbigniew Herbert—Would They Had Stay'd—Late in the Day—Arion—Bodies and Souls—Clonmany to Ahascragh—Sruth—Seeing the Sick—Electric Light.

b. *first edition in wrappers*

SEAMUS HEANEY | Electric Light | [short rule] | ff | *faber and faber*
19.5 × 13 cm.

Pagination as in A75a.

Perfect bound in stiff bright orange paper covers and flaps with a matte finish, lettered in grey and white.

Published 2001 at £8.99; printed in Italy.

Contents: As in A75a.

Note: Published at the same time as A75a.

c. *limited edition*

SEAMUS HEANEY | Electric Light | [short rule] | ff | *faber and faber*
21.5 × 13.5 cm.

[i], limitation statement with number and author's signature; [ii], blank; [iii], half-title: ELECTRIC LIGHT; [iv], *also by Seamus Heaney*; [v], title-page as above; [vi], publishing information, printing information, rights, copyright, ISBNs; [vii], dedication: for Matthew and Caroline; [viii], blank; [ix]–[x], Contents; [1]–81, text; [82]–[88], blank.

Cream paper-covered boards with black cloth spine; front and back covers blank; white pasted-on paper label on spine, lettered in black: SEAMUS HEANEY Electric Light; issued in a cream paper-covered slipcase with black cloth top and bottom.

Published 2001; 325 numbered copies signed by the author, 300 copies numbered 1–300 for sale, 25 copies numbered I–XXV reserved for the author; printed in Italy.

Contents: As in A75a.

d. ***first American edition in boards***

[other than the title, all the following in grey letters] SEAMUS | HEANEY | [title in black] Electric | Light | Farrar, Straus and Giroux | New York | [three grey vertical dots]
21 × 13.5 cm.

[a], blank; [b], ALSO BY SEAMUS HEANEY; [i], half-title: ELECTRIC | LIGHT | [three grey vertical dots]; [ii], blank; [iii], title-page as above; [iv], copyright, rights, publishing information, Library of Congress Cataloging-in-Publication Data; [v], dedication: *For Matthew and Caroline*; [vi], blank; [vii]–[ix], CONTENTS; [x], blank; [1]–98, text; [99]–[100], blank.

Flecked, mint-green, paper-covered boards; front and back cover blank; yellow cloth-covered spine stamped lengthwise, top to bottom, in gold: SEAMUS HEANEY · Electric Light · FSG; tan and green dust-jacket, lettered in green and brown with colour photograph of electric light-bulb on front and sepia photograph of Seamus Heaney on back.

17,000 copies published 8 April 2001 at $20.00; printed in the United States of America.

Contents: As in A75a.

e. ***first American edition in wrappers***

[other than the title, all following in grey letters] SEAMUS | HEANEY | [title in black] Electric | Light | Farrar, Straus and Giroux | NewYork | [three vertical grey dots]
21 × 14 cm.

[a], author's name, title, biographical note; [b], ALSO BY SEAMUS HEANEY . . . pagination continues as in A75d.

Perfect bound in stiff paper covers with matte finish, printed in black, greyish green, pale orange yellow and greyish yellow, with a photograph of the first electric light bulb on the front cover.

Published 3 April 2002 at $13.00; printed in the United States of America.

Contents: As in A75a.

Note: Copyright page states '*First Farrar, Straus and Giroux paperback edition, 2002*'.

A76 TOWERS, TREES, TERRORS 2001

first edition

Università degli Studi di Urbino | Facoltà di Lingue e Letterature Straniere | *Saluto del Rettore* | Giovanni Bogliolo | *Laudatio* | Stefano Pivato | *Lectio Magistralis* | Seamus Heaney | Conferimento della laurea *honoris causa* in Lingue e Letterature Straniere a | Seamus Heaney | Premio Nobel per la Letteratura 1995 | Urbino, 23 novembre 2001
29.5 × 21 cm.

[i], title-page as above; [ii], blank; I–IV, Laudatio; [1], half-title: Lectio Magistralis | Seamus Heaney | Premio Nobel per la Letteratura 1995 | Towers, Trees, Terrors/Torri, Alberi e Terrori; 2–15 bilingual text with English on even numbered pages and Italian on odd numbered pages; [16]–[18], blank.

Stapled green paper wrappers; front cover same as title-page lettered in black with woodcut of woman with books above her head; back cover blank; presented in stiff white folder lettered in black and brown.

No publishing information; printed by l'asterisco copisteria.

Contents: 'Towers, Trees, and Terror: A Reverie in Urbino.'

A77 SOMETHING TO WRITE HOME ABOUT 2001

a. *limited edition in card covers*

[large brown calligraphic] *S* [the following in black] *omething* | *to write* | *home* | *about* | [brown rule] | [in black] BY SEAMUS HEANEY | [in brown] A MEDITATION FOR TELEVISION | [publisher's logo] | [in black] FLYING FOX FILMS | [in brown] 2001
21 × 15 cm.

[i]–[ii], blank; [iii], title-page as above; [iv], illustration: river motif by Basil Blackshaw; *one-twelve*, text [Seamus Heaney's text printed in black towards the right of page, camera directions printed in brown in left margin]; [*thirteen*], colophon; [*fourteen*], ISBN and copyright; [*fifteen*]–[*sixteen*], blank.

Printed in black and brown and sewn in card covers over red inner paper wrappers; the covers are printed with a marbled paper effect and have a salmon coloured strip along the spine; front cover is lettered in brown and black; back cover is blank.

Published in 2001 by Flying Fox Films (David Hammond) in an edition of 350 copies of which 274 unnumbered copies are in card covers (A77a); 50 copies numbered 1–50 have a wrap-around dust-jacket and are signed by Seamus Heaney and David Hammond (A77b); a further 26 signed copies are lettered A–Z and are hand bound and cased by Sydney Aiken (A77c). Printed Northern Ireland by Nicholson & Bass Ltd.

Notes: 1. Although the title pages all give 2001 as the publication date, the various issues were published late 2001–2002, with the lettered issue being delayed in binding and completion of the slip-cases until late 2002–early 2003. 2. The television programme *Something to Write Home About*, described as a 'meditation for television' by Seamus Heaney, was commissioned by BBC Northern Ireland and produced by David Hammond's Flying Fox Films. It was first transmitted on 4 March 1998.

b. ***signed numbered edition***

Title-page as in A77a.
21 × 14.5 cm.

Pagination as in A77a.

An edition of 50 copies sewn in plain white card covers over red inner wrappers, with a wrap-around dust-jacket printed and lettered as are the covers on A77a. Each numbered and signed in ink by Seamus Heaney and David Hammond.

c. ***signed lettered edition***

Title-page same as A77a.
21 × 14.5 cm.

Pagination as in A77a.

An edition of 26 copies of A77a without the red inner wrappers, lettered A–Z and signed by Seamus Heaney and David Hammond, bound in paper-covered boards with a gold-tooled leather spine; the paper-covered boards are printed and lettered as the covers in A77a; tan end papers. Issued in an orange cloth-covered slipcase.

A78 THE WHOLE THING: ON THE GOOD OF POETRY 2002

first edition

SEAMUS HEANEY | THE WHOLE THING: | ON THE GOOD OF POETRY | *Annual Distinguished Lecture* | [ornament] | *Department of International Health and* | *Tropical Medicine* | *The Royal College of Surgeons in Ireland* | *November 5, 2001* | THE RECORDER | *The Journal of the American Irish Historical Society*
23 × 15.5 cm.

[1], title-page as above; [2], copyright; 3–18, text; [19], colophon; [20], blank.

Printed in black from Minion type on Cougar Opaque paper and stapled in greenish grey wrappers; front wrapper has 'SEAMUS HEANEY | THE WHOLE GOOD THING: | ON THE GOOD OF POETRY | [ornament]' all printed in green; back cover blank.

Published in Spring 2002 by *The Recorder* in an edition of 500 copies designed by Jerry Kelly.

Note: The lecture was first published in *The Recorder*, Volume 15, Number 1, Spring 2002.

A79 FINDERS KEEPERS: SELECTED PROSE 1971–2001 2002

a. *first edition in boards*

SEAMUS HEANEY | Finders Keepers | SELECTED PROSE | 1971–2001 | ff | *faber and faber*
21.5 × 13.5 cm.

[i], half-title: FINDERS KEEPERS; [ii], *by the same author*; [iii], title-page as above; [iv], publishing information, printing information, rights, copyright, ISBN; [v], dedication: for Dennis O'Driscoll and Julie O'Callaghan; [vi], blank; vii–viii, Contents; ix–x, Preface; [1]–416, text; [417]–[422], blank.

White cloth-covered boards; front and back covers blank; spine lettered in black: Finders | Keepers | *Selected* | *Prose* | *1971–2001* | SEAMUS | HEANEY | ff; grey endpapers; slate-blue dust-jacket, front cover and spine lettered in black outline letters and white; back cover bar code and ISBN.

Published April 2002 at £20.00; printed in Italy.

Contents: Preface
Part I: Mossbawn—*from* Feeling into Words—Learning from Eliot—Belfast—Cessation 1994—Something to Write Home About—Earning a Rhyme—On Poetry and Professing

Part II: Englands of the Mind—Yeats as an Example?—Place and Displacement: Recent Poetry from Northern Ireland—The Placeless Heaven: Another Look at Kavanagh—The Main of Light—Atlas of Civilization—*from* Envies and Identifications: Dante and the Modern Poet—*from* The Government of the Tongue—*from* Sounding Auden—Lowell's Command—*from* The Indefatigable Hoof-taps: Sylvia Plath—*from* The Place of Writing: 1 W. B. Yeats and Thoor Ballylee; 2 Thomas Kinsella—Edwin Muir—*from* The Redress of Poetry—*from* Extending the Alphabet: Christopher

Marlowe—John Clare's Prog—A Torchlight Procession of One: Hugh MacDiarmid—*from* Dylan the Durable? On Dylan Thomas—Joy or Night: Last Things in the Poetry of W. B. Yeats and Philip Larkin—*from* Counting to a Hundred: Elizabeth Bishop—Burns's Art Speech—Through-Other Places, Through-Other Times: The Irish Poet and Britain

Part III: Stevie Smith's *Collected Poems*—Joyce's Poetry—Italo Calvino's *Mr Palomar*—Paul Muldoon's *The Annals of Chile*—Norman MacCaig—Joseph Brodsky 1940–1996—On Ted Hughes's 'Littleblood'—Secular and Millennial Milosz

Note: The placement in this edition of the book of 'Earning a Rhyme' and 'Something to Write Home About' do not correspond to their listings in the table of contents. In subsequent editions the table of contents was corrected.

b. *first American edition in boards*

[the following in black] FINDERS | KEEPERS | [the following in grey] SELECTED | PROSE | 1971–2001 | [the following in black] SEAMUS | HEANEY | [the following in grey] [rule] | FARRAR STRAUS GIROUX | NEW YORK
23 × 15 cm.

[a], blank; [b], ALSO BY SEAMUS HEANEY; [i], half-title: FINDERS KEEPERS | SELECTED PROSE 1971–2001; [ii], blank; [iii], title-page as above; [iv], copyright, rights, printing information, publishing information, ISBN; [v], dedication: for Dennis O'Driscoll and Julie O'Callaghan; [vi], blank; [vii]–viii, Contents; [ix]–x, FOREWORD; [1]–450, text; [451]–52, ACKNOWLEDGEMENTS.

Black paper-covered boards with cloth quarter spine; front and back covers blank; spine lettered in gold: FINDERS | KEEPERS | · | SELECTED | PROSE | 1971–2001 | · | SEAMUS | HEANEY | FSG; grey endpapers; dust-jacket lettered in black, yellow, white and red on front cover and spine; back cover has black and white photograph of Seamus Heaney, with bar code and ISBN.

7,500 copies published 26 June 2002 at $30.00; printed in the United States of America.

Contents: As in A79a with the addition of Acknowledgements pages.

c. *first edition in wrappers*

SEAMUS HEANEY | Finders Keepers | SELECTED PROSE | 1971–2001 | ff | *faber and faber*
20 × 12.5 cm.

Pagination as in A79a.

Perfect bound in stiff slate-blue paper covers and flaps with a matte finish, lettered in black and bluish white.

Published 2003 at £12.99; printed by T. J. International Ltd, Padstow, Cornwall.

Contents: As in A79a.

Note: Copyright page states 'This paperback edition first published in 2003.'

d. *first American edition in wrappers*

FINDERS | KEEPERS | [sub-title in grey] SELECTED | PROSE | 1971–2001 | SEAMUS | HEANEY | [rule] | FARRAR STRAUS GIROUX | NEW YORK
21 × 14 cm.

[a], author's name, title, biographical note; [b], ALSO BY SEAMUS HEANEY . . . pagination continues as in A79b.

Perfect bound in stiff paper covers with a matte finish, with five bands of various widths printed in strong red, light yellow and black across the front cover, spine and back cover and lettered in black, light yellow, bluish white and white.

Published 16 April 2003 at $15.00; printed in the United States of America.

Contents: As in A79a except for the additions to p. [a].

Note: Copyright page states *'First American paperback edition, 2003'*.

A80 HALLAIG 2002

first edition

[front cover serves as title-page] Hallaig Shomhairle MacGill-Eain | Translated by | Seamus Heaney
21 × 14.5 cm.

[1], 'Published by | Urras Shomhairle | The Sorley MacLean Trust | 2002'; [2]–[7], bilingual text with MacLean's poem in Scots Gaelic on versos and Seamus Heaney's translation in English on rectos; [8], blank.

Printed in black on cream wove paper and stapled in pale green card covers; front cover lettered in black serves as title-page; back cover contains copyrights, printing and limitation information in black.

Published by Urras Shomhairle: The Sorley MacLean Trust, 2002 in an edition of 200 copies of which the first 50 copies are numbered and signed by Seamus Heaney; printed by Lateral Line.

A81 THE VISIT OF SEAMUS HEANEY TO RHODES UNIVERSITY IN HONOUR OF MALVERN VAN WYK SMITH 2002

first edition

[all the following within a single ruled box] [University coat-of-arms] | RHODES UNIVERSITY | The Visit | of | Seamus Heaney | to Rhodes University | in honour of | Malvern van Wyk Smith | August 2002 [all the preceding printed to the left of a sweep of solid blue]
21 × 14.5 cm.

[1], contents; [2], photograph of Seamus Heaney; [3], photograph of Malvern van Wyk Smith; 4, list of five supporters; 5, introduction by Paul Walters; 6–12; citation for Seamus Justin Heaney by Malvern van Wyk Smith, Public Orator; 13–17, Graduation Address: 'Hope and History' by Seamus Heaney; 18–28, The Public Lecture, 27 August 2002: 'The Guttural Muse' by Seamus Heaney

Printed in black on white wove paper and stapled in light-blue card covers; front cover which is lettered in black to the left of a sweeping blue design, serves as title-page; back cover has publisher's details in black.

Published by the Department of English, Rhodes University, Grahamstown, South Africa, 2002; printed by Dupli-Print.

A82 A KEEN FOR THE COINS 2002

a. *first separate edition*

[the following in black] A KEEN FOR THE COINS | SEAMUS HEANEY | [the following in grey] HICKORY, N.C. | LENOIR-RHYNE COLLEGE | 2002
12.5 × 12.5 cm. (bottom edges untrimmed)

[1]–[3], blank; [4], illustration of eight Irish coins within single rules; [5], title-page as above; [6], blank; [7], poem of six lines; [8], blank; [9], colophon; [10], copyrights; [11]–[12], blank.

Printed in black, grey and brown on laid paper and sewn into grey hand-made paper wrappers over plain white card covers; front wrapper is embossed with the reverse of a 1928 Irish coin; back wrapper blank.

Published on 6 October 2002 by Lenoir-Rhyne College, Hickory, NC, in an edition of 100 copies; printed by Richard Murdoch at Shadowy Waters Press, Winston-Salem, NC; illustrations by Todd Rivers. An undetermined number were signed by Seamus Heaney.

Note: This edition of 'A Keen for the Coins' was published by Lenoir-Rhyne College to mark the opening of *Seamus Heaney's Ars Poetica*, an exhibition of the poet's rare publications and manuscripts at the Hickory Museum of Art, and the reading by him at Lenoir-Rhyne College, 6 October 2002. The poem first appeared in *Irish Pages*, Spring 2002.

b. *lettered edition*

[the following in black] A KEEN FOR THE COINS | SEAMUS HEANEY | [the following in grey] HICKORY, N.C. | LENOIR-RHYNE COLLEGE | 2002
15 × 13.5 cm. (front edges untrimmed)

[1], blank page embossed with the reverse of a 1928 Irish coin; [2], blank; [3], half-title: A KEEN FOR THE COINS; [4], illustration of eight Irish coins within single rules; [5], title-page as above; [6], blank; [7], poem of six lines; [8], blank; [9], colophon, letter [*written in*], author's signature; [10], copyrights; [11], reverse of 1928 Irish coin in brown; [12], blank.

Printed in black, grey and brown on laid paper and sewn in handmade marbled paper wrappers over white card covers; front wrapper has a rectangular label with the title and the author's name in brown; back cover blank.

Published on 6 October 2003 by Lenoir-Rhyne College in an edition limited to 26 copies lettered A–Z and signed by the author; printed by Richard Murdoch at Shadowy Waters Press, Winston-Salem, NC; illustrations by Todd Rivers.

Note: An undetermined number of unbound artist's copies were also produced.

A83 ARION 2002

first separate edition

ARION | [illustration in blue of Arion astride a dolphin] | A poem by ALEXANDER PUSHKIN | Translated into English by SEAMUS HEANEY | With a note on the Russian by Olga Carlisle | And a justification for this keepsake by Andrew Hoyem | ARION PRESS, San Francisco, 2002
24 × 16 cm.

[1]–[2], blank; [3], title-page as above; [4], limitation and copyrights; [5]–[9], justification by Andrew Hoyem; [10], text in Russian, in Cyrillic type; [11], text in English, printed in blue; [12]–[16] note on Puskin's *Arion* by Olga Carlisle; [17]–[18], 'Other Poets' Employment of the Arion Legend'; [19]–[20], blank.

Printed in black and blue on wove paper and sewn in dark blue paper wrappers; front wrapper lettered in black: 'ARION | by | ALEXANDER PUSHKIN | translated by | SEAMUS HEANEY | [drawing of a harp]'; back cover blank.

Published in 2002 by Arion Press, San Francisco, in an edition of 400 copies as a keepsake for subscribers.

AA

BROADSIDES AND CARDS

AA1 THE LAST MUMMER 1969

Christmas card

THE LAST MUMMER
Stiff card folded to 17.5 × 11 cm.

[1], text; [2]–[4], blank.

Card with top, front and bottom of pages [1] and [2] deckled and tipped in silver; pages [3] and [4] trimmed. Page [1] contains the poem printed in black within a blind-stamped rectangle.

Note: Subsequently published in *Honest Ulsterman*, March/April 1970 (C126); collected with revisions and extended in *Wintering Out*.

AA2 LAND 1971

first edition

Title 'LAND' to the left of poem of 34 lines in 3 numbered sections, all within single black rules; printing and publishing information at bottom of sheet.
Broadside: 38 × 28 cm.

Printed in black on cream laid paper watermarked '[crown] | Abbey Mills | Greenfield' and signed by the author.

Published by Poem-of-the-Month Club Ltd; printed by John Roberts Press Ltd.

Note: The prospectus for 'Land' announced an edition of 1,000 copies.

AA3 SERVANT BOY 1971

first separate edition

[at left] SERVANT BOY | by | Seamus Heaney | [illustration: The Tarot Fool] | [at right: poem of 20 lines in five verses] | *free* | printed in Detroit, June 20, 1971 | The Red Hanrahan Press

Broadside: 30.5 × 20 cm. (bottom edge untrimmed).

Printed in blue on cream card and published 20 June 1971 by The Red Hanrahan Press, Detroit.

Notes: 1. Some copies do not have the word '*free*' printed above the publishing information; no priority has been determined.
2. First published in *Responses* (B9); collected in *Wintering Out*.

AA4 CHAPLET 1971

first edition

BROADSIDE II | *December 1971* | CHAPLET | *BY* | SEAMUS HEANEY | [drawing of a flower] | [poem of 22 lines in three numbered sections] | [colophon] | [publishing information]
Broadside: 50.5 × 21 cm.

Printed at St. Sepulchre's Press (Dublin) in a limited edition of 50 copies, numbered and signed by the author.

Published December 1971 by Tara Telephone Publications.

Note: This was the second in a series of five broadsides published by Tara Telephone Publications (editor, Peter Fallon). Parts I and III were later printed as parts III and IV, of 'Summer Home' in *Wintering Out*.

AA5 JANUARY GOD 1972

first edition

JANUARY GOD | [poem of four four-line verses surrounded by green and black illustrations] | poem · Seamus Heaney image · T.P. Flanagan an Arts Council of N. Ireland publication
Broadside: 76 × 56 cm.

Text printed in black on white card. T. P. Flanagan's illustration is printed in black and green.

Published by the Arts Council of Northern Ireland, 1972.

Note: The broadside was issued later on a stiff, 23 × 23 cm. card with a section of the illustration missing. Publication information on back of card: 'From a poster commissioned by the N. I. Arts Council, 1972. Image: T. P. Flanagan. Words: Seamus Heaney'.

AA6 CATHERINE'S POEM 1976

Christmas card

CATHERINE'S POEM | text
Card unfolded.

Privately printed for the author; lettered on one side only in blue ink on cards of pink, green, white, and blue; the blue card has deckled edges. The four cards measure: pink, 8.5 × 11.5; white, 9 × 10 cm.; green, 9.5 × 11.5; blue, 8.5 × 11.

Notes: 1. According to the poet, the Christmas cards were printed in County Wicklow in an edition of 75.
2. The poem was collected in (B85).

AA7 CHRISTMAS EVE 1978

Christmas card

Christmas Eve [with drawing of lighted candle in a candlestick]
Card folded to: 18 × 11 cm.

[1], cover-title as above; [2], blank; [3], text; [4], blank.

Single sheet of yellow laid paper, folded once to make a four-page leaflet; title as above on front page; all printed in brown.

125 copies printed by Peter Fallon, Dublin, 1978.

AA8 CHANGES 1980

Christmas card

CHANGES
20 × 13 cm.

[1], blank; [2]–[3], text; [4], blank.

Issued in handsewn olive double wrappers; front cover serves as title-page; front cover foldover: 'Seamus Heaney 1980'; back cover blank; back cover foldover: Privately printed for the author | by Peter Fallon. Christmas 1980; lettered in black.

125 copies printed December 1980; sewn with red thread; printed on tan paper.

Note: The poem first appeared in the *London Review of Books*, 18 September–1 October 1980 (C322).

AA9 HOLLY 1981

Christmas card

HOLLY
21 × 15 cm.

[1]–[2], blank; [3], text; [4], blank.

Green paper wrappers handsewn with red thread; front cover: HOLLY; on front fold-in: copyright Seamus Heaney 1981; on back fold-in: Privately printed for the author by Peter Fallon. Christmas 1981. 121 copies printed.

AA10 REMEMBERING MALIBU 1982

a. *first edition*

[at top left] Remembering Malibu | by Seamus Heaney | [centre] *for Brian Moore* | [poem of 13 two-line stanzas] | Printed in an edition of 200 copies at the | Scripps College Press Claremont California 1982 | [at bottom right] Linoleum block by Carol Wehrmann | Typography by Eileen Walsh
Broadside: 44.5 × 29 cm. (right edge untrimmed).

Printed on thin greenish-tan paper; the title and text are printed in black over a linoleum block illustration in green suggesting hills and a shoreline with waves, seaweeds, gulls, rocks and spray.

Printed in an edition of 200 copies at the Scripps College Press, Claremont, California, 1982.

Note: It is reported that as many as 160 copies were destroyed because of dissatisfaction with the appearance of the mixture of text and illustration.

b. *second edition*

[top and centre left] REMEMBERING MALIBU | [multi-colour linoleum print of hills, sand and sea] [top right] for Brian Moore | [poem of 13 two-line stanzas, in italics] | Seamus Heaney
Broadside: 32.5 × 46.5 cm. (top and right edges untrimmed).

Greenish-tan paper with the title above, and the poem to the right of, a hazy multi-colour print of hills, sand and sea.

The reverse of the broadside states: '*180 copies printed at the Scripps College Press, Claremont, California. The types are Garamond Roman and Italic; the linoleum print is by Carol Wehrmann. Copyright 1983 by Seamus Heaney. This is copy number* [number written in pencil].'

AA11 SWEENEY AND THE SAINT 1982

Christmas card

Seamus Heaney | Sweeney and the Saint | *From the Middle Irish*
20 × 13 cm.

[1], title-page as above; [2], introductory note; [3]–[5], text; [6], blank; [7], copyright and printing information; [8], blank.

Sewn in burnt-orange paper covers; back cover blank; front cover: Sweeney and the Saint; lettered in black.

Published December 1982; 125 copies printed for the author by Peter Fallon, Loughcrew, Co. Meath.

Note: The text comprises sections 74–75 of the subsequently published *Sweeney Astray*. The narration (section 74) was revised for *Sweeney Astray*. The verse dialogue (section 75 in *Sweeney Astray*) includes changes in verses 1, 4–9, 11, 13–15.

AA12 THE NAMES OF THE HARE 1982

first separate edition

Les nouns de vn leure en engleis The Names of the Hare
Broadside: 56 × 43.5 cm.

White coated card with a large blue domed panel containing the Middle English text and Seamus Heaney's translation in two parallel columns, and three golden hares by Barry Flanagan frolicking in the dome above the texts. The blue in the panel is shaded from dark at the top to light at the base. The texts are printed in black, each with its initial letter in gold.

Published 1982 by Waddington Galleries Ltd, London, in an edition of 250 numbered copies signed in pencil by Seamus Heaney and Barry Flanagan. Printed at the Hillingdon Press.

Note: The poem had first appeared in *Poetry Ireland Review*, spring, 1981 (C332).

AA13 A HAZEL STICK FOR CATHERINE ANN 1983

Christmas card

A Hazel Stick | for Catherine Ann
Card folded to: 19.5 × 10.5 cm.

Cover title.
[1]–[2], blank; [3], text; [4], blank.

Purple fold-over wrappers; front fold-over: copyright Seamus Heaney; back fold-over: Privately printed by Peter Fallon for the author.

AA14 THE RAILWAY CHILDREN 1986

first separate edition

[Left side, within thick-thin rules] THE RAILWAY | CHILDREN | [ornament] | SEAMUS HEANEY | 1939 – | [ornament] | *born in County Derry, Northern Ireland;* | *studied at Queen's University, Belfast;* | *taught at Queen's, Berkeley, Harvard;* | *now lives and teaches in Dublin;* | *gives poetry readings all over the world.* | *Reprinted by permission of Faber & Faber* | *from* Station Island © *Seamus Heaney.* | [outside borders] Poems on the Underground | *The Compton Poetry Fund* | *Faber and Faber Publishers Ltd* | *Oxford University Press*
[Right side] poem of thirteen lines
Broadside: 27 × 60.5 cm.

Printed in black on white poster paper.

Published by the Poems on the Underground January 1986.

Note: The poem had first appeared in the *Poetry Book Supplement 1981* (B49).

AA15 VILLANELLE FOR AN ANNIVERSARY 1986

a. *first edition*

VE RI TAS | 350 [blind stamped inside shield] | *Villanelle for an Anniversary* | [poem of 19 lines printed in italics] | *Composed by Seamus Heaney, Boylston Professor of Rhetoric and Oratory, for Harvard's 350 Anniversary Celebration and delivered by him at the Second Convocation, held on Friday, September fifth, nineteen hundred and eighty six.*
Card: 23 × 16 cm.

Engraved in black within an embossed rectangle on a cream card.

Published by Harvard University in celebration of its 350th Anniversary 5 September 1986.

b. ***second edition***

[Harvard 350 insignia] | *Villanelle for an Anniversary* | [poem of 19 lines printed in roman] | [note as in AA15a].
Card: 18.5 × 12.5 cm.

The Harvard 350 insignia is printed in red and the title, text, and note are printed in black, all within an embossed rectangle on a cream card.

Published as in AA15a.

AA16 [FROM] THINGS TO SHARE 1986

first separate edition

'In the last minutes he said more to her . . .' | *from Things to Share: in memoriam M.K.H., 1911–1984* | *The manuscript of this sonnet was given to Boston College by the poet Seamus Heaney* | *to commemorate the second annual Friends of Irish Studies dinner, Dec. 9, 1986.*
Broadside: 27 × 21 cm.

Untitled sonnet printed in green on cream textured card and issued in a green linen-like paper folder with a green band tipped inside to hold the broadside in place. Two short red ribbons to the front of the folder held by gold stick-on star.

Published by the Friends of Irish Studies, Boston College, 9 December 1986.

Note: *Things to Share* was a working title for the *Clearances* sequence. This sonnet was collected with revisions as sonnet 7 in *Clearances* (A40) and later in its collected form as 'Clearances' sonnet 7 in *The Haw Lantern*. This is the first appearance of this poem in this form. The poem first appeared in *Field*, Spring 1986 (C436).

AA17 IN MEMORIAM 1986

first edition

Seamus Heaney [leaf design] *In memoriam*
Single leaf folded to: 24 × 15.5 cm.

[i], cover title as above; [ii], blank; [iii], text; [iv], colophon.

Folded Hahnemühle's Ingres paper; front cover serves as title-page; colophon on back cover.

Published and printed by Sunday Printers, Amstelveen, The Netherlands, 1986, in a *feuille volante* edition of 20 copies 'for the poet's and printers' kin and kith'.

Note: Seamus Heaney considered this poem for the *Clearances* sequence as it appeared in *The Haw Lantern*.

AA18 I THOUGHT OF WALKING ROUND AND ROUND A SPACE 1987

first separate edition

I thought of walking round and round a space . . . | [followed by the rest of the sonnet]
Broadside: 76 × 48 cm.

Monoprint lithograph of untitled sonnet, reproduced in the poet's holograph on a variety of background illustrations by Robert Perkins. The illustrations are based on images suggested by the sonnet and are different in each of the 54 copies; the only constant is the poet's handwritten text. All copies signed by the poet and the artist. Issued in five series, the prints in each being numbered by a combination of a series symbol and roman numerals.

Published by the Char Press, Cambridge, Massachusetts, in 1987; printed by Robert Perkins.

Note: The poem had first appeared in the *Honest Ulsterman*, Spring 1986 (C435), collected as 'Clearances No. 8' in *The Haw Lantern*.

AA19 DANGEROUS PAVEMENTS 1987

a. *Christmas card*

[double rule, one thick, one thin] | Dangerous pavements. | But I face the ice this year | With my father's stick. [double rule, one slender, one broad]
Card: 25 × 18 cm. folded to 22 × 15 cm.

Folded white card; rules and lettering in green.
Back of card: Seamus Heaney 1987 | Published for the author by Peter Fallon | The Gallery Press, Loughcrew.

Published 1987; no printer specified.

b. *second edition (1993)*

Dangerous pavements. | But I face the ice this year | With my father's stick. | ·–Seamus Heaney
Card: 25 × 18 cm. folded to 12.5 × 18 cm.

[1], blank; [2], illustration; [3], poem of three lines; [4], blank.

Folded white card with the illustration printed in blue and black, and poem and author's name printed in black uncial lettering.

Published by the artist, Henry Pearson, in 1993 in a limited edition of 100 hand-numbered copies, signed by him at the bottom. He also issued 30 artist's proof copies numbered in roman numerals, and an undetermined number of out-of-series copies.

AA20 VALEDICTORY VERSES 1988

first edition

Valedictory | Verses | *Composed for the* | *Carysfort Graduation Exercises, 1988* [all of the preceding to the left of sketch of Carysfort College] | [poem of nineteen lines] | *Seamus Heaney* | *13 May 1988*
Broadside: 29.5 × 22 cm.

Printed in black on a cream card; limitation unknown.

Note: The poem of 19 lines in six stanzas was composed for the final graduation exercises held at Carysfort College on 13 May 1988. Carysfort College was a teachers' training college for women situated in the southern suburbs of Dublin. Seamus Heaney had been appointed as a faculty member in the English department there in October 1975 and became head of the department in 1976, a post he held until his resignation in 1981.

AA21 DUBLIN 4 1988

first edition

Printed in three vertical groupings:
On the extreme left: Dublin 4 | [production and design information]
Left of centre: Seamus Heaney | 1939 – | [biographical sketch in two columns]
Right: poem of four lines | publication information
Broadside: 26 × 74 cm.

Printed in green on white card.

Published by Poems on the Dart 1988.

Note: 'Dublin 4' was written expressly for Poems on the Dart; it is collected in *Between the Lines* (B144).

AA22 A RICH HOUR 1988

Christmas card

A Rich Hour | [illustration of lighted candle in candlestick]
Card folded to: 21 × 14.5 cm.

[1], cover title as above; [2], blank; [3], text; [4], copyright, printing information.

Stiff ivory card, lettered and decorated in brown throughout.

Published Christmas, 1988; 125 copies printed for the author by Peter Fallon, Loughcrew, Oldcastle, Co. Meath.

AA23 THE FIRE GAZE 1989

a. *first edition*

[wood engraving] | THE FIRE GAZE | [poem of twelve lines] | *Seamus Heaney* | *Printed for the Friends of The Cheltenham Festival of Literature,* | *1989. Wood-engraving by Hellmuth Weissenborn.*
Broadside: 31.5 × 22 cm.

Brownish-red engraving featuring a salamander followed by poem of four tercets printed on cream paper.

Published in 1989 by the Friends of the Cheltenham Festival of Literature.

b. *first limited edition*

[wood engraving] | THE FIRE GAZE | [poem of twelve lines] | *Seamus Heaney* | *No:* [number written in] *of a limited edition of 125 copies on mould-made paper,* | *printed at The Whittington Press and signed by the author.*| *Printed for the Friends of the Cheltenham Festival of Literature,* | 1989. *Wood-engraving by Hellmuth Weissenborn.*
Broadside: 38 × 26.5 cm.

Brownish-red engraving featuring a salamander, followed by poem of four tercets, printed on mould-made paper and signed by the author.

Published in 1989 by the Friends of the Cheltenham Festival of Literature in an edition of 125 hand-numbered copies signed by the author; printed at The Whittington Press. Issued in a brown paper portfolio together with three other broadsides. (see NOTE 2)

Notes: 1. A postcard-size (18.5 × 11.5 cm.) version of the broadside was also issued.
2. 'The Fire Gaze' was issued as one of a set of four broadsides by four poets, each of whom wrote a poem based on one of the four elements: fire, water, air, earth. In 1989, the other three broadsides were 'First Spring Dawn' by Jenny Joseph; 'The Three Winds' by Laurie Lee; and 'Water' by Lawrence Sail. In each of the three

subsequent years, each poet wrote on a different element so that by the end of four years each had written on all the elements.
3. The set of limited edition broadsides was issued in a brown paper portfolio with an orange paper label, lettered in black: 'The Four Elements | [engraving in brownish-red] | *The Friends of the Cheltenham Festival of Literature*'. The general edition broadsides were issued loose.

AA24 FROM THE REPUBLIC OF CONSCIENCE 1989

a. *Amnesty International Council edition*

From the Republic | of Conscience | [illustration of a sailing boat with sails depicted by three grey panels representing the eye, ear and mouth, and the mast depicted by a pen] | Written to commemorate the | 25th Anniversary of | Amnesty International | by | SEAMUS HEANEY | Presented to each delegate at the | 1989 International Council Meeting of | AMNESTY INTERNATIONAL | Dublin, Ireland
Printed as a 25.5 × 10 cm. tri-fold brochure

[1], outer panel serves as title-page, as above; [2]–[4], text of poem on the three inner panels; [5], fold-in panel, blank; [6], back panel has Amnesty logo, design and printing credits.

Published 1989; printed by Irish Printing Resources.

Note: The poem was first published in 1987; see (D21).

b. *Broadside issue*

From the Republic Of Conscience | [text in three numbered sections] | Seamus Heaney | From the Anthology From the Republic of Conscience, a collection of Poetry reflecting human rights | issues from around the world published by White Pine Press in conjunction with Amnesty International.
Broadside: 35.5 × 21.5 cm.

Printed on stiff white paper; title and author's name printed in dark green, section numbers I, II, III and publishing information in bright yellow and the text in black.

Published 1993 by White Pine Press in conjunction with Amnesty International; number of copies printed unknown.

AA25 THE SETTLE BED 1989

Christmas card

THE | SETTLE | BED | [illustration]
Cream card folded to 21 × 15 cm.

[1], title-page as above; [2]–[3], text; [4], colophon.

Printed and illustrated in brown. Illustration of a settle bed by Catherine Ann Heaney on cover.

Published Christmas 1989; privately printed by Peter Fallon.

AA26 THE EARTH HOUSE 1990

a. ***first edition***

[wood engraving] | THE EARTH HOUSE | [poem of twelve lines] | Seamus Heaney | Printed for the Friends of the Cheltenham Festival | of Literature. Wood-engraving by John O'Connor.
Broadside: 31.5 × 22 cm.

Orange engraving of a woodland scene followed by poem of four tercets, printed on cream paper.

Published 1990 by the Friends of the Cheltenham Festival of Literature.

b. ***first limited edition***

[wood engraving] | THE EARTH HOUSE | [poem of twelve lines] | Seamus Heaney | No: [number written in] of a limited edition of 125 copies on | mould-made paper, printed at the Whittington | Press, and signed by the author. Printed for the | Friends of the Cheltenham Festival of Literature. | Wood-engraving by John O'Connor.
Broadside: 38 × 26.5 cm.

Orange engraving of a woodland scene followed by poem of four tercets, printed on mould-made paper and signed by the author.

Published 1990 by the Friends of the Cheltenham Festival of Literature in an edition of 125 hand-numbered copies signed by the author; printed at the Whittington Press. Issued in a deep-pink paper portfolio together with three other broadsides. (see Notes)

Notes: 1. Like AA23, 'The Earth House' was issued in a set of four broadsides. The other three broadsides were: 'From Persephone' by Jenny Joseph; 'Field of Autumn' by Laurie Lee; and 'Air' by Lawrence Sail.
2. The set of limited edition broadsides was issued in a deep-pink paper portfolio with a tan paper label lettered in black: 'The Four Elements | [engraving in green] | *The Friends of the Cheltenham Festival of Literature*'. The general edition broadsides were issued loose.

AA27 FIELD OF VISION 1990

Christmas card

FIELD OF | VISION | [line drawing of gate between pillars]
Card: folded to 21 × 15 cm.

[1], cover title as above; [2], blank; [3], text; [4], colophon.

Green folded card; printed and decorated in black. Illustration by Catherine Ann Heaney.

Published Christmas 1990; printed privately by Peter Fallon, Oldcastle, Co. Meath.

AA28 THE WATER PAUSE 1991

a. *first edition*

[wood engraving] | THE WATER PAUSE | [poem of twelve lines] | *Seamus Heaney | Printed for the Friends of The Cheltenham | Festival of Literature, 1991. Wood-engraving | by Gwenda Morgan.*
Broadside: 31.5 × 22 cm.

Greenish-blue engraving of a river valley followed by poem of four tercets, printed on cream paper.

Published in 1991 by the Friends of the Cheltenham Festival of Literature.

b. ***first limited edition***

[wood engraving] | THE WATER PAUSE | poem of twelve lines] | *Seamus Heaney* | *No:* [number written in] *of a limited edition of 125 copies on* | *mould-made paper, printed at The Whittington* | *Press and signed by the author.* | *Printed for the Friends of The Cheltenham* | *Festival of Literature, 1991. Wood-engraving* | *by Gwenda Morgan.*
Broadside: 38 × 26.5 cm.

Greenish-blue engraving of river valley followed by poem of four tercets, printed on mould-made paper and signed by the author.

Published in 1991 by the Friends of the Cheltenham Festival of Literature in an edition of 125 hand-numbered copies signed by the author; printed at The Whittington Press. Issued in a greyish-blue paper portfolio with three other broadsides. (see NOTES)

Notes: 1. Like AA23 and AA26, 'The Water Pause' was issued in a set of four broadsides. This time the other three broadsides were: 'Upside Down' by Jenny Joseph; 'Equinox' by Laurie Lee; and 'Fire' by Lawrence Sail.
2. The set of limited edition broadsides was issued in a greyish-blue paper portfolio with a tan paper label lettered in black: 'The Four Elements | [engraving in grey-brown] | The Friends of the Cheltenham Festival of Literature'; the general edition broadsides were issued loose.

AA29 THE UNDERGROUND 1991

first separate edition

[title and poem printed in facsimile of the author's hand] The Underground | [three underlining strokes] | [poem of four 4-line verses] | *April 7, 1991* | *Nineteen Twenty-five F Street Club* | *Folger Poetry Board Reading*

Broadside: 28 × 21.5 cm.

Printed in black on purple card.

Published on 7 April 1991 by the Folger Shakespeare Library, limitation unknown.

Note: This broadside was distributed gratis at the reading given by Seamus Heaney on 7 April 1991 inaugrating the Folger Poetry Board Reading series. An earlier 1985 edition of the broadside may exist (not seen). The poem was first printed in *Thames Poetry*, February 1981 (C329) and collected in *Station Island*.

AA30 MINT 1991

first edition

[woodcut engraving] | MINT *by Seamus Heaney* [in green] | [poem of sixteen lines] | WILLIAM B. EWERT, PUBLISHER · CONCORD, NEW HAMPSHIRE [in green] | [in black] ' "Mint" is dedicated to the Corbett family of Boston, in whose home the | author has enjoyed many a meal of minty soup and lamb. Text copyright | 1991 by Seamus Heaney. Original woodcut copyright 1991 by Mary | Azarian. 136 copies, designed by John Kristensen, were printed at Firefly | Press, Sommerville, Massachusetts, in May 1991. This is copy [written in].'

Broadside: 48 × 25.5 cm. (bottom edge untrimmed).

Printed on heavy white paper and signed by the artist at the foot of the woodcut and by the poet at the foot of the poem. There are 100 copies, numbered 1–100, in which the woodcut is printed in reddish brown and 36 copies, numbered 1–36, in which the woodcut is hand-coloured.

Published in May, 1991 by William B. Ewert.

Note: Although not indicated on the broadside, there were 11 *hors commerce* copies of the ordinary issue and 8 *hors commerce* copies of the hand-coloured issue.

AA31 A TRANSGRESSION 1991

Christmas card

SEAMUS HEANEY | *A Transgression*
Card folded to 22.5 × 16 cm.

[1], cover title as above; [2], blank; [3], text; [4], back cover with colophon at foot.

Light-grey folded leaf; printed in black.

Published Christmas 1991; 125 copies printed for the author by Peter Fallon.

AA32 DIPTYCH 1992

first edition

DIPTYCH | [text] | Broadside [quill pen design]
Broadside: 28 × 21.5 cm.

Stiff cream sheet; printed in black with rule border.

Published by Goshen College, Goshen, Indiana, 23 January 1992. According to the publisher 250 copies were printed; no printer specified.

Note: Collected under the title 'St. Kevin and the Blackbird'. This is not the 'Diptych' that appeared under the same title in *London Review of Books*, 3 July 1986 (C440), nor the 'Diptych' that appeared in *The Irish Times*, 7 January 1989 (C505).

AA33 IRON SPIKE 1992

first separate edition

[lino cut of a spike representing 'I'] RON SPIKE [preceding printed in rust] | [poem of twenty-four lines] | Seamus Heaney | WILLIAM B. EWERT, PUBLISHER · CONCORD, NEW HAMPSHIRE [printed in rust] | publication information and dedication [printed in black]
Broadside: 44.5 × 23 cm. (bottom edge untrimmed).

Poem of six 4-line verses printed in black on cream paper, watermarked '[crown of three towers] | UMBRIA | ITALIA | C. M. | F.'

Published in June 1992 by William B. Ewert in an edition of 100 copies signed by the author; designed by John Kristensen and printed at Firefly Press; linoleum block vignette of spike cut by Gino Lee.

Note: The poem first appeared in the *American Poetry Review*, July/August 1983 (C370) and was collected in *Station Island*.

AA34 THE AIR STATION 1992

a. *first separate edition*

[wood engraving] | *The Air station* | [poem of twelve lines] | *Seamus Heaney* | *Printed for the Friends of the Cheltenham Festival of Literature.*| *Wood-engraving by Miriam Macgregor.*
Broadside: 31.5 × 22 cm.

Engraving of a quarry face on a hillside followed by poem of four tercets, printed on cream paper.

Published in 1992 by the Friends of the Cheltenham Festival of Literature; limitation unknown.

b. *first limited edition*

[on the left, wood engraving] | [on the right] *The Air station* | [poem of twelve lines] | *Seamus Heaney* | *No:* [number written in] *of a limited edition of 125 copies on mould-made* | *paper, printed at The Whittington Press, and signed by the* | *author. Printed for the Friends of the Cheltenham Festival* | *of Literature. Wood-engraving by Miriam Macgregor.*
Broadside: 38 × 26.5 cm.

Engraving in black of a quarry face on a hillside followed by poem of four tercets, printed on mould-made paper and signed by the author.

Published in 1992 by the Friends of the Cheltenham Festival of Literature in an edition of 125 hand-numbered copies signed by the author; printed at the Whittington Press. Issued in a pale green paper portfolio with three other broadsides. (see Notes)

Notes: 1. Like AA23, AA26 and AA28, 'The Air Station' was issued in a set of four broadsides. This time the other three broadsides are: 'By Lake Huron in Winter' by Jenny Joseph; 'Fish and Water' by Laurie Lee; and 'Earth' by Lawrence Sail.
2. The set of limited edition broadsides was issued in a pale-green paper portfolio with a light-blue paper label lettered in black: 'The Four | Elements | [engraving in black] | *The Friends of the* | *Cheltenham Festival* | *of Literature*'. The general edition broadsides were issued loose.
3. Previously collected in *Seeing Things* as 'Squarings x'.

AA35 AN INVOCATION 1992

first separate edition

[publisher's logo, name, address and telephone number] | An Invocation | [poem of twelve tercets]
Card: folded to 30 × 21 cm.

[1], cover blank; [2]–[3], poem, copyright, publishing information; [4], blank.

Poem in three numbered sections, each of four tercets, printed in black on grey card.

Published September 1992 by Bernard Stone and Raymond Danowski, The Turret Book Shop, London; limitation unknown.

Notes: 1. The poem first appeared in the *London Review of Books*, 6 August 1992, and was collected in *The Spirit Level*.
2. Over time a further five issues were published, all as broadsides in different layouts or on different coloured paper (two on grey, one each on blue, orange and purple).

AA36 VILLANELLE OF NORTHWEST ORIENT FLIGHT 4 1993

first edition

[shamrocks in green] | *The Villanelle of Northwest Orient Flight* 4 | [poem of nineteen lines] | publishing information | Seamus Heaney
Card: 18.5 × 12.5 cm.

The shamrocks are printed in green, the text and publishing information in black, all on a cream card.

Published in a limited edition of 500 copies to mark the inaugural Emerald Ball in Tokyo on 12 March 1993.

AA37 THE RIVERBED, DRIED-UP, HALF FULL OF LEAVES 1993

first separate edition

[illustration] | [poem in two lines] | – Seamus Heaney
Card: 25.5 × 18 cm. folded to 12.5 × 18 cm.

[1], blank; [2], illustration; [3], poem; [4], blank.

Folded stiff white card with the illustration printed in brown, and the poem and author's name in black uncial lettering.

Published by the artist Henry Pearson in 1993 in a limited edition of 100 hand-numbered copies signed by him at the illustration. He also issued 30 artist's proof copies and 52 out-of-series copies, both numbered in roman numerals.

Note: The poem first appeared in the dedication page of *The Haw Lantern*.

AA38 POET'S CHAIR 1993

a. ***first limited edition***

[linoleum print] | *Poet's Chair* | [poem of nine lines] | *Seamus Heaney* | WILLIAM B. EWERT, PUBLISHER · CONCORD NEW, HAMPSHIRE | publishing information and note
Broadside: 47 × 25.5 cm.

An issue of 1,000 copies on flecked tan paper (out of a total edition of 1,100 copies) printed in green at the office of the Harvard University Publisher.

Published by William B. Ewert, Concord, New Hampshire; designed by Gino Lee; linoleum block illustration by Dimitri Hadzi.

Note: The following information appears at the bottom of broadsides. 'This broadside was produced for distribution at a gala celebration held on May 15, 1993, to honor Robert and Jana Kiely in their twentieth year of service as Master and Associate Master of Adams House, Harvard University.'

b. ***limited signed edition***

Collation as in AA38a.
Broadside: 64 × 31 cm.

100 copies, numbered 1–100 and signed by the poet and the artist, were printed by hand on cream coloured bond paper at Bow and Arrow Press, Cambridge, Massachusetts.

Though not stated in the publishing information, 50 roman numeral copies and an undetermined number of *hors commerce* copies, all signed by poet and artist, were also issued.

Note: The following information appears at the bottom of broadsides. 'This broadside was produced for distribution at a gala celebration held on May 15, 1993, to honor Robert and Jana Kiely in their twentieth year of service as Master and Associate Master of Adams House, Harvard University.'

AA39 LOOK FAR 1994

first separate edition

[illustration] | [poem of eight lines] | – Translated by Seamus Heaney from the Old Irish.
Card; 25 × 18 cm. folded to 12.5 × 18 cm.

[1], blank; [2], illustration; [3], poem; [4], blank.

Folded stiff white card with the illustration printed in greenish-blue and the poem and author's name printed in black uncial lettering.

Published by the artist, Henry Pearson, in 1994 in a limited edition of 100 copies and signed by him at the illustration. He also issued 30 artist's proof copies and 24 out-of-series copies, both numbered in roman numerals.

Note: The poem first appeared as the second of two poems under the joint-title 'After the Irish' in 1980 in the Field Day Theatre programme for Brian Friel's play *Translations* (D12).

AA40 A DOG WAS CRYING TO-NIGHT IN WICKLOW ALSO 1994

first edition

[all the following within box with thick, thin rules] Seamus Heaney | [photograph of a cottage with dog in the foreground] | *photo by Rachel Brown* | A DOG WAS CRYING TO-NIGHT IN WICKLOW ALSO | *in memory of Donatus Nwoga* | [poem of twenty-eight lines] | Seamus Heaney | [credits, copyright, acknowledgements, publishing information]
Broadside: 89 × 38 cm.

Printed on white glossy card; all lettering in black; photograph in black and white.

Published 1994 as number 4 in Heaven Poster Series by 'White Fields Press for the literary renaissance', Louisville, Kentucky; price $25.00 a copy; no limitation stated.
100 copies of the broadside were numbered and signed by the author, price $100.00.

Note: Donatus Nwoga was a Nigerian student attending Queen's University Belfast when Seamus Heaney first met him. The photograph first appeared in Rachel Brown's book, *Donegal Pictures*.

AA41 THE FORGE 1994

first separate edition

The Forge by Seamus Heaney | Etching by Breon O'Casey
Single leaf folded to 51 × 38 cm.

[1], SEAMUS HEANEY | THE FORGE | [design of Celtic spiral]; [2], title-page as above; [3], THE FORGE | text | coloured etching of forge; [4], colophon.

Issued in paper portfolio; front and backs covers as above; printed and designed in black on untrimmed hand-made paper.

The edition is limited to 50 signed and numbered copies plus 5 artist's proofs. Text printed by Simon King. The etching was printed by Hugh Stoneman.

Note: The poem first appeared in the *Times Literary Supplement*, 19 May 1966 (C61) and was collected in *Door into the Dark*. Although there is no publication date listed, the poet recalls *The Forge* as being issued in 1994.

AA42 TOLLUND 1994

Christmas card

TOLLUND | Seamus Heaney
Card folded to: 21 × 15 cm.

[1], front cover serves as title-page; [2], blank; [3], text | *September 1994*; [4], back cover with colophon.

Stiff cream paper, lettered in brown.

Privately printed for the author by Peter Fallon/the Gallery Press, Loughcrew, Oldcastle, County Meath, September 1994.

AA43 THE SINGER'S HOUSE 1995

first separate edition

Screenprint | [the following printed in the author's hand] The Singer's House [poem in four two-verse columns] Seamus Heaney
Broadside: 76 × 94 cm.

Printed on white Somerset mould-made paper, watermarked 'SOMERSET ENGLAND'; the top four-fifths of the broadside is taken up by James Allen's 54 × 76 cm. colour screenprint. Printed left to right across the bottom in facsimile of author's hand are: the title, followed by four columns each with two 4-line verses, the author's signature. Each print is embossed with the mark of the Belfast Print Workshop on bottom-left corner.

Commissioned and published by David Hammond in 1995 in an edition of 30 copies and 6 artist's proofs. The 30-copies issue was signed in pencil by David Hammond, Seamus Heaney and James Allen; the 6 artist's proofs were signed in pencil by Seamus Heaney and James Allen.

Note: The poem first appeared in *Thames Poetry*, November 1977 (C260) and was collected in *Field Work*.

AA44 THE CLAY PIPES 1995

first separate edition

[all the following within box with thick, thin rules] | CATHAL O'SEARCAIGH | [photograph by Rachel Brown] | [the following in two columns, on left in Irish] NA PÍOPAÍ CRÉAFÓIGE | [poem in thirty-five lines in Irish] | [on right in English] THE CLAY PIPES | [poem in thirty-five lines in English] | [on right] *translated by Seamus Heaney* | [on bottom left, copyrights, acknowledgements, credits, publishing information] | [on bottom right] publisher's logo.
Broadside: 63.5 × 28 cm.

Printed on white glossy card; all lettering in black; photograph printed in black and white.

Published in 1995 as number 29 in Heaven Poster Series by 'White Fields Press in support of the literary renaissance', Louisville, Kentucky; price $25.00; no limitation stated.
100 hand-numbered copies of the broadside were signed by Cathal Ó Searcaigh, Rachel Brown and Seamus Heaney, price $100.00. Later, 26 copies, signed by Cathal Ó Searcaigh, Seamus Heaney and Rachel Brown and lettered A–Z, were issued, price $225.00.

Note: Rachel Brown's photograph, *Rathlin*, originally appeared in *Sweeney's Flight*.

AA45 THE STRAND 1995

first edition

[1], illustration; [2], blank; [3], text; [4], colophon
Card folded to: 11 × 15.5 cm.

Stiff oatmeal paper; front cover illustrated with a watercolour by Felim Egan.

Privately published by Peter Fallon of The Gallery Press, Loughcrew for the author in November 1995 in an edition of 500. The poem's title, 'The Strand' appears on the last page.

Note: The card was printed for Seamus Heaney's use following his Nobel Prize for Literature.

AA46 LAMENT 1996

first separate edition

[colour photograph occupying the entire left two-thirds of the sheet] | [all of the following on right-hand third] Caoineadh | (I gcuimhne mo mháthar) | le Cathal ÓSearcaigh | [poem of twenty-seven lines in Irish] | Lament | (In memory of my mother) | [poem of twenty-eight lines in English] | *translated by* Seamus Heaney | publishing information in Irish.
Broadside: 63.5 × 43.5 cm.

Printed on glossy paper; colour photograph by Kevin McKiernan of the head of a girl looking out over the tail gate of a truck; the poems are printed in black on a dull-yellow background.

Published by Coiscéim Feirste in 1996; printed by Johnswood Press, Belfast.

Note: The poem first appeared in Cathal ÓSearcaigh's *Homecoming/ An bealach 'na bhaile* (B131).

AA47 I AM RAFTERY 1996

first edition

[heavy rule above all of the following] | [on left] *Mise Raifteri* | [poem of three 4-line verses in Irish] | *Antoine Raftery* | (c. 1784–1835) | [on right] *I Am Raftery* | [poem of three 4-line verses in English] | *Seamus Heaney* | [at centre bottom] © *Seamus Heaney 1996* | Mise Raifteri/I Am Raftery *is published on the occasion of* | *Seamus Heaney's reading at Deerfield Academy, 13 December 1996.* | *The edition is limited to 300 copies.* | *The Deerfield Press* | *Deerfield, Massachusetts 01342*
Broadside: 28 × 34 cm. (bottom edge untrimmed).

Printed in black on cream textured card; the untrimmed bottom edge is dipped in green.

Published on 13 December 1996 by the Deerfield Press in an edition of 300 copies.

Note: Published on the occasion of a poetry reading given by Seamus Heaney at Deerfield Academy.

AA48 IN BELLAGHY GRAVEYARD 1996

first edition

[drawing of tree stump with figure in the background] | In Bellaghy Graveyard [printed in the author's hand] | [poem in nineteen lines] | Seamus Heaney [printed in the author's hand] | 1996
Broadside: 42 × 29.5 cm.

Printed in black on pale greyish-tan card.

Published in 1996 by the Northern Ireland Department of the Environment in conjunction with the opening of Bellaghy Bawn; printed by Robin Wade, London, in an edition of 500 copies.

Note: Bellaghy Bawn is a historical and cultural centre near Seamus Heaney's birthplace with a permanent exhibition of his manuscripts, books and other materials associated with him.

AA49 DIGGING 1996

first separate edition

[drawing of a right-hand holding a pen] | Digging [printed in the author's hand] | [poem in thirty-one lines] | Seamus Heaney [printed in the author's hand] | from DEATH OF A NATURALIST
Broadside: 42 × 29.5 cm.

Printed in black on pale greyish-tan card.

Published in 1996 by the Northern Ireland Department of the Environment in conjunction with the opening of Bellaghy Bawn; printed by Robin Wade, London, in an edition of 500 copies.

AA50 GOOD-NIGHT 1996

first separate edition

[from left to right in three vertical sections] *Poetry in Motion* above the following: logo, list of five sponsors, publishing and design information | full height colour illustration by Beate Pionke | the following in purple quotation marks: poem of two 4-line verses in italics | Good-night – Seamus Heaney
Broadside: 28 × 48 cm.

The above is printed on both sides of the glossy white poster card; the logo and the text, title and author's name are in blue, all other lettering in black.

Note: The poem first appeared in *The Listener*, 22 May 1969 (C108) and was first collected in *Wintering Out*.

AA51 JESUS AND THE SPARROWS 1996

Christmas card

JESUS | AND THE | SPARROWS | [woodcut sparrow design] |
Card folded to 23.5 × 14.5 cm.

[1], cover as above; [2], blank; [3], text, *from the Irish, 7th century*; [4], publishing information, printing information, copyrights

Stiff duck-egg blue paper; lettered and designed in black; deckled front fore-edge; woodcut by Timothy Engelland.

One hundred and seventy-five copies privately printed for the author by Peter Fallon/The Gallery Press from Box 13, Deerfield ma 01342, Christmas 1996.

AA52 THE RESCUE 1997

first separate edition

The Rescue | [poem of four lines] | [publishing information on bottom left] | [on bottom right] Seamus Heaney (b. 1939) | [copyright information]
Broadside: 28 × 60.5 cm.

Printed on white paper; the title is printed in red, other text in black and grey, the London Underground logo in red and blue.

2,000 copies published for Poems on the Underground, London, 1997.

Note: The poem first appeared in *Seeing Things*.

AA53 SEAMUS HEANEY ON W. H. AUDEN 1997

first edition

[pen and ink portrait of W. H. Auden] | SEAMUS HEANEY *ON* W. H. AUDEN | [poem of seven lines]
Card: 17.5 × 12.5 cm.

The back of a postcard has a portrait of W. H. Auden, taken from the pen and ink drawing by Don Bachardy, followed by the title 'SEAMUS HEANEY *ON* W. H. AUDEN' printed in white and grey across a thick brown strip, and the poem printed in black on an orange-yellow background.

Published 1997 by the National Portrait Gallery (London). The card was sold singly and also as one in a pack of 25 pull-out postcard biographies.

AA54 WOULD THEY HAD STAY'D 1997

Christmas card

'WOULD THEY HAD STAY'D'
Card folded to 15 × 21 cm.

[1], front cover image of deer; [2]–[3], text; [4], publishing information.

Glossy stock card; front cover 'The Deer' from Basilica San Clemente, Rome.

Privately published for the author by Peter Fallon/the Gallery Press, Christmas 1997.

AA55 A DRINK OF WATER 1998

first separate edition

ANNA LIVIA BOOKS BROADSHEET 2 | A Drink of Water | [poem of fourteen lines] | Seamus Heaney—1979 | facsimile of Seamus Heaney's signature | The American Ireland Fund | San Francisco Dinner | March 6, 1998 | shamrock design
Broadside: 33 × 16.5 cm. (bottom edge untrimmed).

Printed on cream card with the title and holograph signature in dark blue and all other printing in black.

Published by the American Ireland Fund for the San Francisco Dinner, 6 March 1998. Conor Howard (Anna Livia Books) informed us that the broadside was printed at The Hillside Press, San Francisco.

A later issue of 200 copies was published by Anna Livia Books on which the facsimile of Seamus Heaney's signature and everything after it is replaced by a facsimile of an old Irish two-penny postage stamp.

Note: The poem first appeared in *St. Stephen's*, autumn 1974.

AA56 REQUIEM FOR THE CROPPIES 1998

first separate edition

Poets' Corner [lettered in white against an olive green postcard-size background] | Seamus Heaney [lettered in black] | [short green rule] | (born 1939) | REQUIEM FOR THE CROPPIES | text | publishing information, copyright, and design information [all of the above in green and white designed border with an image of a DART train speeding across the bottom]
Broadside: 59.5 × 42 cm.

Printed on glossy white poster stock; lettered in black except as noted above.

Published by Poetry in Motion, Dublin 1998 as a poster; no printer specified.

Note: The poem first appeared in the *Dublin Magazine*, Summer 1966 (C63).

AA57 THE STICK 1998

first edition

The Stick | [poem of twenty-one 3-line verses in two columns] | [woodcut of boy with a stick] | [copyright and publishing information]
Broadside: 45 × 28 cm.

Printed in black on cream card.

Published privately by Peter Fallon at the Gallery Press on 18 August 1998 in an edition of 100 copies each of which is signed by the author; 26 copies are lettered A–Z and the remainder numbered 1–74.

Note: The broadside was published '*to mark the presentation of the Parnell Stick by Seamus Heaney to Nuala Ní Dhomhnaill in the presence of Conor Cruise O'Brien, Guest of Honour*', from whom Seamus Heaney had received it.

AA58 WHINLANDS 1998

first separate edition

[sepia print of a cottage in ruins] | Whinlands | [poem of six 4-line verses] | – Seamus Heaney | [celtic design] | 'The Whinlands,' *From Door into the Dark* by Seamus Heaney © 1969 | Design by Kristine Pelzer. 1998
Broadside: 43 × 27.5 cm.

Printed in dark brown over a background of light yellow celtic script on flecked cream card.

Published in October 1998 by the English Department of Meredith College, Raleigh, North Carolina, in an edition of 100 copies to celebrate a reading given there by Seamus Heaney on 4 October 1998.

Note: The poem first appeared in *Listener*, 24 April 1969, and was collected in *Door into the Dark* (1969).

AA59 THE MANGER 1998

Christmas card

THE MANGER | text
Card folded to 5.5 × 15.5 cm.

[1], front cover with painting; [2], blank; [3], title and text as above; [4], publishing information, copyright information

Glossy white card; front cover, painting by Basil Blackshaw; title and poem printed in black; back cover as above.

Privately published for the author by Peter Fallon/Gallery Press, Christmas 1998.

Note: Collected with revisions as the third section of 'The Loose Box' in *Electric Light*.

AA60 A SKILLED POET 1999

first edition

A Skilled Poet | *For William Alfred* [all the preceding to the left of illustration of tree printed in blue] | [poem of eleven lines] | *Seamus Heaney* | [the following printed in blue] *This translation of Beowulf, lines 88–98, was published by Katherine* | *McCanless at the Bow & Arrow Press, Adams House, Harvard* | *University. The edition of 75 numbered copies and 20 lettered* | *artists proofs was produced during the winter of 1999.*
Broadside: 30.5 × 20.5 cm. (all edges untrimmed).

Printed in black and blue on cream laid paper. All copies are signed in pencil by Seamus Heaney.

Published in late 1999; printed at the Bow & Arrow Press, Harvard University; the price of the numbered copies was $100.

AA61 A LIGHT APPEARED 1999

Christmas card

'A LIGHT APPEARED . . .'
Card folded to: 10.5 × 15.5 cm.

[1], front cover with woodcut; [2], blank; [3], text; [4], publishing information and copyright information.

Grey linen-textured card stock; front cover has woodcut of sun shining through clouds; poem (*Beowulf*, lines 1570–72), printed in black; back cover as above.

Privately published for the author by Peter Fallon/Gallery Press, Christmas 1999.

AA62 THE CHILD THAT'S DUE 1999

first edition

The Child That's Due | *from 'Bann Valley Eclogue'* [in grey] | *by Seamus Heaney* [all of the preceding printed over large light-grey lettering taken from the poem] | [poem of four 6-line verses]
Broadside: 29.5 × 21 cm.

Printed in black and light-grey italic type on cream card.

Published December 1999 by Bank of Ireland Group Treasury. According to the author the edition was split as follows: 300 signed plus 20 unsigned copies for Bank of Ireland Group Treasury, 20 numbered and signed copies for Irish Peatlands Conservation and an unspecified number of unsigned copies.

Note: Bank of Ireland Group Treasury made a donation to the Irish Peatland Conservation Council's 'Save the Bog Campaign' in recognition of Seamus Heaney's permission to print this poem. Seamus Heaney read the poem live on Radio Telefis Eireann on the eve of the millennium.

AA63 BEOWULF 2000

[on left, thirteen lines from the English translation] [on right, six lines from the Anglo-Saxon manuscript] | BL Cotton MS. Vitellius A XV by permission of the British Library Board | from [black] BEOWULF [red] | Translated by Seamus Heaney | Reprinted by permission of Faber from *Beowulf*, translated by Seamus Heaney (1999) | [sheet-wide rule] | [London Underground logo, publisher's name, list of sponsors], Poems on the Underground | [in red] 1,000 YEARS OF POETRY IN ENGLISH
Broadside: 28 × 61 cm.

Printed in black, grey and red on white poster paper.

Published in 2000 by Poems on the Underground.

AA64 THE CLOTHES SHRINE 2000

first edition

[all of the following in red outline letters] THE | CLOTHES | SHRINE | [all of the following printed in black to the right of 'THE'] SEAMUS | HEANEY
Card folded to 24.5 × 18.5 cm. (bottom edges untrimmed)

[1], front cover serves as title-page as above; [2], *for Marie*; [3], poem of seventeen lines; [4], colophon.

Printed in black and red on cream wove paper, bottom edges untrimmed; laid in dark greyish-yellow tri-fold wrappers with the title printed in black outline letters on front wrapper.

Published 14 September 2000. Printed for the author in an edition of one hundred copies by Hans van Eijk at the Bonnefant Press of Banholt. Each copy is numbered in the press and signed by Seamus Heaney.

Note: 'The Clothes Shrine' is a 17-line poem written on the occasion of the poet's wife's 60th birthday.

AA65 AT THE HILLHEAD 2000

Christmas card

If I wasn't there | text
Card folded to: 11 × 15.5 cm.

[1], front cover with woodcut; [2], blank; [3], first line and text as above; [4], publishing information, copyright information and title 'At The Hillhead'.

Cream card; front cover has woodcut of shepherd looking at a rising sun; poem printed in black; back cover as above.

Privately published for the author by Peter Fallon/Gallery Press, Christmas 2000.

AA66 ELECTRIC LIGHT 2001

first separate edition

SEAMUS | HEANEY [preceding in gold outline calligraphic letters] | [following in large bold calligraphic letters] ELECTRIC | LIGHT
Single 20 × 50 cm. sheet folded twice vertically to make a 20 × 16.5 cm. overlapping trifold (front and bottom edges untrimmed).

[1], cover title as above; [2]–[4], poem with five tercets on each page; [5], blank; [6], colophon.

Printed on hand-made paper, the text in black, the title and colophon in gold.

Printed by Brian Molanphy at the Press at Colorado College in an edition of 100 copies 'to commemorate Seamus Heaney's reading on 16 April 2001. The type is Spectrum printed from polymer plates. Tom Leech made the paper and Pat Musick calligraphed the title.'

AA67 FOR ALMA MATER 2001

a. *first edition*

[Queen's University arms printed in brown] | The Queen's University of Belfast Foundation [printed in pink] | [all following in black] FOR ALMA MATER | *On the occasion of the Launch of the Campaign for Queen's* | [poem of nineteen lines]
Broadside: 29.5 × 21 cm.

The villanelle, printed in black on white wove paper, was inserted loose in the brochure distributed on 8 November 2001 advertising the start of the *Campaign for Queen's* fundraising. The following day, 9 November 2001, the poem appeared in the newspaper, *The Irish News*.

b. *second edition*

For Alma Mater | On the occasion of the Launch of the Campaign for Queen's | text | Mark's Club, Thursday 15th November 2001 |

Guest of Honour, Dr. Seamus Heaney [all the preceding in calligraphy]
Card: 20.5 × 15 cm.

Light yellow card with laid cream card pasted in centre (17.5 × 12.5); title and text only on cream card; information printed on cream card.

Note: The card was distributed at the official launch of the Campaign for Queen's.

AA68 THE LOOSE BOX 2001

first edition

[the title printed in red; the etching and the author's name, in black] The | [etching of man cutting wheat with a sickle] | Loose Box | by | Seamus Heaney
Single sheet folded twice to make 8 pages: 23 × 14.5 cm. (top edges uncut)

[1], cover title as above; [2]–[3], blank; [4]–[5], [text]; [6]–[7], blank; [8], text and colophon.

Printed in black and red on bluish-grey laid paper.

Published in 2001 by the *Parnassus: Poetry in Review* in an edition of 101 numbered copies, signed by the author; there were also 19 numbered and signed Artist's Copies. Printed at the Oliphant Press, New York.

Note: Issued on the occasion of the 25th anniversary of Parnassus.

AA69 THE YELLOW BITTERN 2002

first separate edition

[top left, colour illustration of the head of a Yellow Bittern] [at right] THE YELLOW | BITTERN | Seamus Heaney | [poem of five 8-line verses] | A translation of *An Bonnán Buí* | by Cathal Mac Giolla Ghunna (*c.* 1680–1756) | [across the bottom] Published by the Keogh-Notre Dame Centre, Dublin to celebrate the fourth

IRISH SEMINAR, July 2002. Design by Caroline Moloney. Limited edition of 50 of which this is [ ]
Broadside: 29 × 21 cm.

Lettered in black on yellow flecked card with the head of the Yellow Bittern in colour in the top left corner and the poem printed down the right half of the broadside.

Published in July 2002 by the Keough-Notre Dame Centre, Dublin in a hand-numbered edition of 50 copies. In addition to the regular edition, Kevin Whelan, director of the Keogh-Notre Dame Centre, stated that there were 10 unnumbered out-of-series copies.

Note: First published in *Poetry Ireland Review*, summer 1996 (C681).

AA70 POSTSCRIPT 2002

first separate edition

ANNA LIVIA BROADSHEET VI | postscript [in blue uncial] | [poem of sixteen lines] | – *Seamus Heaney* | [facsimile of author's signature in blue] | *Montalvo Literary Arts Program* | *Fox Theatre (John Anagnostou)* | *October 9, 2002* | *The American Ireland Fund* | [shamrock design]
Broadside: 33 × 16.5 cm. (bottom edge untrimmed).

Printed in black and blue on cream card and issued to mark a reading by Seamus Heaney at 'A Night of Irish Poetry', 9 October 2002 at the Fox Theatre, Redwood City, California.

Published 9 October 2002 by Anna Livia Books; printed by Hillside Press; limitation unknown. A later issue was published by Anna Livia Books on which the facsimile of Seamus Heaney's signature and everything after it is replaced by a facsimile of an old Irish two penny postage stamp.

Note: Collected in *The Spirit Level*.

AA71 HORACE AND THE THUNDER 2002

first separate edition

HORACE AND THE THUNDER | *After* Horace, *Odes*, I, 34 | [poem of four 4-line verses] | – Seamus Heaney | THIS PRESSED WAFER BROADSIDE MARKS SEAMUS HEANEY'S READING AT MIT, CAMBRIDGE, MASS. ON OCTOBER 17, 2002. | 26 COPIES HABE (sic) BEEN LETTERED AND SIGNED BY THE POET
Broadside: 28 × 21.5 cm.

Printed in black on poor-quality orange card.

Printed on 17 October 2002 by Pressed Wafer in an undetermined number of copies, of which 26 have been lettered A to Z by hand and signed in ink by the poet, price $90.

Note: The poem was first published as 'Horace and Thunder' in *The Times Literary Supplement*, 18 January 2002.

AA72 THE LIFT 2003

first edition

THE LIFT [printed in reddish brown] | [poem of 31 lines] | – Seamus Heaney | An unpublished poem by the Nobel Laureate, printed at The King Library Press | as a keepsake for Helen Vendler's lecture 'W.B. Yeats and Lyric Form' | opening the exhibition 'Irish Literature 1699–1944' at the University of Kentucky, 13 February 2003
Broadside: 39 × 26.5 cm. (all edges untrimmed).

Printed in black with the title in reddish brown on cream Hahnemühle Biblio paper.

Published on 13 February 2003 by the University of Kentucky in an edition of 350 numbered copies; copies numbered 1–100 are printed in Victor Hammer's American Uncial with copies numbered 1–75 signed by the poet; copies numbered 101–350 are printed in Caslon ATF with copies numbered 101–175 signed by the poet.

Printed by Paul Evans Holbrook of the King Library Press.

Note: The poem, which recounts a scene from the funeral of the poet's sister, Anne, is greatly revised from the early version that was published in *Poetry Ireland Review*, summer 2002 (C846).

AA73 [*from*] VITRUVIANA 2003

first separate edition

from VITRUVIANA [in pale green] | [following in black] Seamus Heaney | Felim Egan
Card folded to: 20 × 15 cm.

[1], cover-title as above; [2], 'VITRUVIANA [in pale green] | | Seamus Heaney 2001' [in black]; [3], poem of five lines printed in gold over Felim Egan's watercolour; [4], '© Hieroglyph Editions 2003 | From "Vitruviana" by Seamus Heaney · Watercolour by Felim Egan | Published by Hieroglyph Editions in an edition of 1000 | 1 to 100 numbered and signed by the artists'.

Glossy white card; published by Hieroglyph Editions in May 2003. An additional 500 cards were published with the poem translated into Russian and printed on page [2]. These cards were distributed in St Petersburg where the artists participated in the celebration of the 300th anniversary of that city's founding.

Note: The poem first appeared in *Felim Egan*, an exhibition catalogue for the Stedelijk Museum, Amsterdam and was later collected as the third section of 'Vitruviana' in *Electric Light*.

AA74 THE COMET AT LULLWATER 2003

first edition

[at left, printed in black in large outline letters and surrounded by six comet/stars printed in blue] SEAMUS HEANEY [at right] The Comet at Lullwater | *for Bill and Joan Chace* | [poem of fourteen lines] | [across the bottom of the broadside]
Printed in honor of Dr. William M. Chace on the conclusion of his tenure as the eighteenth President of Emory University, and on the

occasion of the acquisition of the Seamus Heaney papers by the Robert W. | *Woodruff Library. Set from Bembo types and printed letterpress on Nideggen paper at Sutton Hoo Press in an edition of one hundred twenty-six copies, twenty-six of which are lettered and signed by the poet.*
Broadside: 28 × 38 cm. (bottom edge untrimmed).

Printed in black and blue on greyish-yellow laid paper.

Published 23 September 2003 by Emory University.

AA75 TESTIMONIES 2003

first separate edition

[from top left down] Testimonies [in bold red calligraphy] | [illustration of trees in black] | [publishing information] [from top right down] | SEAMUS HEANEY | [poem of twenty-three lines in two numbered sections]
Broadside: 28 × 40 cm. (bottom and right edges untrimmed).

Hand-set and printed in red and black on cream wove paper in an edition of 200 copies, signed by the author.

Published 'to mark the occasion of the Truman Capote Award presented to the author on September 25, 2003. Two hundred copies were printed by Shari DeGraw and Nichole Flores at the University of Iowa Center for the Book, with gracious support from the Writers' Workshop and the International Writing Program. Calligraphy by Glen Epstein'.

AA76 THE GAELTACHT 2003

first separate edition

[printed in blue down the left half of the sheet] The Gaeltacht | Seamus Heaney | [poem of fourteen lines in four sections] | [design] | [publication and limitation details] [the right half of the sheet has Eileen Ferguson's mixed media, *Land Link* 2002]
Broadside: 20.5 × 25.5 cm.

The text is printed in blue on matte wove paper in an edition of one hundred copies numbered by hand.

Published in September 2003. 'Printed by the Keough Institute for Irish Studies on the occasion of Seamus Heaney's reading at Dante's Cultures: Le Culture di Dante, University of Notre Dame, September 2003. Limited edition of 100 of which this is no. [*written in*].' Although not stated on the broadside, 26 lettered copies, signed by the poet, were also issued.

AA77 I SING OF A MAIDEN 2003

Christmas card

I sing of a Maiden . . .
Card folded to 21 × 15 cm.

[1], front cover with illustration; [2], blank; [3], text; [4], copyright information, publishing information.

White card; front cover greyish-blue with image by Catherine Heaney, c.1978; poem printed in black; back cover as above.

Privately published for the author by Peter Fallon/Gallery Press.

Note: 'I sing of a maiden . . .' from the Middle English.

B

CONTRIBUTIONS TO BOOKS

B1 UNIVERSITIES' POETRY FIVE 1963

UNIVERSITIES' | POETRY FIVE | *EDITED BY* | Tom Lowenstein | Cambridge | Ken Smith | Leeds | Advisory and Managing Editor: Anthony C. Smith | Cover design: John Holden | Business Assistant: Bill Bailey
22 × 14 cm.; pp. 44.

Stiff white paper wrappers, front and back covers lettered and decorated in black and white; spine blank.

Published 1963 by the Managing Committee of Universities' Poetry; printed by Albert E. Allen (Printers) Ltd.

Contents: 'Turkeys Observed'; 'Fair', pp. 6–7.

Note: 'Turkeys Observed' collected with revisions in *Death of a Naturalist*.

B2 YOUNG COMMONWEALTH POETS '65 1965

Young | Commonwealth | Poets | '65 | Edited | by | P. L. BRENT | [publisher's logo] HEINEMANN: LONDON | *in association with* | Cardiff Commonwealth Arts Festival | *Director:* Bill Harpe
21.5 × 14 cm.; pp. 220.

Black paper-covered boards, lettered and decorated in gold on spine; red dust-jacket lettered in white and pink.

Published 1965; printed by Clarke, Doble & Brendon Ltd, Cattedown, Plymouth.

Contents: 'Scaffolding'; 'Soliloquy for an Old Resident', pp. 136–138.

B3 CAHIERS FRANCO-ANGLAIS ANTHOLOGY OF YOUNG BRITISH POETS 1967

POESIE VIVANTE | Cahiers | Franco-Anglais | *No 3 – Anthology of Young* | *British Poets* |*compiled by Jeremy Robson* | *All French*

translations by | *and copyright Jean-Jacques Celly* | Poésie Vivante, | 11, rue Hoffmann, Genève, Suisse
17 × 12 cm.; pp. 96.

Stiff paper wrappers; front and back covers lettered in black.

Published 1967; no printer specified.

Contents: Photograph of Seamus Heaney on p. [30]; 'Gate (Barrière)'; 'The Peninsula (La Péninsule)', pp. 31–33.

B4 ROOM TO RHYME 1968

ROOM TO RHYME [in decorated outline letters] | [the following three lines to the left] *an anthology of poems by* | SEAMUS HEANEY AND | MICHAEL LONGLEY | [the following two lines in the centre] *and of ballads collected by* | DAVID HAMMOND | [the following three lines to the right] *An Arts Council* | *publication* | *price three shillings* | [nine illustrations in three rows of three each]
23 × 18 cm.; pp. [32].

Stiff paper wrappers; front cover, which serves as title-page, in red, lettered and decorated in black; back cover blank.

Published [1968]; no printer specified.

Contents: 'Elegy for a Still-Born Child', pp.[11]–[12]; 'Requiem for the Croppies', p.[14]; 'Last Look', p.[23]. Also six previously collected poems.

Note: 'For Marie' previously collected as 'Poem' in *Death of a Naturalist.*

B5 MODERN POETS FOUR 1968

Modern Poets | [ornament] | FOUR [ornament] | edited by | JIM HUNTER | *Senior English Master* | *Bristol Grammar School* | FABER AND FABER | 24 Russell Square | London
18.5 × 12.5 cm.; pp. 142.

Glassine on white paper-covered boards, lettered and decorated in blue and tan.

Published 1968; issued simultaneously in a paperback edition; printed by Latimer Trend & Co. Ltd, Plymouth.

Contents: 'May Day', p.137; also ten previously collected poems.

B6 TWELVE TO TWELVE 1970

TWELVE | TO | TWELVE | EDITED BY JENI COUZYN | POETRY D-DAY | CAMDEN FESTIVAL 1970 | POETS TRUST LONDON 1970
23.5 × 18 cm.; pp. 52.

a. ***trade edition***

Stiff paper covers; front cover in black; lettered and decorated in red; back cover and spine in white.

2,000 copies published for Poetry D-Day, 9 May 1970; printed by the Hillingdon Press, Uxbridge.

Contents: 'Bye-child', pp. 45–46.

Note: Collected with revisions in *Wintering Out*.

b. ***limited edition***

A special edition of 100 copies in orange cloth was also issued; front and back covers blank; spine lettered in red; orange dust-jacket printed in black on front cover; each copy was signed by the 12 contributors.

Contents: Same as B6a.

B7 THINGS WORKING 1970

Edited by Penny Blackie | Penguin English Project Stage One Things Working [all above a photograph of a train covering two pages]
21 × 15 cm.; pp. 128.

Light-green stiff paper covers; front cover lettered in black with image of sculptured gear-box; back and spine white lettered in black.

Published 1970 by Penguin Books; printed by Ebenezer Baylis & Son, Ltd.

Contents: 'Frogman', pp. 96–97.

B8 NEW POEMS 1970–71 1971

[ornament] | NEW POEMS | 1970–71 | A P.E.N. Anthology | of Contemporary Poetry | [ornament] | *Edited by* | ALAN BROWNJOHN | SEAMUS HEANEY | JON STALLWORTHY | HUTCHINSON OF LONDON
19.5 × 13 cm.; pp. 112.

Black paper-covered boards; spine lettered and decorated in gold; grey endpapers; dust-jacket front cover printed in green and black, lettered in white; back cover lettered in black.

Published 1971; printed at the Anchor Press, Tiptree, Essex.

Contents: 'Introduction' by the editors, unsigned, pp. [9]–[11].

B9 RESPONSES 1971

RESPONSES | The National Book League and the Poetry Society | 1971
25.5 × 19.5 cm.; pp. 44.

Red paper covers; front cover with title in purple; back cover blank; top edges trimmed.

Published 1971; 500 hand-numbered copies printed by the Westerham Press on handmade paper from Hodgkinson's Wookey Hole Mill.

Contents: 'Servant Boy', p.24; also published as broadside in 1971 (AA3).

B10 THE YOUNG BRITISH POETS 1971

THE YOUNG | BRITISH POETS | *Edited by* | JEREMY ROBSON | 1971 | CHATTO & WINDUS | LONDON
19.5 × 13 cm.; pp. 156.

Purple paper-covered boards; front and back covers blank; spine lettered and decorated in gold; white dust-jacket lettered in black with photographs of contributors on front.

Published 1971; printed by Richard Clay (the Chaucer Press) Ltd, Bungay, Suffolk. A paperback edition was published in 1972 by Corgi Books. Published in the United States in 1973 by St. Martin's Press.

Contents: 'Shore Woman', pp. 71–72; also four previously collected poems.

Note: 'Shore Woman' was collected with revisions in *Wintering Out*. This is a different version of (B11).

B11 CORGI MODERN POETS IN FOCUS: 2 1971

Corgi Modern Poets | in Focus: 2 | Edited by | JEREMY ROBSON | [publisher's logo] | CORGI BOOKS | TRANSWORLD PUBLISHERS LTD | A National General Company
18 × 11 cm.; pp. 144.

Stiff paper covers in black, brown, green, orange and blue; lettered in black and white.

Published 1971; printed by Cox & Wyman Ltd, London, Reading and Fakenham. A hardbound edition was published by the Woburn Press (London) in 1973.

Contents: '*Seamus Heaney writes*', pp. 101–102; 'Limbo,' p. 116; also nine previously published poems.

Note: 'Shore Woman' was collected with revisions in *Wintering Out*. This is a different version of (B10).

B12 SOUNDINGS '72 1972

Soundings '72 | Edited by Seamus Heaney | An annual Anthology of New Irish poetry | Blackstaff Press Belfast 1972
24 × 18 cm.; pp. 72.

Glossy black wrappers; front cover lettered in white with aquamarine design on front; back cover has price '£1.00' in top-left corner; spine lettered in white; black and white spiralling psychedelic endpapers.

Published 1972; printed by Belfast Litho Printers Ltd.

Contents: 'Editor's Note', pp. 5–6; 'Mossbawn Sunlight'; 'Sile na Gig,' pp. 23–24.

Note: 'Sile na Gig' was reprinted with revisions in *The Kilpeck Anthology* (B52) and then collected in *Station Island* as 'Sheelagh na Gig'.

B13 NEW POEMS, 1971–72 1972

[ornament] | NEW POEMS | 1971–72 | A P.E.N. Anthology | of Contemporary Poetry | [ornament] | *Edited by* | PETER PORTER | HUTCHINSON OF LONDON

20 × 13 cm.; pp. 184.

Red paper-covered boards; front and back covers blank; spine lettered and decorated in gold; grey endpapers; red and white dust-jacket printed and decorated in black.

Published 1972; printed by Benham and Company Limited, Colchester, Essex, and bound by Wm Brendon, Tiptree, Essex.

Contents: 'Elegy for a Postman', p. 86; also one previously collected poem.

B14 NEW POEMS, 1972–73 1973

[ornament] | NEW POEMS | 1972–73 | A P.E.N. Anthology | of Contemporary Poetry | [ornament] | *Edited by* | DOUGLAS DUNN | HUTCHINSON OF LONDON

20 × 13 cm.; pp. 184.

Red paper-covered boards; front and back covers blank; spine lettered and decorated in gold; orange and brown dust-jacket printed and decorated in black.

Published 1973; printed by R. F. Acford Ltd, Chichester, Sussex.

Contents: 'Bog Bower', p. 85.

Note: Collected with revisions as 'Come to the Bower' in *North*.

B15 POEMS FOR SHAKESPEARE 2 1973

Poems for | Shakespeare 2 | *Edited with an* | *Introduction by* | *Graham Fawcett* | The Globe Playhouse | Trust Publications | London 1973
20 × 13 cm.; pp. 80.

a. *limited edition*

Red cloth-covered boards with leather spine; illustration stamped in gold on front cover; spine lettered and decorated in gold; white endpapers; trimmed, gilded edges. Issued in a red cloth-covered slipcase. All copies signed by the 14 poets. Published 1973 in advance of the regular issue; 100 numbered copies printed by Whitstable Litho, Straker Brothers Ltd.

Contents: 'A Flourish for the Prince of Denmark', p. 37.

Note: The Globe Playhouse Trust gave 14 poets the choice of writing '(i), an "occasional" poem for Shakespeare on his birthday; (ii), a poem developing a Shakespearean theme or character; (iii), a neo-Shakespearean lyric; or (iv) a poem adopting or containing a phrase or line from Shakespeare . . . The new poems are set here alongside earlier examples of the genre . . .'

b. *trade edition*

Poems for | Shakespeare 2 | *Edited with an* | *Introduction by* | *Graham Fawcett* | The Globe Playhouse | Trust Publications | London 1973
20 × 13 cm.; pp. 80.

Stiff cream paper covers; lettered and decorated in red and black.

Published 1973; 1,000 copies printed by Whitstable Litho, Straker Brothers Ltd.

Contents: Same as B15a.

B16 LET THE POET CHOOSE 1973

Let the | *Poet Choose* | edited by | JAMES GIBSON | [publisher's logo] | HARRAP LONDON

21.5 × 13.5 cm.; pp. 192.

Orange cloth-covered boards; front and back covers blank; spine stamped in black; dust-jacket in brown and yellow lettered in white.

Published 1973; issued simultaneously in a paperback edition; no printer specified.

Contents: 'Bogland' and 'The Peninsula' and an introductory note for the poems pp. 72–74; both poems had previously been published.

B17 CHOICE 1973

CHOICE | an anthology of Irish poetry | selected by the poets themselves | with a comment on their choice | edited by Desmond Egan | and Michael Hartnett

23 × 17 cm.; pp. 124.

Brown cloth-covered boards; front and back covers blank; spine lettered and decorated in gold; issued in a clear acetate dust-wrapper.

Published 1973; printed at the Goldsmith Press, Castleknock, Dublin.

Contents: 'Servant Boy', and note on the poem pp. 38–39.

Note: A paperback edition was published in 1979; issued with black wrappers lettered in white. In this edition Seamus Heaney's note and poem appear on pages 46–47.

B18 DESCARTES' DREAM 1973

DESCARTES' DREAM | W. J. HARVEY | A CARCANET PRESS PUBLICATION

19 × 12.5 cm.; pp. 36.

Stiff canary paper wrappers; lettered and decorated in black.

Published 1973; 600 copies; printed by Derek Maggs, London.

Contents: 'Preface', p. 7.

Note: This is the third collection of poems by Harvey, who had died in 1967. Seamus Heaney had met him in 1962 at a gathering of the 'Group' in Belfast, an informal writers' workshop in Belfast facilitated by Philip Hobsbaum and in which Michael Longley, Derek Mahon and Paul Muldoon also participated.

B19 MACBETH 1973

[publisher's logo] Erasmus Series | SHAKESPEARE | Macbeth | FOLENS & CO. LTD. | John F. Kennedy Drive, Naas Road, Dublin 12.
20.5 × 12.5 cm.; pp. viii, 144.

Stiff paper wrappers, lettered and decorated in red and white.

Published 1973; 'printed in 150 copies for the benefit of our Consultants and Contributors'; printed on the Press of the Publisher.

Contents: 'Introduction', pp. 5–22.

Note: A trade edition of this publication was planned but never issued.

B20 NEW POEMS 1973–74 1974

NEW POEMS | 1973–74 | A P.E.N. Anthology | of Contemporary Poetry | *Edited by* | STEWART CONN | [publisher's logo] | HUTCHINSON OF LONDON
20 × 13 cm.; pp. 184.

Orange boards; front and back covers blank; spine lettered in gold; orange dust-jacket lettered and designed in black and blue.

Published 1974; printed by Benham and Company Ltd, Essex.

Contents: 'Act of Union'; 'Bone Dreams'; 'Bog Queen', pp. 69–74.

Note: All three poems were collected with revisions in *North*.

B21 THE FABER BOOK OF IRISH VERSE 1974

a. *first English edition*

The Faber Book of | IRISH VERSE | *edited by* | JOHN MONTAGUE | FABER AND FABER | 3 Queen Square | London
19.5 × 12.5 cm.; pp. 400.

Green cloth-covered boards; front and back covers blank; spine lettered in gold; green endpapers; green and white dust-jacket lettered in black.

Published 1974; printed by Robert MacLehose and Co.

Contents: 'Mossbawn Sunlight', pp. 361–362; also three previously collected poems.

b. *first American edition*

The Book of | IRISH VERSE | AN ANTHOLOGY OF IRISH POETRY | FROM THE SIXTH CENTURY TO THE PRESENT | *edited by* | JOHN MONTAGUE | MACMILLAN PUBLISHING CO., INC. | *New York*
21 × 14 cm.; pp. 400.

Green cloth-covered boards; front and back covers blank, spine lettered in gold; pale yellow dust-jacket lettered in red, black and green.

Published 1976; no printer specified; a paperback edition was issued in 1983.

Contents: Contents same as B21a.

B22 WORLDS 1974

WORLDS | SEVEN MODERN POETS | CHARLES CAUSLEY | THOM GUNN | SEAMUS HEANEY | TED HUGHES | NORMAN MacCAIG | ADRIAN MITCHELL | EDWIN MORGAN | Photographs by | Fay

Godwin, Larry Herman and Peter Abramowitsch | [rule] | Edited by Geoffrey Summerfield | Penguin Education
21 × 15 cm.; pp. 288.

Stiff cloth-grained paper covers; lettered and decorated in black, brown and orange; portraits of poets at bottom on front and back.

Published 1974; printed by Butler & Tanner Ltd, Frome and London.

Contents: [Autobiographical Note], pp. 92–95; [Notes on the Poems], 266–267. Also 19 previously collected poems.

Note: Photographs by Larry Herman showing Heaney appear on pp. [90], [96]–[105], 115. 'The photographs aim either to show the poets in their various worlds or to offer representations of local facts, particular places, particular people which at some time or other have provided these poets with pleasure or significant memory . . .' Preface.

B23 THE WEARING OF THE BLACK 1974

The wearing | of the black | AN ANTHOLOGY OF CONTEMPORARY ULSTER POETRY | Edited by Padraic Fiacc | Blackstaff Press Belfast
21 × 14 cm.; pp. vii, 177.

Stiff white wrappers; lettered in black, with green, black, decoration on front cover; back cover and spine lettered in black.

Published 1974; printed by Belfast Litho Printers Limited.

Contents: 'Whatever You Say, Say Nothing', pp. 38–40; 'From Singing School', pp. 42–43; 'Romanist', p. 44; 'July', pp. 45–46; 'A Constable Calls', pp. 46–47; 'Trial Runs', pp. 51–52; also 3 previously collected poems.

B24 TWO DECADES OF IRISH WRITING 1975

Douglas Dunn | TWO DECADES | OF IRISH WRITING | –A Critical Survey– | [publisher's logo] | A CARCANET PRESS PUBLICATION
21.5 × 13.5 cm.; pp. 268.

Green paper-covered boards; front and back covers blank; spine lettered and decorated in gold; green endpapers; pea-green dust-jacket lettered in black.

Published 1975; printed by Eyre & Spottiswoode Ltd at Grosvenor Press, Portsmouth.

Contents: 'The Poetry of Patrick Kavanagh: from Monaghan to the Grand Canal', pp. [105]–117.

B25 IMAGES OF STONE 1976

IMAGES OF STONE | HELEN HICKEY | Photographs by Bill Porter | Blackstaff Press
20 × 21 cm.; 120 pp.

Glossy paper wrappers; front cover lettered in black over photograph of stone head; back cover and spine lettered in black.

Published by Blackstaff Press, 1976; printed by Litho printers Limited, Belfast.

Contents: 'January God', p. 12.

B26 HAND AND EYE 1977

HAND AND EYE | *An Anthology for* | *Sacheverell Sitwell* | Edited by | Geoffrey Elborn | *Privately printed at* | THE TRAGARA PRESS | EDINBURGH | 1977
22.5 × 14.5 cm.; pp. [32]; unpaginated.

Olive-green paper-covered boards; front and back covers blank; black cloth spine with paper label lettered and decorated in black. Issued in plain un-printed dust-jacket.

Published on Sitwell's eightieth birthday, 15 November 1977; 175 copies hand-set and printed at the Tragara Press; copies 1–20 were signed by the 16 contributors. Each contributor also received a copy, and extra copies were reserved for the editor.

Contents: 'The Otter', pp. [19]–[20].

B27 A WORLD OF STONE: THE ARAN ISLANDS 1977

a world of | *stone* | [lower right corner wrapping around publisher's logo] O'BRIEN EDUCATIONAL · 11 CLARE ST. DUBLIN 2
22 × 15 cm.; pp. 80.

Glossy paper wrappers; front cover lettered in black and printed over black and white photograph of cliffs and crashing waves with title in a blue rectangle; blue back cover lettered in white and black with oval black and white photograph of stone walls; spine lettered in black.

Published in 1977; printed by E. & T. O'Brien Ltd, Dublin.

Contents: 'The Evening Land', p. 6; 'Inisheer', p. 34; 'The Oarsmen's Song', p. 49.

Note: The poems first appeared in *The Island People* (A3).

B28 SEAMUS HEANEY 1977

Seamus | Heaney | Skoleradioen 1977 [all on right hand side of vertical rule]
21 × 14 cm.; pp. 64.

Brown-green wrappers; lettered in orange and white and designed in white.

Published by Skoleradioen, Copenhagen 1977.

Contents: the following essays, 'Mossbawn', p. 17; 'Farm Work', p. 18; 'The Trade of an Irish Poet', pp. 32, 34; 'untitled', p. 39; 'The Bog', 39–40; 'Author's Note', back cover, (on P. V. Glob's *The Bog People* and Denmark). Also previously collected poems and two radio interviews that appear here for the first time.

B29 IN THEIR ELEMENT 1977

in their element | a selection of poems by Seamus Heaney & Derek Mahon | [illustration]
23 × 18.5 cm.; pp. [24]; unpaginated.

Stiff silver-paper covers; front cover same as title-page lettered and decorated in black and purple; back cover blank.

Published 1977; printed by Dorman & Sons Ltd, Belfast for the Arts Council of Northern Ireland.

Contents: 'The Badgers', p. [12].

Note: Collected with revisions in *Field Work*; also 12 previously collected poems.

B30 RICHARD MURPHY: POET OF TWO TRADITIONS 1978

Richard Murphy: | Poet of Two Traditions | Interdisciplinary Studies | *Edited by* | Maurice Harmon | Wolfhound Press
23 × 14.5 cm.; pp. 128.

Tan rexine-covered boards; front and back covers blank; spine lettered in black; black endpapers; dust-jacket, lettered in black and white, has photograph of seagull in flight on front.

Published 1978; no printer specified.

Contents: 'The Poetry of Richard Murphy', pp. 18–30.

Note: This is a special edition of the *Irish University Review*, Richard Murphy issue, spring 1977 (C252).

B31 THE PUSHCART PRIZE 1978

BEST OF THE SMALL PRESSES | [publisher's logo] | EDITED BY BILL HENDERSON | published by THE PUSHCART PRESS | 1978–79 EDITION | THE PUSHCART PRIZE, III: [ornaments]
23.5 × 16 cm.; pp. 552.

Green cloth-covered boards, front and back covers blank; spine lettered in black and red; dark brown endpapers; top and bottom edges trimmed, top edge stained green.

Published 1978; no printer specified.

Contents: Untitled commentary, p. 251; 'Sweeney Astray', pp. 251–259.

B32 MICHAEL MCLAVERTY: COLLECTED SHORT STORIES 1978

a. *first edition*

Collected Short Stories | Michael McLaverty | POOLBEG PRESS: DUBLIN
18 × 11.5 cm.; pp. 278.

Stiff paper wrappers with a multicoloured photograph of fabrics; lettering in white except for Michael McLaverty (black); blue spine with same lettering colour scheme.

Published 1978; printed by Cahill (1976) Ltd, East Wall Road, Dublin.

Contents: 'Introduction,' pp. 7–9.

b. *revised edition*

Collected | *Short Stories* | MICHAEL MCLAVERTY | SOPHIA HILLAN |*wood engravings by* | BARBARA CHILDS | *Introduction by* | SEAMUS HEANEY | THE | BLACKSTAFF | PRESS | [short rule] | BELFAST
19.5 × 12.5 cm.; pp. xiv, 298.

Black cloth-covered boards; front and back covers blank; spine lettered and decorated in silver; grey endpapers; grey dust-jacket with black illustration, lettered in white on front and black on spine.

Published 2002; printed by Betaprint.

Contents: 'Introduction', pp. xi–xiii.

Note: Seamus Heaney's 'Introduction', revised from B32a.

B33 THE FIRST TEN YEARS 1979

The First Ten Years | Dublin Arts Festival Poetry | Edited by Peter Fallon and Dennis O'Driscoll | Dublin Arts Festival 1979
21 × 14.5 cm.; pp. 62.

Black cloth-covered boards; front and back covers blank; spine lettered in gold; grey-green endpapers; tan dust-jacket lettered and decorated in black.

Published 1979; printed by E. & T. O'Brien Ltd, 11 Clare Street, Dublin. A paperback edition was issued in tan wrappers, lettered and designed in black.

Contents: 'An Afterwards'; 'Homecomings', pp. 20–21.

B34 IMAGE AND ILLUSION 1979

Image & Illusion | Anglo-Irish Literature | and its Contexts | A Festschrift for Roger McHugh | Edited by | Maurice Harmon | Wolfhound Press
24 × 16 cm.; pp. 174.

Black cloth-covered boards; front and back covers blank; spine lettered in gold; dust-jacket in red, lettered in black and white with photograph of Roger McHugh on rear.

Published 1979; no printer specified.

Contents: 'Funeral Rites'; 'Punishment'; 'Act of Union', pp. 70–91.

Note: The texts of the poems as published previously in *North* and the worksheets for these poems as they first appeared in *Quarto*, November 1975 (C231), are reprinted here in an article 'The Craft of Diction: Revisions in Seamus Heaney's Poems' by Arthur E. McGuinness, pp. 62–91.

B35 IRISH POETRY AFTER YEATS 1979

Irish Poetry | After Yeats | SEVEN POETS | Austin Clarke Richard Murphy | Patrick Kavanagh Thomas Kinsella | Denis Devlin John Montague | Seamus Heaney | Edited by | MAURICE HARMON | WOLFHOUND PRESS
21 × 15 cm.; pp. 232.

Light tan rexine-covered boards; front and back covers blank; spine lettered in gold; white dust-jacket with black, blue and green lettering and decoration.

Published 1979; no printer specified.

Contents: 'Casualty' collected with revisions in *Field Work*; 'A Post Card from North Antrim'; 'Glanmore Sonnet III'; 'Glanmore Sonnet VII', collected as 'Glanmore Sonnet VIII' in *Field Work*; 'Otter';'Song', pp. 218–225; also 14 previously collected poems.

B36 BEST OF THE POETRY YEAR 6 1979

Selected by DANNIE ABSE | BEST OF THE POETRY YEAR | Poetry Dimension Annual 6 | [publisher's logo] Robson Books
19.5 × 12.5 cm.; pp. 202.

Maroon cloth-covered boards; front and back covers blank; spine lettered and decorated in gold; dust-jacket in blue and green, lettered in green, white and blue.

Published 1979; issued simultaneously in a paperback edition; printed by Redwood Burn Limited, Trowbridge & Esher.

Contents: 'The Skunk', p. 149.

B37 POETRY BOOK SOCIETY: THE FIRST TWENTY-FIVE YEARS 1979

Poetry | Book Society | THE FIRST | TWENTY-FIVE | YEARS | *edited by* | Eric W. White | *for members of* | *the Society* | LONDON | Poetry Book Society | 1979
21.5 × 13.5 cm.; pp. 72.

Burnt-orange cloth-covered boards; front and back covers blank; spine lettered in gold; light-grey dust-jacket, printed and decorated in brown and red.

Published 1979; printed by the John Roberts Press, London.

Contents: 'North', p. 54.

Note: This prose piece had first appeared as 'Seamus Heaney writes . . .' in *Poetry Book Society Bulletin* Summer 1975 (C223).

B38 A CENTENARY SELECTION OF MOORE'S MELODIES 1979

A Centenary | *Selection of* | MOORE'S | MELODIES | *EDITED BY* | DAVID HAMMOND | *with an introduction by* | SEAMUS HEANEY | GILBERT DALTON

18.5 × 11.5 cm.; pp. 64.

Glossy white paper wrappers; front and back covers lettered and designed in green and brown.

Published 1979 by Gilbert Dalton, Skerries, Co. Dublin; printed by Cahill Ltd.

Contents: 'Introduction', pp. 8–9.

B39 CELEBRATION 1979

CELEBRATION | *A salute to* | *a visiting artist* | [swelled rule in outline] | *edited by* | JIM FITZGERALD | VERITAS PUBLICATIONS

21.5 × 13.5 cm.; pp. 56.

Stiff yellow paper wrappers; front cover lettered in white with image of John Behan's sculpture *St. Francis and the Birds*; back cover lettered and decorated in white and blue-grey; spine lettered in white.

Published 1979; printed by Cahill Printers Ltd.

Contents: 'Sweeney Praises the Trees', pp. 10–11.

Note: Seamus Heaney's translation from the Middle Irish; collected with revisions in *Sweeney Astray. Celebration* is a tribute by 19 Irish poets to Pope John Paul II on the occasion of his visit to Ireland. In addition to Heaney, the poets included Richard Murphy, Michael Longley, Eavan Boland and John Hewitt.

B40 ESSAYS BY DIVERS HANDS 1979

ESSAYS BY DIVERS HANDS: | INNOVATION IN | CONTEMPORARY LITERATURE | *being the transactions of* | *the Royal Society of*

Literature, | *New Series: Volume XL* | EDITED BY VINCENT CRONIN, FRSL | *Published for* | *the Royal Society of Literature* | *by the Boydell Press*
21.5 × 13.5 cm.; pp. xi, 161.

Blue cloth-covered boards; front and back covers blank; spine lettered in silver; red dust-jacket lettered in black.

Published 1979; printed by Fletcher & Son Ltd, Norwich.

Contents: 'Feeling Into Words', pp. 83–100.

Note: Collected with revisions in *Preoccupations*. Text of the lecture read before the Society on 17 October 1974.

B41 THE POET'S WORK 1979

The Poet's Work: | [rule] | 29 *Masters of 20th Century Poetry* | *on the Origins and Practice* | *of Their Art* | edited by Reginald Gibbons | Houghton Mifflin Company Boston 1979
21 × 14 cm.; pp. xi, 295.

Black cloth-covered boards; front cover and spine lettered and decorated in gold; back cover blank; black dust-jacket lettered and decorated in white and tan.

Published 1979; no printer specified.

Contents: 'Feelings into Words', pp. 263–282.

B42 THE WEE BLACK TIN 1980

The Wee Black Tin | Poems from Ballinascreen [all of the preceding in heavy Gothic type] | FOREWORD BY SEAMUS HEANEY | POEMS SELECTED AND COMPILED BY | GRAHAM MAWHINNEY | AND | JENNIFER JOHNSTON | BALLINASCREEN HISTORICAL SOCIETY | 1980
22 × 15.5 cm.; pp. 66.

Stapled white paper wrappers; front cover lettered and decorated in black and red; back cover lettered and decorated in black.

Published 1980; printed by Johnston Printing Ltd, Kilrea.

Contents: 'Foreword', p. [v].

B43 THE WRITERS: A SENSE OF IRELAND 1980

a. *trade edition*

THE WRITERS | A Sense of Ireland | [ornament] | *New work by 44 Irish writers selected and edited by* | ANDREW CARPENTER | *and* | PETER FALLON | *with photographs of the writers by* | MIKE BUNN | [publisher's logo] | THE O'BRIEN PRESS | DUBLIN 1980
24 × 17 cm.; pp. 224.

Black rexine-covered boards; front and back covers blank; spine lettered and decorated in gold; grey endpapers; photographic dust-jacket lettered in black and white.

Published 1980; printed by A. Folens & Co. Ltd, Dublin.

Contents: 'A Peacock's Feather'; 'Sweeney Astray'; 'A Lighting Plot', pp. 51–55.

Note: 'Sweeney Astray' was collected as 'King of the Ditchbacks' in *Station Island*.

b. *limited edition*

Leather bindings of various colours with matching slipcase of paper and leather. Stamped in different colours.

Published by O'Brien Press, Dublin in an edition of 24: 12 presentation copies numbered I–XII and 12 numbered 1–12, which were for sale. Signed by all 44 writers, the photographer, the editors, the publisher and the designer.

Contents: Same as in B43a.

B44 SOFT DAY 1980

a. *first American cloth edition*

SOFT DAY | *A Miscellany* | *of Contemporary Irish Writing* | EDITED BY | Peter Fallon & Sean Golden | UNIVERSITY OF NOTRE DAME PRESS | NOTRE DAME LONDON
23 × 15 cm.; pp. xviii, 228.

Green cloth-covered boards; front and back covers blank; spine lettered and decorated in gold.

Published 1980; no printer specified; issued simultaneously in a paperback edition.

Contents: 'A Strange House', p. 132. Also five previously collected poems.

b. ***first Irish cloth edition***

SOFT DAY | *A Miscellany* | *of Contemporary Irish Writing* | EDITED BY | Peter Fallon & Sean Golden | WOLFHOUND PRESS
23 × 15 cm.; p. 246.

Green cloth-covered boards with light-green dust-jacket lettered in white and black. Wolfhound Press; issued in a paperback edition; no printer specified.

Published 1980; no printer specified; issued simultaneously in a paperback edition.

Contents: Same as B44a.

B45 A GARLAND OF POEMS FOR LEONARD CLARK 1980

A GARLAND OF POEMS | for LEONARD CLARK on | his 75th birthday | as a tribute to his achievements | as a poet and in the cause of poetry | Compiled by | R. L. COOK | THE LOMOND PRESS, Kinnesswood and | THE ENITHARMON PRESS, London | 1980
21 × 15 cm.; pp. 36.

Stapled stiff blue wrappers; front and back covers lettered and decorated in black.

Published 1 August 1980 (Leonard Clark's birthday); 400 copies printed by Central Printers (Arbroath) Ltd.

Contents: 'A Vision of Master Murphy on Station Island', pp. 17–18.

Note: Collected with revisions in *Station Island* as section V of 'Station Island'.

B46 YEATS, SLIGO AND IRELAND 1980

YEATS, | SLIGO AND IRELAND | Essays to mark the 21st Yeats International | Summer School | edited by | A. Norman Jeffares | Irish Literary Studies 6 | [publisher's logo] | COLIN SMYTHE | Gerrards Cross, 1980
21.5 × 13.5 cm.; pp. 278.

Blue cloth-covered boards; front and back cover blank; spine lettered in gold; dust-jacket in blue printed in white with photograph of Ben Bulben on front cover.

Published 1980; printed by Billing & Sons Ltd. An American edition was published by Barnes & Noble Books, 1980.

Contents: 'Yeats as an Example?', pp. 56–72.

Note: Text of lecture given at the University of Surrey in 1978.

B47 IRISH STUDIES 1980

IRISH | STUDIES | 1 | EDITED BY P.J. DRUDY | FELLOW OF ST EDMUND'S HOUSE, CAMBRIDGE | CAMBRIDGE UNIVERSITY PRESS | LONDON NEW YORK NEW ROCHELLE | MELBOURNE SYDNEY
21.5 × 13.5 cm.; viii, 160.

Green cloth-covered boards; front and back cover blank; spine lettered and decorated in gold; dark green dust-jacket lettered in white designed in light green.

Published 1980; printed at the Pitman Press, Bath.

Contents: 'A tale of two islands: reflections on the Irish Literary Revival', pp. 1–20.

B48 FEATHERS & BONES 1981

FEATHERS & BONES | Ten Poets of the Irish Earth | [illustration: drawing of bird on harp by Sevrin Housen] | Edited by Sevrin

Housen | Halcyon Press | 1700 49th Street | Sacramento, CA 95819
21.5 × 14 cm.; pp. 96.

Dark yellow wrappers; front cover lettered and decorated in brown; back cover blank; text printed in brown. An edition of 100 copies were issued in brown cloth, numbered and signed by Sevrin Housen, with the front wrapper of the paper issue mounted on front cover.

Published 1981; no printer specified.

Contents: 'Preludes', pp. 12–17; all previously collected prose-poems from *Stations*.

B49 POETRY SUPPLEMENT 1981

Poetry Supplement | COMPILED BY | ANDREW MOTION | FOR THE | POETRY BOOK | SOCIETY | *CHRISTMAS* | 1981 | *The Poetry Book Society is subsidised by* | *the Arts Council of Great Britain*
21 × 14 cm.; pp. [60].

Light blue wrappers; front and back covers lettered and decorated in black.

Published 1981; printed by the John Roberts Press, London.

Contents: 'The Railway Children', p. [16].

B50 LONDON REVIEW OF BOOKS: ANTHOLOGY ONE 1981

[rule] | London Review | OF BOOKS | [rule] | ANTHOLOGY ONE | [rule] | WITH AN INTRODUCTION BY | KARL MILLER | JUNCTION BOOKS | LONDON | [rule]
21 × 13.5 cm.; pp. xi, 309.

Black cloth-covered boards; front and back covers blank; spine lettered in gold; light blue dust-jacket lettered in black, blue and white.

Published 1981; printed by Whitstable Litho Ltd, Kent.

Contents: 'Changes', p. 13.

Note: Collected with revisions in *Station Island.*

B51 EIGHT IRISH WRITERS 1981

IRISH WRITERS | A series of | eight charcoal drawings by | Louis le Brocquy | printed by collotype lithography | on Rives paper by the Imprimerie Arte | Adrien Maeght, Paris, in an individually | numbered and signed edition of 100 with | 25 copies *hors commerce* and an independent | display edition, without text, of 15 Artist's proofs. | texts edited by | Andrew Carpenter | preface by Seamus Heaney | DUBLIN 1981
Eleven sheets folded to 33 × 28.5.

Of these bifolia, eight are dedicated to an individual author with a charcoal drawing inserted; three have publication information, contents, preface, 'editor's note', statement of limitation. Dark linen solander box lettered in white on front cover.

Contents: 'Preface' [5]; the poem 'Digging' appears in the Heaney section.

B52 THE KILPECK ANTHOLOGY 1981

the kilpeck anthology [the word 'kilpeck' printed in red] | [panel of illustrations by Enok Sweetland] | Edited by Glenn Storhaug [line ornament] Five Seasons Press 1981
28.5 × 20 cm.; pp. 54.

a. *trade edition*

Issued in light-brown patterned paper wrappers; lettered in black on front and spine; back cover blank; tan endpapers.

Published 1981; printed at the Senecio Press Ltd.

Contents: 'Sile na Gig', pp. 18–19.

Note: Collected with revisions and with title, 'Sheelagh na Gig at Kilpeck', in *Station Island*. A completely different version was published with the same title in *Soundings '72* (B12).

b. *limited edition*

A special edition of fifty copies was printed letterpress on hand-made paper at the Five Seasons Press; this special edition was issued in linen boards with morocco spine in canvas slipcase; Brian Nevitt made colour silkscreen prints of Jeff Nuttall's water-colour paintings and Al Vandenberg's photographs.

Contents: As in B52a.

B53 ARVON 1980 ANTHOLOGY 1982

Arvon | Foundation | Poetry Competition | 1980 ANTHOLOGY | Edited and introduced | by | TED HUGHES and | SEAMUS HEANEY | Kilnhurst Publishing Company
23.5 × 15.5 cm.; pp. 174.

Cream paper covers; front and back covers lettered and decorated in grey.

Published 1982; printed by Mackays of Chatham Ltd.

Contents: 'Introduction by Seamus Heaney and Ted Hughes', pp. 5–7.

Note: The first part of the introduction, by Seamus Heaney (pp. 5–6), had first been published in the *The Observer*, 15 February 1981 (C331) as 'Panegyric for Three Voices'.

B54 LARKIN AT SIXTY 1982

Larkin at Sixty | [double rule, top rule heavy] | Edited by | ANTHONY THWAITE | [publisher's logo] | *faber and faber*
21.5 × 13.5 cm.; pp. 148.

Grey cloth-covered boards; front and back covers blank; spine lettered in metallic red. Tan dust-jacket lettered and decorated in black on spine and back cover; front cover lettered in tan within red panel with publisher's logo lettered in black below panel.

Published 1982; printed by Latimer Trend & Company Ltd, Plymouth.

Contents: 'The Main of Light', pp. 131–138.

B55 THE HARPER'S TURN 1982

Tom Mac Intyre | The Harper's Turn | *with an introduction by Seamus Heaney* | [publisher's logo] Gallery Books
21.5 × 13.5 cm.; pp. 66.

Black cloth-covered boards; front and back covers blank; spine lettered in gold; light-blue dust-jacket lettered and decorated in black and purple.

Published 1982; issued simultaneously in a paperback edition; no printer specified.

Contents: 'Introduction', pp. 8–9.

B56 POEMS FOR CHARLES CAUSLEY 1982

Poems for | Charles Causley | [list of 26 contributors in two columns] | LONDON [solidus] THE ENITHARMON PRESS [solidus] 1982
21.5 × 14 cm.; pp. 40.

Black cloth-covered boards; front and back covers blank; spine lettered in gold; grey-blue endpapers; grey-blue dust-jacket lettered in blue and black.

Published 1982; 500 copies printed, of which 200 are bound in cloth as above; printed by Skelton's Press, Ltd. The paper edition: light-blue wrappers; front cover lettered in blue and black; back cover and spine lettered in black only.

Contents: 'Sweeney's Praise of Farranan', p. 16.

Note: Collected with revisions in *Sweeney Astray*, section 73.

B57 THE CRANE BAG BOOK OF IRISH STUDIES 1982

The Crane Bag Book | of | Irish Studies | (1977–1981) | [publisher's logo] | BLACKWATER PRESS DUBLIN
24 × 17 cm.; pp. 944.

Black cloth-covered boards; front cover and spine lettered and decorated in gold; back cover blank; grey dust-jacket with front cover lettered in black and white; back cover and spine lettered in black only.

Published 1982; printed by Folens Publishers, Airton Road, Tallaght, Co. Dublin.

Contents: 'Preface', pp. [7]–[8].

Note: *The Crane Bag Book of Irish Studies* is a reprint in book form of the issues of the periodical *The Crane Bag*, vols 1–5, 1977–1981, with a preface by Seamus Heaney.

B58 THE RATTLE BAG 1982

THE RATTLE BAG | [swelled rule] | *An Anthology of Poetry* | *selected by* | SEAMUS HEANEY and TED HUGHES | publisher's logo | *faber and faber*
21.5 × 13.5 cm.; pp. 498.

Yellow cloth-covered boards; front and back covers blank; spine lettered and decorated in gold; dust-jacket in blue and yellow, lettered and decorated in black and red.

Published 1982; printed by Fakenham Press Ltd, Fakenham, Norfolk; issued simultaneously in a paper edition.

Contents: 'Introduction', unsigned, p. 19; 'The Names of the Hare' (from the Middle English, version by Seamus Heaney), pp. 305–306; 'Sweeney Praises the Trees' (from the Irish, translation by Seamus Heaney), pp. 411–413; statement by editors on front flap of dust-jacket.

B59 THE ART OF SEAMUS HEANEY 1982

THE ART OF | SEAMUS HEANEY | edited and introduced by | *Tony Curtis* | POETRY WALES PRESS | 1982
22 × 13.5 cm.; pp. 152.

Green paper-covered boards; front and back covers blank; spine lettered and decorated in gold; dust-jacket in white and green, lettered and decorated in black.

Published 1982; 1,000 copies printed by D. Brown & Sons Ltd, Bridgend, Mid Glamorgan.

Contents: 'The Manuscript Drafts of the poem "North" ', pp. [53]–[62].

B60 CONTEMPORARY IRISH ART 1982

CONTEMPORARY | IRISH ART | A DOCUMENTATION COMPILED AND EDITED BY | RODERIC KNOWLES | WOLFHOUND PRESS
29.5 × 21 cm.; pp. 232.

Tan cloth-covered boards; front and back covers blank; spine lettered and decorated in black; dust-jacket in black, blue and white with reproduction of painting by John Devlin in colour on front; black endpapers.

Published 1982 by Wolfhound Press; printed by Cahill Printers Ltd, East Wall, Dublin; issued simultaneously in a paperback edition. An American edition was published by St Martin's Press in 1983.

Contents: 'T.P. Flanagan: Ghosted Forms of Landscape', p. 74.

B61 JAMES JOYCE AND MODERN LITERATURE 1982

JAMES JOYCE AND | MODERN LITERATURE | Edited by W.J. McCormack and | Alistair Stead | [publisher's logo] | Routledge & Kegan Paul | London, Boston, Melbourne and Henley
21.5 × 13.5 cm.; pp. xiii, 223.

Dark-blue paper-covered boards; front and back covers blank; spine lettered in gold. Yellow dust-jacket lettered and decorated in blue.

Published 1982; printed by Billing & Sons Ltd, Guildford and London.

Contents: 'Leaving the Island', pp. 74–76.

Note: First printed in *The Irish Times*, 2 February 1982 under title, 'A Familiar Ghost' (C342); collected with revisions as Section XII of the 'Station Island' sequence in *Station Island*.

B62 PERSPECTIVES ON READING 1982

PERSPECTIVES ON READING | [rule] | A SYMPOSIUM ON THE THEORY | AND TEACHING OF READING | [rule] | EDITED BY DESMOND SWAN | [publisher's logo] | THE GLENDALE PRESS
20.5 × 14.5 cm.; pp. 190.

Slate-blue paper wrappers; front cover lettered in white with red rules over abstract triangular design; back cover lettered in white; spine lettered in white.

Published 1982; printed by Uniprint.

Contents: 'A Poet's View of Reading', pp. 152–157.

B63 TENFOLD 1983

Tenfold | *Poems for* | FRANCES | HOROVITZ
24.5 × 13.5 cm.; pp. [20].

Stiff grey wrappers; back cover blank, front cover lettered in maroon.

Published 30 October 1983 by Martin Booth on behalf of the Frances Horovitz Benefit to coincide with a reading given by the contributors at the Colston Hall, Bristol; 550 copies printed, of which 50 copies were stitched in blue wrappers and numbered and signed by the contributors; printed on St Cuthbert's Mill rag paper by Skelton's Press, Wellingborough, Northamptonshire.

Contents: 'Song of the soul that delights in knowing God by faith' (from the Spanish of St John of the Cross), pp. [9]–[10].

Note: Collected with revisions as 'Station Island' section XI in *Station Island*.

B64 THE AMERICAN IRISH REVIVAL 1984

THE AMERICAN IRISH REVIVAL | A Decade of the Recorder – 1974–1983 | Edited by | Kevin M. Cahill, M.D. | ASSOCIATED FACULTY PRESS, INC. | Port Washington, N. Y. [center dot] New York City [center dot] London
25.5 × 17.5 cm.; pp. xxii, 810.

Light-tan cloth-covered boards; front and back covers blank; spine lettered in gold; light-blue dust-jacket lettered and decorated in black and white.

Contents: 'A Cart For Edward Gallagher'; 'Ulster Quatrains'; 'Remembering Malibu', pp. 39–45; 'A Night Piece For Tom Flanagan', pp. 120–122.

B65 MANDEVILLE'S TRAVELLERS 1984

MANDEVILLE'S | TRAVELLERS | 1984 [all above on two panels within coloured illustrated title]
25.5 × 18 cm.; pp. [16]; unpaginated.

Sewn brown wrappers; front cover lettered in black with illustration in garnet; back cover blank.

Published 1984; 300 copies printed and published by the Mandeville Press, 2 Taylor's Hill, Hitchin, Herts, of which 50 copies were hand coloured, numbered and signed by the artist, Carola Scupham.

Contents: 'Stone from Delphi', p. [8].

Note: Collected with revisions in *Station Island*.

B66 DÁNTA IDIR GHAEILGE AGUS BHÉARLA 1984

DÁNTA | IDIR GHAEILGE | AGUS | BHÉARLA | WAKE FOREST UNIVERSITY PRESS | WINSTON-SALEM NORTH CAROLINA | 1984
23 × 15 cm.; pp. [20]; unpaginated.

Tan wrappers; front cover lettered in umber; back cover blank.

Published 1984; 275 copies privately printed by Richard Murdoch for distribution by Wake Forest University Press at the XXII Annual Meeting of the American Committee for Irish Studies.

Contents: 'Hailstones', pp. [10]–[11].

B67 THE LITTLE BROWN HOUSE 1984

THE LITTLE BROWN HOUSE [lettered lengthwise from bottom to top] | [all following within laurel wreath] | A | *Garland for* | *Robert* | *McGlynn*
23 × 15.5 cm.; pp. 22.

Brown wrap-around wrappers; back cover blank, verso gives table of contents; the two front wrappers overlap; the outer (left) wrapper has publisher's logo on bottom right, verso serves as colophon; inner (right) wrapper serves as title-page and is printed in black and olive, verso is blank.The text of the book is printed in black with titles and authors' names in olive.

600 copies were printed by the Gallery Press, Dublin; of which 100 were reserved for the Gallery Press and 500 were issued by the Deerfield Press.

Contents: 'A Winter Visit', pp. [4]–[5].

B68 BETWEEN COMETS 1984

Between Comets | *for Norman Nicholson at 70* | Edited by | WILLIAM SCAMMELL | TAXVS [short rule] | 1984
21.5 × 13.5 cm.; pp. 68.

Paper wrappers with coloured scenic illustration on front and back covers; spine lettered in brown.

Published September 1984; 700 copies printed by C.W.S. Printing Works, Gateshead, Tyne & Wear. 50 additional copies were case-bound in maroon linen-covered boards, gold stamped on front cover and on spine, hand numbered and signed by Norman Nicholson and William Scammell; one special presentation copy in boards enclosed in a solander box with maroon and grey hand-marbled lining paper was inscribed by editor and publisher for presentation to Norman Nicholson.

Contents: 'A Paved Text', pp. 22–23.

B69 LIVING WITH ART: DAVID HENDRIKS 1985

Edited by Séan McCrum and Gordon Lambert | Living With Art | David Hendriks | Wolfhound Press
21 × 15 cm.; pp. 80.

Stiff grey paper wrappers; portrait of David Hendriks by Robert Ballagh reproduced in colour on front cover; lettered in black and white.

Published 1985; 2,000 copies printed by O'Brien Promotions Limited, errata slip inserted.

Contents: 'Personal recollection', p. 48.

B70 MUST TRY HARDER 1985

'Must Try | Harder' | [all above within triple ruled border and one uneven border] | 'Tales out of School' from sixty well-known | personalities | Compiled by John Quinn | *All proceeds in aid of Open Door | Day Activity Centre, Bray*
21.5 × 15 cm.; pp. 72.

Stiff paper covers, lettered and decorated in blue, red and white.

Published 1985; printed by Mount Salus Press, Dublin.

Contents: 'Cloistered', pp. 30–31.

B71 LIFE LINES 1985

a. ***first edition, first issue***

[rule made of the following symbol: ***********] | LIFE-LINES | THE UNDERGROUND PRESS | WESLEY COLLEGE | DUBLIN | [rule made of the following symbol: ***********]

25 × 20 cm.; pp. 94.

Stapled light-blue covers; front cover, LIFE LINES in outline letters over solid black image of African continent within black border; back cover blank; last text page pink.

Published June 1985; (sold out in 7 days); printed at Wesley College by the Mavis Machine. Reprinted in August 1985.

Contents: Note on 'Cuchulain Comforted', p. [84].

b. *second issue*

[rule made of the following symbols: +=+=+=] | LIFE-LINES | THE UNDERGROUND PRESS | Wesley College | Dublin | [rule made of the following symbols: +=+=+=]
23 × 20 cm.; pp. 94.

Stapled light-green covers; front cover, LIFE LINES in outline letters over solid black image of African continent within black border; back cover blank.

Published August 1985; printed at Wesley College by the Mavis Machine.

Contents: Same as B71a.

c. *trade edition*

LIFELINES | LETTERS FROM FAMOUS PEOPLE ABOUT THEIR FAVOURITE POEM | Compiled by | [list of compilers] | Edited by Niall MacMonagle | FOREWORD by Seamus Heaney | publisher's logo | Town House, Dublin
24 × 16.5 cm.; pp. xiii, 338.

Brown cloth-covered boards; front and back covers blank; spine lettered in gold; cream dust-jacket lettered in red, blue and black with cover illustration of 'The Penitent Magdelan' by Georges de la Tour.

Published 1992; printed by Colour Books.

Contents: 'Foreword', XI–XII; Note on 'Cuchulain Comforted', pp. 71–72.

Note: Seamus Heaney's 'Foreword' only appears in 1992 edition.

B72 IRELAND'S FIELD DAY 1985

Ireland's | Field Day | *Field Day* | *Theatre Company* | HUTCHINSON | *London Melbourne Sydney Auckland Johannesburg*
23.5 × 15.5 cm.; pp. 128.

Black cloth-covered boards; front and back covers blank; spine lettered in silver; green glossy dust-jacket lettered in silver, black and white.

Published 1985; printed by Anchor Brendon Ltd, Tiptree, Essex. An American edition was issued in 1986 by University of Notre Dame Press, Notre Dame, Indiana.

Contents: 'An Open Letter', pp. 19–29; 'Notes', p. 30.

B73 IMAGES 1985

[front cover serves as title-page] [all of the following printed vertically bottom to top on the right side] IMAGES | ARTS AND THE PEOPLE IN NORTHERN IRELAND
31.5 × 26.5 cm.; [20] pp.; unpaginated.

Stapled black glossy wrappers; front cover lettered in black with yellow, red and blue crayon design and black and white photograph; design continued on back and lettered in white; back flap lettered in white with black and white photograph of Seamus Heaney and daughter in Dublin kitchen and the portrait of Seamus Heaney by Edward McGuire.

Published by the Northern Ireland Information Services/Arts Council of Northern Ireland, 1985; printed by W. & G. Baird Ltd.

Contents: 'Probity, originality, and discretion', [back flap].

B74 DIMENSIONS OF READING 1986

Dimensions of Reading | Vincent Greaney and Brendan Molloy | *Editors* | *THE EDUCATIONAL COMPANY*
22.5 × 15.5 cm.; pp. vi, 186.

Stiff paper wrappers, lettered and decorated in purple, green and white.

Published 1986; printed by Iona Print, Dublin.

Contents: 'Words Alone', pp. 1–13.

Note: First printed in *An Múinteoir Naisiunta*, Autumn 1982 (C353); collected here with revisions.

B75 WILLIAM GOLDING 1986

William Golding | The Man and his Books | [double rule, top rule heavy] | *A Tribute on his 75th Birthday* | Edited by John Carey | [publisher's logo] | *faber and faber* | LONDON · BOSTON
21.5 × 13.5 cm.; pp. 192.

Black paper-covered boards; front and back covers blank, spine lettered and decorated in gold; black dust-jacket printed in white, black and beige with photograph of Golding by Phil Sayer on front.

Published September 1986; printed by Butler and Tanner Ltd, Frome and London.

Contents: 'Parable Island', pp. 169–170.

B76 SORLEY MACLEAN 1986

SORLEY MACLEAN | *CRITICAL ESSAYS* | *Edited by* | RAYMOND J. ROSS | JOY HENDRY | SCOTTISH ACADEMIC PRESS | EDINBURGH
24.5 × 15 cm.; pp. 240.

Dark-green paper-covered boards; front and back covers blank, spine lettered and decorated in gold; dust-jacket has portraits of Maclean reproduced on front (drawing by John R. McWilliam) and back (photograph).

Published 1986; 1,500 copies. Printed by Latimer Trend & Company Ltd, Plymouth.

Contents: 'Introduction', pp. [1]–7.

Note: Reprinted under title 'Seamus Heaney Praises the Scottish Poet Sorley MacLean' in *London Review of Books*, 6 November 1986 (C447); reprinted, with revisions under title 'The Voice of a Bard' in *Antaeus*, spring 1988.

B77 THE POETRY BOOK SOCIETY ANTHOLOGY 1986/87 1986

The | Poetry Book Society | Anthology 1986/87 | *Edited with an Introduction by* | *JONATHAN BARKER* | Hutchinson | London Melbourne Auckland Johannesburg
19.5 × 12.5 cm.; pp. 94.

Stiff light-purple paper wrappers; lettered in white, blue and red.

Published 1986; printed by Anchor Brendon Ltd, Essex.

Contents: '*from* Clearances (i, ii, iii and vi)', pp. 49–50.

Note: This is the same selection as *The Honest Ulsterman*, spring 1986 (C435).

B78 A PORTRAIT OF THE ARTIST AS A YOUNG GIRL 1986

A PORTRAIT OF | THE ARTIST AS | A YOUNG GIRL | [short rule]
21.5 × 13.5 cm.; pp. xiv; 146.

Grey paper-covered boards; front and back covers blank, spine lettered and decorated in gold; dust-jacket has Pauline Bewick's painting 'Holly, Daffodils and Doves' reproduced in colour on front and 'edited by John Quinn with a foreword by Seamus Heaney' as well as a list of contributors printed in black.

Published 1986 by Methuen London Ltd; in association with RTE; printed by Richard Clay Ltd, Bungay, Suffolk; a paperback edition was issued 1987.

Contents: 'Foreword', pp. [xi]–xii.

B79 POETS FOR AFRICA 1986

Poets for Africa | Edited by Lynda Moran | [all following within ruled border] | Proceeds to Band Aid
21.5 × 15.5 cm.; pp. 160.

Stiff white paper wrappers; front and back covers lettered and decorated in black.

Published 1986; printed by the Leinster Leader Ltd.

Contents: 'The Haw Lantern'; 'A Daylight Art', pp. 83–84.

B80 HONEY TO THE EAR 1987

[all of the following printed in brown] *Honey to the Ear* | *A Collection of Poems by* | *Mick McAtamney &* | *Liam McAllister* | Researched and Edited by | William O'Kane & Anne Kerr | Foreword by | Seamus Heaney | *Published by* | SOUTH DERRY BRANCH, IRISH WORLD CITIZEN ORGANIZATION | 54A Main Street, Maghera. Phone: 43187 | [ornament] | Printed by MACPRINT
21 × 14 cm.; pp. iv, 68.

Stiff green wrappers; front cover lettered and decorated in black; back cover with price in black; spine blank; text printed in brown on light yellow paper.

Published 1987; 1,000 copies; printed by MacPrint.

Contents: 'Foreword', p. iv.

B81 FIRST LINES 1987

First [in bold script lettering] | Lines [in bold script lettering] | *poems* | *written in youth,* | *from Herbert to* | *Heaney* | edited and introduced by | Jon Stallworthy | CARCANET [in hand lettered type]
21.5 × 14 cm.; pp. 122.

Black paper-covered boards; front and back covers blank; spine lettered in gold; beige dust-jacket lettered in brown, red, and white; back cover in red.

Published 1987; printed by SRP Ltd, Exeter.

Contents: 'October Thought', p. 115.

B82 DANTE READINGS 1987

Dante Readings | EDITED BY | Eric Haywood | *Published for* | *The Foundation for Italian Studies* | *University College Dublin* | IRISH ACADEMIC PRESS DUBLIN
21.5 × 13.5 cm.; pp. 152.

Dark-green cloth-covered boards; front and back covers blank; lettered in gold on spine; issued without a dust-jacket.

Published 1987; Antony Rowe Ltd, Wiltshire.

Contents: 'Envies and Identifications: Dante and the Modern Poet', pp. [29]–46.

B83 THE BIGGEST EGG IN THE WORLD 1987

MARIN | SORESCU | The Biggest | EGG | in the World | [publisher's logo] | Bloodaxe Books
21.5 × 14 cm.; pp. 80.

Stiff paper covers lettered in white, yellow, red and blue, with colour photographs by Michael Davis and Apollo 17.

Published 1987; printed by Tyneside Free Press Workshop Ltd, Newcastle upon Tyne.

Contents: 'Angle', p. 64; 'The tear', p. 65; 'Old people in the shade', p. 69; 'The first words', p. 71; 'Proper names', p. 72; 'Fountains in the sea', p. 76.

Note: The poems by Marin Sorescu were translated by Seamus Heaney with Joana Russell-Gebbett.

B84 CAUSLEY AT 70 1987

Causley At 70 | edited by Harry Chambers | [publisher's logo] | PETERLOO POETS
21.5 × 14 cm.; pp. 120.

Stiff paper wrappers; lettered and decorated in blue, yellow and grey; cover drawing of Causley by Robert Tilling, RI; spine lettered in blue; back cover lettered in blue with black.

Published October 1987; printed by Latimer Trend & Company Ltd, Plymouth.

Contents: 'The Scop', p. 70.

Note: Seamus Heaney's translation of *Beowulf*, lines 89–98.

B85 ISLAND OF THE CHILDREN 1987

ISLAND | OF | THE | CHILDREN | [ornament] | *An Anthology of New Poems* | [ornament] | COMPILED BY | ANGELA HUTH | DECORATIONS BY | JANE RAY | [publisher's logo] | ORCHARD BOOKS | London
25.5 × 18.5 cm.; pp. 128.

Blue cloth-covered boards; front and back cover blank; spine lettered and decorated in gold; maroon endpapers; dust-jacket illustration in colour by Jane Ray.

Published 1987; printed by A. Wheaton & Co. Ltd, Exeter.

Contents: 'Catherine's Poem', p. 51.

B86 FOUR POETS FOR ST MAGNUS 1987

FOUR POETS | FOR ST MAGNUS | [the following four lines printed in umber] George Mackay Brown | Ted Hughes | Seamus Heaney | Christopher Fry | MCMLXXXVII
31.5 × 23.5 cm.; pp. [48]; unpaginated.

Brown paper-covered boards with parchment spine; front cover has illustration printed in black; spine printed in gold; off-brown endpapers.

Published on St Rognvald's Day, 20 August 1987; 100 copies printed of which 85 copies, numbered 1–85, were for sale; numbers 1–5 were individually bound. All copies were signed by the contributors. 15 copies, lettered A–O were not for sale. Designed by Ron Costley, printed by the September Press, Wellingborough, Northants and Smith Settle, Otley, West Yorkshire. Issued in a cloth-covered slipcase.

Contents: 'In Memoriam', pp. [35], [37].

Note: This poem in Seamus Heaney's autograph is reproduced and mounted on p. [35], the text is printed on p. [37]. This is not the same poem as 'In Memoriam' (AA17).

B87 THE ESSENTIAL WORDSWORTH 1988

a. *first edition*

[rule] | [ornament] The Essential [ornament] | WORDSWORTH | Selected and with an | Introduction by | SEAMUS HEANEY | The Ecco Press | [ornament] New York [ornament] | [rule]
16.5 × 11.5 cm.; pp. 188.

Stiff paper wrappers, lettered and decorated in teal blue, purple, white and black; portrait of Wordsworth on front cover; cover design by Reg Perry; no printer specified.

Published 1988; no printer specified; a cloth edition was published in 1993 by Galahad Books.

Contents: 'Introduction', pp. 3–13.

b. *first British edition*

WILLIAM WORDSWORTH | Poems selected by | SEAMUS HEANEY | ff | *faber and faber*
18 × 10.5 cm.; pp. xii, 148.

Cream paper wrappers; front cover lettered in black with green rule; back cover bar code and price in black; green spine lettered in white; green flaps lettered in white.

This edition published by faber and faber, 2001; printed in Italy.

Contents: 'Introduction', vii–xii.

Note: Text and 'Introduction' first published in a different version by the Ecco Press in 1988.

B88 PHILIP LARKIN 1922–1985: A TRIBUTE 1988

Philip Larkin | 1922–1985 | *A Tribute* | *edited by* | George Hartley | [publisher's logo] | THE MARVELL PRESS
21.5 × 13.5 cm.; pp. xii, 312.

Maroon paper-covered boards; front and back covers blank; spine lettered and decorated in gold.

Published 1988; printed by Woolnough Bookbinding, Irthlingborough, Northants; a paperback edition was issued simultaneously in dark pink covers printed in black.

Contents: 'MCMLXXXV, December 2nd', p. 39.

Note: Collected as 'The Journey Back' in *Seeing Things*.

B89 ON MODERN POETRY 1988

On | *Modern* | *Poetry* | [ornament] | Essays | Presented to | Donald Davie | *Edited by* |Vereen Bell |*and* |Laurence Lerner | VANDERBILT UNIVERSITY PRESS | *Nashville, 1988*
23 × 15 cm.; pp. x, 250.

Black cloth-covered boards; front and back covers blank; spine lettered in gold; illustrated endpapers; issued without dust-jacket.

Published 1988; 1,000 copies; no printer specified.

Contents: 'Or, Solitude: A Reading', pp. 81–87.

B90 LITERATURE AND THE ART OF CREATION 1988

LITERATURE AND THE ART | OF CREATION | Essays and Poems in honour of | A. NORMAN JEFFARES | edited by | Robert Welch | Suheil Badi Bushrui | 1988 | COLIN SMYTHE | Gerrards Cross Bucks | BARNES & NOBLE BOOKS | Totowa, New Jersey
21.5 × 13.5 cm.; pp. ix, 327.

Dark-blue paper-covered boards; front and back covers blank; spine lettered in gold.

Published 1988; Gloucester; printing and binding by Billing & Sons Ltd, Worcester.

Contents: 'The Dark Wood', pp. 247–251.

Note: Seamus Heaney's translation of Dante, *Inferno*, Canto I.

B91 IN THE PRISON OF HIS DAYS 1988

IN THE PRISON | OF HIS DAYS | THE LILLIPUT PRESS | 1988
21.5 × 13.5 cm.; pp. viii, 96.

a. *trade edition*

Stiff paper wrappers, lettered and decorated in black, brown and white African weaving design; back cover lettered in black; spine in white.

Published 1988; printed by Billing & Sons Ltd, Worcester.

Contents: 'New Worlds', p. 62.

b. *limited edition*

IN THE PRISON OF HIS DAYS | A MISCELLANY FOR NELSON MANDELA | Edited by W. J. McCormack | CATHAIR BOOKS | 1990
21.5 × 13.5 cm.; pp. viii, 96.

Black, green and yellow cloth-covered boards; lettered in yellow on front cover. A special edition of 112 copies was issued to celebrate Nelson Mandela's visit to Ireland, 1 July 1990: twelve presentation copies lettered A–L, and 100 numbered copies for sale.

Contents: Same as B91a.

B92 FIRST AND ALWAYS 1988

FIRST AND | ALWAYS | [rule] | *Poems for The* |*Great Ormond Street* |*Children's Hospital* | illustration (drawing of crying child's

face)| Compiled and edited by | Lawrence Sail | Introduction by Ted Hughes | [all of the above in a double line box] | publisher's logo | *faber and faber* | LONDON · BOSTON
19.5 × 12.5 cm.; pp. ix, 71.

Black paper cover with publisher's logo in yellow, blue, green, and red; title-page box reproduced in panel on front cover.

Published 1988; printed by Richard Clay Ltd.

Contents: 'The Butter-Print', p. 30.

Note: Collected with revisions in *The Spirit Level.*

B93 KEIMELIA 1988

KEIMELIA | STUDIES IN MEDIEVAL ARCHAEOLOGY | AND HISTORY IN MEMORY OF | TOM DELANEY | *Edited by* | Gearoid Mac Niocaill | *and* | Patrick F. Wallace | GALWAY UNIVERSITY PRESS | OFFICINA TYPOGRAPHICA
25 × 17.5 cm.; pp. xvi, 628.

Maroon cloth-covered boards; front cover and spine lettered and decorated in gold; back cover blank; grey endpapers; oat-meal dust-jacket lettered in red on front cover and spine; back cover blank.

Published 1988; Clódóirí Lurgan, Indreabhán.

Contents: 'Scrabble', p. [VII].

Note: Collected with revisions in *Seeing Things.*

B94 THE LITERATURE OF REGION AND NATION 1988

The Literature of | Region and Nation | [rule] | *Edited by* | R. P. DRAPER | *Regius Chalmers Professor of English* | *University of Aberdeen* | M | MACMILLAN | PRESS
21.5 × 13.5 cm.; pp. 276.

Black paper-covered boards; back and front cover blank; spine lettered and decorated in gold.

Published 1988; title-page verso states: 'First published 1989'; dark-blue dust-jacket, front cover lettered in white and light blue with illustration; spine lettered in white and light blue; back cover blank. Reissued in the United States in 1989 with St. Martin's Press (New York) imprint substituted.

Contents: 'The Regional Forecast', pp. 10–23.

Note: This essay is based on papers originally presented at the International Conference on the Literature of Region and Nation, University of Aberdeen, 19–23 August 1986.

B95 HILL FIELD 1989

a. *trade edition*

Hill Field [in blue] | POEMS AND MEMOIRS FOR JOHN MONTAGUE | ON HIS SIXTIETH BIRTHDAY, 28 FEBRUARY 1989 | COMPILED AND EDITED BY THOMAS DILLON REDSHAW | Coffee House Press, Minneapolis: Gallery Books, Oldcastle
22.5 × 15.5 cm.; pp. 122.

Glossy stiff blue wrappers; lettered in white with S. W. Hayter's 'Hill Field' reproduced on front cover.

Published 1989; 1,700 copies printed by Coffee House Press.

Contents: 'Fosterling', p. 16.

Note: 'Fosterling' collected with revisions in *Seeing Things*. *Seeing Things* version same as *The Tree Clock* version.

b. *limited edition*

22.5 × 15 cm.

Blue cloth-covered boards; spine lettered in gold. Glossy blue dust-jacket, lettered in white with S. W. Hayter's 'Hill Field' reproduced on front wrapper. 150 copies printed

Contents: Same as B95a.

c. *presentation edition*

22.5 × 15 cm.

Marbled paper-covered boards with linen spine bound by Dennis Ruud, St Paul. 26 lettered copies.

Contents: Same as B95a.

B96 THE ART OF TRANSLATION 1989

THE ART OF | TRANSLATION | [ornament] voices from the field | EDITED BY ROSANNA WARREN | *Northeastern University Press* | BOSTON

23 × 15 cm.; pp. 300.

Mauve cloth-covered boards; lettered in silver with design stamped in white on front cover; back cover blank; spine blank; mauve endpapers; dust-jacket in garnet lettered and decorated in light blue, garnet and mauve.

Published 1989; printed by the Hamilton Printing Company, Rensslaer, New York.

Contents: 'Earning a Rhyme: Notes on Translating *Buile Suibhne*', pp. 13–20.

Note: This is a revised version of a lecture given at Boston University at one of the weekly meetings of the Translation Seminar; first printed in *Poetry Ireland Review*, Spring 1989 (C513) under title: 'Earning a Rhyme'; reprinted here with the addition of an introductory paragraph.

B97 THE POETRY BOOK SOCIETY ANTHOLOGY 1989–1990 1989

The | Poetry Book Society | Anthology 1989–1990 | *Edited with an introduction by* | *CHRISTOPHER REID* | Hutchinson | London Sydney Auckland Johannesburg

20 × 12.5 cm.; pp. 110.

Stiff maroon paper wrappers; front cover illustration: *Boxing Hares* by Sophie Ryder; lettered and decorated in yellow and white; back cover blank.

Published 1989; printed by Courier International, Tiptree, Essex.

Contents: from *Lightenings*, pp. 47–51.

Note: Collected in *Seeing Things* as 'Squarings' numbers: ix; x (with revisions); xii (with revisions); xxii (with revisions); xxiv (with revisions).

B98 32 COUNTIES 1989

a. *trade edition*

32 COUNTIES [all within grey ruled border] | Photographs of Ireland by Donovan Wylie | with new writing by thirty-two Irish writers | *Secker & Warburg*
28 × 23.5 cm.; pp. 256.

Black paper-covered boards; front and back covers blank; cream lettering on spine; light-grey endpapers; glossy cream dust-jacket with black and white photographs on front and back; the back contains a list of contributors printed in black and white.

Published 1989. Printed and bound by Butler and Tanner Ltd, Frome, Somerset.

Contents: 'Five Derry Glosses', pp. 69–71.

Note: Only one of these 'Squarings,' 'Memory as a building or city,' was collected in *Seeing Things* as 'xix.'

b. *limited edition*

Bindings as in B98a. Issued in black cloth-covered slipcase and contains an extra print signed by the photographer; numbered 1–100 and signed by all 32 authors. Also issued, 50 copies signed by the contributors, numbered with Roman numerals, presented to authors, photographer and publishers.

Contents: Same as B98a.

B99 THE ORANGE DOVE OF FIJI 1989

THE ORANGE | DOVE OF FIJI | *Poems for the World Wide Fund for Nature* | *Edited by* | *Simon Rae* | *Preface by* | *H.R.H. The Duke of Edinburgh* | Hutchinson | London Sydney Auckland Johannesburg
21.5 × 13.5 cm.; pp. xiii, 131.

Stiff black paper wrappers; lettered in white and yellow with reproduction of painting by David Hockney on front cover; back cover and spine lettered in white and yellow.

Published 1989; printed by Courier International Ltd, Tiptree, Essex.

Contents: 'The Road at Frosses', p. 53.

Note: Collected as 'Squarings' 'xxxi' in *Seeing Things*.

B100 PADRAIC FALLON COLLECTED POEMS 1990

PADRAIC FALLON | Collected Poems | introduction by Seamus Heaney | edited, with an afterword and notes | by Brian Fallon | CARCANET [outline letters] | GALLERY
21.5 × 13.5 cm.; pp. 284.

Black cloth-covered boards; front and back covers blank; spine lettered in gold; dust-jacket in orange, black and white.

Published 1990; printed by SRP Ltd, Exeter; issued simultaneously in a paperback edition.

Contents: 'Introduction', pp. 11–17.

Notes: Printed also under title, 'Padraic Fallon: a Modern with an Irish voice' in *The Irish Times*, June 26, 1990 (C547); reprinted in *Erect me a Monument of Broken Wings: An Anthology of writings by and on Padraic Fallon* (1992).

B101 THE BIRMINGHAM SIX: AN APPALLING VISTA 1990

a. ***trade edition***

THE BIRMINGHAM SIX: | AN APPALLING VISTA | [design of scales] | *Editor:* | OSCAR GILLIGAN | *Sub Editors*: | JÜRGEN SCHNEIDER | RALF SOTSCHECK | LITERÉIRE PUBLISHERS DUBLIN | DECEMBER 1990
21.5 × 13.5 cm.; pp. 240.

Glossy grey paper wrappers; front cover lettered in white with colour illustration; back cover lettered in black and white; spine lettered in black.

Published 1990; printed by Elo Press Ltd, Dublin.

Contents: 'Excerpt from *The Cure at Troy. A Version of Sophocles' Philoctetes*', pp. 66–69.

Note: An international anthology of support for the Birmingham Six by 55 writers and artists.

b. ***limited edition***

20.5 × 13 cm.

Cloth-covered boards, spine lettered in gold; grey dust-jacket lettered in white and black with reproduction of Louis le Brocquy's painting 'Condemned Man' on front; limited to 100 specially bound numbered copies, signed by Seamus Heaney, Thomas Kinsella, Patrick Galvin, Francis Stuart, Seamus Deane, Paul Durcan, and Louis le Brocquy. There were also 27 unsigned and unnumbered copies for presentation.

Contents: Same as B101a.

B102 HIGH ON THE WALLS 1990

HIGH ON | THE WALLS | AN ANTHOLOGY CELEBRATING | TWENTY-FIVE YEARS OF | POETRY READINGS AT | MORDEN

TOWER | * | edited by | Gordon Brown | MORDEN TOWER | in association with | BLOODAXE BOOKS
21.5 × 14 cm.; pp.144.

Stiff glossy paper wrappers; front and back covers with abstract design; lettered in white, black and orange.

Published 1990; printed by Billing & Sons Ltd, Worcester.

Contents: Note on Morden Tower by Seamus Heaney, p. 65; 'Three Rich Hours', pp. 66–67.

Note: 'Three Rich Hours' collected in *Seeing Things* as 'Squarings' 'xiv' (with revisions), 'xv', 'xvi' (with revisions).

B103 THE MAYO ANTHOLOGY 1990

THE MAYO | ANTHOLOGY | [short rule] | EDITED BY | RICHARD MURPHY | [short rule] | MAYO COUNTY COUNCIL
22 × 15.5 cm.; pp. 194.

Stiff glossy white paper wrappers; front cover lettered in black with colour image; back cover blank; spine lettered in black.

Published 1990; printed by *The Western People*, Ballina, County Mayo.

Contents: 'Belderg' on pp. 128–129; note on 'Belderg', p. 129.

B104 MIGRATIONS 1990

Migrations | The IRISH | at Home & Abroad | *Edited by* | Richard Kearney | WOLFHOUND PRESS
21.5 × 13.5 cm.; pp. 128.

Black paper-covered boards; front and back covers blank; spine lettered and decorated in gold; dust-jacket lettered in black, white and blue, with illustration from the series 'People Looking at Paintings' by Robert Ballagh.

Published 1990; printed by Colour Books Ltd.

Contents: 'Correspondences: Emigrants and Inner Exiles', pp. 21–31.

B105 THISTLEDOWN 1990

THISTLEDOWN | *Poems for* UNICEF | Edited by John F Deane | [publisher's logo] DEDALUS
29.5 × 21 cm.; pp. 64.

Stiff paper wrappers; front cover painting by Robert Ballagh; back cover and spine in pale blue; lettered and decorated in black, white, yellow and red.

Published 6 November 1990; no printer specified.

Contents: 'The Wishing Chair', p. 21.

Note: Collected with revisions as 'Squarings' xxxix in *Seeing Things*.

B106 PHARAOH'S DAUGHTER 1990

Nuala Ní Dhomhnaill | PHARAOH'S | DAUGHTER | [publisher's logo] | Gallery Books
21 × 13.5 cm.; pp. 160.

Black paper-covered boards; front and back covers blank; spine lettered in gold; gold dust-jacket lettered and decorated in black and white with cover monoprint 'Looking at a Man' by Constance Short.

Published 22 November 1990; published simultaneously in a paperback edition. A revised edition was published by Wake Forest University Press, Winston–Salem, North Carolina in March 1993.

Contents: 'Miraculous Grass', pp. 33, 35; 'Mo Mhíle Stór', p. 49.

Note: Seamus Heaney's translation from the original Irish of Nuala Ní Dhomhnaill, the Irish text is included.

B107 ROBERT GREACEN A TRIBUTE AT THE AGE OF SEVENTY 1991

Robert Greacen | A Tribute at the Age of Seventy | [decoration] | Poetry Ireland

20.5 × 14.5 cm.; pp. 34.

Stapled green paper wrappers; front and back covers printed and designed in black with a photograph of a bust of Greacen on back cover.

Published in February 1991 in a special edition of 50 copies numbered and signed by Robert Greacen; no printer specified.

Contents: 'The Settle Bed', p. 8.

B108 A TRIBUTE TO KEVIN SULLIVAN 1991

A Tribute to | Kevin Sullivan | by Thomas Flanagan, Seamus Heaney, Benedict Kiely, | Sean White and June K. Davison | edited by June K. Davison
21.5 × 14 cm.; pp. 18.

Stapled stone-grey laid paper wrappers; the front cover is lettered and decorated in black and is folded over to form an inner sleeve.

Published 26 February 1991; no publishing information; no printer specified.

Contents: 'Introduction to memorial reading for Kevin Sullivan, Queens College, New York, 2 May 1988', pp. 3–5.

Note: There was a limited edition of 25 numbered copies, signed by all five contributors.

B109 HOCKNEY'S ALPHABET 1991

a. *first trade edition*

HOCKNEY'S ALPHABET | DRAWINGS BY DAVID HOCKNEY | & | Written contributions edited by | Stephen Spender | *faber and faber* | *for the* | *Aids Crisis Trust*
32.5 × 24.5 cm.; pp. [120]; unpaginated.

Dark-blue buckram covers; front and back covers blank; spine lettered in gold; white dust-jacket, the front is decorated and lettered in black, blue, orange, red and green, the back contains a yellow panel with the names of the contributors and the letters they were allocated printed in black.

Published in 1991; printed by Westerham Press, Westerham, Kent.

Contents: 'G as in Gaelic', p. [37].

Note: The book consists of 27 full-page letters drawn by David Hockney appearing opposite texts by 27 contributors. The letter 'Q' is printed twice with contributions from T. S. Eliot and William Golding.

b. ***special edition***

Yellow buckram, front and back covers blank; dark-blue panel on spine lettered in gold; in grey cloth slipcase; each copy signed by the artist and the editor. Printed by Westerham Press, Westerham, Kent.

Contents: Same as B109a.

c. ***limited edition***

A signed de luxe edition of 300 numbered copies, of which 250 were for sale, was also issued at $2,000. This de luxe edition was bound by Smith Settle in quarter vellum with handmade Fabriano Roma paper sides, top edge gilt, blocked in gilt on spine. Issued in matching slipcase with paper label.

Contents: Same as B109a.

d. ***first American edition, withdrawn***

HOCKNEY'S | ALPHABET | [all of the preceding in multi-coloured outline letters] | DRAWINGS BY DAVID HOCKNEY | With | Written Contributions | edited by Stephen Spender | [publisher's logo in red] | Random House | in Association with the American Friends | of AIDS Crisis Trust
29 × 23 cm.; pp. xiii, 99.

Published 1991; no printer specified.

Contents: Same as B109a, 'G as in Gaelic', p. 21.

e. ***second American edition***

Same typesetting as above, except title-page imprint is '*Random House | in association with | the American Friends of | Aids Crisis Trust*'. Verso title has 'Manufactured in Great Britain | [printing code; 2–3] | Random House, Inc., 1992 Edition'.

32.5 × 24.5 cm.

Black boards, spine stamped in gold; cream endpapers. Dust-wrapper as in a, with changes appropriate to American issue; on back flap.

'Printed in Great Britain. 9/92'. On front cover, a circular sticker specifying the charitable destination of the proceeds.

Contents: Same as B109a

B110 THE POETRY BOOK SOCIETY ANTHOLOGY 2 1991

The Poetry Book Society | Anthology 2 | *Edited by* | Anne Stevenson | Hutchinson | London Sydney Auckland Johannesburg
20 × 12.5 cm.; pp. 96.

Blue and green paper wrappers; lettered in white over a continuous design of fish on front and back covers; spine lettered in white.

Published 1991; printed by Cox and Wyman Ltd, Reading.

Contents: 'An Architect', p. 67.

Note: Collected with revisions in *The Spirit Level.*

B111 THE FIELD DAY ANTHOLOGY OF IRISH WRITING 1991

THE FIELD DAY | ANTHOLOGY | OF IRISH WRITING | VOLUME II | [design] | General Editor: Seamus Deane | Associate Editors: Andrew Carpenter, Jonathan Williams | Derry | Field Day Publications | Distributed by Faber & Faber Limited
23.5 × 18 cm.; pp. xv; 1245.

Blue cloth-covered boards; front and back covers blank; spine lettered and designed in gold.

Published 1991; issued with two other volumes in a blue cloth-covered slipcase.

Contents: 'William Butler Yeats (1865–1939)': 'Introduction', pp. 783–790; 'Annotations', pp. 790–830.

B112 FOOD WITH THE FAMOUS 1991

food [all of the following to the right of a large script 'f'] with | the | amous | [end of title] | FOREWORD | [text of foreword] | Pamela Devlin | Easter 1991
30 × 22 cm.; 72 pp.

Stapled stiff paper wrappers; front cover lettered in red over black and white photographs of contributors; back cover with black and white photographs of contributors.

Published by Alison Publications for St Patrick's Girls' Secondary School, Dungannon, 1991; Ronan Press Ltd.

Contents: 'Poached Salmon', p. 37.

B113 EVERY STONEY ACRE HAS A NAME 1991

Every Stoney Acre Has a Name: | a celebration of the Townland in Ulster | Edited by Tony Canavan | Federation for Local Studies
29 × 21 cm.; pp. xii, 64.

Glossy paper wrappers; continuous embroidered map illustration on front and back covers; lettered in white on blue panels.

Published 1991; printed by Coleraine Printing Co.

Contents: 'Preface', pp. xi–xii.

B114 SOMHAIRLE, DÁIN IS DEILBH 1991

Somhairle | Dáin is Deilbh | A celebration on the 80th birthday | of Sorley MacLean | Edited by Angus Peter Campbell | acair | 1991
30 × 21 cm.; pp. 136.

Pale-green paper wrappers; front cover lettered and designed in black with a black and white photograph of Sorley MacLean; back cover contains a publisher's statement and a list of contributors.

Published 1991; no printer specified.

Contents: 'To Sorley MacLean', pp. 59–60.

B115 SOHO-FOUR 1991

[heavily designed title-page; all of the following in and around egg-shaped black-and-white pen design from top to bottom] Edited by Bill Manhire | SOHO SQUARE FOUR | BLOOMSBURY
21 × 17 cm.; pp. 288.

Glossy paper wrappers folded over to create inside flap; front cover heavily designed and lettered in red, black, yellow, and white; back cover contains list of contributors; spine lettered in black and red.

Published by Bloomsbury Publishing, 1991; printed by Butler & Tanner Ltd, Frome and London.

Contents: 'Mint'; 'The Articulation of Siberia', pp. 102–103.

Note: 'Mint' collected with revisions in *The Spirit Level*. 'The Articulation of Siberia' collected with revisions as 'M.' in *The Spirit Level*.

B116 CONFOUNDED LANGUAGE 1991

CONFOUNDED | LANGUAGE | IMAGES BY NOEL CONNOR | NEW POEMS BY NINE IRISH WRITERS | [publisher's logo] | BLOODAXE BOOKS
21.5 × 14 cm.; pp. 48.

Stiff salmon paper covers lettered and decorated in black, red and rust.

Published 1991; printed by Peterson Printers, South Shields, Tyne & Wear.

Contents: 'The Lost People', p. 13.

Note: Seamus Heaney's translation of Dante's *Inferno*, Canto III, lines 22–52. This translation of Canto III, ll. 22–52 differs from those in *Dante's Inferno* (B133).

B117 HANDS BEHIND MY BACK 1991

Marin Sorescu | HANDS BEHIND | MY BACK | SELECTED POEMS | Translated by Gabriels Dragnea, | Stuart Friebert, and | Adriana Varga | Introduction by Seamus Heaney | Oberlin College Press: | FIELD Translation Series 18
19 × 12.5 cm.; pp. 168.

White cloth-covered boards, lettered in black on spine; white dust-jacket lettered and decorated in black, with colour reproduction of painting by Sorescu on front.

Published 1991; issued simultaneously in a paperback edition; no printer listed.

Contents: 'Introduction', pp. 9–15.

B118 ART IS MY LIFE 1991

ART IS MY LIFE | *A Tribute to* JAMES WHITE | [publisher's logo] | THE NATIONAL GALLERY OF IRELAND
28 × 21.5 cm.; pp. xvi, 200.

White cloth-covered boards; front and back covers blank; spine lettered in gold; dust-jacket with painting of *The Conjuror* by Nathaniel Hone the Elder on the front cover and a black-and-white photograph of James White on the back, spine is lettered in black.

Published in 1991; printed by Nicholas & Bass.

Contents: 'The Biretta', p. 83.

Note: Collected with revisions in *Seeing Things*. The poem was commissioned by the book's editor, Brian P. Kennedy, and is Seamus Heaney's response to the painting *The Sick Call* by Matthew James Lawless.

B119 EDWARD MCGUIRE 1991

Edward McGuire, RHA | Brian Fallon | [ornament] | WITH A CATALOGUE BY SALLY MCGUIRE | AND POEMS AND MEMOIRS BY |

Anthony Cronin, Paul Durcan, Michael Hartnett, | Seamus Heaney, Pearse Hutchinson, Michael Longley, | John Montague and Francis Stuart | FOREWORD BY JAMES WHITE | [publisher's logo] | IRISH ACADEMIC PRESS
24.5 × 18.5 cm.; pp.144.

Dark-blue cloth-covered boards; front and back covers blank; spine lettered and decorated in silver; dust-jacket with self-portrait of Edward McGuire on front and lettered in blue, brown and black.

Published 1991; printed by Abacus (Colour Printers) Ltd, Lowick, and Billing and Sons Ltd, Worcester.

Contents: 'A Basket of Chestnuts', p. 94; portrait of Seamus Heaney by Edward McGuire on p. 95.

B120 A GARLAND FOR STEPHEN 1991

a | garland | for | Stephen | [all above within floral wreath border lettered and decorated in green] | *Arranged by Barry Humphries* | The Tragara Press | EDINBURGH | 1991
25 × 16.5 cm.; pp. 56.

Green wrappers; front cover lettered in black with David Hockney's drawing of Stephen Spender; back cover blank.

Published 1991; 150 numbered copies printed of which 75 were for sale; no printer specified.

Contents: 'Two Settings', p. 24.

Note: Both 'Settings' collected with revisions as 'Squarings' xix and xx in *Seeing Things*.

B121 THE ODYSSEY 1992

HOMER | *The Odyssey* [within decorated border] | Translated by Robert Fitzgerald | Illustrated by Barnaby Fitzgerald | [publisher's logo] | EVERYMAN'S LIBRARY | 94
20.5 × 12.5 cm.; pp. xxii, 522.

Cinnamon-brown cloth-covered boards; front and back covers blank; spine has black panel lettered and decorated in gold; white dust-jacket lettered and designed in grey, black and red.

Published 1992; printed and bound in Germany.

Contents: 'Introduction', pp. v–xx.

B122 THE POETRY BOOK SOCIETY ANTHOLOGY 3 1992

The Poetry Book Society | Anthology 3 | *Edited by* | William Scammell | Hutchinson | London
20 × 12.5 cm.; pp. 96.

Purple paper wrappers; lettered in white over a continuous design of flying insects on the front and back covers; spine lettered in white.

Published 1992; printed by Cox and Wyman Ltd, Reading.

Contents: 'The Gravel Walks', pp. 27–28.

Note: Same as 'The Gravel Walks' (A52). Collected with revisions in *The Spirit Level*.

B123 CONTEMPORARY IRISH POETRY 1992

Contemporary Irish | Poetry | [rule] | A Collection of Critical Essays | *Edited by* | ELMER ANDREWS | *Lecturer in English* | *University of Ulster at Coleraine* | M
21.5 × 14 cm.; pp. x, 334.

Blue cloth-covered boards; front and back blank; spine lettered in gold; glossy white dust-jacket; front cover lettered in white; back cover lettered in blue.

Published by Macmillan in 1992; printed by Anthony Rowe Ltd, Wiltshire.

Contents: 'Place and Displacement: Reflections on Some Recent Poetry from Northern Ireland', pp. 124–144.

Note: Seamus Heaney's Pete Laver Memorial Lecture at Grasmere, 1984.

B124 THE MODERN MOVEMENT 1992

a. *first edition*

A TLS COMPANION | [swelled rule] |THE MODERN | MOVEMENT | *Edited and with an Introduction by* | John Gross | [publisher's logo] | HARVILL | An *Imprint of* HarperCollins *Publishers*
25.5 × 13.5 cm.; pp. xxiv, 312.

Stiff white paper wrappers; lettered in black and decorated with a reproduction of a painting by Charles Demuth on front cover; back cover lettered in black and white; spine lettered in black, blue and red.

Published in London in 1992, printed by Hartnoll, Ltd, Bodmin, Cornwall.

Contents: 'Small Fantasia for W. B.', p. 304.

Note: This is a reprint of 'Small Fantasia For W. B.' which originally appeared in *The Times Literary Supplement*, 27 January 1989 (C508). The poem was collected with revisions in *Seeing Things* as 'Squarings' xxii.

b. *first American edition*

THE MODERN | MOVEMENT | [swelled rule] | A TLS COMPANION | *Edited and with an Introduction by* | John Gross | [publisher's logo] | The University of Chicago Press
21.5 × 13.5 cm.; pp. xxiv, 312.

Stiff white paper wrappers; lettered in black, yellow, blue and orange with a reproduction of a painting by Mark Gertler on the front; back cover lettered in black, white and orange.

Published 1993; no printer specified.

Contents: Same as B124a.

B125 FROM ERUDITION TO INSPIRATION 1992

From Erudition to Inspiration | *A Booklet for Michael* | [rule] | BELFAST BYZANTINE TEXTS AND TRANSLATIONS | [rule] 1992
21 × 15 cm.; xxv, 87 pp.

Stiff paper wrappers decorated with classical design in brown and ivory, and lettered in white.

Published in 1992 in Belfast Byzantine Enterprises, Department of Greek and Latin, Queen's University Belfast; Priory Press, Holywood.

Contents: 'Triptych', pp. 1–2.

Note: Sections I and III comprise the poem 'Saint Kevin and the Blackbird' collected in *The Spirit Level*. Section II begins: 'Compared with Atlas posted faithfully.' The book is a collection of essays by former students in honour of Professor Michael McGann on the occasion of his retirement from the Queen's University of Belfast, September 1992.

B126 THE MAGIC OF LINEN 1992

The Magic of | LINEN| Flax Seed to Woven Cloth | *Linda Heinrich* | Orca Book Publishers
28 × 21.5 cm.; pp. xiii, 219.

Glossy paper wrappers; front cover with a photograph of flax and linen towels against a blue background, lettered in white except 'LINEN' in tan; back cover with photograph of author and lettered in linen and white; spine lettered in black.

Published in 1992; printed in Hong Kong.

Content: 'Memories of Flax', p. 158.

Note: This is a short letter from Seamus Heaney to the author.

B127 FORWARD INTO THE PAST 1992

a. *trade edition*

FORWARD INTO THE PAST [all in burnt umber] | *For May Sarton* | *On Her Eightieth Birthday* | *May 3, 1992* | [ornament printed in burnt umber] | PRINTED BY SPECIAL ARRANGEMENT WITH | WILLIAM B. EWERT, PUBLISHER | CONCORD, NEW HAMPSHIRE
24 × 15.5 cm.; pp. [90]; unpaginated.

Dark wine wrappers; lettered and decorated in gold on front cover and spine; back cover blank.

Published [20 June], 1992; 150 copies, printed at Firefly Press, Somerville, MA.

Contents: 'A Wave from the Distance', p. [28].

Note: The poem is an early version of 'A Sofa in the Forties', collected in *The Spirit Level.*

b. *limited edition*

FORWARD INTO THE PAST [all in burnt umber] | *For May Sarton* | *On Her Eightieth Birthday* | *May 3, 1992* | [ornament printed in burnt umber] | PRINTED BY SPECIAL ARRANGEMENT WITH | WILLIAM B. EWERT, PUBLISHER | CONCORD, NEW HAMPSHIRE
24 × 15.5 cm.; pp. [104]; unpaginated.

Half-bound in dark red leather over textured grey paper; title in gold on front cover and spine; marbled endpapers.

Published simultaneously; 15 copies.

Contents: Same as B127a.

B128 CRITICAL ESSAYS ON TED HUGHES 1992

[rule] [ornament] [rule] | *Critical Essays on* | TED HUGHES | [rule] [ornament] [rule] | *edited by* | LEONARD M. SCIGAJ | *G. K. Hall & Co. /New York* | *Maxwell Macmillan Canada / Toronto* | *Maxwell Macmillan International / New York Oxford Singapore Sidney*

23.5 × 15.5 cm.; pp. 288.

Wine cloth-covered boards; front and back covers blank; spine lettered and decorated in gold.

Published 1992; no printer specified.

Contents: 'The New Poet Laureate', pp. 45–46.

Note: Reprinted from the *Belfast Review*, March/April/May 1985 (C407).

B129 FRANCIS LEDWIDGE: SELECTED POEMS 1992

Francis Ledwidge: | Selected Poems | Edited by Dermot Bolger | Introduced by Seamus Heaney | [publisher's logo] | Dublin
21.5 × 14 cm.; pp. 80.

Blue rexine-covered boards; front and back covers blank; spine lettered and decorated in gold; white dust-jacket lettered and illustrated in sepia.

Published 1992; issued simultaneously in a paper edition; printed by Colour Books, Ltd.

Contents: 'Introduction', pp. 11–20.

Note: Seamus Heaney's poem 'In memoriam Francis Ledwidge' is reprinted, pp. 79–80.

B130 THE ACHIEVEMENT OF BRIAN FRIEL 1993

THE | ACHIEVEMENT OF | BRIAN FRIEL | Edited by | Alan J. Peacock | *Ulster Editions and Monographs:* 4 | COLIN SMYTHE | Gerrards Cross, 1993
21.5 × 13.5 cm.; pp. xix, 269.

White glossy wrappers; lettered in blue on front and back covers and spine; colour photograph of Brian Friel on front cover.

Published 1993; printed by T. J. Press, Padstow.

Contents: 'For Liberation: Brian Friel and the Use of Memory', pp. 229–240.

B131 HOMECOMING 1993

Homecoming | [double rule] | *An bealach 'na bhaile* | Selected Poems / Rogha Danta | Cathal Ó Searcaigh | arna chur in eagar ag / edited by | Gabriel Fitzmaurice | réamhrá le / introduction by | Lillis Ó Laoire | [double rule] | Cló Iar-Chonnachta, Indreabhán, Conamara, Éire.
21 × 14.5 cm.; pp. xii, 200.

Chartreuse-paper wrappers; front cover lettered and designed in melon yellow with colour cover painting; back cover lettered in melon yellow and white; spine lettered in melon yellow.

Published 1993; Clódóri Lurgan Teo, Indreabhan; a second edition was also published in 1993.

Contents: 'Will Travel', p. 81; 'Exile's Return', p. 93; 'The Clay Pipes', pp. 199–201; 'Lament', p. 209.

Note: Seamus Heaney's translations from the Irish of Cathal Ó Searcaigh. 'The Clay Pipes' was reprinted as a broadside (AA44); 'Lament' was also reprinted as a broadside (AA46).

B132 THE ORDERING MIRROR 1993

The | Ordering Mirror | Readers and Contexts | THE BEN BELITT LECTURES AT | BENNINGTON COLLEGE | *Introduction by* | PHILLIP LOPATE | [college coat-of-arms] | FORDHAM UNIVERSITY PRESS | New York | 1993
23 × 15 cm.; xviii, 306 pp.

Burgundy cloth-covered boards; front and back covers blank; spine stamped in gold; dust-jacket with painting of medieval scholar on front cover lettered in yellow and white; back cover and spine lettered in black, yellow, and white.

Published by Bennington College 1993; no printer specified.

Contents: 'Dylan the Durable', pp. 255–275.

B133 DANTE'S INFERNO 1993

a. *limited edition*

Dante's Inferno [in red] | TRANSLATIONS BY | TWENTY CONTEMPORARY POETS | *Introduced by James Merrill* | *With an Afterword by Giuseppe Mazzotta* | *Edited by Daniel Halpern* | *Frontispiece by Francesco Clemente* | [publisher's logo] | THE ECCO PRESS

33 × 25.5 cm.; pp. xiv, 206.

Quarter black leather over deep-red silk; front and back cover blank; spine stamped in gold with publisher's name; black silk slipcase; printed letterpress on heavyweight paper; fore-edges untrimmed.

Published 1993; 145 copies. 125 copies numbered 1 to 125 have been signed by all 20 poets. Each book contains a signed unbound colour etching created specially for this edition by Francesco Clemente. 20 additional copies, numbered I–XX, are reserved as the Poets' Edition.

Contents: Cantos I, II and III, pp. 3–15.

b. *trade edition*

Dante's Inferno | TRANSLATIONS BY | TWENTY CONTEMPORARY POETS | *Introduced by James Merrill* | *With an Afterword by Giuseppe Mazzotta* | *Edited by Daniel Halpern* | [publisher's logo] | THE ECCO PRESS

23 × 15 cm.; pp. xiii, 201.

Black paper-covered boards with cloth spine; publisher's logo blind-stamped on front cover; back cover blank; spine lettered in gold; dark-green dust-jacket letter in red, yellow and white with illustration of 'The Tribulations of St. Anthony', on front. The Ecco Press. Issued simultaneously in a paper edition.

Contents: Same as B133a.

B134 THE MAY ANTHOLOGY OF OXFORD AND CAMBRIDGE POETRY 1993 1993

the May Anthology | of Oxford and Cambridge Poetry 1993 | Varsity/Cherwell
18 × 11 cm.; pp. x, 78.

Stiff paper wrappers with coloured photograph by Bruce Head on front cover and spine and spilling over onto back cover; lettered in white.

Published 1993; printed and bound by Ennisfield Print and Design, Telfords Yard, 6–8 The Highway, Wapping, London.

Contents: Introduction, [ix]–[x], by Seamus Heaney, who also made the selection.

B135 SANDYMOUNT STRAND 1993

a. ***limited edition***

Text by Seamus Heaney | and James Joyce | Etchings Felim Egan | [design]
45 × 37.5 cm.; pp. [28].

Slate-grey hardboard covers loose; scallop-shaped pages inserted; hand-printed on hand-made paper; 40 copies in loose sheets in a solander box. The paper with a watermark of the artist was made at the Kaldewey Press.

Published 1993; printed in the Tower of Poestenkil, New York 1993. All copies signed by Seamus Heaney & Felim Egan.

Contents: 'The dotted line . . .', p. [5]; 'The tide is so far out . . .', p. [23].

Note: 'The dotted line . . .' collected with revisions as 'The Strand' in *The Spirit Level*.

b. *deluxe edition*

12 deluxe copies hand-coloured by Felim Egan and bound in calf leather by Christian Zwang.

Published 1993; printed at the Kaldewey Press, New York 1993. All copies signed by Seamus Heaney & Felim Egan.

Contents: Same as B135a.

B136 POEMS FOR ALAN HANCOX 1993

a. *limited edition*

[wood-engraving printed in burnt orange] | *Poems for Alan Hancox* | *Melvyn Bragg, D. J. Enright, U. A. Fanthorpe,* | *Michael Foot, Duncan Forbes, John Fuller, Seamus Heaney,* | *Michael Horovitz, Ted Hughes, Adrian Mitchell,* | *Jenny Joseph, P. J. Kavanagh, Laurie Lee, Peter Levi,* | *Brian Patten, Lawrence Sail, Jon Silkin, Jon Stallworthy,* | *Charles Tomlinson* [all lettering in black] | [wood-engraving in burnt orange]
28 × 20 cm.; pp. [42]; unpaginated.

Garland decorated pink paper-covered boards; quarter-bound in brown cloth; front and back covers blank; spine lettered in gold; printed on mould-made paper; top edges gilt; rust-brown endpapers.

Published 1993 in an edition of 300 numbered copies signed by all of the contributors.

Printed by the Whittington Press, Herefordshire.

Contents: 'A Sofa in the Forties' pp. [20]–[21].

Note: 'A Sofa in the Forties' was collected with revisions in *The Spirit Level*.

b. *special limited edition*

[wood-engraving printed in burnt orange] | *Poems for Alan Hancox* | *Melvyn Bragg, D. J. Enright, U. A. Fanthorpe,* | *Michael Foot, Duncan Forbes, John Fuller, Seamus Heaney,* | *Michael Horovitz, Ted Hughes, Adrian Mitchell,* | *Jenny Joseph, P. J. Kavanagh, Laurie Lee, Peter Levi,* | *Brian Patten, Lawrence Sail,*

Jon Silkin, Jon Stallworthy, | *Charles Tomlinson* [all lettering in black] | [wood-engraving in burnt orange]
28 × 20 cm.; pp. [48].

Garland decorated pink paper-covered boards quarter-bound in Oasis leather; front and back covers blank; spine lettered in gold; printed on mould-made paper; top edges gilt; rust-brown end-papers. This edition includes an additional signed proof of the title-page wood-engraving; in slipcase.

Published 1993 in an edition of 50 copies; signed by all of the contributors.

Printed by the Whittington Press, Herefordshire.

Contents: 'A Sofa in the Forties', pp. [22]–[23].

B137 TOWARD HARMONY 1993

TOWARD HARMONY | A CELEBRATION: | for TONY O'MALLEY | on the occasion of his 80th Birthday | September 25th 1993 | [publisher's logo] DEDALUS
29.5 × 21 cm.; pp. 48.

Stiff glossy paper wrappers; front cover lettered in black with a painting by Tony O'Malley; list of contributors lettered in black on back cover; spine lettered in black.

Published 1993; printed by the Dedalus Press.

Contents: 'The Morning Light', p. 26.

Note: Seamus Heaney's translation from the Irish of the opening lines from Brian Merriman's *The Midnight Court* with an occasional quatrain to Tony O'Malley included at the end. The poet's translation is a different version from that which appears in *The Midnight Verdict* (1993).

B138 LIQUORICE ALL-SORTS 1993

Liquorice All-Sorts | A GIRL GROWING UP | by | Muriel Breen | [publisher's logo] | MOYTURA PRESS | [short rule] | DUBLIN
21.5 × 14 cm.; 174 pp.

Glossy paper wrappers; front cover, spine and one-quarter of back cover lettered in white, mustard and purple over illustration based on *The Beach Scene* by Tom Carr; white back cover lettered in black.

Published 1993; printed by Colour Books Ltd.

Contents: 'Acrostic for a Lady', pp. [7].

B139 I REMEMBER, I REMEMBER 1993

I REMEMBER, | I REMEMBER | *Illustrated by* | *Trevor Newton* | *Compiled by Rob Farrow* | *Edited by Jennifer Curry* | [publisher's logo] | RED FOX
20 × 13 cm.; pp. 194.

Stiff glossy paper covers; front cover with illustration by Emma Chichester Clark of a child reading stretched out on the grass under an apple tree spilling over to back cover; spine lettered in black.

Published 1993; printed by Cox & Wyman Ltd, Reading, Berkshire.

Contents: 'Note', p. 113.

Note: Seamus Heaney selected Blake's 'The Tyger'. ' "The Tyger" was given to our class not for "appreciation" but for "comprehension", but its hypnotic beat, its mixture of radiance and menace, were unforgettable.'

B140 SOHO SQUARE SIX 1993

[all of the following printed in child-like printing with no breaks between words] | sohosquaresixe | ditedbycolmToi | binbloomsbury | sohosquaresixedi | tedbycolmtoibinb | loomsburysixsqu | aresohotoibinco | lmbyeditedb | loomsburysohosi
25 × 21cm.; pp. 256.

Green paper wrappers; front cover and spine lettered in white, black, red and green; back cover lettered in black with an illustration in colour.

Published 1993; printed by St Edmundsbury Press.

Contents: 'Skims and Glances', pp. 30–31.

B141 WRITERS AND THEIR HOUSES 1993

WRITERS AND THEIR HOUSES | A GUIDE TO THE WRITERS' HOUSES OF ENGLAND, | SCOTLAND, WALES, AND IRELAND | ESSAYS BY MODERN WRITERS | [double rule] | EDITED BY | KATE MARSH | WITH PHOTOGRAPHS BY | HARLAND WALSHAW AND PETER BURTON | [publisher's logo] | HAMISH HAMILTON · LONDON
24.5 × 18.5 cm.; pp. x, 534.

Black cloth-covered boards; front and back covers blank; spine lettered in gold; dust-jacket, lettered in black, gold and white, has photograph of Dylan Thomas's boat house at Laugharne on front cover.

Published 1993; printed by Butler & Tanner Ltd, Frome and London.

Contents: 'W. B. Yeats: Thoor Ballylee, Gort, Galway', pp. 481–495.

Note: Part of the contents of Heaney's essay appeared in a slightly different form in *The Place of Writing* (A45).

B142 OXFORD COMPANION TO TWENTIETH-CENTURY POETRY IN ENGLISH 1994

THE OXFORD COMPANION TO | Twentieth-century | Poetry in English | [dotted rule] | Edited by IAN HAMILTON | Oxford New York | OXFORD UNIVERSITY PRESS | 1994
23.5 × 15.5 cm.; pp. xvi, 602.

Dark-blue cloth-covered boards; Oxford University seal stamped on front cover; back cover blank; spine lettered and decorated in gold; grey dust-jacket lettered in white with reproduction of Matisse's 'The Conversation' on the front.

Published 1994; printed by the Bath Press, Bath, Avon.

Contents: 'Robert Lowell', pp. 312–315.

B143 JOHN CLARE IN CONTEXT 1994

JOHN CLARE IN CONTEXT | EDITED BY | HUGH HAUGHTON | *University of York* | ADAM PHILLIPS | *Charing Cross Hospital* | GEOFFREY SUMMERFIELD | *New York University* | [the following to the right of the Cambridge University coat-of-arms] | CAMBRIDGE | UNIVERSITY PRESS

23 × 15 cm.; pp. xv, 317.

Green cloth-covered boards; front and back covers blank; spine lettered in gold; dust-jacket illustrated and lettered in grey-green.

Published 1994; printed at the University Press, Cambridge.

Contents: 'John Clare—a bi-centenary lecture', pp. 130–147.

Note: 'Seamus Heaney delivered this lecture on Clare as Professor of Poetry at the University of Oxford in October 1992.'

B144 BETWEEN THE LINES 1994

Between | the Lines | [rule] | *Poems on the* DART | [rule] | JONATHAN WILLIAMS | EDITOR | THE LILLIPUT PRESS | MCMXCIV

21.5 × 13 cm.; pp. xii, 180.

Glossy chalk paper wrappers with foldovers front and back; lettered in black and green on front and back covers and spine; blue, green and white design on front.

Published 1994; printed in Dublin by Betaprint.

Contents: 'Dublin 4', p. 11.

B145 AFTER OVID 1994

a. *first edition*

AFTER OVID | NEW METAMORPHOSES | [design] | EDITED BY | MICHAEL HOFMANN | AND JAMES LASDUN | publisher's logo | *faber and faber*

21.5 × 13.5 cm.; pp. xiv, 306.

Blue cloth-covered boards; front and back cover blank; spine lettered in white; dust-jacket has publisher's logo in black on blue background; title, editors and illustration by Picasso in white panel on front; spine has white panel lettered in black; back has list of contributors printed in black in white panel.

Published 1994; issued simultaneously in a paperback edition; printed by Clays Ltd, St. Ives plc.

Contents: 'Orpheus and Eurydice' (x, 1–85), pp. 222–225; 'Death of Orpheus' (xi, 1–84), pp. 226–229.

b. *first American edition*

AFTER OVID | NEW METAMORPHOSES | [design] | EDITED BY | MICHAEL HOFMAN | AND JAMES LASDUN | *Farrar, Straus and Giroux* | NEW YORK
23.5 × 15.5 cm.; pp. xiii, 301.

Grey cloth-cover boards; front and back covers blank; spine lettered in black, dust-jacket has black and white photographic negative on front lettered in bright orange; black back cover lettered in bright orange; bright-orange spine lettered in black.

Published 1995; no printer specified.

Contents: Same as B145a.

B146 TURNING TIDES 1994

TURNING TIDES | [short rule] | MODERN DUTCH & FLEMISH VERSE | IN ENGLISH VERSIONS | BY IRISH POETS | EDITED BY PETER VAN DE KAMP | ASSOCIATE EDITOR: FRANK VAN MEURS | WITH AN INTRODUCTION BY | PROFESSOR THEO D'HAEN [all of the preceding within a double rule box] | STORY LINE PRESS | 1994
21 × 13.5 cm.; pp. xliii, 437.

Bright-green paper covers; front cover lettered in white over windmill image; back cover lettered in white, black and green; spine lettered in white and black.

Contents: 'Turning Tides . . .', p. [v]; 'After Liberation', p. 133.

Note: Only the first four lines of 'Turning Tides . . .' as collected in *The Spirit Level* appear here. 'After Liberation' collected with revisions as part '2' of 'To a Dutch Potter in Ireland' in *The Spirit Level.*

B147 TRANSVERSE II 1994

CUMANN AISTRITHEOIRÍ na hÉIREANN | IRISH TRANSLATORS' ASSOCIATION | Transverse II | SEAMUS HEANEY IN TRANSLATION | Seamus Heaney | Giovanni Bandini | Stanislaw Baranczak | Ulrike Einspieler | Uffe Harder | Ditte König | Maya Koreneva | Tatsuo Murata | Francesc Parcerisas | Dídac Pujol Morillo | Gabriel Rosenstock | Yoshiharu Sakamoto | Toru Sugino | Koichi Yakushigawa | EDITED BY HANS-CHRISTIAN OESER

20.5 × 14.5 cm.; 148 pp.

Cream paper covers; front cover lettered brown; back cover and spine blank; mauve endpapers.

Published by the Irish Translators' Association 1994; printed by Kopyprint.

Contents: 'A Sofa in the Forties', pp. 129–130; 'At Banagher', p. 133; 'At the Wellhead', p. 135.

Note: The poems appear with their respective translations under the heading 'Poems in Progress'.

B148 SWEET KILLOUGH LET GO YOUR ANCHOR 1994

SWEET KILLOUGH | LET GO YOUR ANCHOR | [short rule] | MAURICE HAYES | THE | BLACKSTAFF | PRESS | [short rule] | BELFAST

21 × 13.5 cm.; pp. x, 222.

Cream paper wrappers; illustrations on front and back covers; lettered in white, black and maroon; spine lettered in black and maroon.

Published 1994; printed in Ireland by Colourbooks Limited.

Contents: 'Introduction', pp. [vii]–x.

B149 BOOK 'IM 1994

Book 'im! [hand lettering by Ralph Steadman] | [photograph of Bernard Stone] | Published by Friends of Bernard Stone | London 1994 | Compiled by Martina Berne and Miles | With help from Ralph Steadman and Raymond Danowski | Edited by Miles | Assisted by Jackie Ainsworth | Typesetting, artwork and design by kd digital | with Julia Salisbury and Edwin Jones | Individual authors 1994
27.5 × 21 cm.; pp. [96]; unpaginated.

White paper wrappers; the front cover hand-lettered and decorated in black, red, purple, and blue by Ralph Steadman; colour photographic montage on back cover.

Published 1994; no printer specified.

Contents: 'A Treat in the Book Shop', in Seamus Heaney's holograph on postcard of 'The Peacóck' from *The Ashmole Bestiary*; p. [74].

Note: The poem is an occasional quatrain.

B150 A WHISTLE OVER THE WATER 1994

A Whistle | Over the | Water | A *Broadside* Sampler | *Edited by* | *Carmen Horst* | *Wanda Kraybill*
23 × 15 cm.; pp. 120.

Blue paper covers lettered in black with a drawing of a heron on the front cover.

Published in 1994 by Pinchpenney Press, Goshen College, Goshen, Indiana.

Contents: 'Diptych'.

Note: Collected as 'St Kevin and the Blackbird' in *The Spirit Level*.

B151 SALUTE TO OUTPOSTS 1994

SALUTE TO POSTS | ON ITS FIFTIETH ANNIVERSARY | edited by | Wolfgang Görtschacher | James Hogg | & Roland John | UNIVERSITY OF SALZBURG | 1994
21 × 15 cm.; pp. x, 168.

Light-blue paper covers lettered in black; front cover has photograph of Howard Sergeant and Roland John (respectively, the magazine's founding editor and successor); back cover carries a partial list of contributors.

Published 1994 by Salzburg University.

Contents: 'Saint Patrick's Stone', p. 123.

B152 THE CLIFDEN ANTHOLOGY 1995

The Clifden Anthology | editor Brendan Flynn | Clifden Community Arts Week | 1995
21 × 15 cm.; pp. 196.

White paper wrappers; front cover lettered in white and black and illustrated; back cover and spine lettered in black, white and brown.

Published 1994; printed by Yellow Banana, Dublin.

Contents: 'Saint Kevin and the Blackbird', p. 46.

Note: Collected with revisions in *The Spirit Level*.

B153 A PARCEL OF POEMS 1995

A PARCEL OF POEMS for Ted Hughes | on his Sixty-Fifth Birthday | *17th August 1995*
21.5 × 13.5 cm.; pp. 80.

White stiff paper covers over a yellow-coloured leaf front and back; grey-brown outer wrappers; spine has tipped-on yellow label lettered in black.

Published for private distribution by Faber and Faber; 300 copies printed by Smith Settle, Otley, West Yorkshire.

Contents: 'Sea Interlude, with Hero', pp. 56–58.

Note: Seamus Heaney's translation of *Beowulf*, lines 194–285.

B154 NORMAN MACCAIG: A CELEBRATION 1995

Norman MacCaig | A CELEBRATION | *Tributes from writers in honour of Norman* | *MacCaig's 85th birthday* | *Chapman Publishing* | *1995* | Limited edition of: | 500 [written in ink] | This is number: [number written in ink]
21 × 15cm.; pp. 62.

Stiff glossy white wrappers; front cover has reproduction of coin with Norman MacCaig's face drawn on it, lettered and designed in pea green; back cover advertisement for Chapman Magazine.

Contents: 'A Norman Simile', p. 41.

B155 MY FIRST LOVE & TURNING POINTS 1995

M [in uncial] Y | FIRST LOVE | & *Turning Points* | *Edited by* | GRAHAM REILLY | JULIE MORGAN [publisher's logo] MARKETING
24 × 17.5 cm.; pp. 152.

Red paper wrappers; front lettered in white and tan with colour illustration; back cover lettered and decorated in tan and white with colour illustration; spine lettered and decorated in tan and white.

Published 1995; printed by Impact Printing.

Contents: 'Seamus Heaney', pp. 89–93.

Note: In this essay Seamus Heaney discusses the post-colonial politics of language and place.

B156 MODERN IRISH POETRY 1995

MODERN | IRISH | POETRY | *An* | *Anthology* | [centred dot] | *Edited by* | PATRICK CROTTY | THE | BLACKSTAFF | PRESS | [short rule] | BELFAST
23 × 14.5 cm.; pp. 448.

Glossy paper wrappers; front cover, spine and partial back cover decorated with colour photograph by Dermott Dunbar; front and back covers lettered in orange, tan and white; spine lettered in orange, white and black.

Published 1995; printed by ColourBooks Limited.

Contents: 'Keeping Going', pp. 217–219, and fourteen previously collected poems.

Note: Collected with revisions in *The Spirit Level.*

B157 LES PRIX NOBEL 1995 1996

LES PRIX NOBEL | THE NOBEL PRIZE | 1995 | [small photograph of Nobel medal in lower right corner and all of the following under it] | NOBELPRISET | The Nobel Prize | [very small black rectangle]
24 × 16 cm.; pp. 388.

White paper-covered boards; front cover lettered in orange and green; back cover blank; spine lettered and designed in orange and green; transparent tissue dust-jacket.

Published by the bodies responsible for awarding the Nobel Prizes 1996; printed by Norstedts Tryckeri AB, Stockholm.

Contents: '[Biographical essay]', pp. 317–320; 'Crediting Poetry', pp. 321–333.

B158 AUSTIN CLARKE REMEMBERED 1996

Austin Clarke | Remembered | Edited by | R Dardis Clarke | Introduction by | Seamus Heaney | The Bridge Press 1996

21 × 15 cm.; pp. 136.

Black paper-covered boards; front and back covers blank; spine lettered in gold; glossy white dust-jacket; front cover lettered in black with black and white photograph; back cover and spine lettered in black.

Published 1996 in a hardback edition of 200, of which 10 (in a white slipcase) are numbered and signed by the editor and Seamus Heaney; printed by ColourBooks Ltd, Dublin. A paperback edition of 400 copies was also issued in 1996.

Contents: 'Introduction', pp. 9–11; 'The Yellow Bittern', pp. 49–50.

Note: 'The Yellow Bittern' is Seamus Heaney's translation from the Irish of Cathal Buí MacGiolla Ghunna (c. 1680–1756).

B159 THE FLIGHT PATH 1996

THE FLIGHT | PATH | [the following in red] *Writings by the Winners of* | *The American Ireland Fund Literary Award* | *1972–1996* [end of red] | *Edited by Maurice Hayes* | *Privately published by* | The Gallery Press | *for* | The American Ireland Fund
23 × 16 cm.; pp. 96.

Cream paper-covered boards; maroon cloth spine; front cover stamped with the American Ireland Fund logo [shamrock] in gold in bottom right corner, back cover blank; mauve endpapers; cream paper-covered slipcase with maroon cloth top and bottom.

Published 19 June 1996 in an edition of 500 copies; 400 copies for Friends and Benefactors and Supporters of the American Fund; 100 copies retained for the authors and publishers; printed by Betaprint and binding by Antiquarian Bookcrafts Ltd.

Contents: 'Up and Away', p. 18.

Note: This is a section of 'The Flight Path', collected in *The Spirit Level.*

B160 INTERNATIONAL ASPECTS OF IRISH LITERATURE 1996

INTERNATIONAL ASPECTS | OF | IRISH LITERATURE | Edited by Toshi Furomoto et al. | Irish Literary Studies Series 44 | IASAIL–Japan Series 5 | [publisher's logo] | COLIN SMYTHE | Gerrards Cross, 1966
21.5 × 13.5 cm.; pp. xii, 452.

Grape cloth-covered boards; front and back covers blank; spine lettered in gold; grape dust-jacket lettered in white.

Published 1996; no printer specified.

Contents: 'Keeping Time: Irish Poetry and Contemporary Society', pp. 247–262.

B161 IRISH WRITERS AND THEIR CREATIVE PROCESS 1996

IRISH WRITERS | AND | THEIR CREATIVE PROCESS | edited by | Jacqueline Genet | and | Wynne Hellegouarc'h | IRISH LITERARY STUDIES 48 | [publisher's logo] | COLIN SMYTHE | Gerrards Cross, 1996
21.5 × 13.5 cm.; pp. viii, 152.

Green cloth-covered boards; front and back covers blank; spine lettered and designed in gold; green dust-jacket lettered in white with colour illustration on front cover.

Published 1996; printed by T. J. Press (Padstow) Ltd, Cornwall.

Contents: 'The Frontier of Writing', pp. 3–16.

B162 THE LITERARY MAN 1996

The Literary Man | Essays Presented to Donald W. Hannah | Edited by Karl-Heinz Westarp | [publisher's logo] | AARHUS UNIVERSITY PRESS
24 × 17 cm.; pp. 228.

Red glossy paper wrappers; lettered in white on front and back covers and spine; front cover includes illustration.

Published 1996; no printer specified.

Contents: 'The Welcome to Denmark', pp. 7–8.

Note: Seamus Heaney's translation of *Beowulf*, lines 286–319 collected with revisions in *Beowulf* (A72).

B163 WHEN THE TUNNELS MEET 1996

WHEN THE | TUNNELS | MEET | CONTEMPOPARY | ROMANIAN POETRY | EDITED BY | JOHN FAIRLEIGH | publisher's logo | BLOODAXE BOOKS
21.5 × 14 cm.; pp. 112.

Glossy paper wrappers; front and back cover and spine lettered in tan, red and black; front cover illustrated with reproduction of 'Steeple' by Horia Bernea.

Published 1996; printed by Cromwell Press Ltd, Wiltshire.

Contents: 'Do you remember the beach'; 'The country we come from'; 'Sometimes I dream'; 'Maybe there's somebody dreaming me'; 'It's snowing hostility'; 'The morning after I die'; 'Inhabited by a song'; 'Loneliness'; 'Hunt'; 'As if', pp. 26–32.

Note: Versions from the Romanian of Ana Blandiana by Seamus Heaney based upon literal translations by Simeon Dumitrache and Heather Brett.

B164 DIMITRI HADZI 1996

Dimitri Hadzi | Introduction by Seamus Heaney | Interview by Albert Elsen | Essays by Peter Selz, Joseph Masheck, and Debra Bricker Balken | Hudson Hills Press, New York
30.5 × 23 cm.; pp. 176.

Olive-green cloth-covered boards; front stamped in gold; spine stamped in gold; back cover blank; brown endpapers. White dust-jacket illustrated on front with photograph of Hadzi's sculpture, 'Helmet Bell' and on the back with a photograph of Hadzi.

Published 1996; printed by Toppan Printing Company (Japan).

Contents: 'Introduction', pp. 14, 17.

B165 HOMAGE TO ROBERT FROST 1996

a. *first American edition*

HOMAGE TO | ROBERT FROST | [the following down to and including design, in grey] | JOSEPH BRODSKY | SEAMUS HEANEY | DEREK WALCOTT | [design] | FARRAR STRAUS GIROUX | NEW YORK
21 × 13.5 cm.; pp. 128.

White paper-covered boards with black cloth spine; small design in black on front cover; back cover blank; spine lettered in silver; black-and-white dust-jacket with photograph of Frost in top left corner and continued on right bottom corner, lettered in black and white.

Published 1996; issued simultaneously in a paperback edition; no printer specified.

Contents: 'Above the Brim', pp. 61–88.

b. *first British edition*

HOMAGE TO ROBERT FROST | Joseph Brodsky, Seamus Heaney | Derek Walcott | [publisher's logo] | *faber and faber* | LONDON [centre dot] BOSTON
19.5 × 12.5; pp. 128.

Sky-blue glossy wrappers with a photograph of Frost on front, lettered in red and white; back cover lettered in black; spine lettered in black and white.

Published 1997; printed by Mackays of Chatham plc, Chatham, Kent.

Contents: As in B165a.

B166 DOVE-MARKS ON STONE 1996

DOVE-MARKS | ON STONE [all of the preceding in brown] | * | Poems for | George Mackay Brown | BABEL
24.5 × 16.5 cm.; pp. 20.

Taupe laid-paper wrappers, sewn; front cover lettered in black; back cover ISBN in black; both covers folded over to form flaps; back flap: BABEL [vertical]; bottom edges uncut; printed on rag paper.

Published 1996; 225 copies printed by Martino Mardersteig at the Stampería Valdonega, Verona, Italy, of which 25 are signed by the poets and contain a photograph of George Mackay Brown.

Contents: 'A Landfall', p. 9.

B167 MICHAEL J. DURKAN 1996

[cross design] | MICHAEL J. DURKAN | 1925–1996
21 × 15 cm.; folded sheet; pp. [4]; unpaginated.

Letterpress text paper; front page lettered and decorated in red and black; back page lettered in black.

Published by Swarthmore College 1996; 550 copies printed by Michael Peich, at the Aralia Press.

Contents: 'A Grace Note for Michael', p. [2].

Note: 'Seamus Heaney and Paul Muldoon read at the celebration of the life of Michael J. Durkan held at Swarthmore College on November 15, 1996.' Paul Muldoon's poem 'Hay' is on page [3].

B168 THE SCHOOL BAG 1997

a. *first edition*

The School Bag | *edited by* | SEAMUS HEANEY *and* TED HUGHES | [publisher's logo] | *faber and faber*

21.5 × 13.5 cm.; pp. xviii, 590.

Blue cloth-covered boards; front and back covers blank; spine lettered in light yellow; bright-blue dust-jacket lettered in black with illustrations in bright orange and yellow.

Published 1997; printed by Clays Ltd, St Ives plc.

Contents: 'Foreword', p. XVII; 'The Yellow Bittern', pp. 349–351; '*from* The Midnight Court', pp. 358–365; '*from* Lament for Fergal Rua', p. 495.

Note: The three poems listed are Seamus Heaney's translations from the Irish of Cathal Buí Mac Giolla Ghunna (c. 1680–1756), Brian Merriman (1749–1805) and Tadhg Óg Ó hUiginn (?–1447).

b. *limited presentation edition*

Title-page same as B168a.
21.5 × 13.5 cm.; pp. xviii, 592.

Bright-red cloth covers; front and back blank; spine lettered in gold with black panel; sky-blue endpapers.

Published 1997, 200 numbered copies, specially bound and signed by the editors for presentation at a Gala Evening for the Arvon Foundation; printed by Clays Ltd, St Ives plc.

Contents: Same as B168a.

c. *limited edition*

Title-page same as B168a.
21.5 × 13.5 cm.; pp. xviii, 592.

Yellow paper-covered boards with dark blue cloth spine; front and back blank; spine lettered in gold within a black panel; dark-blue endpapers; clear acetate dust-wrapper; issued in a dark-blue slipcase.

Published 1997, 310 numbered copies signed by the editors, 1–300 for sale, 10 copies numbered I-X reserved for the editors; printed by Clays Ltd, St Ives plc.

B169 ROBERT BURNS AND CULTURAL AUTHORITY 1997

ROBERT BURNS | AND | CULTURAL AUTHORITY | [short rule] | Edited by | Robert Crawford | EDINBURGH UNIVERSITY PRESS
23.5 × 15.5 cm.; pp. xiii, 247.

Dark-blue cloth-covered boards; front and back covers blank; spine lettered in gold; light-blue dust-jacket; front cover lettered in white over image of Burns; back cover has the same image of Burns; spine lettered in black.

Published 1997; no printer specified. American edition published by University of Iowa Press, 1997.

Contents: 'Burns's Art Speech', pp. 216–234.

B170 HUMANIZING THE CITY 1997

HUMANIZING | THE CITY | Politics, Religion, | The Arts in Critical | Conversation | Edited by | PATRICK PRIMEAUX | Catholic Scholars Press | San Francisco – London – Bethesda | 1997
21 × 13.5 cm.; pp. vii, 153.

White glossy wrappers; front and back covers and spine lettered in black.

Published 1997; no printer specified.

Contents: 'Seamus Heaney', pp. [87]–105.

Note: This is the transcript of a paper presented at St John's University in March 1993 as part of a conference entitled: 'Humanizing the City: Politics, the Arts, and Religion in Critical Conversation'. Seamus Heaney's essay also includes an early version of 'Poet's Chair', which was collected in *The Spirit Level.*

B171 MODERN ART IN IRELAND 1997

DOROTHY WALKER | MODERN | ART IN | IRELAND | FOREWORD BY SEAMUS HEANEY | THE LILLIPUT PRESS

28 × 24 cm.; pp. 240.

Black cloth-covered boards; front and back covers blank; spine lettered in gold; yellow endpapers; dust-jacket in black lettered in red, white and purple with illustration by Sean Scully on front and by Dorothy Cross on back.

Published 1997; printed by Betaprint of Clonshaugh. A limited edition of 100 copies signed by the author and Seamus Heaney was issued simultaneously in red cloth-covered boards with black endpapers, in a black cloth-covered slip case.

Contents: 'Foreword', pp. 9–11.

B172 LEABHAR SHEÁIN UÍ THUAMA 1997

Leabhar Sheáin Uí Thuama | arna chur in eagar | ag Louis de Paor | Coisceim
21 × 15 cm.; pp. xi, 205.

Grey designed paper wrappers; front cover with title in black-and-white outline letters and author's name white; back cover blank; spine lettered in white.

Published 1997; printed by Johnswood Press.

Contents: 'Poet to Blacksmith', p. 1.

Note: Seamus Heaney's translation of 'Eoghan Rua O Suilleabhain's instructions to Seamus MacGearailt' from the Irish. The volume contains poems in English, Irish, and Scots–Gaelic.

B173 TRYING THE LINE 1997

Trying The Line | A volume of tribute to | Gillian Clarke | Edited by | Menna Elfyn | Gomer
21 × 15 cm.; pp. 112.

Glossy wrappers; front cover printed in black-and-white over illustration of 'Llyn-y-Fan' by Mary Lloyd Jones spilling over to back cover and spine.

Published 1997; printed at the Gomer Press, Llandysul.

Contents: 'Penworker' (from the eleventh-century Irish), p. 38.

Note: This is a version of 'Colmcille the Scribe'.

B174 WILDE THE IRISHMAN 1998

Wilde the Irishman | EDITED BY | JERUSHA MCCORMACK | Yale University Press | New Haven and London
23.5 × 15.5 cm.; pp. xvi, 208.

Green cloth-covered boards; front and back covers blank; spine lettered in gold; dust-jacket lettered in white and black; has a reproduction of a portrait of Wilde on the front cover and of a sculpture of Wilde on the back.

Published 1997; printed by Bookcraft, Somerset.

Contents: 'Oscar Wilde Dedication: Westminster Abbey, 14 February 1995', pp. 174–176.

B175 SEAN O'CASEY: PLAYS ONE 1998

SEAN O'CASEY | Plays One | *Juno and the Paycock* | *Within the Gates* | *Red Roses for Me* | *Cock-A-Doodle Dandy* | Introduced by | Seamus Heaney | [publisher's logo] | *faber and faber*
20 × 12.5 cm.; pp. x, 422.

Cream paper wrappers; front and back covers and spine lettered in black with illustration by Breon O'Casey on front cover.

Published 1998; printed by Mackays of Chatham plc, Chatham, Kent.

Contents: 'Introduction', pp. vii–x.

B176 OR VOLGE L'ANNO: AT THE YEAR'S TURNING 1998

OR VOLGE L'ANNO | AT THE YEAR'S TURNING | AN ANTHOLOGY OF IRISH POETS | RESPONDING TO LEOPARDI | Edited,

Introduced and Annotated by | Marco Sonzogni | DEDALUS [to the right of logo] | Dublin 1998
21 × 14.5 cm.; pp. 304.

Blue and black mottled leather-textured boards; front and back covers blank; spine lettered in gold; glossy dust-jacket; front cover illustrated with colour photograph and lettered in red; back cover contains a photograph and short biography of the editor and a note on the edition; spine letter in black and red; light blue endpapers.

Published 1998; issued simultaneously in a paperback edition 1998; no printer specified.

Contents: 'Ballynahinch Lake', pp. 146–147. There is also a quotation 'Whatever is given can always be reimagined' SEAMUS HEANEY, p. 11 (other than that the page is blank).

B177 IN MEMORIAM DARCY O'BRIEN 1998

IN MEMORIAM | DARCY O'BRIEN |1939–1998 | CHRISTOPHER CAHILL ◇ STANLEY CROUCH | THOMAS FLANAGAN · ADRIAN FRAZIER | SEAMUS HEANEY · BENEDICT KIELY · J.C.C. MAYS · MAIRE MHAC AN TSAOI · CONOR CRUISE O'BRIEN
23 × 15 cm.; pp. 32.

Stiff cream wrappers, stapled, front cover: IN MEMORIAM | DARCY O'BRIEN, printed in blue; back cover blank.

Published as a supplement to *The Recorder: The Journal of the American-Irish Historical Society*, Fall 1998; printed at the Stinehour Press.

Contents: 'NON-U', pp. 22–23.

B178 A WRITING LIFE 1998

A writing life | Celebrating Nadine Gordimer | Edited by | ANDRIES WALTER OLIPHANT | Photographs by | David Goldblatt | [publisher's logo] | [short rule] | VIKING | [short rule]

23.5 × 15.5 cm.; pp. xxiv, 510.

Black paper wrappers; front cover lettered in white with a photograph of Nadine Gordimer; grey back cover lettered in black and white; spine lettered in white.

First published by Penguin Books (South Africa) 1998; printed and bound by ABC Press.

Contents: 'An Image from Beowulf', p. 121. Collected with revisions as 'The Border Campaign' in *Electric Light*.

B179 IDEAS MATTER 1998

IDEAS MATTER | Essays in Honor of Conor Cruise O'Brien | [rule] | Edited by Richard English and Joseph Morrison Skelly | POOLBEG
21.5 × 13 cm.; pp. 416.

Glossy wrappers; front cover lettered in blue and red with colour photograph of Conor Cruise O'Brien; back cover lettered in blue, red and black; spine lettered in blue, red and black.

Published 1998; printed by the Guernsey Press Ltd, Channel Islands.

Contents: 'The Stick', pp. 51–53.

Note: The poem is introduced by a short note by Seamus Heaney.

B180 BARRIE COOKE 1998

Profile [preceding lettered vertically, bottom to top] Barrie Cooke | GANDON EDITIONS
22.5 × 22.5 cm.; pp. 48.

Glossy wrappers; front cover lettered in white with painting *Algal Growth* by Barrie Cooke; back cover blank in tourquoise; spine lettered in white.

Published 1998; printed by Nicholson and Bass, Belfast.

Contents: 'Total Absorption', pp. 5–7.

B181 ECRIRE LES FRONTIERES. LE PONT DE L'EUROPE 1999

ECRIRE LES FRONTIERES. LE PONT DE L'EUROPE | GRENZUBERSCHREIBUNG. DIE EUROPABRUCKE | Council of Europe Publishing
16 × 24.5 cm.; pp. 184.

Glossy paper wrappers lettered in white, black and red; front cover has a colour photograph of bridges and publisher's logo; photograph continued on spine and one-eighth of back cover; back cover has publisher's description of the book in French, English and German, and a list of the forty contributors.

Published by the Council of Europe Publishing in a tri-lingual edition (French, German, English) in April 1999; no printer specified.

Contents: 'Steady under the strain and strong through tension', p. 65; French translation p. 66; and German translation p. 67.

Note: Collected with revisions as 'The Bridge' (section 3 in 'Ten Glosses') in *Electric Light*. Seamus Heaney wrote this untitled seven-line poem expressly for *Ecrire Les Frontiers*. The book is a collection of prose, poems and personal recollections inspired by the bridge, The Pont de L'Europe, which connects France and Germany. Each text is given in its original language first.

B182 THE EPIC POISE 1999

THE EPIC POISE | [short rule] | A CELEBRATION OF | Ted Hughes | [bold short rule] | [short rule] | *edited by* | NICK GAMMAGE | ff | *faber and faber*
21.5 × 13.5 cm.; pp. xv, 289.

Olive paper wrappers lettered in ivory; front wrapper has photograph of Ted Hughes; back wrapper has list of contributors.

Published 1999; printed by Clays Ltd, St Ives plc.

Contents: 'Omen and Amen: On "Littleblood" ', pp. 59–61.

B183 LOST LIVES 1999

LOST | LIVES [all of the preceding in outline letters] | The stories of the men, women, and children | who died as a result of the Northern Ireland troubles |DAVID MCKITTRICK, SEAMUS KELTERS | [the following in large caps] BRIAN FEENEY [the following in small caps] AND [the following in large caps] CHRIS THORNTON | [short rule] | MAINSTREAM | [short rule] | PUBLISHING | [short rule] | EDINBURGH AND LONDON
25 × 15.5 cm.; 1632 pp.

Black cloth-covered boards; front and back covers blank; spine stamped in silver; black dust-jacket; front cover lettered in black, red and white with black-and-white photograph of night-time street confrontation; back cover with black-and-white photograph of bomb site; spine lettered in black, red and white.

Published 1999; printed by the Bath Press, Great Britain.

Contents: 'Letter from Seamus Heaney to the *Irish News*, 1997, condemning the killing of Sean Brown', pp. 1407–1408.

Note: The editors reprint Seamus Heaney's letter (C701) written while the poet was in Greece. Sean Brown was a family friend from Bellaghy who was shot 12 May 1997.

B184 SOURCES 1999

SOURCES | [in grey] *Letters* | [in grey] *from* | *Irish People* | [in grey] *on Sustenance* | [in grey] *for the Soul* | EDITED BY | MARIE HEANEY | [publisher's logo] | TOWN | HOUSE | DUBLIN
21.5 × 14 cm.; pp xii, 236.

Turquoise paper covers lettered in white and black; front cover has rectangular cut-out exposing detail of Howard Hodgkin's painting 'Mrs. K.'.

Published 1999; printed by ColourBooks Ltd.

Contents: Letter, beginning 'Dear Marie' and signed 'Seamus', discussing William Blake's poem 'Auguries of Innocence', pp. 160–161. The poem is printed in full on pp. 161–164.

B185 THE FABER BOOK OF WRITERS ON WRITERS 1999

The Faber Book of | WRITERS ON WRITERS | *edited by Sean French* | ff | *faber and faber* | LONDON [centred dot] NEW YORK
23.5 × 15 cm.; pp. xxiii, 217.

Red paper-covered boards; front and back covers blank; spine lettered in black; white dust-jacket lettered in black, olive and grey, with a design of pen nibs on front and back covers.

Published 1999; printed by Clays Ltd, St Ives plc.

Contents: 'Robert Lowell', p. 197.

Note: Reprinted from *Erato*: *The Harvard Book Review*, Winter and Spring 1988 (C479).

B186 THE PORTABLE CREATIVE WRITING WORKSHOP 1999

The | Portable | *Creative Writing* | *Workshop* | PAT BORAN | Salmon | Publishing
21.5 × 14 cm.; pp. 216.

Black paper wrappers, lettered and decorated in white and green with image of typewriter keys on front cover; back cover and spine blank.

Published 1999; printed by Sciprint, County Clare.

Contents: 'Seamus Heaney (poet/playwright)', p. 192.

Note: Seamus Heaney's contribution is a short paragraph in the book's section titled 'Advice for Beginning Writers'.

B187 WATCHING THE RIVER FLOW 1999

watching the river *flow* | A Century of Irish Poetry | Edited by Noel Duffy and Theo Dorgan | 100 poems selected by | Eavan Boland | Eiléan Ni Chuilleanáin | Bernard O'Donoghue | Thomas Kinsella | Ciaran Carson | John Montague | Michael Longley |

Seamus Heaney | Cathal Ó Searcaigh | Nuala Ní Dhomhnaill | [publisher's logo] | Poetry Ireland | Éigse Éireann
25.5 × 15.5 cm.; pp 272.

Black paper wrappers printed in white and tan and decorated with photographs of water scenes on front and back covers.

Published 1999; printed by Colourbooks Limited, Dublin.

Contents: 'Meaning Business: 1970–79', pp. 159–162.

Note: Ten poets were invited to choose 100 significant poems of the century. Each poet was allotted a decade and asked to select ten poems that mark, characterise, or are emblematic of that particular decade. Seamus Heaney was allotted the 1970s and in '1970–1979 Meaning Business' he discusses the rationale behind his choices. The poems he selected are: Thomas Kinsella's 'His Father's Hands'; Derek Mahon's 'A Disused Shed in Co. Wexford'; Michael Longley's 'Wounds'; John Montague's 'Small Secrets'; Michael Hartnett's 'Death of an Irishwoman'; Paul Durcan's 'Wife Who Smashed Television Gets Jail'; Eavan Boland's 'Conversation with an Inspector of Taxes about Poetry'; Eilean Ni Chuilleanain's 'The Second Voyage'; Pearse Hutchinson's 'Gaeltacht'; and Paul Muldoon's 'Wind and Tree'. The poems are on pp. 163–181.

B188 MODERN POETRY IN TRANSLATION 1999

Modern Poetry In Translation | New Series/No. 15 | Edited by Daniel Weissbort | Published by | King's College London | University of London | Strand, London WC2R 2LS | Arts Council funded
21.5 × 13.5 cm.; pp. 280.

Stiff baize paper covers; front and back covers printed and decorated in black, red, brown, green and grey.

Published 1999; printed by Short Run Press, Exeter.

Contents: 'The Civil Power', p. 174.

Note: Seamus Heaney's translation of Alexander Pushkin's poem 'Mirskaia Vlast'.

B189 THE CRACKED LOOKING GLASS 1999

THE CRACKED LOOKING GLASS | CONTRIBUTIONS TO THE STUDY | OF IRISH LITERATURE | edited by | Carla de Petris, Jean M. Ellis D'Alessandro | and Fiorenzo Fantaccini | BULZONI EDITORE

21 × 15 cm.; pp. 308.

Green paper wrappers; front cover lettered in black with cream rectangle design; back cover lettered in black; white spine lettered in black.

Published 1999; Grafica Universal per conto della GESP.

Contents: 'Further Language', pp. 45–58.

Note: Reprinted from *Studies in the Literary Imagination*, fall, 1997 (C709).

B190 PODIUM IV 1999

PODIUM IV | [long rule] | Podium 4 | an anthology of poetry from | Samhlaíocht Chiarraí | Kerry Arts | Edited by | Noel King, Samhlaíocht Chiarraí

20 × 14.5 cm.; 78 pp.

Purple paper wrappers; front cover lettered in white and yellow with photograph; back cover lettered in white and yellow; spine lettered in white.

Published by Samhlaiocht Chiarrai, Kerry Arts, 1999; no printing information.

Contents: 'Would They Had Stay'd', pp. 20.

Note: Collected with revisions in *Electric Light*.

B191 BOG BODIES, SACRED SITES, AND WETLAND ARCHAEOLOGY 1999

Bog Bodies, Sacred Sites and | Wetland Archaeology | Edited by Bryony Coles, John Coles | and Mogens Schou Jorgensen [all of

the preceding within a rectangle] | Proceedings of a conference held by WARP and | the National Museum of Denmark, in conjunction | with Silkborg Museum, Jutland, September 1996. | WARP [in outline letters] | ISBN
21 × 30 cm.; pp. 236.

Light purple-tint glossy paper covers; front cover has a photograph in purplish tones of bog grass and title and author's name printed in dark purple; back cover has list of contents; blank spine.

Published 1999; printed by Short Run Press, Exeter.

Contents: 'The Man and the Bog', pp. 3–6; 'Tollund Man', p. 6.

Note: Photograph of Seamus Heaney with the Queen of Denmark and Christian Fisher, curator of the Silkborg Museum, appears on p. 7.

B192 AFTER PUSHKIN 1999

AFTER | PUSHKIN | *Versions of the poems of* | *Alexander Sergeevich Pushkin* | *by contemporary poets* | Edited and introduced by | Elaine Feinstein | Preface by | Marita Crawley | *Drawings by Alexander Pushkin* | London | The Folio Society | 1999
24.5 × 15.5 cm.; pp. 96.

Light-blue cloth-covered boards; front cover lettered in gold and dark blue; back cover blank; spine lettered in gold; dark-blue paper-covered slipcase.

Published 1999; printed by Butler and Tanner Ltd, Frome. A paperback edition was published by Carcanet Press.

Contents: 'Arion', p. 83.

B193 LEWIS'S LOUGHINSHOLIN (1837) 1999

a. *first trade edition*

LEWIS'S | LOUGHINSHOLIN | (1837) | [short rule] | Foreword by Seamus Heaney | Introduction by Graham Mawhinney | Ballinascreen Historical Society | 1999
15.5 × 11.5 cm.; pp xvi, 80.

Orange paper covers; front and back covers and spine lettered in black.

Published 1999; no printer specified.

Contents: 'Foreword', pp. i–iii.

b. *limited edition*

15.5 × 11.5 cm.; pp xvi, 80.

Dark-blue simulated leather; lettered in gold on front and spine; back cover blank.

Published 1999 in an edition of 100 hand-numbered copies; no printer specified.

Contents: Same as B193a.

B194 DERRY AND LONDONDERRY: HISTORY AND SOCIETY 1999

Derry and | Londonderry | [thick grey rule] | HISTORY & SOCIETY | Interdisciplinary Essays on the | History of an Irish County | *Editor*: | Gerard O'Brien | *Series Editor*: | William Nolan | [publisher's logo] GEOGRAPHY PUBLICATIONS
23 × 15 cm.; pp. xxiv, 744.

Red cloth-covered boards; front and back covers blank; spine lettered in gold; dust-jacket front is lettered in red, yellow and slate across a reproduction of a painting of Derry by John Noah Gossett, back has photograph by Tom Russell. Errata slip pasted on back free endpaper.

Published 1999; printed by Colour Books Ltd.

Contents: 'Preface', pp. xxii–xxiii.

B195 TRANSLATION OF POETRY AND POETIC PROSE 1999

TRANSLATION OF | *POETRY AND* | *POETIC PROSE* [the preceding underlined by three page-wide rules] | *Proceedings of Nobel*

Symposium 110 | Editor | Sture Allen | *Swedish Academy, Stockholm* | [publisher's logo] World Scientific | *Singapore* [centre dot] *New Jersey* [center dot] *Hong Kong*
22 × 15 cm.; pp. xv, 351.

Dark-blue paper-covered boards; front cover, back cover and spine lettered in silver; light-blue endpapers; blue dust-jacket lettered and decorated in white and gold.

Published 1999; printed by Uto-Print, Singapore.

Contents: 'Report on Session 6: "The Role of the Author" ', pp. 262–265; 'Report on Session 7: "Several Translations of the Same Text" ', pp. 330–333.

B196 THE NORTON ANTHOLOGY OF ENGLISH LITERATURE 1999

[double rule] | [ornament] | [double rule] | The Norton Anthology | of English Literature | [long rule] | SEVENTH EDITION | VOLUME 1 | M. H. Abrams, *General Editor* | CLASS OF 1916 PROFESSOR OF ENGLISH EMERITUS, | CORNELL UNIVERSITY | Stephen Greenblatt, *Associate General Editor* | HARRY LEVIN PROFESSOR OF LITERATURE, | HARVARD UNIVERSITY | [publisher's logo] | [long rule] | W [centre dot] W [centre dot] NORTON & COMPANY [center dot] *New York* [centre dot] *London*
23.5 × 15 cm.; pp. lxi, 2978.

Grey cloth-covered boards; front and back covers blank; spine lettered and decorated in gold; dust-jacket has portrait of Elizabeth I on front and spine.

Published 1999; no printer specified.

Contents: 'Beowulf', pp. 32–99.

Note: This version is slightly different from that published by Faber and Faber (A72a).

B197 THE WHOSEDAY BOOK 1999

a. *first edition*

THE WHOSEDAY BOOK [the preceding in black; the following in grey] A MILLENNIUM JOURNAL
19 × 24 cm.; pp. 392.

Black cloth-covered boards; front cover THE WHOSEDAY BOOK stamped in copper over small copper square.; back cover blank; spine has small copper square stamped MM [in black]. Issued with ribbon page marker; dust-jacket illustrated with a photograph of Seamus Heaney's hands; lettered in black, white, grey and copper.

Published by the Irish Hospice Foundation 1999; printed Modus Media International.

Contents: Introduction, p. [7]; 'Exile's Return', [translation from the Irish of Cathal ÓSearcaigh's 'Pilleadh An Deorai'], 5 February 2000; 'Hygeia,' 15 May, 2000.

Note: Seamus Heaney is a patron of the Irish Hospice Foundation.

b. *special edition*

THE WHOSEDAY BOOK [the preceding in black; the following in grey] A MILLENNIUM JOURNAL
19 × 24 cm.; pp. 392.

Black cloth-covered boards; front cover THE WHOSEDAY BOOK stamped in copper over small copper square; back cover blank; spine has small copper square stamped MM [in black]. Issued with ribbon page marker in a black cloth-covered slipcase with spine stamped to match book.

Contents: Same as B197a.

c. *limited edition*

Binding same as B197a.

Issued in a post-production format with a limitation page inserted: a limited edition of 129 copies signed by Seamus Heaney of which 42 of this edition were also signed by at least 35 other contributors.

Contents: Same as B197a.

B198 W. B. YEATS 2000

W. B. YEATS | Poems selected by SEAMUS HEANEY | ff | *faber and faber*
18 × 10 cm.; pp. xxv, 135.

Stiff white paper wrappers with green flaps; the front cover printed in black with the names YEATS and HEANEY underlined in green; back cover blank; spine lettered in black.

Published 2000; no printer specified.

Contents: 'Introduction', pp. xi–xxv.

Note: 'The Introduction of this book is a revised version of the Introduction to a slightly less comprehensive selection of W. B. Yeats's poems published in Volume II of *The Field Day Anthology of Irish Writing*.'

B199 FIRST LOVES 2000

FIRST LOVES | [ornament] | *Poets Introduce the Essential Poems* | *That Captivated and Inspired Them* | EDITED BY | Carmela Ciuraru | SCRIBNER | New York London Toronto Sydney Singapore
21 × 14 cm.; pp. 272.

Green paper-covered boards; front and back covers blank; black cloth spine lettered in silver; grey and green dust-jacket lettered in black and maroon, front and back panels contain list of contributors and their contributions.

Published in 2000; no printer specified; issued simultaneously in a paper edition.

Contents: 'Seamus Heaney on the Dactyls of Derry', pp. 106–107.

B200 WELCOME ABOARD THE POETRY OLYMPICS PARTY 2000

Welcome aboard the [the following in flowing letters over musical grand staff] Poetry Olympics Party [end of flowing letters] | Anthology | Published in 2000 by New Departures | PO Box 9819, London W11 2GQ | [rights] |Copyright to this selection and the Introduction | © 2000 Michael Horovitz |[copyrights, ISBN]
21 × 15 cm.; pp. 128.

Red paper wrappers; front and back covers and spine lettered and decorated in yellow and black.

Published 2000, printed by Sterling, London College of Printing.

Contents: 'Audenesque', pp. 47–49.

B201 CASTALIAN SPRING/LOOSE FOR A LITTLE WHILE 2000

[Broadside printed in two side-by-side columns; first column] *Castalian Spring* | text of sonnet | Seamus Heaney | [second column] *Loose for a Little While* | for Seamus | text | Stratis Haviaras | [across the bottom of the broadside] *This Pressed Wafer publication celebrates the inaugural Stratis Haviaras Lecture delivered by Seamus Heaney on April 6, 2000. Printed by Katherine McCanless at the Bow & Arrow* | *Press in an edition of one hundred and fifty copies, twenty-six of which are lettered A–Z and signed by both authors.*
28 × 39.5 cm.; broadside.

Printed in black on tan laid paper.

Published 2000; printed by Katherine McCanless at the Bow & Arrow Press in an edition of 150 copies, 26 of which are lettered A–Z and signed by both authors.

Contents: 'Castalian Spring'.

B202 MY BEST ADVICE! 2000

[the following in gold] My best advice! [end of gold] | Over 100 famous Irish people share the | best advice they ever received | [image of gold nuggets] |[the following in gold] Gong Publishing
10 × 10 cm.; [144] pp.

Dark-blue paper wrappers; front and back covers and spine lettered and decorated in gold and white.

Published 2000; printed by Grafton Litho Ltd.

Contents: 'My late editor, Charles Monteith, once told me: Never call a book by a title that people aren't sure how to pronounce', p. [58].

B203 INTERPRETING SYNGE 2000

INTERPRETING | SYNGE | *Essays from the Synge Summer School* |1991–2000 | Edited by Nicholas Green | THE LILLIPUT PRESS | DUBLIN
23.5 × 15.5 cm.; pp. 224.

Blue cloth-covered boards, front and back covers blank; spine lettered in gold; dust-jacket has photograph of Synge with his mother and two friends across both front and back covers, front panel lettered in yellow and white on blue background, back panel lettered in black, spine lettered in grey and white.

Published 2000; printed by MPG Books, Bodmin, Cornwall.

Contents: 'Glanmore Eclogue', pp. 17–19.

Note: Collected with revisions in *Electric Light*.

B204 STRONG WORDS 2000

STRONG WORDS | modern poets on modern poetry | *edited by* | W. N. HERBERT | & MATTHEW HOLLIS | [publisher's logo] | BLOODAXE BOOKS
21.5 × 14 cm.; pp. 320.

Glossy paper wrappers; front cover lettered in blue, red and black with painting, *A Reading of Ovid (Tyros)* by Percy William Lewis; back cover lettered in blue, red and black; spine lettered in blue, red and black.

Published 2000; printed by Cromwell Press Ltd, Wiltshire.

Contents: 'Craft and Technique', pp. 158–160.

Note: This is a revised excerpt from 'Feeling into Words', collected in *Preoccupations*: *Selected Prose 1968–1978* (A25).

B205 EXCALIBUR 2000

Excalibur | *A Tribute to Seamus Heaney* | *William David Martin*
18 × 12 cm.; pp. 62.

Stiff glossy paper covers; front cover lettered in black on white, blue, and red background; back cover lettered in black and outline letters on blue background.

Published 2000; printed by Forward Press Ltd, Peterborough.

Contents: Typed letter, signed 'Seamus Heaney', p. 62.

B206 THE NAMES UPON THE HARP 2000

a. *first edition*

IRISH MYTH AND LEGEND | The Names Upon | The Harp | MARIE HEANEY | ILLUSTRATED BY | P. J. LYNCH | ff | *faber and faber*
28 × 21.5 cm.; pp. 96.

Green paper-covered boards; front and back covers have full-page illustrations by P. J. Lynch; front cover has title in gold outline letters, other lettering in orange on cover and spine; grey end-papers with celtic design; green dust-jacket repeats the cover illustrations on front and back panels; title in outline letters on front, other lettering in gold on front and spine.

Published 2000; printed by Tien Wah Press in Singapore.

Contents: 'Summer', p. [71].

Note: Seamus Heaney's translation from the Irish.

b. *limited edition*

120 numbered copies of which 100 were for sale signed by the author and illustrator; issued in green paper covered boards with quarter vellum in cream slipcase. An American edition was published in 2000 by Arthur A. Levine Books.

Contents: Same as B206a.

c. *first American edition*

[in gold] IRISH MYTH AND LEGENDS | [in green calligraphy] The | Names Upon | The Harp | [in gold] BY MARIE HEANEY ILLUSTRATED BY P. J. LYNCH | [in black] [publisher's logo] | ARTHUR A. LEVINE BOOKS | *An Imprint of Scholastic Press* [all of the foregoing within coloured borders]
28 × 21.5 cm.; pp. 96.

Reddish-brown paper-covered boards with Celtic designs across front and back; spine lettered in gold; green endpapers with Celtic designs; illustrated dust-jacket lettered in gold.

Published 2000; printed at Tien Wah Press, Singapore.

Contents: Same as B206a.

B207 MAJORING IN THE REST OF YOUR LIFE 2000

Majoring In the | Rest of Your Life | College and Career Secrets for Students | Carol Carter | Lynn Quitman Troyka | Prentice Hall | Upper Saddle River, NJ 07458
27.5 × 21 cm.; pp. xix, 333.

Bright-green glossy paper wrappers; front and back covers lettered in white and yellow; spine lettered in white, yellow and black.

Published 2000; no printer specified.

Contents: 'Commencement Ceremony at the University of North Carolina at Chapel Hill, May 12, 1996', pp. 302–305. See (A66).

B208 THE LIVING STREAM: A FESTSCHRIFT FOR THEO DORGAN 2000

the living stream | A FESTSCHRIFT FOR THEO DORGAN | EDITED BY NIAMH MORRIS
24 × 20.5 cm.; pp. 72.

Oatmeal-white paper wrappers; front cover lettered in black with purple designs; spine lettered in black; back cover black with designs purple.

Published by Why Go Bald? Books, 13 December 2000 in an edition of 250 copies; no printer specified.

Contents: 'Three glosses for Theo', p. 34.

B209 DÁNTA DEIREADH SAOIL POEMELE SFÁRSÍTULUI 2000

Marin Sorescu | Dánta deireadh saoil | Poemele Sfársítului | Aistrithe ag Aodh Ó Canainn | agus Anamaria Maior
21 × 15 cm.; pp. xvii, 95.

Orange and red paper wrappers; front cover lettered in white with painting of flowers in a vase; back cover with black and white photograph of Marin Sorescu; red spine lettered in white.

Published by Coiscéim, 2000; printed by Johnswood Press.

Contents: 'Foreword' [in Irish], p. xi.

B210 THE PEOPLE OF THE SEA 2000

The | People | of the Sea | *A Journey in Search of the Seal Legend* | David Thomson | Introduction by Seamus Heaney | Decorations by Jonathan Heale | COUNTERPOINT | WASHINGTON, D. C.
21 × 13.5 cm.; pp. xxiv, 214.

Gold paper-covered boards with green spine; front cover stamped DT in gold; back cover blank; spine stamped in gold; green endpapers; dark green dust-jacket lettered in yellow, white and grey; woodcut of seal on front cover by Jonathan Heale.

Published 2000; no printer specified. A paperback edition was also published in England by Canongate Classics, 2000.

Contents: 'Introduction', pp. xii–xix.

Note: *The People of the Sea* was first published in 1954. Seamus Heaney's introduction is dated September 1999.

B211 FIGURES OF SPEECH 2000

figures | of | speech | [initial 'f' and 's' calligraphic; all of the preceding printed over a large, grey M] | AN ANTHOLOGY OF | MAGDALENE WRITERS | *edited by* | M E J Hughes | John Mole | Nick Seddon | MAGDALENE COLLEGE | CAMBRIDGE | MM
25 × 13.5 cm.; pp. xviii, 254.

Red cloth-covered boards; front and back covers blank; spine lettered in gold; red dust-jacket lettered in robin-egg blue and white.

Published 2000; printed by the St. Edmundsbury Press, Bury St. Edmunds.

Contents: 'The Loose Box', pp. 212–214.

Note: Collected with revisions in *Electric Light*.

B212 PER VANNI SCHEIWILLER 2000

per Vanni Scheiwiller | [publisher's logo] | LIBRI SCHEIWILLER |MILANO 2000
22 × 15 cm.; pp. 308.

Slate-blue paper wrappers; front cover lettered in white; back cover blank; spine lettered in white.

Published by Vanni Scheiwiller, 2000; printed in Italy.

Contents: 'Vanni Scheiwiller', p. 158.

Note: This is a brief prose appreciation of Vanni Scheiwiller.

B213 ADULT EDUCATION: UNIVERSITY COLLEGE DUBLIN 2000

[abstract design of heads with 50 on top left and bottom right corners] | *Adult* | *Education* | *University College Dublin* | [short rule] | *Celebrating* | *50 Years* | *Of Lifelong Learning* | *at* UCD | [short rule] [all of the preceding printed in blue]
21 × 15 cm.; pp. [30]; unpaginated.

Stapled white glossy covers; front cover lettered and decorated in white and blue; back cover lettered in blue.

Published by the Office of Adult Education 2000; no printer specified.

Contents: 'Draw a line and add up': front cover.

B214 THE PUSHCART PRIZE 2001 2001

25th Anniversary Edition [the preceding across the top of the title-page] | [all of the following within a single rule box] THE | PUSHCART | PRIZE 2001 | XXV | [the following in a black panel at the top right] BEST OF | THE SMALL PRESSES | [at the bottom left: publisher's logo above a black panel containing the following] EDITED BY | BILL HENDERSON | WITH THE PUSHCART | PRIZE EDITORS | [end of single rule box] PUSHCART PRESS | WAINSCOTT, NEW YORK
23.5 × 15.5 cm.; pp. 624.

Grey paper-covered board quarter-bound blue cloth spine; front and back covers blank; spine lettered and decorated in silver; blue endpapers; dust-jacket printed in white, purple and blue.

Published 2001; no printer specified.

Contents: 'New Staves', pp. 93–98.

B215 A WAY OF LIFE, LIKE ANY OTHER 2001

A WAY OF LIFE | LIKE ANY OTHER | DARCY O'BRIEN | Introduction by | SEAMUS HEANEY | NEW YORK REVIEW OF BOOKS | [publisher's logo] | New York
20.5 × 13 cm.; pp. xiv, 162.

Glossy paper wrappers; front cover has yellow block lettered in pink and blue over a photograph of a dog, woman and child by a seaside pool; back cover lettered in pink and blue; spine lettered in pink and blue.

Published 2001; no printer specified.

Contents: 'Introduction', pp. ix–xiv.

Notes: *A Way of Life, Like Any Other* was first published in 1977. Seamus Heaney's 'Introduction', 2001.

B216 JOSEPH BRODSKY: NATIVITY POEMS 2001

JOSEPH BRODSKY [the preceding in grey] | [black and white photograph of a church dome with Christmas lights in foreground] | NATIVITY POEMS

19 × 12 cm.; pp. vii, 120.

Dark-blue paper-covered boards with cloth spine; front cover stamped in silver: J * B; back cover blank; spine stamped in silver; dust-jacket lettered in blue and white with illustration by Alexander Anno on front and back covers.

Published by Farrar, Straus and Giroux 2001; no printer specified.

Contents: 'Imagine striking a match that night in the cave', p. 79; 'Flight into Egypt (2)', pp. 99, 101.

Note: Seamus Heaney dates his translations from the Russian of Joseph Brodsky of 'Imagine striking a match that night in the cave' as 1989 and the date of 'Flight into Egypt (2)' as December 1995.

B217 BRIAN MOORE 2001

Brian Moore | 1921–1999 | Leighton House | 28th October 1999

24 × 17 cm.; pp. 40.

Cream paper wrappers; front cover same as title-page; back cover and spine blank.

No publishing or printing information. Not for sale.

Contents: 'Untitled Memorial Address', pp. 21–24.

Note: This is the transcript produced in 2001 of a memorial evening for Brian Moore held on 28 October 1999 at Leighton House.

B218 IRELAND & POLAND 2001

Janusz Skolimowski | Cezary Lusinski | Ireland | and | Poland | Common | Perspectives | Embassy of the Republic of Poland | Dublin 2001
21 × 15 cm.; pp. 92.

Glossy paper wrappers; front cover and back cover wrap-around colour photograph of office building; front and back covers lettered in orange; green spine lettered in white.

Published 2001; no printer specified.

Contents: 'Remarks at a ceremony in Polish Embassy in Dublin, April 1998, marking the award of the Order of Merit for Polish Culture', pp. 59–60.

B219 HOTEL EUROPA 2001

HOTEL EUROPA [the preceding in grey] | 12 Europese dichters over de euro | Samenstelling en redactie | Hans van de Waarsenburg
19 × 11.5 cm.; pp. [36].

Stapled cream wrappers; front cover lettered in red, white and black and orange with an abstract watercolour image of a sun shining on a riverside village; back cover lettered in black.

Published by Gemeente Maastricht, 2001; printed by MTB, Maastricht.

Contents: [untitled poem published later as 'A Keen for the Coins'], p. [13].

Notes: 1. The pamphlet is accompanied by a set of 12 cards issued in decorated envelope; each card contains one poem by each author. (15 × 4.5 cm.)
2. See 'A Keen for the Coins' (A82).

B220 THE BAG APRON 2001

THE BAG APRON | or, The Poet and His Community | [thick rule] | The Inaugural Lecture of the Ireland Chair of Poetry | by | John Montague | with Introductory Remarks by | Seamus Heaney
21 × 15 cm.; 40 pp.

Sewn grey paper wrappers; front cover lettered in silver; back cover blank; front and back flaps lettered in silver.

Published by the Lagan Press, 2001; printed by Eastwood Printing, Belfast, in a limited edition of 750 numbered copies, numbers 1–50 have been signed and are not for sale.

Contents: 'Introductory Remarks', pp. 9–13.

Note: Seamus Heaney's 'Introductory Remarks' appear under the title: 'Remarks at the Announcement of John Montague's Appointment to the post of Ireland Professor of Poetry, 14th May, 1998'.

B221 LAST BEFORE AMERICA 2001

Essays in honour of Michael Allen | Last before America | Irish and American Writing | edited by | Fran Brearton and Eamonn Hughes | THE | BLACKSTAFF | PRESS | [short rule] | BELFAST
23.5 × 15.5 cm.; pp. xiv, 234.

Blue paper wrappers; front cover lettered in brown, dark blue, light blue and tan over *Dawn, Killary Harbour* by Paul Henry (painting wraps around spine to back quarter); back cover lettered in tan and black; spine lettered in light blue, dark blue and black.

Published 2001; printed by ColourBooks Ltd.

Contents: 'The Two Mice', pp. 29–35.

Note: 'A fable translated by Seamus Heaney from the fifteenth-century Scots of Robert Henryson.'

B222 ITALO CALVINO 2001

[rule] | *Modern Critical Views* | [rule] | ITALO CALVINO | *Edited and with an introduction by* | Harold Bloom | Sterling Professor of the Humanities | Yale University | CHELSEA HOUSE PUBLISHERS | Philadelphia

23.5 × 15.5 cm.; pp. vii, 129.

Cream cloth-covered boards with black leather spine; front cover blank; back cover stamped in gold; spine stamped in gold; dust-jacket lettered in white and black; front cover has a photograph of Italo Calvino against an image of stars.

Published 2001; no printer specified.

Contents: 'The Sensual Philosopher: *Mr. Palomar*', pp. 77–80.

Note: Reprint of 'The Sensual Philosopher' (C416).

B223 THE POET'S DANTE 2001

The Poet's Dante | [short rule] | *Edited* | *by* | *Peter S. Hawkins* | *and* | *Rachel Jacoff* | [short rule] | Farrar, Straus and Giroux | New York

21 × 13.5 cm.; pp. xxvi, 406.

Maroon paper-covered boards with black paper spine; front and back covers blank; spine lettered in gold; dust-jacket decorated in maroon and black and lettered in yellow and brown; front cover image, *Dante in his Study* by Tom Phillips.

Published 2001; no printer specified.

Contents: 'Envies and Identifications: Dante and the Modern Poet', pp. 239–258.

B224 WHEN HOPE AND HISTORY RHYME 2002

a. *trade edition*

When Hope and History Rhyme | [short rule] | *The* NUI, *Galway* | *Millennium Lecture Series* | Ruth Curtis | EDITOR | [publisher's logo] | FOUR COURTS PRESS

23.5 × 15.5 cm.; pp. 80.

Maroon paper-covered boards; front and back covers blank; spine stamped in gold; dust-jacket has photographs of lecture series participants and title in outline letters on front cover; back cover has National University of Ireland, Galway, coat-of-arms; spine lettered in white.

Published 2002; printed by Betaprint Ltd, Dublin.

Contents: '*Us* as in Versus: Poetry and the World', pp. 49–66.

b. ***limited edition***

500 numbered copies were also issued in a red cloth-covered slip-case stamped in gold on the front cover, back over and spine blank. Numbered in ink in an embossed seal on front page.

Contents: Same as B224a.

B225 AMID OUR TROUBLES 2002

AMID OUR TROUBLES | Irish Versions of Greek Tragedy | Edited by | Marianne McDonald and | J. Michael Walton | Introduction by | Declan Kiberd | Methuen
23.5 × 15 cm.; pp. xiii, 291.

Black cloth-covered boards; front and back covers blank; spine lettered in silver; black dust-jacket lettered in white and gold with photograph of a Greek statue on the front.

Published 2002; printed by Creative Print and Design, Wales.

Contents: 'The Cure at Troy: Production Notes in No Particular Order', pp. 171–180.

B226 THE DEBATEABLE LAND 2002

The | Debateable | Land | [all of the preceding in yellow outline letters] | Ireland's | border counties | Edited by | Brian S Turner
23.5 × 15.5 cm.; 96 pp.

Glossy paper wrappers, front cover lettered in orange, black and white over colour photograph of castle; back cover lettered in black with colour photograph of Seamus Heaney; orange spine lettered in black.

Published 2002 by The Ulster Local History Trust; printed by W.&G. Baird.

Contents: 'Keeping the Accent', pp. 11–18.

B227 HOPKINS VARIATIONS 2002

HOPKINS VARIATIONS | *Standing round a Waterfall* | JOAQUIN KUHN | AND | JOSEPH J. FEENEY, S. J. | EDITORS | SAINT JOSEPH'S UNIVERSITY PRESS | PHILADELPHIA | AND | FORDHAM UNIVERSITY PRESS | NEW YORK
21.5 × 14 cm.; pp. xxi, 311.

Grey cloth-covered boards; front and back covers blank; spine lettered in silver; grey endpapers; dust-jacket has photograph of a waterfall on front cover and is lettered in white outline letters.

Published 2002; no printer specified.

Contents: ' "INCERTUS" as GMH as Seamus Heaney', pp. 3–4.

Note: Seamus Heaney's contribution includes a brief prose note on Hopkins and his relation to his own work and the poems 'October Thought' and 'Seeing the Sick'.

B228 CHILDHOOD AND ITS DISCONTENTS 2002

CHILDHOOD | AND ITS DISCONTENTS | *The First Seamus Heaney Lectures* | *Edited by* | Joseph Dunne *and* James Kelly | The Liffey Press | Dublin
23 × 15.5 cm.; pp. xvi, 224.

Glossy paper wrappers; front cover illustration *A Boy Blowing Bubbles* by Walter Osborne, back cover lettered in black over blue white background; white spine lettered in black and blue.

Published 2002; printed by Colour Books Ltd.

Contents: 'Foreword', pp. [xiii]–xvi.

B229 THE BEST SPIRITUAL WRITING 2002 2002

THE BEST | SPIRITUAL | WRITING | 2002 | EDITED BY | PHILIP ZALESKI | INTRODUCTION BY NATALIE GOLDBERG | [publisher's logo] | HarperSanFrancisco | *A Division of HarperCollinsPublisher*
20.5 × 13 cm.; pp. xix, 281.

Oatmeal-textured paper wrappers; front cover lettered in black, gold, white and dark red; back cover lettered in black and dark red; spine lettered and decorated in gold, dark red and white.

Published 2002; no printer specified.

Contents: 'A Dream of Solstice', pp. 85–86.

B230 MIDSUMMER FEAST 2002

Midsummer Feast | Incline Press: Oldham: 2002
23 × 15 cm.; pp. 42.

Marbled paper-covered boards with leather quarter spine; front cover pasted title plate; back cover blank; spine pasted title plate.

Published and printed by Oldham Press, England in an edition of 230 numbered copies. The colour and pattern of the marbled paper-covered boards and leather quarter spine vary throughout the print run.

Contents: 'A Snapshot', p. 11; 'Rookery', p. 12; 'from Sharping Stone', p. 15; 'The Wishing Tree', p. 16; 'A Peacock's Feather (for Daisy Garnett)', pp. 22–23; 'Sister Clare', p. 25; 'Watercolour', p. 28; 'The Clothes Shrine (for Marie)', p. 31; 'Santiago de Compostela', p. 33; 'An Epithalamium for Rose and Tom', pp. 35–40; '–and for George', p. 41.

Note: Published in celebration of an extended family gathering of which Seamus Heaney took part.

B231 THE CLIFDEN ANTHOLOGY 2002

THE CLIFDEN ANTHOLOGY | Edited by Brendan Flynn | Clifden Community Arts Week | *2002*
21 × 15 cm.; 138 pp.

Bronze paper wrappers; front cover lettered in black and white with cover image of a child pulling back a curtain; back cover lettered in black and white with partial continuation of cover image; spine lettered in black and white.

Published 2002: printed by ColourBooks Ltd.

Contents: 'Raftery's Killeadan', pp. 66–67.

Note: Seamus Heaney's translation from the Irish of Antoine Raftery (1784–1835).

B232 JAN HENDRIX, DIARIO DE FATIGAS 2002

Jan Hendrix | diario de fatigas [the preceding all on one line] | Seamus Heaney | Issa Maria Benitez
25 × 22 cm.; pp. 160.

Designed in grey and black paper wrappers; front cover lettered in black; spine and back cover blank.

Published by Turner/ Fundacion Cultural Artencion, 2002; printed in Spain.

Contents: 'Ramifications: A Note on Jan Hendrix' [bilingual], pp. 7–11.

B233 TO STANLEY KUNITZ, WITH LOVE 2002

TO STANLEY KUNITZ, | WITH LOVE | From Poet Friends | for his 96th birthday | THE SHEEP MEADOW PRESS | RIVERDALE-ON-HUDSON, NEW YORK
23 × 15 cm.; pp. 160.

Black paper wrappers; front cover lettered in white with photograph of Stanley Kunitz; back cover lettered in red and white; spine lettered in white with red short rule.

Published 2002; no printer specified.

Contents: 'The Boiling House', p. 29.

B234 BELIEVING IN ACTION 2002

Believing in Action | *The first thirty years* | *of Concern* | *1968–1998* | Tony Farmar| A. & A. Farmar
21.5 × 14 cm.; pp. viii, 248.

Glossy paper wrappers; front cover lettered in burgundy, white and black with photograph of child; back cover purple; spine lettered in white.

Published 2002; printed by ColourBooks.

Contents: 'Foreword', pp. 1–3.

B235 POEMS FOR REFUGEES 2003

Pippa Haywood (ed.) | POEMS FOR REFUGEES | With a foreword by Martin Jarvis | [publisher's logo] | VINTAGE
20 × 13 cm.; xiv, 226.

Paper wrappers; front cover with colour photograph of a child in a refugee camp lettered in orange, red, and white; back cover lettered in orange, black and white; red spine lettered in white and orange.

Published 2002; printed by Cox & Wyman Ltd, Reading, Berkshire.

Contents: 'Chosen by Seamus Heaney', pp. 93–94.

Note: Seamus Heaney comments on 'To a Mouse' by Robert Burns.

B236 101 POEMS AGAINST WAR 2003

101 POEMS AGAINST WAR | *edited by* | MATTHEW HOLLIS | *and* | PAUL KEEGAN | ff | *faber and faber*
19.5 × 12.5 cm.; 156 pp.

Bright-red paper wrappers; front cover lettered in white and blue with lower third of cover in blue; back cover lettered in blue and white; spine lettered in white.

Published 2003; printed by Mackays of Chatham plc, Chatham, England.

Contents: 'Sophoclean', p. 15; 'Testimony', p 113.

B237 IRISH WRITERS AGAINST WAR 2003

IRISH | WRITERS | AGAINST | WAR | Edited by | Conor Kostick and Katherine Moore | [publisher's logo] | THE O'BRIEN PRESS | DUBLIN

Paper wrappers; front cover lettered in white and black with photograph in green tones of anti-war protesters; back cover in green tones lettered in black and white; spine lettered in white and yellow.
19.5 × 13 cm.; 144 pp.

Published 2003; printed by The Woodprintcraft Group Ltd.

Contents: 'News of the Raven (adapted from *Beowulf*)', pp. 53–54.

Note: This is a newly revised version of lines 2897–3028 from Seamus Heaney's translation of *Beowulf*.

B238 PERIPHERY – CENTRE 2003

ACTA PHILOSOPHICA UNIVERSITATIS LULENSIS | Luleå Studies in the Arts and Social Sciences 3 | *Seamus Heaney – Folke Isaksson:* |*Periferi – centrum* | *Periphery – Centre* | *Seamus Heaney and Folke*

Isaksson | *on their Backgrounds and Art* | *Editor/Redaktör* | *Gunnar Persson* | Luleå 2003 | SWEDISH SCIENCE PRESS
24 × 17 cm.; 152 pp.

Light-green paper wrappers; front cover lettered in black with cover illustration by Hilda Persson of a small boy staring into a lake; back cover lettered in black with a colour photograph of Gunnar Persson; spine lettered in black.

Published 2003; printed by The Printing Office of Lulea University of Technology.

Contents: 'The Guttural Muse is a Global Age', pp. 5–17; *Crediting Poetry*, pp. 33–48.

Note: This bilingual publication appears in conjunction with the Nobel Prize Centenary and Seamus Heaney's visit to the Luleå University of Technology.

B239 THE WAY YOU SAY THE WORLD 2003

The Way You Say | The World | a celebration for | ANNE STEVENSON | compiled by John Lucas and Matt Simpson | Shoestring [publisher's logo] Press
21 × 15cm.; pp. 224.

Green paper wrappers; front cover lettered in white over *Window*, a watercolour by Pauline Lucas; back cover lettered in black; spine lettered in black.

Published 2003; no printer specified.

Contents: 'A Note-Spurt', pp. 64–65.

Note: The subtitle of Heaney's contribution is: 'Five Poems from the Old Irish.' They are: 1. 'The Blackbird of Belfast Lough'; 2. 'Comcille's Derry'; 3. 'The Monk's Tryst'; 4. 'Grainne's Words about Diarmait'; 5. 'North-East'.

B240 WAXWING POEMS 2003

Waxwing Poems | from the House of Icarus | 20: February 2003 |[all of the preceding above green rule] | [the following lettered within blue in orange rectangle] *these cards are sent as a cry* | *against the ongoing violence of* | *our times: and they are an at-* | *tempt to stay in touch:* |[the following over green rule] | Seamus Heaney | [the following in black ruled square box] | *John F. Deane* | 24 The Heath | Cypress Downs | Dublin 6W | Ireland

Card folded to: 21 × 15 cm.; pp. [4].

Cream stock paper; title-page [above] serves as cover; back cover lettered in black with blue rectangular lines continued from front cover with John F. Deane's poem, 'The Visitor' and colour photograph of a flower.

Published 2003; no printer specified.

Contents: 'Nonce Words', p. [2].

C

CONTRIBUTIONS TO PERIODICALS

1959

C1 REAPING IN HEAT [poem]
OCTOBER THOUGHT [poem]
Both by 'Incertus'.
Q, Michaelmas 1959: 27.

C2 NOSTALGIA IN THE AFTERNOON [poem]
By 'Incertus'.
Gorgon, November 1959: 17.

1960

C3 ARAN [poem]
By Seamus J. Heaney.
Gorgon, February 1960: 7.

C4 LINES TO MYSELF [poem]
By Seamus Heaney.
Gorgon, December 1960: no page number.

1961

C5 THE SEDUCTIVE MUSE [editorial]
By Seamus J. Heaney.
SONG OF MY MAN-ALIVE [poem]
By 'Incertus'.
THERE'S ROSEMARY . . . [short story]
By 'Incertus'.
Gorgon, Hilary Term, 1961: 4–6, 19, 29–32.

C6 SHALL WE JIVE THIS JIG? [essay]
By Seamus J. Heaney.
Irish Digest, April 1961: 10–12.
Seamus Heaney discusses modern dancing and the ceilidhe.

C7 HER HOME [poem]
By 'Incertus'.
Gorgon, Michaelmas Term, 1961: 18.

C8 MODERN, FUNCTIONAL, BEAUTIFUL [essay]
By Seamus J. Heaney.

Newman, Michaelmas Term, 1961: 9–11.
On the new chapel at St. Joseph's Training College for Post-Graduate Training.

1962

C9 TRACTORS [poem]
By Seamus J. Heaney.
Belfast Telegraph, 24 November 1962: 5.

C10 TURKEYS OBSERVED [poem]
Belfast Telegraph, 15 December 1962: 5.
By Seamus J. Heaney.

1963

C11 SCOTCH FIR IN CITY CEMETERY [poem]
Going in [poem]
Interest, January 1963 : 13.

C12 MID-TERM BREAK [poem]
Kilkenny Magazine, spring 1963: 25.

C13 AN ADVANCEMENT OF LEARNING [poem]
Irish Times, 9 March 1963: 8.
Collected with revisions in *Death of a Naturalist*.

C14 OUR OWN DOUR WAY [essay]
Hibernia, April 1963: 15.
On literary magazines and publishing in Northern Ireland and the Republic of Ireland.
Hibernia was published in Dublin.
This essay was reprinted as an editorial in *Trench* (St. Joseph's Training College) April 1964: 3–4.

C15 ESSENCES [poem]
WELFARE STATE [poem]
Interest, May 1963: 16.

C16 POOR MAN'S DEATH [poem]
Dubliner, summer 1963: 54.

C17 THE IMMORTAL NEWSMEN [review]
Hibernia, July 1963: 17.

Review of *Later Poems* by Austin Clarke; *Come Dance with Kitty Stobling* by Patrick Kavanagh; *Six Irish Poets* by Robin Skelton; *Another September* by Thomas Kinsella; *Forms of Exile* by John Montague; *Sailing to an Island* by Richard Murphy; *Lady and Gentleman* by Richard Weber.

C18 MACKENNA'S SATURDAY NIGHT [poem]
Kilkenny Magazine, autumn/winter 1963–1964: 17.

C19 POETS PROTEST [letter]
POETRY FROM A CO-OPERATIVE SOCIETY [review]
Hibernia, September 1963: 2, 15.
Seamus Heaney's letter responds to criticism of his review 'The Immortal Newsmen' (*Hibernia* July 1963, C17). James Liddy, Michael Harnett (*sic*) and Richard Weber had criticised Heaney in August, and Richard Weber replied to Heaney's letter in the October *Hibernia*.
The review is of *A Group Anthology* edited by Edward Lucie-Smith and Philip Hobsbaum.

1964

C20 FISHER [poem]
By James Heaney.
Irish Times, 8 February 1964: 10. This version of 'Fisher' differs from those of C23 and A42.

C21 THE INDOMITABLE IRISHRY [poem]
Poetry Ireland, spring 1964: 104.

C22 EASTER SON [poem]
English, spring 1964: 15.

C23 SUCH MEN ARE DANGEROUS [poem]
Fisher [poem]
Interest, May 1964: 9–10. This version of 'Fisher' differs from those of C20 and A42.

C24 THE BREAD OF TRUTH [essay]
Trench, June 1964: 5–6.
On the poetry of R. S. Thomas.

C25 THE PLAY WAY [poem]
Outposts, autumn 1964: 14. 'The Play Way' collected with revisions in *Death of a Naturalist*.

C26 EDUCATING THE EPSILONS [review]
Hibernia, September 1964: 10–11.
Review of *English for the Rejected* by David Holbrook.

C27 WRITER AND TEACHER [poem]
YOUNG BACHELOR [poem]
SOLILOQUY FOR AN OLD RESIDENT [poem]
Interest, November 1964: 16–17.

C28 DIGGING [poem]
STORM ON THE ISLAND [poem]
SCAFFOLDING [poem]
New Statesman, 4 December 1964: 880.

C29 THE FOLK SINGERS [poem]
Envoi, 24, 1964: 10.

1965

C30 ST. FRANCIS AND THE BIRDS [poem]
Irish Times, 9 January 1965: 8.

C31 TWICE SHY [poem]
Listener, 28 January 1965: 156.
Collected with revisions in *Death of a Naturalist*.

C32 TROUT [poem]
Listener, 4 February 1965: 193.

C33 WRITER AND TEACHER [poem]
Irish Times, 20 February 1965: 8.

C34 END OF A NATURALIST [poem]
VALEDICTION [poem]
Poetry Ireland, spring 1965: 8–9.
'End of a Naturalist' collected with revisions as 'Death of a Naturalist' in *Eleven Poems* and *Death of a Naturalist*.

C35 POOR WOMEN IN A CITY CHURCH [poem]
DOCKER [poem]

Dublin Magazine, spring 1965: 69.
The poems appeared under the title 'Belfast Snapshots'.

C36 THE EARLY PURGES [poem]
TAKING STOCK [poem]
Kilkenny Magazine, spring 1965: 42–43.

C37 IN SMALL TOWNLANDS [poem]
Interest, March 1965: 48.
Collected with revisions in *Death of a Naturalist*.

C38 POEMS-PENNY EACH [review]
Trench, March 1965: 26.
Review of poems by Austin Clarke, Tony Connor and Charles Tomlinson.

C39 PERSONAL HELICON [poem]
New Statesman, 19 March 1965: 446.

C40 ON HOGARTH'S ENGRAVING 'PIT TICKET FOR THE ROYAL SPORT' [poem]
Irish Times, 10 April 1965: 8.

C41 IN SMALL TOWNLANDS [poem]
New Statesman, 16 April 1965: 611.

C42 SAINT PATRICK'S STONE [poem]
CONFESSIONS AND HISTORIES [review]
Outposts, summer 1965: 3; 21–23.
Review of *Confessions and Histories* by Edward Lucie-Smith; *Selected Poems* by Anne Sexton; *77 Dream Songs* by John Berryman; *The Arctic Ox* by Marianne Moore. 'Saint Patrick's Stone' is reprinted in *Salute to Outposts on Its Fiftieth Anniversary* (B151).

C43 EVANGELISTS [review]
New Statesman, 9 July 1965: 54–55.
Review of *How Children Fail* by John Holt and *Experiments in Education at Sevenoaks* [Seamus Heaney is not listed as the author of the review].

C44 MID-TERM BREAK [poem]
Listener, 29 July 1965: 158.

C45 BLACKBERRY PICKING [poem]
SYNGE ON ARAN [poem]
New Statesman, 30 July 1965: 156.
Both poems collected with revisions in *Death of Naturalist.*

C46 LINT WATER [poem]
Times Literary Supplement, 5 August 1965: 681.

C47 A CHESTER PAGEANT [essay]
Use of English, autumn 1965: 58–60.

C48 THE BARN [poem]
LOVERS ON ARAN [poem]
WATERFALL [poem]
ANCESTRAL PHOTOGRAPH [poem]
Vogue, 1 September 1965: 134–135.
'The Barn', 'Waterfall' and 'Ancestral Photograph' collected with revisions in *Death of a Naturalist.*

C49 KICKING AGAINST THE CODE [review]
New Statesman, 12 November 1965: 748.
Review of *English Versus Examinations* edited by Brian Jackson, and *Escape from the Classroom* by R. F. Mackenzie.

C50 TIED AND TAPED [review]
New Statesman, 26 November 1965: 848.
Review of *Talking to Women* by Nell Dunn and *Five Women* by Tony Parker.

C51 FOLLOWER [poem]
New Statesman, 3 December 1965: 888.

C52 THE DIVINER [poem]
Poetry Supplement, Poetry Book Society, Christmas 1965: [5].
Collected with revisions in *Death of a Naturalist.*

C53 IN SMALL TOWNLANDS [poem]
THE EARLY PURGES [poem]
POEM [poem]
Northern Review, vol. 1, no. 2, [1965]: 7–8.

1966

C54 THE SALMON FISHER TO THE SALMON [poem]
PROSPERO IN AGONY [review]
Outposts, spring 1966: 1; 21–23.
Review of *For the Union Dead* by Robert Lowell. 'The Salmon Fisher to the Salmon', collected with revisions in *Door into the Dark*.

C55 THE PENINSULA [poem]
GATE [poem]
Dublin Magazine, spring 1966: 38. 'The Peninsula' was collected with revisions in *Door into the Dark*.

C56 HONEYMOON FLIGHT [poem]
Kilkenny Magazine, spring/summer 1966: 19.

C57 FOR A YOUNG NUN [poem]
Tomorrow, March 1966: 7.

C58 DAWN SHOOT [poem]
New Statesman, 1 April 1966: 473.

C59 CANA REVISITED [poem]
Irish Times, Saturday, 8 and 9 April 1966: 8.

C60 FOR THE COMMANDER OF 'THE ELIZA' [poem]
THE PENINSULA [poem]
Cambridge Review, 7 May 1966: 389.
'For the Commander of "The Eliza" ' collected with revisions in *Death of a Naturalist*. 'The Peninsula' was collected with revisions in *Door into the Dark*.

C61 THE FORGE [poem]
The Times Literary Supplement, 19 May 1966: 426.
Collected with revisions in *Door into the Dark*.

C62 THAW [poem]
Irish Times, 28 May 1966: 8.

C63 REQUIEM FOR THE CROPPIES [poem]
GIRLS BATHING, GALWAY 1965 [poem]
[Review]
Dublin Magazine, summer 1966: 48–49; 91–92.

'Requiem for the Croppies' and 'Girls Bathing, Galway 1965' were both collected with revisions in *Door into the Dark*. Review of *Selected Poems* by John Heath-Stubbs, *American Scenes* by Charles Tomlinson and *The Striders* by A. K. Ramanujan.

C64 ARIES [poem]
Encounter, June 1966: 40.

C65 PERSEPHONE [poem]
Cambridge Review, 4 June 1966: 464.
Collected with revisions under title of 'Rite of Spring' in *Door into the Dark*.

C66 JACOB AND JOSIE [review]
New Statesman, 17 June 1966: 899.
Review of *Folktales of Ireland* translated and edited by Sean O'Sullivan and *The Outer Hebrides and Their Legends* by Otta Swire.

C67 OUT OF LONDON: ULSTER'S TROUBLES [essay]
New Statesman, 1 July 1966: 23–24.

C68 WORDS AND RHYMES [review]
Times Literary Supplement, 14 July 1966: 616.
Unsigned review of *The Northern Fiddler* by Brian Higgins; *The Mind has Mountains* by Elizabeth Jennings; *Pieta* by R. S. Thomas; *The Burning Hare* by J. C. Hall; *Fables from Life* by W. Price Turner.

C69 ROOKERY [poem]
ORANGE DRUMS, TYRONE 1966 [poem]
Listener, 29 September 1966: 475.
'Orange Drums, Tyrone 1966' collected with revisions as part 3 of 'Singing School' in *North*.

C70 ANTAEUS [poem]
Hibernia, October 1966: 17.
Collected with revisions in *North*.

C71 RELIC OF MEMORY [poem]
MAY DAY [poem]
AUBADE [poem]
New Statesman, 14 October 1966: 556.

'Relic of Memory' collected with revisions in *Door into the Dark*. 'May Day' collected as part I of 'A Retrospect' in *Seeing Things*.

C72 POOR WHITES [review]
New Statesman, 2 December 1966: 840–841.
Review of *Realities of Irish Life* by W. Steuart Trench, and *The South As It Is* by John Richard Dennett.

C73 TRIPTYCH FOR THE EASTER BATTLERS [poem]
The New Statesman, 23 December 1966: 942.

C74 AT A POTATO DIGGING [poem]
New Ireland, 1966: 37–38.
Collected with revisions in *Death of a Naturalist*.

C75 BLACKBERRY-PICKING [poem]
CHURNING DAY [poem]
Critical Quarterly Poetry Supplement Number 7, 1966: 8–9.

1967

C76 WRITER AT WORK [essay]
THE FORGE [poem]
St. Stephen's, Hilary Term, 1967: 20–21.
'Writer at Work' and 'The Forge' were reprinted in *The Honest Ulsterman*, December 1968: 13–14.

C77 BOY DRIVING HIS FATHER TO CONFESSION [poem]
ELEGY FOR A STILL-BORN CHILD [poem]
THE OUTLAW [poem]
Phoenix, March 1967: 35–37.
This is the first appearance of 'Boy Driving his Father to Confession'; it was published separately with revisions in December 1970 (A7); it was collected in *Poems and a Memoir* (A32). 'Elegy for a Still-born Child' was reprinted in *Room to Rhyme* and collected in *Door into the Dark*. 'The Outlaw' first appeared in the *Cheltenham Festival of Literature*, October 3–8, 1966: 43 (D2).

C78 FOLLOWER [poem]
SCAFFOLDING [poem]
Threshold, summer 1967: 31–32.

C79 THE WIFE'S TALE [poem]
Phoenix, summer 1967: 10–11.
Collected with revisions in *Door into the Dark*.

C80 SOUTH DERRY EVENING [poem]
Hibernia, July 1967: 21.

C81 KILLING TIME [review]
Listener, 19 October 1967: 508.
Review of *Gladiators* by Michael Grant; *Gurkhas* by David Bolt; *Highwaymen* by Christopher Hibbert; *Nihilists* by Ronald Hingley.

C82 CORNCRAKE [poem]
BOGLAND [poem]
Listener, 2 November 1967: 573. 'Corncrake' collected with revisions in *Poems and a Memoir* (A32).

C83 A LOUGH NEAGH SEQUENCE [poem]
University Review, winter 1967: 286–290.
This is the first appearance of 'A Lough Neagh Sequence'; it was published separately in 1969 (A4).

C84 CHESTNUT TIME [poem]
Words, December 1967: no page number.

C85 IRISH EYES [review]
Listener, 28 December 1967: 851–853.
Review of *Dublin* by V. S. Pritchett; *Portrait of Dublin* by Desmond Guinness; *Ireland: Munster* edited by Sean Jennett; *Irish Gardens* by Edward Hyams.

C86 [UNTITLED REVIEW] [review]
Northern Review, 1967: 50–52.
Review of *Wodwo* by Ted Hughes.

1968

C87 VICTORIAN GUITAR [poem]
Listener, 18 January 1968: 85.

C88 LAST LOOK [poem]
Outposts, spring 1968: 7.
Different from the poem of the same title collected in *Station Island*.

C89 THE PLANTATION [poem]
Phoenix, spring 1968: 16–17.

C90 UNDINE [poem]
NIGHT DRIVE [poem]
Listener, 11 April 1968: 474.

C91 CHILD LOST [poem]
THE SURVIVOR [poem]
Square Times, May 1968: 15.

C92 LAST LOOK [poem]
Broadsheet 4 [May 1968]: [single leaf].
Different from the poem of the same title collected in *Station Island*. Hayden Murphy's *Broadsheet* was published in Dublin.

C93 SHORELINE [poem]
Phoenix, summer/autumn: 1968: 13.
Collected with revisions in *Door into the Dark*.

C94 BACHELOR DECEASED [poem]
Honest Ulsterman, June 1968: 5.

C95 FROGMAN [poem]
Listener, 4 July 1968: 11.

C96 BACKWARD LOOKS [review]
Manchester Guardian, 5 July 1968: 7.
Review of *The Autobiography of William Carleton Penny in the Clouds* by Austin Clarke.

C97 CANTICLES TO THE EARTH [review]
Listener, 22 August 1968: 245–246.
Review of *Collected Poems* by Theodore Roethke.

C98 DRIVING IN THE SMALL HOURS [poem]
Poetry Review, autumn 1968: 166–167.

C99 A GATHERING OF POEMS [review]
Irish Press, 28 September 1968: 10.
Review of *Collected Poems 1932–1967* by John Hewitt.

C100 THE THATCHER [poem]
Honest Ulsterman, October 1968: 3.

C101 CIVIL RIGHTS, NOT CIVIL WEEKS [essay]
Gown, 22 October 1968: 5.

C102 OLD DERRY'S WALLS [essay]
Listener, 24 October 1968: 521–523.

C103 THE IMPORTANCE OF BEING MICHEAL [interview]
BIRDWATCHER [poem]
Everyman, no. 1, 1968: 10–13, 126.
'Seamus Heaney interviews the Irish actor Micheal Mac Liammoir on the Arts in Ireland.' Heaney is listed on the Editorial Board. This is a different version of 'Birdwatcher' than that of (C120).

C104 PERSEPHONE [poem]
Broadsheet 2, 1968: [single leaf].
Published for the Poetry Workshop, University College, Dublin; edited by Richard Ryan.

1969

C105 SHORE WOMAN [poem]
Irish Press, 1 March 1969: 7.
Collected with revisions in *Wintering Out*.

C106 WHINLANDS [poem]
BANN CLAY [poem]
Listener, 24 April 1969: 571.

C107 IN AN AIRPORT COACH [poem]
Honest Ulsterman, May 1969: 16.

C108 GOOD-NIGHT [poem]
Listener, 22 May 1969: 729. Collected with revisions in *Wintering Out*.

C109 FOREWORD [essay]
THE POETRY OF JOHN HEWITT [review]
Threshold, summer 1969: [3]; 73–77.
Review of *Collected Poems 1932–67* by John Hewitt.
Seamus Heaney was also the editor of this issue.

C110 SEAMUS HEANEY WRITES . . . [essay]
Poetry Book Society Bulletin, summer 1969: [1].
On *Door into the Dark*.

C111 AT ARDBOE POINT [poem]
BLOOD BROTHERS [review]
Phoenix, summer 1969: 6, 30–31.
Review of *Selected Poems* by Louis Simpson.

C112 CELTIC FRINGE, VIKING FRINGE [review]
Listener, 21 August 1969: 254–255.
Review of *An Orkney Tapestry* by George Mackay Brown and of *Conor Cruise O'Brien Introduces Ireland* by Conor Cruise O'Brien.

C113 SERENADES [poem]
MIDNIGHT [poem]
NAVVY [poem]
FIRST CALF [poem]
MEDALLION [poem]
ICON [poem]
IDYLL [poem]
Listener, 4 September 1969: 311.
'Serenades', 'Midnight', 'Navvy' and 'First Calf' collected with revisions in *Wintering Out*.

C114 A WINTER'S TALE [poem]
Listener, 30 October 1969: 592.
Collected with revisions in *Wintering Out*.

C115 TURNIP MAN [poem]
HIGH STREET, 1786 [poem] (see C118)
FROM CAVE HILL [poem]
SEPTEMBER SONG [poem]
Honest Ulsterman, November 1969: 4–6.

The poems were numbered one to four and published under the title 'Offerings'. 'High Street, 1786' was collected with revisions as 'Linen Town' in *Wintering Out*. This 'September Song' is uncollected. It is not the same as the poem of the same title published in *The Honest Ulsterman*, January/February 1977 (C249) and subsequently collected in *Field Work*.

C116 DELIRIUM OF THE BRAVE [review]
Listener, 27 November 1969: 757, 759.
Review of *The Year of Liberty* by Thomas Pakenham.
'Seamus Heaney writes about the Ireland of Wolfe Tone and the persistence of anachronistic passions.'

C117 MAIGHDEAN MARA [poem]
AN EVENING AT KILLARD [poem]
The Irish Press, 29 November 1969: 9.
'Maighdean Mara' collected with revisions in *Wintering Out*. (See C156, C157, C159.)

C118 HIGH STREET, BELFAST, 1786 [poem] (see 103)
TWEED [poem]
DAWN [poem]
Critical Quarterly, winter 1969: 293–295.
The three poems were collected in *Wintering Out*: 'High Street, Belfast, 1786' was collected with revisions as 'Linen Town'; 'Tweed' appears under the title 'The Wool Trade'.

C119 THEIR BROTHER [poem]
CROWING MAN [poem]
LICTOR [poem]
Listener, 18 December 1969: 864.

C120 BIRDWATCHER [poem]
A TWILIGHT [poem]
ROOKERY [poem]
GOOD NIGHT [poem]
CORNCRAKE [poem]
three, 1969: 38.
'The poems in the magazine were written at different times over the last two years but Mr Heaney has put them together in sequence because he feels they all

contribute to a similar mood.' This version of 'Corncrake' is different from that of (C82) and (A32).

C121 YANK [poem]
Everyman, no. 2, 1969: 14–15.

C122 UNDINE [poem]
Broadsheet 3, 1969: [single leaf].
Published for the Poetry Workshop, University College, Dublin; edited by Richard Ryan.

C123 THE WIFE'S TALE [poem]
UNDINE [poem]
THE FORGE [poem]
Critical Quarterly Poetry Supplement Number 10, 1969: 2–3.

1970

C124 LIMBO [poem]
ELEGY FOR A POSTMAN [poem]
Listener, 5 February 1970: 182.

C125 DREAM OF THE TRENCHES [poem]
Broadsheet 7, March 1970: [single leaf].
Collected with revisions as 'Veteran's Dream' in *Wintering Out*.

C126 THE LAST MUMMER [poem]
The Honest Ulsterman, March/April, 1970: 15.
The table of contents lists the poem as 'Last Summer'. A revised version of 'The Last Mummer' appeared in *The Honest Ulsterman* (C149) and the poem was collected with further revisions in *Wintering Out*.

C127 KING CONCHOBOR AND HIS KNIGHTS [review]
Listener, 26 March 1970: 416–417.
Review of *The Tain* translated by Thomas Kinsella.

C128 NAVVY [poem]
FIRST CALF [poem]
Capella 4, April 1970: 26–27.
'Navvy' collected with revisions in *Wintering Out*.

C129 THIRD DEGREE [poem]
The New Statesman, 10 April 1970: 515.

C130 DREAM OF THE TRENCHES [poem]
The New Statesman, 17 April 1970: 557.
Collected with revisions as 'Veteran's Dream' in *Wintering Out*.

C131 SHORE WOMAN [poem]
Listener, 7 May 1970: 611.
Collected with revisions in *Wintering Out*.

C132 TINDER [poem]
New Statesman, 15 May 1970: 704.
Collected with revisions in *Wintering Out*.

C133 WEDDING DAY [poem]
Phoenix, summer 1970: 5. Collected with revisions in *Wintering Out*. See also D6.

C134 RETORT [poem]
THE LAST MUMMER [poem]
ICON [poem]
Michigan Quarterly Review, summer 1970: 165–167.
'The Last Mummer', collected as part 1 of 'The Last Mummer' in *Wintering Out*.

C135 THE TOLLUND MAN [poem]
Threshold, summer 1970: 5–6.
Collected with revisions in *Wintering Out*.

C136 LAST CAMP [poem]
New Statesman, 12 June 1970: 840.

C137 LAST MUMMER [poem]
NOCTURNE [poem]
Manchester Guardian, 9 July 1970: 11.

C138 VIEWS [essay]
Listener, 31 December 1970: 903.
Seamus Heaney writes about living in Berkeley, California.

C139 MUNRO [radio play]
Everyman, no. 3, 1970: 58–65. Heaney's verse play was written for the BBC and broadcast on 14 January 1970.

C140 AT ARDBOE POINT [poem]
SETTING [poem]
Ardboe, 1970: 38.

1971

C141 AS WE ROVED OUT [poem]
INTIMIDATION [poem]
NOCTURNE [poem]
RUBRIC [poem]
Malahat Review, January 1971: 33–36.
'As We Roved Out' collected with revisions in *Wintering Out* under the title 'Augury'.

C142 SEAMUS HEANEY PRAISES LOUGH ERNE [essay]
Listener, 4 February 1971: 142–143.
Transcript of conversation with John Reihill, Tommy Gunn and T. P. Flanagan, originally broadcast on Radio 4.

C143 A MIDSUMMER [poem]
MUSEUM PIECES FOR MICHAEL S. HARPER [poem]
Irish Times, 13 February 1971: 5.

C144 HOME [poem]
New Yorker, 1 May 1971: 48.
Collected as section II of 'Summer Home' in *Wintering Out*.

C145 MAY [poem]
BYE-CHILD [poem]
The Irish Press, 7 August 1971: 9.
'May' and 'Bye-Child' collected with revisions in *Wintering Out*. Different version of 'Bye-Child' previously collected in *Twelve to Twelve* (B6).

C146 THE SMELL [poem]
Occident, fall 1971: 49.
Collected with revisions as section I of 'Summer Home' in *Wintering Out*.

C147 CRAIG'S DRAGOONS (AIR: 'DOLLY'S BRAE') [poem]
Review, autumn/winter, 1971–1972: 47.
The poem appears in Karl Miller's essay 'Opinion'.

C148 WHATEVER YOU SAY, SAY NOTHING – SEAMUS HEANEY GIVES HIS VIEW ON THE IRISH THING [poem]
Listener, 14 October 1971: 496–497.
Collected with revisions as 'Whatever You Say, Say Nothing' in *North*; part 4 forms the introductory poem to *Wintering Out*.

C149 SERVANT BOY [poem]
THE LAST MUMMER [poem]
LETTER TO AN EDITOR [verse letter]
Honest Ulsterman, November/December 1971: 5–7.
An earlier version 'The Last Mummer' had appeared in *The Honest Ulsterman* (C126); the poem was collected with revisions in *Wintering Out*. The 'Letter to an Editor' is a playful protest against editorial comments directed at Heaney which had appeared in *The Honest Ulsterman*.

C150 EASY RIDER [poem]
Atlantis, November 1971: 50.
Collected under the title 'Westering' in *Wintering Out*.

C151 A POET'S CHILDHOOD [essay]
Listener, 11 November 1971: 660–661.
'From "People at Work," a Northern Ireland Schools Radio Programme.'

C152 AUBADE [poem]
New Yorker, 27 November 1971: 47.
Collected as a section of 'Summer Home' in *Wintering Out*.

C153 SLIEVE GALLON'S BRAE [poem]
Broadsheet 13, December 1971: [single leaf].

C154 WHATEVER YOU SAY, SAY NOTHING [poem]
Irish Press, 11 December 1971: 9.
Collected with revisions in *North*.

C155 A NORTHERN HOARD [poem]
Hibernia, 17 December 1971: 21.
Collected with revisions in *Wintering Out*.

C156 BELFAST'S BLACK CHRISTMAS [essay]
Listener, 23 December 1971: 857–858.
Collected as Part 2 of 'Belfast' in *Preoccupations*.

C157 THE TOLLUND MAN [poem]
MAIGHDEAN MARA [poem] (see C117)
Poetry Supplement, Poetry Book Society, Christmas 1971: [2]–[5].

C158 SEA-WIFE [poem] (see C117)
WOODCUT [poem]
Workshop 11 [1971]: 3–4.
'Sea-Wife' collected with revisions as 'Maighdean Mara' in *Wintering Out*.

C159 FATHER OF THE BRIDE [poem]
MOTHER OF THE GROOM [poem]
IN DEVON [poem]
Aquarius, no. 4, 1971: 44–45.
'In Devon' is the last section of 'Bone Dreams' collected in *North*.

C160 MAIGHDEAN MARA [poem]
LIMBO [poem]
AS WE ROVED OUT [poem]
Criterion, Galway 1971: 34–36.
'As We Roved Out' collected with revisions as 'Augury' in *Wintering Out*.

1972

C161 AFTER THE SYNGE-SONG—SEAMUS HEANEY ON THE WRITINGS OF PATRICK KAVANAGH [review]
Listener, 13 January 1972: 55–56.
Review of *The Green Fool* by Patrick Kavanagh.

C162 GIFTS OF RAIN [poem]
MAY [poem]
Poetry (Chicago), February 1972: 280–283.

C163 THE NATURALNESS OF *ULYSSES* [review]
Listener, 2 March 1972: 281–282.
Review of *Ulysses on the Liffey* by Richard Ellmann.

C164 FODDER [poem]
Times Literary Supplement, 17 March 1972: 314.

C165 ORACLE [poem]
TRADITIONS [poem]
BOG OAK [poem]
CAIRN-MAKER [poem]
NERTHUS [poem]
Listener, 23 March 1972: 372.
All five poems were collected in *Wintering Out*; 'Bog-Oak' and 'Cairn-Maker' collected with revisions.

C166 THE TRADE OF AN IRISH POET [essay]
THE BACKWARD LOOK [poem]
Manchester Guardian, 25 May 1972: 17.
'Seamus Heaney on the proposition: I am an Irish poet. What does that mean?' 'The Trade of an Irish Poet' was collected as '1972', part 3 of the essay 'Belfast' in *Preoccupations*.

C167 SHADOWED [poem]
THE BLINKER [poem]
ORANGE DRUMS, TYRONE 1966 [poem]
THE OTHER SIDE [poem]
Fortnight, July 1972: 20–21.
'Shadowed' is an early version of Part 1 of 'King of the Ditchbacks' collected in *Station Island*.

C168 ANAHORISH [poem]
TOOME [poem]
BROAGH [poem]
Stand, July 1972: 4–5.
The poems were published under the title 'Watermarks', which was dropped when they were collected with revisions, in *Wintering Out*.

C169 BONE DREAMS [poem]
Arts in Ireland, autumn 1972: 52–53.

Includes a prefatory note by Seamus Heaney. The poem is collected with revisions in *North*. See (C188).

C170 THE LABOURER AND THE LORD [review]
The Listener, 28 September 1972: 408–409.
Review of *Francis Ledwidge* by Alice Curtayne; *Lord Dunsany* by Mark Amory; *My Talks with Dean Spanley* and *The Curse of the Wise Woman* by Lord Dunsany.

C171 SCULLIONS [poem]
Irish Times, 7 October 1972: 9.

C172 TRADITION AND AN INDIVIDUAL TALENT [review]
Hibernia, 3 November 1972: 11.
Review of *The Hugh MacDiarmid Anthology* edited by Micheal Grieve and Alexander Scott.

C173 LAND [poem]
Hibernia, 17 November 1972: 15.

C174 GIFTS OF RAIN [poem]
Irish Press, 18 November 1972: 7.

C175 BOG QUEEN [poem]
Listener, 23 November 1972: 713.
Reprinted with revisions in *The James Joyce Quarterly*, spring 1974 (C196) and reprinted with further revisions in *Antaeus*, spring 1975 (C215).

C176 DEEP AS ENGLAND [review]
Hibernia, 1 December 1972: 13.
Review of *Selected Poems* by Ted Hughes.

C177 STAG OF THE CABBAGES [review]
Listener, 21 December 1972: 869.
Review *of The Leaping Hare* by George Ewart Evans and David Thomson.

1973

C178 VIOLENCE AND RESPONSE [review]
Hibernia, 19 January 1973: 13.
Review of *Gradual Wars* by Seamus Deane.

C179 A NEW LIFE [poem]
Listener, 22 February 1973: 239.
Of these four sonnets, the first and last were collected with revisions as 'Act of Union' in *North*. See also (C180).

C180 A NEW LIFE [poem]
Lynx, spring, 1973: 21.
Same version as (C179).

C181 PUNISHMENT [poem]
Broadsheet 17, March 1973: [1].
Revised version appeared in the *James Joyce Quarterly*, spring 1974 (C196); reprinted with further revisions in *The Listener*, 23 May 1974 (C200); collected with revisions in *North*.

C182 A QUESTION OF TASTE [review]
Irish Press, 7 April 1973: 10.
Review of *The Oxford Book of Twentieth Century English Verse* edited by Philip Larkin.

C183 POETIC SWEETNESS AND LIGHT IN CLASSROOM [review]
Education Times, 26 April 1973: 14.
Review of *Poiemata* edited by Desmond Egan and Gerard Rice, and *Focus* 'fifty poems analysed by Desmond Egan and Eugene Watters'.

C184 LOST ULSTERMEN [review]
Listener, 26 April 1973: 550–551.
Review of *The Rough Field* by John Montague.

C185 THE SEED-CUTTERS [poem]
Irish Times, 5 May 1973: 10.
Collected with revisions in *North*.

C186 THE BELFAST HARP FESTIVAL 1792 [poem]
JOHN FIELD [poem]
Cambridge Review, 18 May 1973: 145.

C187 FIRESIDE [poem]
New Yorker, 26 May 1973: 48.

C188 BONE DREAMS [poem]
Phoenix, July 1973: 6–7.
Same version as (C169).

C189 POETRY IN PERSPECTIVE [review]
RTE Guide, 10 August 1973: 15.
Review of *Irish Poets in English: Thomas Davis Lectures* edited by Sean Lucy.

C190 JAGGY CLIMBS [review]
Listener, 26 October 1973: 549–550.
Review of *A Local Habitation* by Norman Nicholson.

C191 THE DIGGING SKELETON (AFTER BAUDELAIRE) [poem]
Fuse, November 1973: 34.
Collected with revisions in *North*.

C192 THE GRAUBALLE MAN [poem]
Listener, 15 November 1973: 663.

C193 MOSSBAWN SUNLIGHT [poem]
Antaeus, winter, 1973: 59.

C194 WHEN LI'L ABNER BREEZED IN FROM CASTLEDAWSON [essay]
Education Times, 20 December 1973: 7.
Collected as Part 2 of 'Mossbawn' in *Preoccupations*.

1974

C195 FAITH, HOPE, AND POETRY [review]
Hibernia, 18 January 1974: 13.
Review of *Selected Poems* by Osip Mandelstam and *Mandelstam* by Clarence Brown.

C196 BOG QUEEN [poem]
PUNISHMENT [poem]
THE GRAUBALLE MAN [poem]
KINSHIP [poem]
James Joyce Quarterly, spring, 1974: 221–232.
Published under the title 'Poems by Seamus Heaney'. 'Punishment' a revised version of *Broadsheet* 17, 1973 (C181), revised version of 'Kinship', printed in *Bog Poems* and collected with further revisions in *North*.

C197 A VISITANT [poem]
American Irish Foundation Report, spring 1974: 999.
Collected with revisions as 'A Drink of Water' in *Field Work*.

C198 NOW AND IN ENGLAND [review]
The Spectator, 4 May 1974: 547.
Review of *The Sleeping Lord* by David Jones.

C199 COOL AND COMPLEX WEAVING OF MYTH AND LANGUAGE [review]
Education Times, 16 May 1974: 12.
Review of *Red Shift* by Alan Garner and of *Welsh Poems: Sixth Century to 1600* translated and introduced by Gwyn Williams.

C200 PUNISHMENT [poem]
The Listener, 23 May 1974: 663.
Revised version of (C196) and (C181).

C201 ACT OF UNION [poem]
Broadsheet 21, [June] 1974: 7.

C202 VIKING DUBLIN: TRIAL PIECES [poem]
New Review, June 1974: 18–19.
Collected with revisions in *North*. An earlier draft appeared in (C207); see also (C226).

C203 LAND-LOCKED [essay]
Irish Press, 1 June 1974: 6.

C204 SUMMONING LAZARUS [review]
Listener, 6 June 1974: 741–742.
Review of *The Mound People: Danish Bronze-Age Man Preserved* by P. V. Glob.

C205 THE DIGGING SKELETON [poem]
Times Literary Supplement, 16 August 1974: 880.

C206 A DRINK OF WATER [poem]
St Stephens, autumn 1974: 17.
Collected with revisions in *Field Work*.

C207 OCEAN'S LOVE TO IRELAND [poem]
NORTH [poem]

VIKING DUBLIN: TRIAL PIECES [poem]
Irish University Review, autumn 1974: 199–203.
All three poems collected with revisions in *North*. A later and longer draft of 'Viking Dublin: Trial Pieces' had appeared in (C202); see also (C226).

C208 FUNERAL RITES [poem]
Irish Times, 9 November 1974: 10.

C209 BELDERG [poem]
Encounter, December 1974: 63.

C210 FUNERAL RITES [poem]
Exile 2, no. 1, 1974: 5–7.
Collected with revisions in *North*.

C211 A CONSTABLE CALLS [poem]
ACT OF UNION [poem]
Aquarius, 1974: 108–109.

1975

C212 PATRICK KAVANAGH [essay]
New Review, January 1975: 57–62.
Collected as 'The Poetry of Patrick Kavanagh: From Monaghan to the Grand Canal' in *Two Decades of Irish Writing* (B24).

C213 ADROITEST OF MAKERS [review]
Education Times, 6 February 1975: 17.
Review of *Thank You, Fog* by W. H. Auden; *Poetry Introduction 3*; and *The Third Book of Criticism* by Randall Jarrell.

C214 KINSHIP [poem]
ANAHORISH [poet's worksheets]
NOTEBOOK ENTRY [diary]
Phoenix 13, spring 1975: 11–13; 39–41.
The 'Worksheets' are photographic reproductions of manuscript versions of 'Anahorish'. The 'Notebook Entry' is for Friday, August 19, 1966, and deals with Gallarus Oratory, County Kerry, Ireland. 'Kinship' was collected with revisions in *North*.

C215 BOG QUEEN [poem]
Antaeus, spring 1975: 43–44.

C216 DIGGING DEEPER [essay]
Times Literary Supplement, 21 March 1975: 306.
On *Volunteers* by Brian Friel.

C217 MAKING POETRY REAL FOR THE STUDENT TEACHERS [essay]
Education Times, 27 March 1975: 12–13.

C218 SEED CUTTERS [poem]
Times Literary Supplement, 28 March 1975: 336.

C219 STRANGE FRUITS [poem]
Times Literary Supplement, 4 April 1975: 352.

C220 FREEDMAN [poem]
New Blackfriars, May 1975: 213.

C221 THE POET CROWNED [poem]
New York Review of Books, 15 May 1975: 41.

C222 HERCULES AND ANTAEUS [poem]
Irish Times, 31 May 1975: 10.

C223 SEAMUS HEANEY WRITES [essay]
Poetry Book Society Bulletin, summer 1975: [1].
Seamus Heaney writes on *North*. Reprinted under the title 'North' in *Poetry Book Society: The First Twenty-Five Years* (B37).

C224 HEDGE SCHOOL [prose poem]
New Blackfriars, June 1975: 265.

C225 REMEMBERING FORECASTS [poem]
THUNDERLIGHT [poem]
Listener, 5 June 1975: 745.
Collected with revisions as 'Glanmore Sonnets' VII and VIII in *Field Work*.

C226 VIKING DUBLIN: TRIAL PIECES [poem]
Irish Press, 7 June 1975: 6. (See also C202, C207.)

C227 MACNEICE'S DARK TOWER [review]
Guardian, 20 June 1975: 15.

Review of *Closing Times* by Dan Davin, *Time was Away* edited by Terence Brown and Alec Reid, and *Louis MacNeice* by Terence Brown.

C228 PATRICK AND OISIN [prose poem]
New Blackfriars, July 1975: 328.

C229 THE SABBATH-BREAKERS [prose poem]
AN ULSTER TWILIGHT [prose poem] (See C265)
ENGLAND'S DIFFICULTY [prose poem]
SWEET WILLIAM [prose poem]
THE GENTS [prose poem]
KERNES [prose poem]
BALLAD [prose poem]
'MO THURAS GO RANN NA FEIRSTE' [prose poem]
Irish Times, 8 July 1975: supplement, 1.
The poems appeared under the title 'Autobiographical Borings' and were introduced by Seamus Heaney: 'I don't know if these can be called prose poems. They could be regarded as autobiographical borings, narrow shafts let down into one stratum of a northern consciousness, bits to drill the compacted years of G.A.A. [Gaelic Athletic Association] sports days and ceilidhe bands, that embattled culture of feiseanna and Gaeltacht scholarships, family rosaries and Faith of our Fathers. They do not form a complete sequence but are extracted from a pamphlet collection of similar pieces which is to appear from *The Honest Ulsterman* later this year.' (See *Stations*, A10.)

C230 IN THE COUNTRY OF CONVENTION [review]
Times Literary Supplement, 11 July 1975: 750–751.
Review of *The Penguin Book of Pastoral Verse* edited by John Barrell and John Bull; collected under the title 'In the Country of Convention' in *Preoccupations*.

C231 A DREAM OF JEALOUSY [poem]
Worksheets for 'Funeral Rites,' 'Punishment,' 'Act of Union,' A Constable Calls' [worksheet]
Quarto (Coleraine), November 1975: 2; 3–17.
'A Dream of Jealousy' collected with revisions in *Field Work*. (See also C234, C266.) The 'Worksheets' show

that early drafts of 'Funeral Rites' were titled 'The Funerals', 'Growing Pains' and 'Elegy'; 'Shame' was the working title for 'Punishment' and 'A Constable Calls' was titled 'Tillage Records'.

C232 OPENED GROUND [poem]
THE TRAIN [poem]
A DRINK OF WATER [poem]
Poetry Wales, vol. 2, no. 1, 1975: 24–25.
All three poems collected in *Field Work*. 'Opened Ground' and 'The Train' collected with revisions as 'Glanmore Sonnets' I and IV.

C233 [INTRODUCTION] [note]
CAULED [prose poem]
HEDGE-SCHOOL [prose poem]
NESTING GROUND [prose poem]
SINKING THE SHAFT [prose poem]
WATER BABIES [prose poem]
PATRICK AND OISIN [prose poem]
ENGLAND'S DIFFICULTY [prose poem]
A VISITANT [prose poem]
THE WANDERER [prose poem]
CLOISTERED [prose poem]
TURAS [prose poem]
BALLAD [prose poem]
ALIAS [prose poem]
Exile, II, nos 3 and 4, 1975: 107–120.
The poems appear under the title 'from Turas'. All of the poems appear with revisions in *Stations* except 'Ballad' and 'Turas'. 'Turas' was collected as 'Stations of the West' in *Stations* and *Selected Poems 1966–1987*. 'Alias' was collected with revisions as 'Incertus' in *Stations* and *Selected Poems 1966–87*.

C234 A DREAM OF JEALOUSY [poem]
HIATUS [poem]
Little Word Machine, no. 7, 1975: 38.
Both poems were collected in *Field Work*. 'A Dream of Jealousy' was collected with revisions (see also C231,

C266). 'Hiatus' was collected with revisions as 'Glanmore Sonnets' VIII.

1976

C235 SUNLIGHT [poem]
KINSHIP [poem]
FUNERAL RITES [poem]
SHORELINE [poem]
THE GRAUBELLE MAN [poem]
OCEAN'S LOVE TO IRELAND [poem]
BOG OAK [poem]
MOTHER OF THE GROOM [poem]
A DRINK OF WATER [poem]
THATCHER [poem]
New Republic, 27 March 1976: 23–27.
All of the poems had been previously collected, except 'A Drink of Water'.

C236 A MEMORABLE VOICE [review]
Irish Times, 3 April 1976: 8.
Review of *Collected Poems* by Stevie Smith.

C237 THE BOG [essay]
Ireland of the Welcomes, May/June, 1976: 20–25.

C238 THE HARVEST BOW [poem]
Times Literary Supplement, 28 May 1976: 634.
Collected with revisions in *Field Work*.

C239 IN MEMORIAM: SEAN O RIADA [poem]
Cyphers, summer 1976: 33.
Collected with revisions in *Field Work* (see also C243, C256).

C240 [UNTITLED] [note]
AN EXTRACT FROM THE MIDDLE IRISH TALE *BUILE SHUIBE* [poem/translation]
Grilled Flowers, fall/winter 1976: 58–62.
Collected with revisions in *Sweeney Astray*.

C241 SHORTS FOR AUDEN [review]
Hibernia, 8 October 1976: 21.
Review of *W. H. Auden: Collected Poems*.

C242 THE BELFAST GROUP: A SYMPOSIUM [essay]
Honest Ulsterman, November/December, 1976: 61–63.
Seamus Heaney's contribution collected as 'The Group' as part 1 of the essay 'Belfast' in *Preoccupations*.

C243 IN MEMORIAM: SEAN O RIADA [poem]
THE BADGERS [poem]
Sewanee Review, winter 1976: 120–122.
'In memoriam Sean O Riada' same as C239; collected with revisions in *Field Work*. 'The Badgers' collected with revisions in *Field Work*.

C244 [UNTITLED] [note]
SWEENEY ASTRAY [poem/translation]
Armadillo 3, 1976: 20–24.
'Sweeney Astray', collected with revisions in *Sweeney Astray* as section 40.

C245 HOMECOMINGS [poem]
mars, no. 1 [1976]: 35.
Collected with revisions in *Field Work*.

C246 A DREAM OF JEALOUSY [poem]
Blue Moon News, 1 no. 2 [1976]: [24].

C247 GLANMORE [poem]
A NIGHT IN THE COLD [poem]
Prospice, no. 5, 1976: 64–65.
'Glanmore' is composed of 'Glanmore Sonnets' I and II, respectively, and 'A Night in the Cold' is 'Glanmore Sonnet' X. All three sonnets were collected with revisions in *Field Work*.

1977

C248 AN AFTERWARDS [poem]
VIA, January 1977: 1.
Collected with revisions in *Field Work*.

C249 SEPTEMBER SONG [poem]
Honest Ulsterman, January/February 1977: 61.
Not the same as 'September Song' in the *The Honest Ulsterman* (C115); this poem was collected with revisions in *Field Work*.

C250 THE PIGEON SHOOT [poem]
New Yorker, 31 January 1977: 34.
Collected with revisions as part III of 'The King of the Ditchbacks' in *Station Island*.

C251 NOW AND IN ENGLAND [essay]
Critical Inquiry, spring 1977: 471–488.
Collected under the title 'Englands of the Mind' in *Preoccupations*.

C252 THE POETRY OF RICHARD MURPHY [essay]
Irish University Review, spring 1977: 18–30.
Reprinted in *Richard Murphy: Poet of Two Traditions* edited by Maurice Harmon (B30).

C253 TRIPTYCH [poem]
Irish Press, 12 March 1977: 9.
Collected with revisions in *Field Work*.

C254 A POET'S VIEW [essay]
Kairos, Educational Magazine, April/May, 1977: 4–5.

C255 TRIPTYCH [poem]
Listener, 23 June 1977: 832.
Collected with revisions in *Field Work*.

C256 IN MEMORIAM: SEAN O RIADA [poem]
Encounter, July 1977: 14.
(See C243)

C257 SECRET NESTS OF COUNTY DERRY [essay]
Listener, 1 September 1977: 265–266.
'The first of a series of BBC Radio 4 talks on "Childhood Landscapes".'

C258 REMEMBERING ROBERT LOWELL [comment]
Listener, 22 September 1977: 379–380.

'A programme of tributes to Robert Lowell, presented by Michael Schmidt, was broadcast on BBC Radio 3 on 13 September.'

C259 JOHN BULL'S OTHER ISLAND [essay]
Listener, 29 September 1977: 397–399.
Edited version of BBC Radio 3 broadcast, September, 1977. 'Seamus Heaney spoke about the problems of Irish writers . . .'

C260 THE SINGER'S HOUSE [poem]
OYSTERS [poem]
A STRANGE HOUSE [poem]
Thames Poetry, November 1977: 11–13.
'The Singer's House' and 'Oysters' were collected with revisions in *Field Work*. 'A Strange House' was reprinted with revisions in *Soft Day* (B44).

C261 IN MEMORIAM FRANCIS LEDWIDGE [poem]
Irish Times, 19 November 1977: 11.
Appears with note: 'Killed in France July 31st, 1917'.

C262 THEATRE OF YEATS [review]
Guardian, 24 November 1977: 19.
Review of *The Noble Drama of W. B. Yeats* by Liam Miller and *W. B. Yeats: The CriticAl Heritage* by A. Norman Jeffares.

C263 LEAVINGS [poem]
THE SKUNK [poem]
Cyphers, Winter 1977–78: 36–37.

C264 FICTIONARIES [review]
Hibernia, 16 December 1977: 23.
Review of *A Hole is to Dig* by Ruth Krauss and illustrated by Maurice Sendak; *Hit or Myth* by James Riddell; *Nonstop Nonsense* by Magaret Mahy; *Archie and the Strict Baptists* by John Betjeman; and *The Sly Cormorant and the Fishes* by Brian Patten.

C265 THE WORKSHOP [poem]
RTE Guide, 23 December 1977: 3.

Published as 'Christmas Eve' (AA7) in December 1978 and collected with revisions under the title 'An Ulster Twilight' in *Station Island*, but not the same poem as (C229).

C266 A DREAM OF JEALOUSY [poem]
'Y', 1977: 9.

C267 OTTER [poem]
Aquarius, no. 9, 1977: 32.
Collected as 'The Otter' with revisions in *Field Work*.

C268 ADJUDICATION [essay]
New Poetry, no. 36, 1977: 38.
Seamus Heaney comments on his adjudication of a poetry competition for the magazine.

1978

C269 THE INTERESTING CASE OF JOHN ALPHONSUS MULRENNAN [essay]
Planet: The Welsh Internationalist, January, 1978: 34–40.
Lecture delivered at the 1977 annual rally of the Department of Extra-mural Studies, the University College of Wales, Aberystwyth. Author: Seumas [*sic*] Heaney.

C270 from SWEENEY ASTRAY [poem/translation]
Quest, January/February 1978: 46; collected with revisions as the 'Sweeney Praises the Trees' stanzas from section 40 of *Sweeney Astray* (A34). The poem accompanies an article with interview material and photographs of Seamus Heaney.

C271 AN AFTERWARDS [poem]
THE SKUNK [poem]
New Review, February, 1978: 24–25.

C272 ON ROBERT LOWELL [essay]
New York Review of Books, 9 February 1978: 37–38.
Extract from Memorial Address; see A22.

C273 LEAVINGS [poem]
THE HARVEST BOW [poem]
Poetry Australia, March 1978: 18–19.

C274 FULL FACE [review]
Irish Times, 1 April 1978: Weekend, 3.
Review of *Day by Day* by Robert Lowell.

C275 ALBA [poem]
Hibernia, 27 April 1978: 22.
Collected with revisions as 'A Snowshoe', part 6 of 'Shelf Life' in *Station Island*.

C276 POSTCARD FROM NORTH ANTRIM [poem]
Irish Press, 29 April 1978: 14.

C277 THE PLEASURES OF THE DAY [poem]
Broadsheet, 26–30 (final issue), June 1978: 3.
This issue was published by Hayden Murphy in Edinburgh.

C278 IN MEMORIAM: SEAN O'RIADA [poem]
Poetry Review, June 1978: 4–5.
Collected with revisions in *Field Work*.

C279 HIGH SUMMER [poem]
POLDER [poem]
Honest Ulsterman, July/October, 1978: 8–9.
'High Summer' and 'Polder' collected with revisions in *Field Work*.

C280 FIELD WORK [poem]
New England Review, autumn 1978: 31.
Collected with revisions in *Field Work*.

C281 THE POET AS A CHRISTIAN [essay]
Furrow, October 1978: 603–606.

C282 FIELD WORK [poem]
Stone Ferry Review, winter 1978: 66–69.

C283 CRITICS' CHOICE [selection]
Hibernia, 21 December 1978: 34.

Seamus Heaney chooses *Day by Day* by Robert Lowell and *Getting Through* by John McGahern.

C284 A POSTCARD FROM NORTH ANTRIM [poem]
Poetry Review, vol. 67, no. 4, 1978: 11–12.

C285 IN MEMORIAM FRANCIS LEDWIDGE [poem]
Stand, vol. 19, no. 2, 1978: 21.

1979

C286 LEAVINGS [poem]
Listener, 18 January 1979: 121.

C287 ELEGY [poem]
Encounter, February 1979: 93.

C288 SONNET [poem]
New Yorker, 26 February 1979: 38.
Collected with revisions as 'Glanmore Sonnet' VI in *Field Work*.

C289 THE STRAND AT LOUGH BEG [poem]
FIELD WORK [poem]
SONG [poem]
THE OTTER [poem]
TRIPTYCH: I. AFTER A KILLING; II. SIBYL; III. SONG OF ERNE [poem]
UGOLINO: (FROM *INFERNO*, CANTOS XXXII AND XXXIII) [poem/translation]
Antaeus, spring 1979: 20–31.
All of the poems were collected in *Field Work*, 'Field Work', 'Song' and 'Triptych' with revisions. 'Song' is a revised version of the poem as it first appeared in *Irish Poetry after Yeats* (B35). 'After a Killing' was written in 1976 on the day Christopher Ewart-Briggs, British Ambassador to Ireland, was murdered.

C290 LEAVINGS [poem]
POLDER [poem]
Paris Review, spring 1979: 233–234.
Both poems collected in *Field Work*; 'Polder' with revisions. This 'Polder' is different from *The Honest*

Ulsterman, July/October 1978 (C279) version; thus, there were three versions of 'Polder'.

C291 THE STRAND AT LOUGH BEG [poem]
THE TOOME ROAD [poem]
Threshold, Spring 1979: 34–35.
Both poems collected with revisions in *Field Work*. Seamus Heaney was the Poetry Editor of this issue of *Threshold*.

C292 THE BADGERS [poem]
Outposts, spring 1979: 4–5.

C293 UGOLINO [poem/translation]
lower stumpf lake review, spring 1979: 6–7.
'After Dante, *Inferno*, Cantos 32, 33.'

C294 CASUALTY [poem]
New Yorker, 2 April 1979: 38.

C295 KAVANAGH OF THE PARISH [essay]
Listener, 26 April 1979: 577–579.

C296 HIGH SUMMER [poem]
POLDER [poem]
Harvard Advocate, May 1979: 6, 9.

C297 THE STRAND AT LOUGH BEG [poem]
London Magazine, June 1979: 3–4.
This issue also contains 'Meeting Seamus Heaney,' an interview with John Haffenden (F11).

C298 THE GUTTURAL MUSE [poem]
New Yorker, 25 June 1979: 28.

C299 IN MEMORIAM FRANCIS LEDWIDGE [poem]
New Republic, 7 July 1979: 32.

C300 AN AFTERWARDS [poem]
New Republic, 25 August 1979: 30.

C301 SEAMUS HEANEY WRITES [essay]
Poetry Book Society Bulletin, autumn 1979: [1]–[2].
Seamus Heaney writes on *Field Work*.

C302 THE LANGUAGE OF EXILE [review]
Parnassus, fall/winter 1979: 5–11.
Review of *The Star-Apple Kingdom* by Derek Walcott.

C303 A KITE FOR MICHAEL AND CHRISTOPHER [poem]
NEAR ANAHORISH [poem]
Ploughshares [September] 1979: 23–24.
'Near Anahorish' collected with revisions as 'Making Strange' in *Station Island*. This issue also contains an interview with Seamus Heaney (F13).

C304 THE TOOME ROAD [poem]
New York Review of Books, 27 September 1979: 8.

C305 A DEER IN GLANMORE [poem]
NEAR ANAHORISH: A VISITATION [poem]
London Review of Books, 25 October 1979: 20.
'A Deer in Glanmore', collected with revisions as 'A Migration' in *Station Island*; 'Near Anahorish: A Visitation' same as (C303), collected with revisions as 'Making Strange' in *Station Island*.

C306 ELEGY [poem]
Cork Review, November/December [1979]: 25.

C307 THE HARVEST BOW [poem]
A POSTCARD FROM NORTH ANTRIM [poem]
Literary Review, winter 1979: 212–214.
This *Literary Review* is published in Madison, New Jersey.

C308 SEAMUS HEANEY [selection]
Sunday Times, 'Books of the Year', 9 December 1979: 33.
Seamus Heaney selected *One and Other Poems* by Thomas Kinsella; *The Year of the French* by Thomas Flanagan and *The Complete Prose of Osip Mandelstam*.

C309 IN TOUCH [poem]
Listener, 20 and 27 December 1979: 871.
'In Touch' collected with revisions as 'M' in *The Spirit Level*.

C310 from GLANMORE SONNETS [poem]
Aquarius, no. 11, 1979: 85.

Identified here as 'Glanmore Sonnets' V and VIII collected as Sonnets VI (with revisions) and IX respectively in *Field Work*.

C311 LEAVINGS [poem]
Straight Lines, no. 2, 1979: 27.

C312 CASUALTY [poem]
Dutch Quarterly Review of Anglo-American Letters, Amsterdam, vol. 9, no. 1, 1979: 2–3.

C313 A CART FOR EDWARD GALLAGHER [POEM]
SONG [poem]
Recorder, vol. 40, 1979: 40–43.
'A Cart for Edward Gallagher' was collected with revisions as 'Last Look' in *Station Island*.

1980

C314 A CART FOR EDWARD GALLAGHER [poem]
Times Literary Supplement, 8 February 1980: 136.
'A Cart for Edward Gallagher' was collected with revisions as 'Last Look' in *Station Island*.

C315 THE SENSE OF PLACE [essay]
Cork Review, March/April, 1980: 12–15.

C316 A HANK OF WOOL [poem]
Times Literary Supplement, 7 March 1980: 261.

C317 TWO VOICES [review]
London Review of Books, 20 March 1980: 8.
Review of *The New Cratylus* by A. D. Hope.

C318 A VILLANELLE FOR MARIE [poem]
Quarto (Coleraine) summer 1980: 34.
Not the same *Quarto* as (C320).

C319 TRIPTYCH: I, AFTER A KILLING; II, SIBYL; III, SONG OF ERNE [poem]
GLANMORE SONNETS I–IV, VII–VIII, X [poem]
DAM: Poetry International Documents, Summer 1980: 24–30.
'Triptych' collected with revisions in *Field Work*.

C320 TREELY AND RURALLY [review]
Quarto, IX, August 1980: 14.
Review of C. H. Sisson's translation of Dante's *Divine Comedy* and of *Dante* by George Holmes. This *Quarto* was published in England.

C321 ELEGY [poem]
ROBERT LOWELL: A MEMORIAL ADDRESS [essay]
Agenda, autumn, 1980: 21–22; 23–28.
'Elegy' collected with revisions in *Field Work*.

C322 CHANGES [poem]
London Review of Books, 18 September–1 October 1980: 10.
Collected with revisions in *Field Work*.

C323 ENGLISH AND IRISH [review]
The Times Literary Supplement, 24 October 1980: 1199.
Review of Dublin Theatre Festival's production of *Translations* by Brian Friel.

C324 THE LINE: A POETS' SYMPOSIUM [essay]
Epoch, winter 1980: 191–192.

C325 A KITE FOR MICHAEL AND CHRISTOPHER [poem]
WIDGEON [poem]
Aquarius, [December] 1980: 34–35.

C326 HERCULES AND ANTAEUS [poem]
Strawberry Fare, 1980: 19.
This issue also contains an interview with Seamus Heaney (F17).

C327 FROM SWEENEY ASTRAY [poem/translation]
Ploughshares, vol. 6, no. 1, 1980: 111–117.
Seamus Heaney was co-ordinating editor of this issue.
'from *Sweeney Astray*' collected with revisons as sections 17–23 in *Sweeney Astray* (A34).

C328 LETTER [facsimile]
THE WELL AT NEW PLACE [poem]
New Departures, no. 12, 1980: 15, 18.

'Special anthology issued on the celebration of the conception of the first Poetry Olympics – launched from the Poet's Corner, Westminster Abbey, London – on Friday, 26 September 1980.' Seamus Heaney's letter to the editor explains why he would not participate in the Poetry Olympics.

1981

C329 THE UNDERGROUND [poem]
Thames Poetry, February 1981: 5.
Collected with revisions in *Station Island*.

C330 THE LOANING [poem]
London Review of Books, 5–18 February 1981: 11.
Collected as Part I of 'The Loaning' in *Station Island*.

C331 PANEGYRIC FOR THREE VOICES [essay]
The Observer, 15 February 1981: 29.
Observer Poetry Prize/Arvon Foundation Poetry Competition 1980 winners introduced by Seamus Heaney.

C332 THE NAMES OF THE HARE [poem/translation]
Poetry Ireland Review, spring, 1981: 8–9.
Seamus Heaney's translation 'From the Middle English'
Collected with revisions in *Opened Ground*.

C333 A SUMMER NIGHT [poem]
Bananas, April 1981: 26.

C334 CURRENT UNSTATED ASSUMPTIONS ABOUT POETRY [essay]
Critical Inquiry, summer, 1981: 645–651.
Text of talk given at the Modern Language Association convention 1979. Panelists with Seamus Heaney were Robert Pinsky and Thomas Parkinson. The session was chaired by Helen Vendler.

C335 AN ULSTER TWILIGHT [poem]
Outposts, Summer 1981: 3. (See C265.)

C336 THE POEMS OF THE DISPOSSESSED REPOSSESSED [review]
Sunday Tribune Magazine, 16 August 1981: 38–39.

Review of *An Duanaire 1600–1900: Poems of the Dispossessed*, curtha i láthair ag Seán ÓTuama and translated by Thomas Kinsella.

C337 OSIP AND NADEZHDA [review]
London Review of Books, 20 August–2 September 1981: 3, 5–6.
Review of *Stone* by Osip Mandelstam, translated by Robert Tracy; *Journey to Armenia* by Osip Mandelstam, translated by Clarence Brown; *Selected Poems* by Osip Mandelstam, translated by Clarence Brown; *The Prose of Osip Mandelstam* by Osip Mandelstam, translated by Clarence Brown; *The Complete Critical Prose and Letters* translated by Jane Gary Harris and Constance Link; *Hope Against Hope* by Nadezhda Mandelstam translated by Max Hayward; *Hope Abandoned* by Nadezhda Mandelstam translated by Max Hayward; *Mandelstam* by Clarence Brown; *Modern Russian Poets on Poetry* by Carl Proffer; *Homage to Mandelstam* edited by Richard Burns and George Gomori.

C338 SEAMUS HEANEY [selection]
Sunday Tribune, 'Books of the Year', 20 December 1981: Review Section, 1.
Seamus Heaney selected: *An Duanaire 1600–1900: Poems of the Dispossessed*, curtha i láthair ag Seán ÓTuama and translated by Thomas Kinsella; reprint of *Kavanagh's Weekly*; John Hewitt's *Selected Poems*.

C339 THE RAILWAY CHILDREN [poem]
Poetry Supplement, Poetry Book Society, Christmas 1981: [16].

C340 A SHOOTING SCRIPT [poem]
THE LOANING [poem]
The Sunday Tribune Magazine, 27 December 1981: 4.
'A Shooting Script' collected with revisions in *The Haw Lantern*. 'The Loaning', Parts I–III, collected with revisions in *Station Island*.

1982

C341 AMONG THE WHINS ('FROM CHEKHOV'S "DONEGAL NOTEBOOK" ') [poem]
CHEKHOV ON SAKHALIN [poem]
New Statesman, 29 January 1982: 21.
Includes a note on the poems by Seamus Heaney.
'Chekhov on Sakhalin', collected with revisions in *Station Island.*

C342 A FAMILIAR GHOST [poem]
Irish Times, 2 February 1982: supplement 'James Joyce 1882–1982', 1.
Reprinted with revisions under the title 'Leaving the Island' in *James Joyce and Modern Literature* (B61); collected with further revisions as section XII of the 'Station Island' sequence in *Station Island.*

C343 COME INTO THE CHAMBER OF DREAMS [essay]
Sunday Tribune Review, 2 February 1982: 18–20.
Seamus Heaney writes on James Joyce's poetry.

C344 CHEKHOV ON SAKHALIN [poem]
THE LOANING [poem]
Cumberland Poetry Review, spring 1982: 28–31.
'Chekhov on Sakhalin' collected with revisions in *Station Island*; not the same as (C341). 'The Loaning', Parts I–III, collected with revisions in *Station Island*; not same as (C340).

C345 THE NERVES IN LEAF [essay]
Ireland of the Welcomes, March/April, 1982: 19–20.
On Sonja Landweer (Dutch Potter).

C346 NORTH-EAST [poem/translation]
SWEENEY'S PRAISE OF FARANNAN [poem/translation]
Harvard Advocate, summer 1982: 40.
'North-East' includes the sub-title 'from the Old Irish'; 'Sweeney's Praise of Farannan' includes the sub-title 'from the Middle Irish.' 'North-East' first appeared under the title 'After the Irish' in *Field Day Theatre* programme

1980 (D12). 'Sweeney's Praise of Farranan' collected with revisions in *Sweeney Astray*.

C347 VERSES FOR A FORDHAM COMMENCEMENT [poem]
Fordham, summer 1982: 8–9.

C348 JOHN FIELD [poem]
PATRICK AND OISIN [prose poem]
INQUISITION [prose poem]
Digraphe, June 1982: 45–47.

C349 HOLLY [poem]
Quarryman, August 1982: 2.
Collected with revisions in *Station Island*.

C350 LAST LOOK [poem]
Illuminations, autumn, 1982: 1.
Collected with revisions in *Station Island*.

C351 VERSES FOR A FORDHAM COMMENCEMENT [poem]
Irish Literary Supplement, fall, 1982: 22–23.

C352 REMEMBERING MALIBU [poem]
Fiction Magazine, autumn 1982: 29.
Collected with revisions in *Station Island*.

C353 WORDS ALONE [essay]
Múinteoir Náisúnta (Journal of the Irish National Teachers Organisation), Autumn 1982: iii–v.
Ninth World Congress on Reading, Dublin 1982. Revised version appears in *Dimensions of Reading* (B74).

C354 A POET HITS HIS STRIDE [review]
Sunday Tribune, 19 September 1982: 20.
Review of *Kist* by Dennis O'Driscoll.

C355 THE BIRTHPLACE [poem]
London Review of Books, 7–20 October 1982: 20.

C356 BENNETT AWARD ACCEPTANCE SPEECH, 1982 [essay]
Hudson Review, winter 1982–1983: 518, 520.

C357 SWEENEY'S LAMENT IN MOURNE [poem/translation]
Belfast Review, winter 1982: 27.

C358 SWEENEY ASTRAY [poem/translation]
Threshold, winter 1982: 35–40.
Collected with revisions as sections 1–17 in *Sweeney Astray*.

C359 AN ULSTER TWILIGHT [poem]
New Statesman, 17/24 December 1982: 43.
Collected with revisions in *Station Island*. (See C265.)

C360 SLOE GIN [poem]
SWEENEY'S LAMENT [poem/translation]
Listener, 23 and 30 December 1982: 38.
'Sloe Gin' collected with revisions in *Station Island*. 'Sweeney's Lament' collected with revisions as section 61 in *Sweeney Astray*.

C361 ULSTER QUATRAINS [poem]
REMEMBERING MALIBU [poem]
Recorder, vol. 43, 1982: 59–62.
'Ulster Quatrains' is in three sections: 1. 'Sectarian Water'; 2. 'Sectarian Latin'; 3. 'Sectarian Alphabet'.

C362 BORGES AND THE WORLD OF FICTION [interview]
Crane Bag, vol. 6, no. 2, 1982: 71–78.
Seamus Heaney and Richard Kearney interview Borges in June 1982, James Joyce's centenary.

1983

C363 SEAMUS HEANEY TALKS TO BORGES [interview]
Sunday Independent, 2 January 1983: 14.
Richard Kearney also participates in this exchange as in (C362).

C364 DAVIN ON THE BROAGH ROAD [poem]
Broadsheet, [February 1983]: [2].
Collected as 'A Bat on the Road' in *Station Island*. Issued in conjunction with an exhibition of Hayden Murphy's Broadsheets 1967–1978 at the National Library of Scotland on 4 February–20 April 1983.

C365 IN A BASILICA [poem]
Observer, 6 February 1983: 33.

Collected with revisions as 'Station Island' III in *Station Island.*

C366 THE FULLY EXPOSED POEM [review]
Parnassus, spring/summer 1983: 4–16.
Review of *Sagittal Section: Poems New and Selected* by Miroslav Holub and *Interferon or On Theater* by Miroslav Holub.

C367 FROM STATION ISLAND [poem]
Studies in Medievalism, summer 1983: 15–17.
Collected as 'Station Island' XII in *Station Island*; the section is identified here as section XIV of the 'Station Island' sequence.

C368 STATION ISLAND [poem]
Hudson Review, summer, 1983: 257–264.
Sections I–III. Section III collected with revisions as 'The Frontier of Writing' in *The Haw Lantern.*

C369 THE BIRTHPLACE [poem]
NOTE [essay]
New England Review and Bread Loaf Quarterly, summer 1983: 567–568.
The accompanying note by Seamus Heaney discusses 'The Horses' by Edwin Muir.

C370 AN IRON SPIKE [poem]
American Poetry Review, July/August 1983: 48.
Collected with revisions as part 4 of 'Shelf Life' in *Station Island.*

C371 SHELF LIFE: I, OLD PERFUME BOTTLE; II, PUSSY WILLOW; III, PEWTERS [poem]
Outposts, Poetry Quarterly, autumn 1983: 72–73.
'Pewters' collected with revisions as 'Old Pewter', part 3 of 'Shelf Life', in *Station Island.*

C372 THE UNDERGROUND [poem]
HOLLY [poem]
REMEMBERING MALIBU [poem]
Sequoia, autumn 1983: 1–3.
All three poems collected with revisions in *Station Island.*

C373 STATION ISLAND (IV, VII, VIII, IX) [poem]
Yale Review, autumn 1983: 136–144.
Section IV uncollected; sections VII, VIII and IX collected with revisions as 'Station Island' V, VI and VII respectively in *Station Island*.

C374 FORKED TONGUES, CEILIS AND INCUBATORS [essay]
Fortnight, September 1983: 18–21.
'This essay is based on the second annual John Malone Memorial Lecture, "Among Schoolchildren" given by Seamus Heaney at Queen's University, Belfast, in June.'

C375 UNWINDING [poem]
IN THE BEECH [poem]
THE OLD ICONS [poem]
London Review of Books, 20 October–2 November 1983: 14.
'In the Beech' collected with revisions in *Station Island*.

C376 FROM A COMMON BED OF FEELING [review]
New York Times Book Review, 20 November 1983.
Review of *The Modern Poetic Sequence: The Genius of Modern Poetry* by M. L. Rosenthal and Sally M. Gall.

C377 FROM STATION ISLAND [poem]
THE UNDERGROUND [poem]
SLOE GIN [poem]
Poetry Ireland Review, winter 1983–1984: 23–24.
'from Station Island' was collected as section VI, stanza 3, in *Station Island*.

C378 A NIGHT PIECE FOR TOM FLANAGAN [poem]
Recorder, vol. 44, 1983: 29–31.

C379 SWEENEY REMINISCES [poem/translation]
SWEENEY IN THE CHESTNUT TREE [poem/translation]
Aquarius, 1983/4: 55–56.
'Sweeney Reminisces' collected with revisions as 'Drifting Off' in *Station Island*. 'Sweeney in the Chestnut Tree' collected with revisions as 'In the Chestnut Tree' in *Station Island*.

C380 THE CRANE BAG OF SEAMUS HEANEY [essay]
Irish Literary Supplement, vol. 2, no. 1, 1983: 1, 31.
'This article is the preface to the *Crane Bag Book of Irish Studies*, . . .' (B57).

1984

C381 AN ISLAND OF HIS OWN [review]
Observer, 8 January 1984: 50.
Review of *The Collected Letters of John Millington Synge: Volume 1, 1871–1907* by Ann Saddlemyer.

C382 IN ILLO TEMPORE [poem]
Observer, 5 February 1984: 52.

C383 SWEENEY DRIFTS OFF [poem]
Runway, February/March 1984: 25.
Collected as 'Drifting Off' in *Station Island*.

C384 THE MASTER [poem]
THE HAG [poem]
THE HERMIT [poem]
Critical Quarterly, spring and summer 1984: 19–20.
'The Master' collected with revisions in *Station Island*.

C385 SWEENEY AND THE CLERIC [poem]
SWEENEY AND THE SCRIBES [poem]
Thames Poetry, March 1984: 28–29.
Collected as 'The Cleric' and 'The Scribes', respectively in *Station Island*.

C386 A NEW AND SURPRISING YEATS [review]
New York Times Book Review, 18 March 1984: 1, 35–36.
Review of *The Poems: A New Edition* by Richard J. Finneran and *Editing Yeats's Poems* by Richard J. Finneran.

C387 A POET'S BLESSING [essay]
Listener, 19 April 1984: 13–14.
'Poet to Poet: Seamus Heaney on Patrick Kavanagh.'

C388 WE IRISH [essay]
New Republic, 30 April 1984: VII–IX, 3–18.

C389 FROM STATION ISLAND [poem]
Agenda, summer 1984: 3–5.
Collected as 'Station Island' VIII in *Station Island*.

C390 LA TOILETTE [poem]
Horizon, June 1984: 27.
Collected with revisions in *Station Island*.

C391 SANDSTONE KEEPSAKE [poem]
New Yorker, 9 July 1984: 36.
Collected with revisions in *Station Island*.

C392 ALPHABETS [poem]
Harvard Magazine, July/August 1984: 31.
Collected with revisions in *The Haw Lantern*.

C393 CHANGES [poem]
THE RAILWAY CHILDREN [poem]
THE LOANING [poem]
Antaeus, autumn 1984: 90–94.

C394 THE BOULE MICHE OF THE NORTH [essay]
Fortnight, September 1984: 19.
On Belfast's Botanic Avenue.

C395 STATION ISLAND VII [poem]
Irish Times, 13 September 1984: 13.
The poem is included in 'Comfortable image belies the serious poet' by Deaglan de Breadun.

C396 STATION ISLAND [poem]
Inside Tribune, 30 September 1984: 1–3, 6.
Excerpts from sections VII and VIII of the 'Station Island' sequence and the entire text of section IX of the 'Station Island' sequence as part of an interview and article titled 'A Pilgrim's Progress' by Fintan O'Toole.

C397 GROTUS AND COVENTINA [poem]
Verse, Issue 1 [October] 1984: 3.

C398 SWEENEY REDIVIVUS [poem]
Times, 11 October 1984.

C399 MAKING IT NEW [review]
New York Review of Books, 25 October 1984: 40–42.
Review of *Children in Exile: Poems 1968–1984* by James Fenton.

C400 HAILSTONES [poem]
TERMINUS [poem]
London Review of Books, 1–14 November 1984: 8.

C401 PILGRIM'S JOURNEY, SEAMUS HEANEY WRITES . . . [essay]
Poetry Book Society Bulletin, winter, 1984: 3.

C402 ALPHABETS [poem]
Harper's, December 1984: 31.

C403 CHANGES [poem]
THE EASTER HOUSE [poem]
DAVIN ON THE BROAGH ROAD [poem]
Pequod, nos 16–17, 1984: 36–38.

C404 INTRODUCTION [essay]
Ploughshares, vol. 10, no. 1, 1984: 11–12.
Seamus Heaney was the coordinating editor of this issue.

1985

C405 ENVIES AND IDENTIFICATIONS: DANTE AND THE MODERN POET [essay]
Irish University Review, spring 1985: 5–19.
Part of the essay was incorporated into 'The Government of the Tongue' in *The Government of the Tongue*.

C406 PLACE AND DISPLACEMENT: RECENT IRISH POETRY FROM NORTHERN IRELAND [essay]
Wordsworth Circle, spring 1985: 48–56.

C407 THE NEW POET LAUREATE [essay]
Belfast Review, March/April/May, 1985: 6.
'Seamus Heaney introduces Ted Hughes.'

C408 THE SENSE OF THE PAST [essay]
Ulster Local Studies, summer 1985: 109–115.
Originally delivered as a lecture to The Friends of the Monaghan County Museum in 1984.

C409 ALPHABETS [poem]
Paris/Atlantic, summer 1985: 50–52.
'The Irish Issue: featuring the new poetry of Ireland.'

C410 BOWSTRING, HARPSTRING [review]
Sunday Tribune, 23 June 1985: 20.
Review of *Poems 1963–1983* by Michael Longley.

C411 Ó DIREÁIN – A DEEP CHORD IN THE COMMON CULTURE [review]
Irish Press, 17 August 1985: 8.
Review of *Máirtín Ó Direáin, Selected Poems – Tacar Dánta* selected and translated by Tomas MacSiomoin and Douglas Sealy.

C412 SONNET: A COBBLE THROWN A HUNDRED YEARS AGO [poem]
Strawberry Fare, autumn 1985: 15.
Collected with revisions as 'Clearances 1' in *The Haw Lantern*.

C413 THE MUD VISION [poem]
Threepenny Review, fall 1985: 8.
Collected with revisions in *The Haw Lantern*.

C414 PLACE, PASTNESS, POEMS: A TRIPTYCH [essay]
Salmagundi, fall/winter 1985–1986: 30–47.

C415 HEANEY ON DANTE [review]
Sunday Tribune, 15 September 1985: Colour Tribune, 16.
Review of Dante's *Divine Comedy* translated and illustrated by Tom Phillips.

C416 THE SENSUAL PHILOSOPHER [review]
New York Times Book Review, 29 September 1985: 1, 60.
Review of *Mr Palomar* by Italo Calvino. Reprinted in B222.

C417 A CHRONICLE OF MIDDLE IRELAND [review]
Sunday Tribune, 6 October 1985: Books Tribune, 21.
Review of *The High Ground* by John McGahern.

C418 A LAST WORD ON THE ISLAND [poem]
Irish Times, 26 October 1985: Weekend, 5.
Collected as 'The Disappearing Island' in *The Haw Lantern*.

C419 POETRY AND POLITICS [discussion]
Magill, November 1985: 40–48.
A conversation between Seamus Heaney and Joseph Brodsky conducted by Fintan O'Toole.

C420 FROM THE FRONTIER OF WRITING [poem]
FROM THE LAND OF THE UNSPOKEN [poem]
Times Literary Supplement, 1 November 1985: 1224, 1227.

C421 A DAYLIGHT ART [poem]
Scotsman, 15 November 1985: 11.
Collected with revisions in *The Haw Lantern*.

C422 SWEENEY AND THE CLERIC [poem]
SWEENEY REMEMBERS THE HERMIT [poem]
THE MASTER [poem]
Graham House Review, winter 1985: 7–9.
Collected as 'The Cleric' and 'The Hermit'; 'The Master' collected with revisions in *Station Island*.

C423 THE BALLAD OF THE BULLETS [poem]
Ploughshares, [Winter] 1985: 38–40.
Collected with revisions as 'The Song of the Bullets' in *The Haw Lantern*.

C424 LARKIN – THE TRANSCENDENT ANTI-ROMANTIC [essay]
Irish Times, 10 December 1985: 12.
'Seamus Heaney writes about the life and poetry of Philip Larkin who died last week.'

C425 THE SPOONBAIT [poem]
THE STONE VERDICT [poem]

THE MUD VISION [poem]
Poetry Australia, no. 102, 1985: 32–34.

C426 PLACE AND DISPLACEMENT: REFLECTIONS ON SOME RECENT POETRY FROM NORTHERN IRELAND [essay]
Agni Review, no. 22, 1985: 158–177.

C427 SEAMUS HEANEY AT THE PIERPONT MORGAN LIBRARY [essay]
MAKING STRANGE [poem]
THE STRAND AT LOUGH BEG [poem]
'STATION ISLAND, III, VIII, XI' [poem]
Envoy (Academy of American Poets), no. 47, 1985: 1–6.
All of the poems were previously collected.

C428 [SEAMUS HEANEY WRITES] [essay]
OLD SMOOTHING IRON [poem]
In Touch 2, 1985: 30.
'Old Smoothing Iron' was collected with revisions in *Station Island*.

1986

C429 AMONG SCHOOLCHILDREN [essay]
Signal, January 1986: 3–16.

C430 THE LATE PAUL CEZANNE [poem]
Word & Image, Poems on Pictures, January/March 1986: 96.

C431 FROM THE CANTON OF EXPECTATION [poem]
Times Literary Supplement, 24 January 1986: 95.

C432 AN AUTHENTIC POETIC VOICE THAT BRIDGES TIME, CULTURES [review]
Boston Globe, 9 February 1986: A27–28.
Review of *Collected Poems 1948–1984* by Derek Walcott.

C433 GENIUS ON STILTS [review]
Observer, 23 February 1986: 28.
Review of *The Collected Letters of W. B. Yeats*, vol. 1, *1865–1895*, edited by John Kelly and Eric Domville.

C434 A DAYLIGHT ART [poem]
Cumberland Poetry Review, spring, 1986: 43–44.

C435 FROM CLEARANCES [poem]
THE OLD TEAM [poem]
Honest Ulsterman, spring 1986: 3–5.
from 'Clearances': 'A cobble thrown a hundred years ago'; 'Polished linoleum shone there. Brass taps shone'; 'When the other woman was away at Mass' (collected with revisions as 'When all the others were away at Mass' in *The Haw Lantern*); 'In the first flush of the Easter holidays'; and 'I thought of walking round and round a space.' The five 'Clearances' sonnets were collected as sonnets: 1, 2, 3, 6, 8 in *The Haw Lantern*.

C436 FROM CLEARANCES [poem]
Field, spring 1986: 44–46.
'Polished linoleum shone there. Brass taps shone'; 'When the other woman was away at mass' (collected as 'When all the others were away at Mass' in *The Haw Lantern*); 'Fear of affectation made her affect'; 'In the last minutes he said more to her'; and 'I thought of walking round and round a space.' The five 'Clearances' sonnets were collected as sonnets: 2, 3, 4, 7, 8 in *The Haw Lantern*.

C437 THREE IRISH POETS TO WATCH [review]
Irish Literary Supplement, spring 1986: 1, 27.
Review of *After Kavanagh* by Michael O'Loughlin; *The Diary of a Silence* by Michael O'Loughlin; *The Burren Days* by John Ennis; *The Berlin Wall Café* by Paul Durcan.

C438 FROM MAECENAS TO MCALPINE [essay]
RIAI Bulletin, March/April 1986: 11–13.
'The following is an edited text of the lecture presented to the RIAI [Royal Institute of the Architects of Ireland] Annual Conference at Dunadry, Co. Antrim.'

C439 STATION ISLAND: JOTTINGS FOR A POEM [essay]
ERATO, Premier Issue, summer, 1986: 1 (cover)-3.
The essay includes early notes for and drafts of 'Station Island'.

C440 DIPTYCH [poem]
London Review of Books, 3 July 1986: 10.

'She taught me . . .' collected as the introductory poem to 'Clearances'; 'I thought of her as a wishing tree,' collected as 'The Wishing Tree' in *The Haw Lantern*. Not the same 'Diptych' as (C505) or (C606) or the broadside, (AA32).

C441 THE UGLY SUCKLING [review]
New Republic, 11–18 August 1986: 33–35.
Review of *The Collected Letters of Dylan Thomas* edited by Paul Ferris.

C442 THE SONG OF THE BULLETS [poem]
An Múinteor, The Irish Teachers Journal, Autumn 1986: 12.

C443 SONNET [poem]
Poetry Ireland Review, [Autumn 1986]: 6.
'The cool that came off sheets just off the line' from 'Clearances' collected as 'Clearances' 5 in *The Haw Lantern.*

C444 HOLDING COURSE [poem]
THE MUD VISION [poem]
A PEACOCK'S FEATHER [poem]
A SHIP OF DEATH [poem/translation]
Numbers, autumn 1986: 91–96.
'A Ship of Death' is Seamus Heaney's translation of *Beowulf*, lines 26–52. (This is the first appearance of any *Beowulf* passage translated by Seamus Heaney. His complete translation of *Beowulf* appeared in October 1999, A130).

C445 VILLANELLE FOR AN ANNIVERSARY [poem]
Erato, fall/winter 1986: front page.
Reproduction of first issue of the poem (A52) and of Seamus Heaney's signature.

C446 FROM THE REPUBLIC OF CONSCIENCE [poem]
Reflections: Journal of the Society of Writers, United Nations Staff Recreation Council, September, 1986: 4–5.

C447 SEAMUS HEANEY PRAISES THE SCOTTISH POET SORLEY MACLEAN [essay]
London Review of Books, 6 November 1986: 6–7.

Reprinted as 'Introduction' to *Sorley MacLean: Critical Essays* (B76); reprinted with revisions under the title 'The Voice of the Bard' in *Antaeus*, Spring 1988 (C483).

C448 SEAMUS HEANEY [selection]
Observer Review, 30 November 1986: 21.
Seamus Heaney selects: *Less Than One* by Joseph Brodsky; *Collected Letters of W. B. Yeats* by John Kelly; *Mephisto* by John Banville.

C449 VILLANELLE FOR AN ANNIVERSARY [poem]
Harvard Magazine, November/December 1986: 48.

C450 THE IMPACT OF TRANSLATION [essay]
Yale Review, December 1986: 1–14. (See C483)

C451 LIKE A GREEDY SHARK [review]
Observer, 28 December 1986: 21.
Review of *The Faber Book of Contemporary American Poetry* edited by Helen Vendler.

C452 A DAYLIGHT ART [poem]
Gown, [1986]: Literary Supplement, 10.

C453 ROBERT PENN WARREN [essay]
Partisan Review, 1986: 606–612.
Discussion by Seamus Heaney, Derek Walcott and Christopher Lydon – conducted by Christopher Lydon.

C454 HAILSTONES [poem]
Seneca Review, vol. 16, no. 2, 1986: 40–41.
Collected with revisions in *Hailstones*.

C455 INTRODUCTION TO TOMAS TRANSTROMER [essay]
Tracks, no. 6, 1986: 11–13.

C456 THE HAW LANTERN [poem]
TWO QUICK NOTES [poem]
THE STONE GRINDER [poem]
WOLFE TONE [poem]
Verse, no. 6, 1986: 23–24.
'The Haw Lantern', 'Two Quick Notes' and 'Wolfe Tone' are collected with revisions in *The Haw Lantern*.

C457 ART AND POLITICS: 4 IRISH EXPRESSIONIST PAINTERS [essay]
Working Papers in Irish Studies, vol. 4, no. 5, 186: 32–38. (See C505.)

1987

C458 [BIRTHDAY TRIBUTE TO MARIE BULLOCK] [poem]
Poetry Pilot, February 1987: 7.
This issue of *Poetry Pilot* is devoted to tributes to Marie Bullock 1911–1986.

C459 [Review]
Erato supplement: The Harvard Book Shelf, spring, 1987: 7–8.
Review of Racine's *Phaedra* translated by Richard Wilbur and of *Happy Hour* by Alan Shapiro.

C460 INFERNO III [poem/translation]
Ploughshares [spring] 1987: 64–69.
Lines 22–51 were reprinted with revisions under the title 'The Lost People' in *Confounded Language* (B116).

C461 THE COOL THAT CAME OFF SHEETS [poem]
DURING HOLY WEEK [poem]
Salmagundi, spring/summer 1987: 42–43.
Collected as 'Clearances' 5 and 3 respectively in *The Haw Lantern*.

C462 AN OPEN LETTER [poem]
Harper's Magazine, March 1987: 39–40.

C463 AN AMICABLE AND A CANDID CHILD [essay]
Poetry Book Society Bulletin, summer 1987: [4].
'Seamus Heaney reflects on the birth and antecedents of his latest collection of poems *The Haw Lantern*.'

C464 THE STONE VERDICT [poem]
University of Toronto Review, summer 1987: 31.
Collected with revisions in *The Haw Lantern*.

C465 THE SUMMER OF LOST RACHEL [poem]
THE WISHING TREE [poem]
Poetry Kanto, summer 1987: 16–17.

C466 SOUNDING AUDEN [essay]
London Review of Books, 4 June 1987: 15–18.

C467 THE SONG OF THE BULLETS [poem]
IN MEMORIAM: ROBERT FITZGERALD [poem]
THE HAW LANTERN [poem]
Irish Press, 20 June 1987: 9.

C468 JOHN HEWITT: 1907–1987 – THE UNIVERSAL POET [essay]
Sunday Tribune, 5 July 1987: Arts Tribune, 18.

C469 FROM THE REPUBLIC OF CONSCIENCE [poem]
A SHOOTING SCRIPT [poem]
THE DISAPPEARING ISLAND [poem]
American Poetry Review, July/August, 1987: 6.

C470 SEAMUS HEANEY [holiday reading] [selection]
The Sunday Tribune, 2 August 1987: 6.
Seamus Heaney lists: *The Youth of Don Quixote* by Marin Sorescu; *Wilfred Owen* by Dominic Hibberd; *The Village of Longing* by George O'Brien,.

C471 WHO IS IRELAND'S MOST NEGLECTED POET?—A SURVEY [note]
Poetry Ireland Review, autumn 1987: 50.
Seamus Heaney selects John Ennis.

C472 A PLACELESS HEAVEN: ANOTHER LOOK AT KAVANAGH [essay]
Massachusetts Review, autumn 1987: 371–380.
'The following is a version of the keynote address delivered in November 1985 to Kavanagh's Yearly, the annual weekend school held at Carrickmacross.'

C473 ATLAS OF CIVILIZATION [essay]
Parnassus, vol. 14, no. 1, 1987: 17–32.
Review of three works by Zbigniew Herbert: *Barbarian in the Garden; Selected Poems; Report from the Besieged City and Other Poems.*

C474 BRODSKY'S NOBEL: WHAT THE APPLAUSE WAS ABOUT [essay]
New York Times Book Review, 8 November 1987: 1, 63, 65.
Part of this essay was reprinted under the title 'Joseph Brodsky: strong poet strong man' in *The Irish Times Weekend*, 11 June 1988 (C489).

C475 THE GLAMOUR OF CRAIG RAINE [essay]
Ploughshares [winter] 1987: 162–166.

C476 IN MEMORIAM: ROBERT FITZGERALD [poem]
New York Review of Books, 17 December 1987: 9.

C477 WOLFE TONE [poem]
New York Times Book Review, 27 December 1987: 27.

C478 THE INTERESTING CASE OF NERO, CHEKHOV'S COGNAC AND A KNOCKER [essay]
Shenandoah, vol. 37, no. 3, 1987: 3–15.
'This essay is a condensed version of a talk given under the auspices of the Glasgow Endowment Committee at Washington and Lee University in May 1987.' The talk was also delivered to the Royal Dublin Society in 1986. (See C494)

1988

C479 GULLIVER IN LILLIPUT: REMEMBERING ROBERT LOWELL [essay]
A FUGITIVE FROM UTOPIA: THE POETRY OF ZBIGNIEW HERBERT [review]
Erato, winter/spring, 1988: 1–2, 2–3 (insert).
'Gulliver in Lilliput: Rembering Robert Lowell' delivered on 28 October 1987, at Boylston Hall, Harvard University, to commemorate the tenth anniversary of Lowell's death.' The review is of *A Fugitive from Utopia: The Poetry of Zbigniew Herbert* by Stanislaw Baranczak.

C480 THE INDEFATIGABLE HOOF-TAPS [essay]
Times Literary Supplement, 5–11 February 1988: 134, 143, 144.
On Sylvia Plath; first delivered as one of the T. S. Eliot Memorial Lectures at Eliot College, University of Kent 1986.

C481 ABOVE RESPECTABILITY [review]
Atlantic, February 1988: 84–86.
Review of *Oscar Wilde* by Richard Ellmann.

C482 THE IMPACT OF TRANSLATION [essay]
End, Journal of European Nuclear Disarmament, February/March, 1988: 22–24.
Revised version of (C450).

C483 THE PITCHFORK [poem]
THE ASH PLANT [poem]
THE VOICE OF A BARD [essay]
Antaeus, spring 1988: 183, 184, 297–306.
'The Voice of the Bard' originally appeared, with additional materials under the title 'Seamus Heaney Praises the Scottish Poet Sorley MacLean' (C447).

C484 DAVID THOMSON [obituary]
Independent (London), 2 March 1988: 19.
'David Thomson, writer, broadcaster and folklorist, born 1914.'

C485 POETRY AND THE BEGGAR AT THE GATE [essay]
Fortnight, April 1988: 24–25.
A condensed version of the introductory essay in *The Government of the Tongue*, where it appeared under the title 'The Interesting Case of Nero, Chekhov's Cognac and a Knocker.'

C486 THE PROGRESS OF A SOUL [review]
Times Literary Supplement, 8–14 April 1988: 381–382.
Review of *Owen the Poet* by Dominic Hibberd.

C487 ANGLO-IRISH OCCASIONS [essay]
London Review of Books, 5 May 1988: 9.
On the occasion of receiving '*The Sunday Times* Award for Excellence' in Writing, London, 28 April 1988.

C488 LUSTRAL SONNET [poem]
THE STRAND HOTEL [poem]
THE PITCHFORK [poem]
Orbis, summer/autumn 1988: 22–23.

C489 JOSEPH BRODSKY: STRONG POET, STRONG MAN [essay]
Irish Times, 11 June 1988: Weekend, 5.

C490 APPLYING THE YEATS CHALLENGE TO THE ANGLO-IRISH AGREEMENT [essay]
Boston Globe, 27 June 1988: 15.
'In London recently, the poet Seamus Heaney received *The Sunday Times* Award for Excellence in Writing. The following are excerpts from his acceptance speech.' Excerpts taken from the same occasion reported in (C486).

C491 THE SCHOOLBAG [poem]
Irish Times, 30 July 1988: Weekend, 7.
Collected with revisions in *Seeing Things*.

C492 SONG AND SUFFERING [essay]
Harper's, August 1988: 35–39.
'From the Introduction to *The Government of the Tongue* . . . An earlier version of this essay appeared last year in *Shenandoah*' (C478).

C493 THE PRE-NATAL MOUNTAIN: VISION AND IRONY IN RECENT IRISH POETRY [essay]
THE SOUNDS OF RAIN [poem]
Georgia Review, fall, 1988: 465–482.
The essay was originally delivered at Emory University 12 April 1988, to inaugurate the Richard Ellmann Lectures in Modern Literature. The poem is dedicated to Ellmann.

C494 LOWELL'S COMMAND [essay]
Salmagundi, fall 1988: 83–101.
This issue also contains an interview with Seamus Heaney (F42).

C495 THE PRIVATE AGONY OF ENGLAND'S CULTURE HERO [review]
Sunday Independent, 25 September 1988: 14.
'Seamus Heaney looks at the life and achievement of T. S. Eliot who was born 100 years ago tomorrow.' Review of *The Letters of T. S. Eliot*, vol. 1, 1898–1922, edited by Valerie Eliot.

C496 THE BUTTER-PRINT [poem]
The Times, 7 October 1988: Section G, 20.

C497 UNRESTING DEATH [review]
Observer, 9 October 1988: 44.
Seamus Heaney reviews *Collected Poems* by Philip Larkin, edited by Anthony Thwaite.

C498 THE JOURNEY BACK [poem]
1973 [poem]
New Nation, Dublin, November 1988: 21.
Both poems collected with revisions in *Seeing Things*. '1973' as section 4 of 'Glanmore Revisited'.

C499 VICTORIOUS ULSTERMAN: [obituary]
Sunday Independent, 6 November 1988: 18.
'Seamus Heaney on the playwright Stewart Parker who died during the week.'

C500 SEAMUS HEANEY. BOOKS OF THE YEAR [essay]
Observer, 4 December 1988: 65.
Seamus Heaney selects: *Collected Poems* by Czeslaw Milosz; *Blood and Family* by Thomas Kinsella; *Battle Cry of Freedom* by James MacPherson; *Modern Ireland 1600–1972* by R. F. Foster.

C501 A FIELD DAY FOR THE IRISH [essay]
Times, 5 December 1988: 18.
'Seamus Heaney describes the work of the Field Day troupe in exploring the links between culture and politics.'

C502 LAUREATE IN THE TIME OF CATASTROPHE [review]
Irish Times, 17 December 1988: Weekend, Books, 9.
Review of *The Collected Poems 1931–1987* by Czeslaw Milosz.

C503 ON IRISH EXPRESSIONIST PAINTING [essay]
Irish Review, no. 3, 1988: 34–39.
'Seamus Heaney: A Reply': 'The above papers were given at a symposium held at the Museum of Fine Arts, Boston, in April 1986, and circulated in "Working Papers in Irish Studies", Northeastern University. They are published here courtesy of Dr Ruthanne Harris and Dr James Doane.' (See C457.)

C504 THE GOVERNMENT OF THE TONGUE [essay]
Partisan Review, vol. 55, no. 2, 1988: 292–308.
Collected with revisions in *The Government of the Tongue*.

1989

C505 DIPTYCH [poem]
Irish Times, 7 January 1989: Weekend, 8.
From 'Lightenings', a sequence of poems in progress. Collected in *Seeing Things* as 'Squarings' vi and vii. Not to be confused with 'Diptych,' *London Review of Books*, 3 July 1986 (C440) or the broadside (AA32) or *CutBank* 42, summer 1993 (C606).

C506 A LIGHTING PLOT [poem]
Sunday Independent, 8 January 1989: Colour Extra, 7.

C507 A YEATS SYMPOSIUM [essay] anniversary
Guardian, 27 January 1989: Review, 25.
'To mark tomorrow's 50th anniversary of his [Yeats's] death nine Irish poets, writers and academics assess the Yeats legacy and explain what he means to them personally.'

C508 SMALL FANTASIA FOR W. B. YEATS [poem]
Times Literary Supplement, 27 January–2 February 1989: 76.
Same version as (B124); collected with revisions in *Seeing Things*.

C509 IN THE MIDST OF THE FORCE-FIELD [essay]
Irish Times, 28 January 1989: Weekend, 9.
On W. B. Yeats, 50th anniversary of his death.

C510 ANOTHER LOVE-CHILD OF ENGLISH [review]
Sunday Telegraph, 26 February 1989. [Page number unknown.]
Review of *Collected Poems 1957–1987*, by Stephen Spender.

C511 THE SPRING [poem]
Sunday Tribune, 26 February 1989: 21.

C512 THE SOUNDS OF RAIN [poem]
THE CROSSING [poem/translation]
FROM LIGHTENINGS [poem]
LEARNING FROM ELIOT [essay]
Agenda, spring 1989: 5–31.
'Seamus Heaney Fiftieth Birthday Issue', 'The Sounds of Rain' is a revised version of (A43). 'The Crossing' is Seamus Heaney's translation of *INFERNO*, CANTO III, lines 82–129. From *Lightenings*: 'Shifting brilliancies. . . .'; 'Roof it again . . .' 'Squarings? In the game . . .'; 'Beneath the ocean of itself, . . .'; 'Strange how things in the offing, . . .'; 'Once, as a child, . . .'; '(I misremembered. . . . .'; 'The annals say: . .', collected as 'Squarings': i, ii, iii, iv, xlviii, vi, vii, viii, in *Seeing Things*. 'Learning from Eliot' is an edited version of remarks first prepared for the T. S. Eliot Centenary Lectures at Harvard University, spring 1988, and developed subsequently as the Cheltenham Lecture in October 1988. The essay is collected with revisions in *Finders Keepers*. An edition of 50 numbered and signed copies in a card slipcase was also issued. Cover reproduces a portrait of Heaney by Louis le Brocquy.

C513 FOSTERLING [poem]
EARNING A RHYME [essay]
Poetry Ireland Review, spring 1989: 1, 95–100.
A revised version of 'Fosterling' appeared in *Hill Field* (B95). The *Poetry Ireland Review* version was reprinted in *The Tree Clock* (A48) and collected in *Seeing Things*. 'Earning a Rhyme' is an edited version of a talk given at Boston University. The essay is reprinted with the addition of an introductory paragraph in *The Art of Translation: Voices from the Field* (B96). The essay is collected with revisions in *Finders Keepers*.

C514 YEATS' NOBILITY [essay]
Fortnight, Supplement, March 1989: II–III.
Extracts from a lecture delivered in the Guildhall, in Derry, on 28 January 1989, Yeats's 50th anniversary.

C515 THE PLACE OF EDWIN MUIR [essay]
Verse, March 1989: 22–33.
'This is an edited version of the Alexander Stone Lecture in Bibliophily delivered in November 1988 at the University of Glasgow.' Collected with revisions in *Finders Keepers*.

C516 A ROYAL PROSPECT [poem]
London Review of Books, 2 March 1989: 9.
Collected with revisions in *Seeing Things*.

C517 THE VISIONARY DARING OF YEATS UNDIMINISHED [essay]
Boston Sunday Globe, 12 March 1989: B16-B17.

C518 LIGHTENINGS [poems]
Irish Times, 8 April 1989: Weekend, 1–2.
'A sequence of poems in progress': 'The annals . . .'; 'A boat . . .'; 'Overhang of grass . . .'; 'And lightening? . . .'; 'Deserted harbour stillness . . .' collected in *Seeing Things* as 'Squarings': viii, ix, x, xii, xxiv, of which x, xii, xxiv have been revised.

C519 CROSSINGS [poem]
New Yorker, 17 April 1989: 35.
'On St. Brigid's Day . . .'; 'Not an avenue . . .'; 'Running water . . .'; 'Be literal . . .'; '*To those who have seen* . . .'; 'Shaving cuts . . .; 'And yes, my friend,. . . .' collected in *Seeing Things* as 'Squarings': xxx, xxxi, xxxii, xxxiii, xxxiv; xxxv, xxxvi, of which xxxii, xxxiv,xxxv, xxxvi have been revised.

C520 CROSSINGS [poem]
London Review of Books, 20 April 1989: 12.
'Travelling south at dawn . . .'; 'Only to come up . . .'; 'Everything flows . . .'; 'The ice was like . . .'; 'Choose one set of tracks . . .' collected in *Seeing Things* as 'Squarings' xxv, xxvi, xxvii, xxviii, xliii, of which xxvi and xliii have been revised.

C521 THE SOUNDS OF RAIN [poem]
Oxford Magazine, Eighth Week, Trinity Term, 1989: 12.

C522 THE CONVERT [essay]
Alpha, 8 June 1989: 15.
'Gerard Manley Hopkins died a hundred years ago today. Seamus Heaney looks at the legacy of a great poet unrecognised during his own lifetime.'

C523 THE PITCHFORK [poem]
Irish Times, 5 August 1989: Weekend: 7.

C524 THE PRIMACY OF INSTINCT [essay]
Weekend Telegraph, August 1989: 9.
'Seamus Heaney celebrates Lorca.'

C525 YEATS' NOBILITY [essay]
Four Quarters, fall 1989: 11–14.

C526 THE GOLDEN BOUGH [poem/translation]
Translation, fall 1989: 197–201.
Seamus Heaney's translation of *Aeneid* Book VI. Collected with revisions in *Seeing Things*.

C527 ANUBIS OF CWMDONKIN DRIVE [essay]
Irish Times, 2 September 1989: Weekend, 9.
Seamus Heaney on Dylan Thomas.

C528 A PILLOWED HEAD [poem]
Observer, 10 September 1989: 50.
Collected with revisions in *Seeing Things*.

C529 INFLUENCES [essay]
Boston Review, October 1989: 7–9, 22.
'Seamus Heaney thinks about the power of T. S. Eliot.'

C530 LITERATURE IS ALWAYS POLITICAL [review]
Sunday Tribune, 1 October 1989: B 6.
Review of *Essays on Politics and Literature* by Bernard Crick.

C531 SIX POEMS [poem]
London Review of Books, 26 October 1989: 20.
'When you sat, far-eyed . . .'; 'I was four but I turned . . .'; 'Sand-bed, they said. . . .'; 'All gone into the world . . .'; 'For certain ones what was written . . .'; 'The visible

sea . . .' collected in *Seeing Things* as 'Squarings' xxxix; xl; xli; xliv; xlv; xlvii.

C532 A LATCH [poem]
A WINDOW [poem]
Times Literary Supplement, 27 October–2 November 1989: 1172.
Collected in *Seeing Things* as 'Squarings' xxix; xlvi.

C533 LUSTRAL SONNET [poem]
SCRABBLE [poem]
SCENE SHIFTS [poem]
1973 [poem]
Owl, November 1989: 9–12.
Published under the title 'Glanmore Revisited'. '1973' collected with revisions in *Seeing Things* and is a different version than that of (C498).

C534 ROBERT FROST'S 'SWEETEST DREAM' [essay]
RESIN [poem]
THE POINT [poem]
Oxford Poetry, winter 1989/90: 12–16.
'The following ['Robert Frost's "Sweetest Dream" '] is the conclusion of Seamus Heaney's second lecture as Professor of Poetry, delivered on October 26th, 1989.' 'Resin' and 'The Point' collected in *Seeing Things*; 'The Point' collected with revisions as Part 1 of 'Three Drawings'.

C535 FROM HOLDINGS [poem]
Poetry Review, winter 1989/1990: 4–5.
Four 'Squarings': 'Cotyledon, flap your . . .'; 'A molten reddishness scudding . . .'; 'What were the virtues. . . .'; 'Staccato and reflexive . . .' of which 'What were the virtues . . .' was collected in *Seeing Things*, the other three are uncollected.

C536 PICK OF THE YEAR [selection]
Irish Times, 9 December 1989: Weekend, 1.
'Who read what in 1989? What did they admire? . . . Kathy Sheridan inquired.' Seamus Heaney selected *The Book of Evidence* by John Banville. In addition he

comments that it was 'a year of notable biographies: Cronin's Flann O'Brien, Holmes' Coleridge, Stevenson's Plath, McCarthy's Eric Gill. I found Ian Gibson's Fredrico Garcia Lorca especially compelling'.

C537 THE POINT [poem]
Alpha, 21 December 1989: Insert, 2A.
Collected with revisions as part I of 'Three Drawings' in *Seeing Things*.

C538 THE REDRESS OF POETRY [essay]
Times Literary Supplement, 22–28 December 1989: 1412, 1413, 1418.
An abridged version of the poet's inaugural lecture as Professor of Poetry at Oxford University, delivered 24 October 1989.

C539 A GLOSS ON DERRY [poem]
Drumragh Parish Magazine, 1989: 5.
Collected with revisions in 32 *Counties* (B98).

C540 POETS' ROUND TABLE: A COMMON LANGUAGE [essay]
PN Review, vol. 15, no. 4, 1989: 39–47.
Transcription of a debate between, Seamus Heaney, Joseph Brodsky, Derek Walcott, and Les Murray on the internationalism of poetry.

C541 PADRAIC FALLON [essay]
PN Review, vol. 16, no. 4, 1989: 19–21.
Review of *Padraic Fallon: Collected Poems*.

1990

C542 A RENT [poem]
QUOTING [poem]
Times Literary Supplement, 19–25 January 1990: 53.
Both poems are 'Squarings' and are collected in *Seeing Things* as poems, xxi and xxxvii respectively.

C543 GLANMORE REVISITED [poem]
Antaeus, spring/autumn, 1990: 48–51.

The poems 'Scrabble'; '1973'; 'Scene Shifts'; 'Lustral Sonnet' became parts 1, 4, 3 and 5 respectively of 'Glanmore Revisited' in *Seeing Things*.

C544 THE SKYLIGHT [poem]
BEDSIDE READING [poem]
Poetry Ireland Review, summer 1990: 3–4.
The poems appear under the title 'from "Glanmore Revisted"'.

C545 NEW AND SELECTED [essay]
Poetry Book Society Bulletin, summer 1990: 7.
Seamus Heaney writes on his *New Selected Poems 1966–1987*.

C546 GEORGE HERBERT'S EXQUISITE REDRESS [essay]
Erato, summer and fall 1990: 1, 6.
This is the text of the 'conclusion of Seamus Heaney's inaugural lecture at Oxford University of 24 October 1989, when, as the newly elected Professor of Poetry, he spoke on "The Redress of Poetry"'.

C547 PADRAIC FALLON: A MODERN WITH AN IRISH VOICE [essay]
Irish Times, 26 June 1990: Arts/Features, 8.
Reprinted as 'Introduction' to: *Padraic Fallon Collected Poems* (B100).

C548 A PILLOWED HEAD [poem]
THE SETTLE BED [poem]
Parnassus [July] 1990: 102–103.
'A Pillowed Head' collected with revisions in *Seeing Things*.

C549 THE SHIP IN THE AIR [poem]
Edge (Japan) autumn 1990: 1.
'The Ship in the Air' collected in *Seeing Things* as 'Squarings' viii.

C550 THE PULSE [poem]
THE JOURNEY BACK [poem]
stet, autumn 1990: 7.
Both poems collected in *Seeing Things*; 'The Pulse' is section II of 'Three Drawings'.

C551 EDITORIAL [essay]
O Write, autumn 1990: [1].

C552 SEEING THINGS [poem]
ABOVE THE BRIM: ON ROBERT FROST [essay]
Salmagundi, fall 1990–winter 1991: 78–81, 275–294.
'Above the Brim' is the text of the second lecture delivered by Heaney as Professor of Poetry at Oxford University on October 26, 1990. Collected in *Homage to Robert Frost* (B165).

C553 CASTING AND GATHERING [poem]
London Review of Books, 27 September 1990: 6.

C554 SCRABBLE [poem]
THE COT [poem]
1973 [poem]
LUSTRAL SONNET [poem]
BEDSIDE READING [poem]
THE SKYLIGHT [poem]
English Review (Oxford), November 1990: 21.
The poems appeared under the title 'Glanmore Sonnets'. With the addition of 'Scene Shifts' these six poems comprised 'Glanmore Revisited' in *Seeing Things*.

C555 FROM SQUARINGS [poems]
Force 10, winter 1990: 31–33.
'In famous poems . . .'; 'We climbed the Capitol . . .'; 'When you sat, . . .'; 'I was four . . .'; 'Sand-bed, they said . . . .'; 'Heather and kesh . . .'; 'Choose one set . . .'; '*All gone into* . . .'; 'For certain ones . . .'; 'Mountain air from . . .'; 'The visible sea . . .'; 'Strange how things . . .' collected in *Seeing Things* as 'Squarings' 'xxxvii, xxxviii, xxxix, xl, xli, xlii, xliii, xliv, xlv, xlvi, xlvii, xlviii.'

C556 THE VULGAR MUSE [review]
Sunday Times, 23 December 1990: Books, 9.
Review of *The Faber Book of Vernacular Verse* edited by Tom Paulin.

C557 SEAMUS HEANEY ON KEITH DOUGLAS [essay]
Poet's House Members' Magazine, vol. 2, no. 1, 1990/1991: 11.

C558 FROM SQUARINGS [poem]
Agni, vol. 29, no. 30, 1990: 168–173.
'When you sat . . .'; 'I was four . . .'; 'Sand-bed, they said . . .'; 'Heather and kesh . . .'; '*All gone into the world of light?* . . .'; 'For certain ones . . .' collected in *Seeing Things* as 'Squarings' xxxix (revised), xl, xli, xlii, xliv, xlv.

C559 GROVE HILL [poem]
BOTHAR BUI [poem]
Thames Poetry, vol. 3, no. 17, 1990: 42–43.
'Bothar Bui' collected in *Seeing Things* as 'Squarings' xiii.

1991

C560 POET AS PROFESSOR [essay]
Poetry Ireland Review, winter/spring 1991: 10–13.

C561 A CHORUS [poem/translation]
New York Times, 1 January 1991: 29.
Collected with revisions in *The Cure at Troy*.

C562 THE BIRETTA [poem]
Times Literary Supplement, 25 January 1991: 3.
Collected with revisions in *Seeing Things*.

C563 FIELD OF VISION [poem]
SEEING THINGS [poem]
The Irish Times, 2 February 1991: Weekend, 9.
Both poems collected in *Seeing Things*; 'Field of Vision' collected with revisions.

C564 A RETROSPECT [poem]
London Review of Books, 7 February 1991: 8.

C565 CHORUS FROM THE CURE AT TROY [poem/translation]
Arion: A Journal of Humanities and the Classics, spring 1991: 131–138.

C566 STIRLING STANZAS [poem]
Airthrey Journal, spring 1991: 14–15.

C567 MAN AND BOY [poem]
THE GOLDEN BOUGH [poem/translation]
Poetry Review, spring 1991: 72–74.
Both poems collected in *Seeing Things*; 'Man and Boy' with revisions. 'The Golden Bough' is Seamus Heaney's translation of *Aeneid*, Book VI, lines 98–177.

C568 MARKINGS [poem]
FIELD OF VISION [poem]
CASTING AND GATHERING [poem]
Field 44, spring 1991: 52–55.

C569 THE PATH BETWEEN INCENSE AND SENSUALITY [review]
Independent on Sunday, 31 March 1991: 27.
Review of *Gerard Manley Hopkins: A Very Private Life* by Robert Bernard Martin.

C570 MARKINGS [poem]
Oxford Today, Trinity Issue, 1991: 21.
Collected with revisions in *Seeing Things*.

C571 THE POET AS WITNESS AND VICTIM [review]
Irish Times, 6 April 1991: Weekend, 9.
Review of *Stone* and *Collected Critical Prose and Letters* by Osip Mandelstam, and *Hope Against Hope* by Nadezhda Mandelstam.

C572 FIELD OF VISION [poem]
Spectator, 13 April 1991: 36.

C573 THE FAIR HILL [poem]
New Yorker, 29 April 1991: 36.
Collected in *Seeing Things* as 'Squarings' xviii.

C574 A BASKET FULL OF CHESTNUTS
New Yorker, 27 May 1991: 36.
Collected as 'A Basket of Chestnuts' in *Seeing Things*.

C575 A ROYAL PROSPECT [poem]
Threepenny Review, summer 1991: 5.

C576 CREWEIAN ORATION 1991 [note]
Oxford University Gazette, 21 June 1991: 1256–1257.

C577 MAN AND BOY [poem]
Tikkun, July/August 1991: 67.

C578 A POET'S EUROPE [essay]
European Poetry Festival Special Issue: A Poet's Europe, October/December 2001: 156–161.

C579 EMIGRANTS AND INNER EXILES [essay]
Ireland at Home and Abroad, 1991: 9–10.

1992

C580 WEIGHING IN [poem]
Times Literary Supplement, 17 January 1992: 28.
Collected with revisions in *The Spirit Level*.

C581 ON CHRISTOPHER MARLOWE'S 'HERO AND LEANDER' [essay]
BEGINNING WITH MY STREETS [review]
Harvard Review, Premier Issue, spring 1992: 35–39; 136–137.
'On Christopher Marlowe's Hero And Leander' is an excerpt from Seamus Heaney's Oxford lecture which is collected in *The Redress of Poetry*. The review is of *Beginning with my Streets* by Czeslaw Milosz.

C582 PART OF HIS OWN POSTERITY [obituary]
Fortnight, May 1992: 31.
Seamus Heaney writes on Michael McLaverty.

C583 AT BANAGHER [poem]
New Welsh Review, summer 1992: 11.
Collected with revisions in *The Spirit Level*.

C584 THE PLACE OF WRITING [essay]
THE GRAVEL WALKS [poem]
Thinker Review, summer 1992: 303–307.
'The Place of Writing' is an excerpt from 'W. B. Yeats and Thoor Ballylee', collected in *The Place of Writing*. 'The Gravel Walks' collected with revisions in *Seeing Things*.

C585 AN INVOCATION [poem]
London Review of Books, 6 August 1992: 16.

C586 A DOG WAS CRYING TONIGHT IN WICKLOW ALSO [poem]
Independent on Sunday, 16 August 1992: Sunday Review, 22.

C587 STYLE [essay]
Georgetown Review, fall 1992: 16–17.

C588 AN INVOCATION [poem]
Harvard Review, fall 1992: 25–26.
Collected with revisions in *The Spirit Level*.

C589 A HUNDRED YEARS AFTER – A TENNYSON SYMPOSIUM [essay]
Times Literary Supplement, 2 October 1992: 8.
'Twelve writers reflect on Tennyson's achievement and influence'; Seamus Heaney is one of the twelve writers.

C590 LARKIN AND HEANEY [letter]
Evening Press, 5 October 1992: 13.
Seamus Heaney responds to Michael O'Toole's article in which O'Toole 'misreads' Heaney's poem 'The Journey Back' dedicated to the memory of Philip Larkin.

C591 POSTSCRIPT [poem]
Irish Times, 10 October 1992: Weekend Books, 9.
Collected with revisions in *The Spirit Level*.

C592 KEEPING GOING [poem]
New Yorker, 12 October 1992: 76–77.

C593 THE FLIGHT PATH [poem]
P. N. Review, November/December 1992: 31–32.
Collected with revisions in *The Spirit Level*.

C594 POET OF THE WALKING WOUNDED [essay]
Irish Times, 21 November 1992: Weekend, 8.
'Seamus Heaney on the art and brief life of Francis Ledwidge.'

C595 A CURLEW IN THE ORKNEYS [essay]
RESOLUTIONS [poem]
Mica, winter 1992: 7–9; 31–32.

The essay is 'extracted from a lecture delivered to the Annual Conference of IASIL (Japan) in July 1990'. 'Resolutions' are three twelve-line untitled poems: 'To refuse the other cheek. To cast the stone'; 'I saw the future in a sunburnt crowd'; 'They were a kind of anti-funeral.' 'To refuse the other cheek. To cast the stone' collected as the third section of 'Weighing In' in *The Spirit Level*.

C596 A SOFA IN THE FORTIES [poem]
Verse, winter 1992: 6–7.

C597 RESOLUTIONS [poem]
AT BANAGHER [poem]
Verso, Oxford Poetry, Hiver 1992: 47–51.
This was a French issue.

C598 FRANK BIDART: A SALUTE [essay]
Agni, no. 36, 1992: 270–271.
'This publication is adapted from the introduction to the March, 1992, Morris Gray Reading at Harvard University.'

C599 AN INVOCATION: IN MEMORIAM HUGH MACDIARMID [poem]
Hermathena (Quatercentenary issue), 1992: 113–114.
Collected with revisions as 'An Invocation' in the *Spirit Level.*

1993

C600 HERE FOR GOOD [poem]
Times Literary Supplement, 22 January 1993: 10.
Collected with revisions as 'Poet's Chair' in *The Spirit Level.*

C601 TO A DUTCH POTTER IN IRELAND [poem]
Threepenny Review, spring 1993: 15.

C602 THE SINGING CLASSES [poem]
Education Today, spring 1993: 20.
'This poem was originally written for the closedown of Carysfort and has since been revised for *Education Today*.'

C603 ON W. B. YEATS'S 'THE MAN AND THE ECHO' [essay]
Harvard Review, spring 1993: 96–99.
'This is the conclusion of a lecture given at Oxford in 1990, during the Hilary Term. The lecture dealt with the contrasting attitudes of W. B. Yeats and Philip Larkin to "last things"'.

C604 THE CLAY PIPES [poem/translation]
Poetry and Audience, March 1993: 28.
Translation from the Irish of 'Na Píopaí Créafóige' by Cathal ÓSearcaigh.

C605 THE RAINSTICK [poem]
New Republic, 22 March 1993: 42.

C606 DIPTYCH [poem]
CutBank 42, summer 1993: 47–48.
Collected as 'Saint Kevin and the Blackbird' in *Seeing Things*. *CutBank* is published by The Associated Students of the University of Montana.

C607 MINT [poem]
New Republic, 21 June 1993: 45.
Collected with revisions in *The Spirit Level*.

C608 JOHN CLARE [note]
John Clare Society Journal, July 1993: 28.

C609 DYLAN THE DURABLE [essay]
Salmagundi, fall 1993: 66–85.

C610 ON A MAGIC CARPET RIDE OF CONVICTION [essay]
Irish Independent, 18 September 1993: 7–9.
'Three of Ireland's foremost poets write on the occasion of the All Ireland Final.' Seamus Heaney writes on his home county of Derry.

C611 THE MODERN MISTRESS [poem]
Verse, winter 1993: 87.
Collected with revisions as 'Two Lorries' in *The Spirit Level*.

C612 THE FLIGHT PATH [poem]
Threepenny Review, winter 1993: 5.

C613 VOICES BEHIND A DOOR: ROBERT FROST [essay]
Poetry Review, winter 1993/1994: 31–32.
'Seamus Heaney, in a revised and edited version of his talk at the ICA on November 24 1993, admires Robert Frost's ability "to stay buoyant, rhythmically and spiritually, while still managing to register the full drag of being alive".'

C614 FROM SANDYMOUNT STRAND [poem]
Irish Times, 18 December 1993: Weekend, 5.

C615 THE MIDNIGHT COURT [poem/translation]
Brangle, New Writing from the School of English, Queen's University, Belfast, 1993: 74–75.
Seamus Heaney's translation from the Irish of Brian Merriman. Collected as part of 'The Midnight Verdict' in *The Midnight Verdict.*

C616 POET'S CHAIR [poem]
Agni, 38, 1993: 1–2.
Collected with revisions in *The Spirit Level.*

1994

C617 BOY DRIVING HIS FATHER TO CONFESSION [poem]
TO A WINE JAR [poem]
Honest Ulsterman, spring 1994: 19–20.
'To a Wine Jar' is Seamus Heaney's translation from Horace, *Odes* III, xxi.

C618 FRONTIERS OF WRITING [essay]
Bullán, spring 1994: 1–15.

C619 MORE RIVER RHYMES [poem]
Irish University Review, spring 1994: 60.

C620 VARIETIES OF IRISHNESS? [essay]
Fortnight, March 1994: 40.
'On the Northern Ireland Peace Process.'

C621 AT THE WELLHEAD [poem]
New Yorker, 28 March 1994: 74.

C622 MAYBE THERE'S SOMEBODY DREAMING ME [poem/translation]
IT'S SNOWING ENEMY SNOW [poem/translation]
INHABITED BY A SONG [poem/translation]
Lift Magazine, April 1994: 133–135.
Seamus Heaney's translations from the Romanian of Ana Blandiana.

C623 THE MIDNIGHT VERDICT [poem/translation]
Printer's Devil, Issue D [summer] 1994: 43–47.
Seamus Heaney's translation from the Irish of Brian Merriman.

C624 LAMENT FOR TIMOLEAGUE [poem/translation]
Recorder, summer 1994: 52–54.
Seamus Heaney's translation from the Irish of Sean Ó Coileain.

C625 TWO LORRIES [poem]
Oxford Poetry, summer 1994: 6–7.

C626 LAMENT 19 OR: A DREAM [poem/translation]
Harvard Review, fall 1994: 7–10.
Translations by Stanislaw Baranczak and Seamus Heaney from the Polish of Jan Kochanowski.

C627 DAMSON [poem]
Antaeus: The Final Issue, autumn, 1994: 278–279.

C628 SEAMUS HEANEY ON ROBERT GRAVES 'THE STRAW' [note]
ORPHEUS AND EURYDICE [poem/translation]
Poetry Review, autumn 1994: 19–20; 41–44.
'Orpheus and Eurydice' is Seamus Heaney's translation of Ovid's *Metamorphoses*, Book X.

C629 LIGHT FINALLY ENTERS THE BLACK HOLE [essay]
Sunday Tribune, 4 September 1994: A9.
'Seamus Heaney writes about his feelings of hope, anger, and elation [in response to the cease-fire in Northern Ireland].'

C630 BURYING THE PAST [essay]
Scotland on Sunday, 4 September 1994: 'Ireland: Days of Hope' Supplement, 1.

C631 FILLING THE CUP ABOVE THE BRIM [essay]
Sunday Independent, 25 September 1994: 8L.
Review of *The Annals of Chile* by Paul Muldoon.

C632 TOLLUND [poem]
New Yorker, 3 October 1994: 92.
Collected with revisions in *The Spirit Level*.

C633 THE CALL OF COAGH [essay]
Age, 15 October 1994: 1, 6.
The Melbourne Writers' Festival Special Edition.

C634 'SEAMUS HEANEY' [essay]
Times Literary Supplement, 2 December 1994: 12.
This is a note on Elizabeth Bishop's *One Art*.

C635 MYCENAE LOOKOUT [poem]
Times Literary Supplement, 16 December 1994: 15.

C636 FAR AWAY [poem]
The New Yorker, 26 December 1994–2 January 1995: 88.
Collected in *The Spirit Level* as section 5 of 'The Flight Path'.

1995

C637 GOD MOVES IN MYSTERIOUS METRES [essay]
Eureka Street (Australia), January/February 1995: 24–27.
'This is an edited and revised version of the talk Seamus Heaney gave at the Melbourne Writers' Festival during the 1994 poetry session sponsored by *Eureka Street*.' It covers issues relating to religion and poetry.

C638 THE WATCHMAN AT MYCENAE [poem]
Notre Dame Review, Inaugural Issue, spring, 1995: 1–2.
Collected with revisions as 'The Watchman's War', section I of 'Mycenae Lookout' in *The Spirit Level*.

C639 KOCHANOWSKI'S LAMENTS: 6, 7, 8 [poem/translation]
Poetry Review, summer, 1995: 30–31.

Translations by Stanislaw Baranczak and Seamus Heaney from the Polish of Jan Kochanowski. These poems were collected as 'Laments' 6, 7 and 8 in *Laments*. This issue also contains a note by Seamus Heaney on translating Kochanowski's sonnets.

C640 POSTSCRIPT [poem]
Tandem, summer 1995: 2.
Tandem is published in Worcester, England.

C641 THE RICHARD ELLMANN PRIZE [essay]
Oxford Poetry, summer/autumn 1995: 4–5.
Seamus Heaney's remarks on adjudicating the Prize he founded.

C642 INHABITED BY SONG [poem/translation]
AS IF [poem/translation]
MAYBE THERE'S SOMEBODY DREAMING ME [poem/translation]
LONELINESS [poem/translation]
HUNT [poem/translation]
THE SWING [poem]
ORPHEUS IN IRELAND: ON BRIAN MERRIMAN'S THE MIDNIGHT COURT [essay]
Southern Review, July 1995: 468–471, 676–678, 786–806.
Seamus Heaney's translations from the Romanian of Ana Blandiana. 'The Swing' is collected with revisions in *The Spirit Level*. 'Orpheus in Ireland' was originally delivered as a lecture at Oxford University on 21 October 1993.

C643 LAMENT I [poem/translation]
Irish Times, 1 July 1995: Weekend, 8.
Translations by Stanislaw Baranczak and Seamus Heaney from the Polish of Jan Kochanowski.

C644 A WATER SEER [poem]
Times Literary Supplement, 7 July 1995: 8.
Collected as 'His Reverie of Water' in *The Spirit Level*.

C645 [UNTITLED][essay]
Independent, 31 August 1995: 15.
Seamus Heaney was asked: 'are you optimistic about the future?' on the occasion of the first anniversary of the first IRA cease-fire.

C646 TRIBUTES TO PETER FALLON: 25 YEARS OF GALLERY PRESS
Irish Literary Supplement, fall 1995: 6.
Seamus Heaney's tribute is one of eight.

C647 SPERANZA IN READING: ON 'THE BALLAD OF READING GAOL' [essay]
Island (Tasmania), autumn 1995: 40–48.

C648 BEOWULF'S BOAST [poem/translation]
THE WATCHMAN REMEMBERS FROM MYCENAE
WAVELENGTHS [poem]
College Green, Trinity College Dublin, Autumn 1995: [46–49].
Seamus Heaney's translation of *Beowulf*, lines 407–459.

C649 WHITBY-SUR-MOYOLA [poem]
Honest Ulsterman, autumn 1995: 40.

C650 LAMENT 1 [poem/translation]
Threepenny Review, fall 1995: 13.
Translation by Stanislaw Baranczak and Seamus Heaney from the Polish of Jan Kochanowski and collected as 'Lament 1' in *Laments*.

C651 TO A DUTCH POTTER IN IRELAND [poem]
Poetry Ireland Review, autumn/winter 1995: 62–64.

C652 THE RAIN STICK [poem]
Observer Review, 10 September 1995: 17.
Includes an article and interview material on *The Redress of Poetry*.

C653 IRELAND'S FINAL FRONTIER: IT'S ALL IN THE MIND [essay]
Irish Independent, 12 September 1995: section 2, 2–3.
'This is an edited version of "Frontiers of Writing" from *The Redress of Poetry*.'

C654 EXILE RUNES [poem/translation]
London Review of Books, 21 September 1995: 8.
Seamus Heaney's translation of *Beowulf*, lines 1117–1140.

C655 A CALL [poem]
Spectator, 23 September 1995: 39.

C656 A DOG WAS CRYING TO-NIGHT IN WICKLOW ALSO [poem]
REMEMBERED COLUMNS [poem]
MYCENAE NIGHTWATCH [poem]
Poetry, October/November 1995: 1–4.
'Mycenae Nightwatch' was collected as 'The Nights' in part 4 of 'Mycenae Lookout' in *The Spirit Level.*

C657 REDRESS OF THE 'HONY OF ROSES' [essay]
Guardian, 7 October 1995: 31.
'This is an edited version of "The Redress of Poetry" from *The Redress of Poetry.*'

C658 LAMENTS [poem/translation]
Times Literary Supplement, 6 October 1995: 32.
Translations by Stanislaw Baranczak and Seamus Heaney from the Polish of Jan Kochanowski collected as 'Lament' 5 and 'Lament' 13 in *Laments.*

C659 THE STRAND [poem]
THE POPLAR [poem]
Sunday Times, 8 October 1995: Books, 8–9.

C660 THE GRAVEL WALKS [poem]
Observer Review, 8 October 1995: 16.

C661 THE SHARPING STONE [poem]
New Yorker, 23 October 1995: 62–63.
Collected with revisions in *The Spirit Level.*

C662 KEEPING GOING [poem]
AT BANAGHER [poem]
SAINT KEVIN AND THE BLACKBIRD [poem]
MINT [poem]
TWO LORRIES [poem]
Fortnight, November 1995: 26–27.

C663 A LANDFALL [poem]
Oar 8, November 1995: 3.

C664 HOMELESSNESS [essay]
Big Issues, 9–22 November 1995: 20.
Seamus Heaney discusses the travelling community.

C665 SAINT KEVIN AND THE BLACKBIRD [poem]
Link-Up, December 1995: 25.

C666 CREDITING POETRY [essay]
New Republic, 25 December 1995: 27–34.

C667 CHARLES MONTEITH [essay]
Independent, 30 December 1995: Magazine, 15.

C668 LAMENTS [poem/translation]
TRANSLATORS' NOTE [essay]
Graph, second series, no. 1: 1995: 38–40; 41.
'Stanislaw Baranczak and Seamus Heaney translate three laments by the sixteenth-century poet Jan Kochanowski.' The poems were collected as 'Laments' 2, 3 and 4 in *Laments*.

C669 WHY I WRITE [essay]
Inscape '95, vol. 50, 1995: 8–11.
Inscape is a publication of Pasadena City College.

C670 LAMENTS [poem/translation]
Partisan Review, no. 3, 1995: 443–445.
Translations by Stanislaw Baranczak and Seamus Heaney from the Polish of Jan Kochanowski collected as 'Lament' 16 and 'Lament' 2 in *Laments*.

C671 CHEERS [poem]
TWO STICK DRAWINGS [poem]
A CALL [poem]
A BRIGID'S GIRDLE [poem]
Parnassus, vol. 20, nos 1 and 2, 1995: ['Cheers' appears on page (10) of the supplement honouring Herb Leibowitz which follows page 8]; 281–284.

1996

C672 LINES TO MYSELF [poem]
Washington Post, 2 January 1996: C10.
One of Seamus Heaney's earliest poems included in an article titled 'Irish Poems that Drown Out Words of War' by Colman McCarthy.

C673 A POET REMEMBERED [essay]
Scotsman, 27 January 1996: 16.
'Seamus Heaney, Nobel Laureate in literature, recalls his delight in first meeting Norman MacCaig the man and his work.'

C674 LISTENING AND WRITING [essay]
Irish Times, 27 January 1996: Weekend, 9.
On Norman MacCaig.

C675 AUDENESQUE [poem]
Times Literary Supplement, 9 February 1996: 11.
In memory of Joseph Brodsky.

C676 GUS MARTIN [memorial tribute]
Roscrea Review, spring 1996: 3.

C677 THE FRAGMENT [poem]
MYCENAE LOOKOUT [poem]
Harvard Review, spring 1996: 12, 15–21.

C678 THE FRAGMENT [poem]
Irish Review, spring/summer 1996: 108.

C679 THE SINGER OF TALES: ON JOSEPH BRODSKY [essay]
New York Times Book Review, 3 March 1996: 31.

C680 AS TARHEELS OF THE MIND [essay]
Chapel-Hill Herald, 18 May 1996: 8.
'Following is Seamus Heaney's speech at Kenan Stadium as part of this year's University of North Carolina at Chapel Hill commencement exercises.'

C681 THE YELLOW BITTERN [poem/translation]
Poetry Ireland Review, summer 1996: 68–69.
Seamus Heaney's translation from the Irish of Cathal Buí MacGiolla Ghunna (1680–1756).

C682 JOSEPH BRODSKY 1940–1996 [essay]
Metre, autumn 1996: 31–34.
The essay appears under the title: 'Secret Sharer: *Seamus Heaney Remembers Joseph Brodsky.*'

C683 THE WALK [poem]
Agenda, autumn/winter 1996: 5.

C684 RAFTERY'S KILLEADAN [poem/translation]
Éire-Ireland, fall/winter 1996: 9.
Seamus Heaney's translation from the Irish of Antoine Raftery (1784–1835).

C685 THE LITTLE CANTICLES OF ASTURIAS [poem]
Slate on Paper, September 1996: 59.
Originally posted Monday, 24 June, in '*Slate* the internet magazine'

C686 THE YELLOW BITTERN [poem/translation]
Ireland of the Welcomes, September/October 1996: 31.
Seamus Heaney's translation from the Irish of Cathal Buí Mac Giolla Ghunna (c. 1680–1756)

C687 WISLAWA SZYMBORSKA [letter]
Times Literary Supplement, 1 November 1996: 20.

C688 CASSANDRA [poem]
Threepenny Review, winter 1996: 9.
Collected with revisions as part 3 of 'Mycenae Lookout' in *The Spirit Level.*

C689 I AM RAFTERY [poem/translation]
Merton Journal, Advent 1996: 33.
Seamus Heaney's translation from the Irish of Antoine Raftery (1784–1835).

C690 AUDENESQUE [poem]
THE ERRAND [poem]
Atlanta Review, vol. 2, no. 2, 1996: 22–25.

C691 SHORTS FOR SIMIC [essay]
Agni, no. 44, 1996: 202–208.
Seamus Heaney writes about Charles Simic.

C692 A TORCHLIGHT PROCESSION OF ONE [essay]
Parnassus, vol. 21, nos 1 and 2, 1996: 11–29.
Seamus Heaney writes about Hugh MacDiarmid.

C693 DIPTYCH [poem]
Tracks, no. 11, 1996: 22–23.
Collected as 'Saint Kevin and the Blackbird' in *The Spirit Level.*

1997

C694 THE ROAD TO DERRY [poem]
Derry Journal, 31 January 1997: 3.
('Air: "The Boys of Mullaghbawn" ') includes a note on the occasion of the song, 'The Road to Derry', which was written just after Bloody Sunday.

C695 THE ROAD TO DERRY [poem]
Guardian, 1 February 1997: 2.
(Air: 'The Boys of Mullaghbawn') includes a note on the occasion of the song, 'The Road to Derry', which was written just after Bloody Sunday.
Published in an article titled 'Heaney's Derry Lament'.

C696 ON THE ART OF DIMITRI HADZI [essay]
Harvard Review, spring 1997: 126–128.

C697 COLMCILLE THE SCRIBE [poem/translation]
THE GLAMOURED [poem/translation]
Recorder, spring & fall 1997: 8–10.
Seamus Heaney's translation of 'Colmcille the Scribe' from the eleventh-century Irish; 'The Glamoured', translated from the Irish of Aodhagan O Rathaille, c. 1675–1729.

C698 BAGS OF WOBBLE AND FLOP: COMMENTS ON 'THE SCHOOL BAG' [essay]
Times, 25 March 1997: 36.
'Ted Hughes and Seamus Heaney reveal what prompted them to compile *The School Bag.*'

C699 SRUTH [poem]
Sunday Times, 30 March 1997: Books, 2.
Collected with revisions in *Electric Light.*

C700 THE FRAGMENT [poem]
Tabla, no. 6, April 1997: 5.
Collected with revisions in *Electric Light*.

C701 THE STAIN OF SPILLED BLOOD [letter]
Irish News, 15 May 1997: 1.
Letter denouncing murder of Sean Brown. Facsimile of Seamus Heaney's hand-written letter is also reproduced. Collected in *Lost Lives* (B183).

C702 LETTER [extract]
Sunday Independent, 18 May 1997: 1.
Published under the title 'Poet begs release from stain of blood'. Version of (C701).

C703 I AM RAFTERY [poem/translation]
Rosebud, summer 1997: 23.
Seamus Heaney's translation from the Irish of Antoine Raftery (1784–1835).

C704 COLMCILLE THE SCRIBE [poem/translation]
Irish Times, 7 June 1997: Weekend, 9.
Seamus Heaney's translation from the eleventh-century Irish. 'Monday is the feast of St. Colmcille, the 1400th anniversary of whose death falls this year.'

C705 SEAMUS HEANEY [selection]
Irish Times, 5 July 1997: Weekend, 1.
Summer reading selections. Seamus Heaney mentions: Volume 2 of Richardson's *Life of Picasso*, Nooteboom's *Roads to Compostela* and works by Andrew Motion and Deirdre Madden.

C706 JESUS AND THE SPARROWS [poem/translation]
Spirituality, July/August 1997: 242.
Seamus Heaney's translation from the eighth-century Irish.

C707 THE LUPINS [poem]
Sunday Times, 17 August 1997: Books, 9.
'The Lupins' was collected with revisons as 'Lupins' in *Electric Light*.

C708 [UNTITLED] [essay]
CANOPY [poem]
Metre, autumn 1997: 15–16, 36–37.
Seamus Heaney contributes to: 'Irish Poetry and the Diaspora'.

C709 FURTHER LANGUAGE [essay]
Studies in the Literary Imagination, fall 1997: 7–16.
'The following is an edited version of a keynote address given at the American Conference for Irish Studies, Queen's University, Belfast, June 26, 1995.'

C710 THE FUNERAL OF BEOWULF [poem/translation]
Times Literary Supplement, 19 September 1997: 4.
Seamus Heaney's translation of *Beowulf*, lines 3137–3182.

C711 SEAMUS HEANEY ON W. H. AUDEN (1907–73) [essay]
Independent on Sunday, 5 October 1997: Review Section, 33.
Postcard Biographies from the National Portrait Gallery. 'After the success of the first series of postcard biographies, written in the 1920s and 1930s and taken from the NPG's archives, we begin a series of new, specially commissioned 70-word biographies of and by major figures of today.'

C712 THREE-PIECE: 1. A SUIT; 2. A TIE; 3. A COAT [poem]
Poetry, October/November 1997: 30–32.
'A Suit' was collected with revisions as section 4 of 'Ten Glosses' in *Electric Light*.

C713 THE GOOD STEWARD [memorial tribute]
Books Ireland, November 1997: 305.
In memory of Lar Cassidy, Literature Officer of Arts Council of Ireland.

C714 ALL IRELAND'S BARD [review]
Atlantic Monthly, November 1997: 155–160.
Review of *W. B. Yeats: A Life* by R. F. Foster.

C715 THE LAST SURVIVOR [poem/translation]
Times Literary Supplement, 14 November 1997: 13.

Seamus Heaney's translation of *Beowulf*, lines 2241–2270.

C716 WOULD THEY HAD STAY'D [poem]
Poetry Review, winter 1997/1998: 7.
Collected with revisions in *Electric Light*.

C717 [INTERNATIONAL BOOKS OF THE YEAR] [selection]
Times Literary Supplement, 5 December 1997: 10–11.
Seamus Heaney selects: *Tales from Ovid* by Ted Hughes and an anthology of Hungarian poetry, *In Quest of the Miracle Stag*.

1998

C718 A WOUNDED POWER RISES FROM THE DEPTHS [review]
Irish Times, 31 January 1998: Weekend, 11.
Review of *Birthday Letters* by Ted Hughes. 'Seamus Heaney celebrates the "undertruths of sadness and endurance" in Ted Hughes's elegy for lost love.'

C719 CARLO [poem]
SOMETHING TO WRITE HOME ABOUT [essay]
Princeton Library Chronicle, spring 1998: 441–443; 621–632.
'Something to Write Home About' – 'The following essay is an edited version of the script for a television film made by Flying Fox Films in the autumn of 1997 and broadcast by the BBC (Northern Ireland) in March 1998.' Published as (A77).

C720 UNHERD MELODIES [essay]
Irish Times, 11 April 1998: Supplement on the Northern Ireland Good Friday Agreement, 1.

C721 INTIMATIONS [essay]
Irish Times, 2 May 1998: Weekend, 11.
Initiates 'Poetry Now': a column on the state of poetry in Ireland and abroad.

C722 A SEA-CROSSING [poem/translation]
River City, summer 1998: 117–118.
Seamus Heaney's translation of *Beowulf*, lines 193–228.

C723 SEAMUS HEANEY [essay]
Art Matters, June 1998: 'Aosdana: A special supplement accompanying *Art Matters*, Issue no 29, June 1998', [3].
Seamus Heaney's response to being conferred 'Saoi of Aosdana' on 1 May 1998.

C724 THE MARCHING SEASON [poem]
Irish Times, 10 July 1998: 1.

C725 BEOWULF [note]
BEOWULF [poem/translation]
Sunday Times, 26 July 1998: Books, 6–7.
In the 'Note' Seamus Heaney discusses his translation of *Beowulf*; the sections of *Beowulf* (with Seamus Heaney's titles) are published here as follows: 'Paths to Power', lines 1–25; 'A Sea-crossing', lines 193–228; 'The Return to Geatland', lines 1880–1924.

C726 THE RECIPROCITY OF TEARS [essay]
Irish Times, 22 August 1998: 7.
Seamus Heaney writes on the Omagh bombing.

C727 CARLO [poem]
AT TOOMEBRIDGE [poem]
Thumbscrew, autumn 1998: 2–4.
'At Toomebridge' was collected with revisions in *Electric Light*.

C728 AN IMAGE FROM BEOWULF [poem]
Crab Orchard Review, fall/winter 1998: 102.
Collected with revisions as 'The Border Campaign' in *Electric Light*.

C729 TWO PAINTINGS BY LE DOUANIER ROUSSEAU [poem]
Graph, autumn/winter 1998: 'Lar Cassidy Memorial Feature', xv.

C730 GETTING THE PICTURE: ON DERMONT SEYMOUR'S PAINTING 'THE RUSSIANS. WILL WATER THEIR HORSES ON THE SHORES OF LOUGH NEAGH' [essay]
Éire-Ireland, fall/winter 1998 and spring 1999: 9–12.

C731 [UNTITLED] [note]
INTO ARCADIA [poem]
BASSAE [poem]
MYCENAE [poem]
Cara, September/October 1998: 14, 16–17.
The poems are published here under the title 'Sonnets from the Peleponnese.'
'Into Arcadia' collected with revisions as 'Sonnets from Hellas' in *Electric Light*.

C732 THE GLAMOURED [poem/translation]
Index, September/November 1998: 131–132.
Seamus Heaney's translation of 'The Glamoured' from the Irish of Aodhagan O Rathaille, c. 1675–1729. A note on the aisling form in seventeenth- and eighteenth-century Irish-language poetry accompanies the poem.

C733 ON FIRST LOOKING INTO TED HUGHES'S 'BIRTHDAY LETTERS' [poem]
New Yorker, 5 October 1998: 64–65.
Collected with revisions as 'On His Work in the English Tongue' in *Electric Light*.

C734 ON A NEW WORK IN THE ENGLISH TONGUE [poem]
Sunday Times, 11 October 1998: Books, 7.
Revised version of (C733) collected with revisions as 'On His Work in the English Tongue' in *Electric Light*.

C735 THE HEDGEHOG AND THE FOX [essay]
Irish Times, 17 October 1998: 1.
Seamus Heaney comments on John Hume and David Trimble being awarded the Nobel Peace Prize for 1998.

C736 [UNTITLED] [memorial tribute]
Irish Times, 31 October 1998: 11.
On the death of Ted Hughes.

C737 BLUE [poem]
Poetry Ireland Review, winter 1998: 75–76.
'Blue' was collected with revisions as 'Blue' of 'Red, White and Blue' in *Electric Light*.

C738 [INTERNATIONAL BOOKS OF THE YEAR][selection]
Times Literary Supplement, 4 December 1998: 10.
'Seamus Heaney selected the following books: Tom Paulin's *The Day-Star of Liberty*; Jonathan Galassi's bilingual edition of *Montale's Collected Poems 1920–1954* and Ted Hughes's *Birthday Letters*.'

C739 THE GLAMOURED [poem/translation]
Aquarius 23/24, 1998: 15–16.
Seamus Heaney's translation from the Irish of Aodhagan O Rathaille, c. 1675–1729.

C740 ENERGY AT EASTER [essay]
Lapis, no. 7, 1998: 11–12.
This essay is a reprint of 'Unherd Melodies' in *The Irish Times*, 11 April 1998 (C720).

C741 A SCHOOL OF POETRY CLOSES [poem/translation]
RAFTERY'S KILLEADAN [poem/translation]
Force 10, no. 9, 1998: 13–15.
Seamus Heaney's translations from the Irish of Tadhg Óg Ó hUiginn (?–1447) and Antoine Raftery (1784–1835) respectively.

C742 SELECTIONS FROM BEOWULF [poem/translation]
Agni 48, 1998: 1–5.
Seamus Heaney's translation of *Beowulf*, the sections of *Beowulf* (with Seamus Heaney's titles) are published here as follows: 'Grendel Attacks Hrothgar's Hall', lines 86–163; 'Beowulf's Departure from Denmark', lines 1880–1924.

1999

C743 [ON BRIAN MOORE] [memorial tribute]
Irish Times, 13 January 1999: 11.
Seamus Heaney's comment on the death of Brian Moore.

C744 THE PEACE OF THE WORD IS ALWAYS WITH YOU [essay]
Sunday Times, 17 January 1999: Culture, 10–11.

C745 REMEMBERING MALIBU [poem]
[ON BRIAN MOORE] [memorial tribute]
Sunday Tribune, 17 January 1999: Review Section, 2.
Seamus Heaney comments on the death of the novelist Brian Moore.

C746 THE PERCH [poem]
A HYPERBOREAN [poem]
New Yorker, 18 January 1999: 30; 56.
'A Hyperborean' was collected with revisions as 'To the Shade of Zbigniew Herbert' in *Electric Light*.

C747 NORTHERN STAR [essay]
Magill, February 1999: 44.
On John Montague.

C748 A SCHOOL OF POETRY CLOSES [poem/translation]
Kestrel, spring, 1999: 62–63.
Seamus Heaney's translation from the Irish of Tadhg Óg Ó hUiginn (?–1447).

C749 COLMCILLE THE SCRIBE [poem/translation]
Gazette of the Grolier Club [spring] 1999: 5.
Seamus Heaney's translation of 'Colmcille the Scribe' from the eleventh-century Irish.

C750 MYCENAE [poem]
CONKERS [poem]
Persephone (Harvard), spring 1999: 34, 36.
'Conkers' collected as sonnet 2 in 'Sonnets from Hellas'; 'Mycenae' collected as 'Pylos', sonnet 3 in 'Sonnets from Hellas'. Both poems were collected in *Electric Light*.

C751 THE REAL NAMES
Irish University Review, spring/summer 1999: 1–5.
Collected with revisions in *Electric Light*.

C752 A PLACE AT THE EDGE [essay]
Cara, March/April 1999: 32.
On Felim Egan.

C753 CARLO
Times, 27 March 1999: Metro Section: 17.

C754 RED, WHITE AND BLUE [poem]
Sunday Times, 11 April 1999: Culture, 13.
Collected with revisions in *Electric Light*.

C755 FROM THE MINISTRY OF FEAR [poem]
[Untitled][note]
Irish Times, 11 May 1999; Education & Living Section, 8.
Seamus Heaney's contributions appear in an article about his old Grammar School, St Columb's, Derry. Brian Friel and John Hume are among the other contributors.

C756 A GREAT MAN AND A GREAT POET [memorial tribute]
Observer, 16 May 1999: Review Section 4.
Seamus Heaney's address at the Ted Hughes Memorial Service.

C757 KNOWN WORLD [poem]
Times Literary Supplement, 21 May 1999: 21.
Collected with revisions in *Electric Light*.

C758 THE HAUNTED MERE [poem/translation]
Threepenny Review, summer 1999: 8.
Seamus Heaney's translation of *Beowulf*, lines 1310–1379.

C759 THE GOD OF THE SEA GREETS BRAN IN THE LAND OF THE WAVES [poem]
New Yorker, 2 August 1999: 48–49.
Seamus Heaney's translation from the Irish.

C760 NEW STAVES: ON THE FUNCTION OF POETRY [essay]
Threepenny Review, fall 1999: 6–7.

C761 MEMORIAL ADDRESS, WESTMINSTER ABBEY, 13 MAY 1999 [memorial tribute]
American Poet, fall 1999: 8–9.
Seamus Heaney's Memorial address for Ted Hughes.

C762 1999 ST. JEROME LECTURE: FRETWORK, ON TRANSLATING BEOWULF [essay]
In Other Words: The Journal for Literary Translators, autumn/winter 1999/2000: 23–33.

This is a version of 'The Drag of the Golden Chain' (C769) and the St Jerome Lecture given at the Elizabeth Hall, South Bank London, 5 October 1999.

C763 THE BRIDGE [poem]
Forbes, 4 October 1999: 95.
Collected with revisions as section 3 of 'Ten Glosses' in *Electric Light*.

C764 BANN VALLEY ECLOGUE [poem]
Times Literary Supplement, 8 October 1999: 32.
Collected with revisions in *Electric Light*.

C765 ARION [poem/translation]
Times Literary Supplement, 15 October 1999: 28.
Seamus Heaney's translation from the Russian of Alexander Pushkin.

C766 A NEW BEOWULF [poem/translation]
New York Review of Books, 4 November 1999: 8.
'Excerpt from Seamus Heaney's Introduction and translation of *Beowulf*.'

C767 THE DRAG OF THE GOLDEN CHAIN – ON TRANSLATING BEOWULF [essay]
Times Literary Supplement, 12 November 1999: 14–16.

C768 [ON IRELAND AND SCOTLAND][essay]
Irish Times, 30 November 1999: Scotland and Ireland (special report), 7.
The 'note' appears in an article titled: 'A heritage in common and yet somehow estranged'.

C769 MILOSZ AND WORLD POETRY [essay]
ROBERT HAAS AND SEAMUS HEANEY [essay]
Partisan Review, winter, 1999: 20–38; 39–48.
Both of these essays are transcripts of discussions that took place at the International Czeslaw Milosz Festival, Claremont-Mckenna College, April 1998. In 'Milosz and World Poetry', Seamus Heaney is one of four commentators; his comments appear on pages 20–24,

34, 35, 36, 37. In 'Robert Haas and Seamus Heaney', Seamus Heaney's comments appear on pages 42–48.

C770 A GATE LEFT OPEN: ON TRANSLATING THE SONGS OF JANACEK'S JOURNAL D'UN DISPARU [essay]
Translation Ireland, December 1999: 1–2.

C771 A DREAM OF SOLSTICE [poem]
Irish Times, 21 December 1999: 1. (See C839.)

C772 THE MANGER [poem]
Ballyscullion Parish Bulletin, 25 December 1999: front page.

C773 BANN VALLEY ECLOGUE [poem]
Sunday Business Post, 26 December 1999: 1.

C774 THE LITTLE CANTICLES OF ASTURIAS [poem]
Chapman, 1999: 38.
Collected with revisions in *Electric Light*.

C775 SCREENPLAY [poem]
Cork Review 99, 1999: 6.

C776 THE CIVIL POWER [poem/translation]
Modern Poetry in Translation no. 15, 1999: 174.
Seamus Heaney's translation from the Russian of Alexander Puskin.

2000

C777 BEOWULF [poem/translation]
American Poetry Review, January/February 2000: 21–28.
Seamus Heaney's translation of *Beowulf*, lines 1–490. The translation appears under the title: 'An Introduction and New Verse Translation', which also includes the poet's comments under 'About this Translation'.

C778 PUSHKIN AND POMEROY [letter]
Irish Times, 22 January 2000: 17.

C779 WHAT DOES 'PEACE' MEAN ANYWAY? [letter]
Irish News, 8 February 2000: 6.

C780 THE REAL NAMES [poem]
Threepenny Review, spring 2000: 34–35.
Collected with revisions in *Electric Light*.

C781 THE HEALING FOUNTAIN [essay]
Prometheus, no. 3 (spring) 2000: 6–11.
This is an abridged version of a BBC talk on poetry given by Seamus Heaney on 17 January 1999.

C782 NIGHTS OF '57 [poem]
IN THE AFTERLIFE [poem]
Harvard Review, spring 2000: 6.
'Nights of '57' collected as section 2 of 'Bodies and Souls' in *Electric Light*.

C783 AN EMPTY SURFBOARD ON A FLAT SEA [poem]
Paris Review, spring 2000: 97–98.
A number of poets were given eight titles and asked to write a poem on the one of their choice: 'Jaws'; 'The English Are So Nice'; 'Howl'; 'An Empty Surfboard on a Flat Sea'; 'Dr. Strangelove'; 'Lines to Seduce a Stranger an Hour Before the Ships Sails'; 'Upon Julia's Breasts'; 'A Lavatory in a Cathedral.'

C784 THRESHOLD AND FLOOR [essay]
URLAR [poem]
Metre, spring/summer 2000: 265–268.
'Author's note': 'úrlár is a term used in relation to the "floor" of sound of Scottish piping'.

C785 SUMMER [poem/translation]
Éire-Ireland, spring/summer 2000: 88–89.
Seamus Heaney's translation from the Irish.

C786 NIGHTS OF '57 [poem]
THE AUGEAN STABLES [poem]
New Yorker, 20 March 2000: 62, 66.
Included in the article 'Famous Seamus' by Seamus Deane. 'Nights of '57' collected as section 2 of 'Bodies and Souls'; 'The Augean Stables' collected as sonnet 4 of 'Sonnets from Hellas' in *Electric Light*.

C787 COMMENCEMENT ADDRESS [essay]
New York Times, 29 May 2000: A11.
Excerpt from Seamus Heaney's Commencement Address at the University of Pennsylvania.

C788 TRANSCENDING BOUNDARIES [essay]
Almanac: University of Pennsylvania, 30 May 2000: 'Commencement/Baccalaureate', Supplement, S2–S3.

C789 THE REAL NAMES [poem]
THE INNER ZODIAC [essay]
Around the Globe, summer 2000: 28–29.
'The Real Names' was collected with revisions in *Electric Light*. The essay comments upon the poem.

C790 [UNTITLED] [essay]
Ireland Fund, summer 2000: 29.
Seamus Heaney comments on Kevin Mallen.

C791 THE REAL NAMES [poem]
PROSE NOTE [essay]
Times Educational Supplement, 16 June 2000: The Friday Magazine, 21–22.
The poem is collected with revisions in *Electric Light*.
Published under the heading 'Heaney on Shakespeare'.

C792 ELECTRIC LIGHT [poem]
New Yorker, 19 and 26 June 2000: 152–153.
Collected with revisions in *Electric Light*.

C793 WHAT MAKES A GOOD POET? [essay]
Portal, 2 July 2000: 4–6.
This is a transcript of Seamus Heaney's talk delivered in the Athenaeum, 8 May 2000.

C794 THE GREEN MAN, THE ART OF BARRIE COOKE [essay]
Modern Painters, autumn 2000: 70–72.

C795 OUT OF THE BAG [poem]
Threepenny Review, fall 2000: 8.

C796 INTO ARCADIA [poem]
CONKERS [poem]

PYLOS [poem]
Mondogreco, fall 2000: 5–7.
The poems appear under the heading 'Sonnets from Hellas'.

C797 AT TOOMEBRIDGE [poem]
THE AUGEAN STABLES [poem]
College Green, September 2000: 6.
'The Augean Stables' collected as sonnet 4 of 'Sonnets from Hellas' in *Electric Light*.

C798 BOOK LEARNING [essay]
Harvard Magazine, September/October 2000: 66–68.
Seamus Heaney's Commencement Address at Harvard University.

C799 AN ARTIST OF THE FLOWING WORLD [essay]
Independent, 13 October 2000: Friday Review, 9.
Seamus Heaney comments on the work of Barrie Cooke.

C800 THE PEOPLE OF THE SEA [essay]
Los Angeles Times, 5 November 2000: Book Review, 5–6.
Reprint of Seamus Heaney's introduction to *The People of the Sea*.

C801 THE DEAREST FRESHNESS [poem]
Threepenny Review, winter 2000: 7.

C802 GREEN MAN – THE ART OF BARRIE COOKE [essay]
Céide, December 2000/January 2001: 11–13.

C803 INTERNATIONAL BOOKS OF THE YEAR [selection]
Times Literary Supplement, 1 December 2000: 11.
Seamus Heaney selects Polish poet Czeslaw Milosz's *Roadside Dog* and *Milosz's ABC*, Saul Bellow's *Ravelstein* and Richard Murphy's *Collected Poems*.

C804 CAN A POEM STOP A TANK: BEI LING AND SEAMUS HEANEY IN THE CONVERSATION BEIJING TRIED TO STOP [essay]
Los Angeles Times, 13 December 2000: Book Review, 7–9.

C805 NATIVITY POEM [poem/translation]
FLIGHT TO EGYPT [poem/translation]
New Yorker, 18 December: 69, 72.
Seamus Heaney's translations from the Russian of Joseph Brodsky.

C806 LINKED VERSES [poem]
Irish Times, 30 December 2000: Weekend, 8.

C807 THE CLOTHES SHRINE [poem]
BRIAN MOORE [obituary]
Harp, Journal of Irish Literature, 2000: 5; 122–124.
'The Clothes Shrine' collected with revisions in *Electric Light*.

C808 FOREWORD [essay]
Pages: Postgraduate Research in Progress, 2000: 5.

2001

C809 NO TREATY I FORESEE, WILL SALVE COMPLETELY [essay]
News Letter, 22 January 2002: Act of Union Supplement, 4–5.
Seamus Heaney comments on his poem 'Act of Union', which is reprinted with the essay.
The News Letter is published in Belfast.

C810 REFLECTIONS [essay]
Magill, 2001 February: 23
Seamus Heaney comments on the 1981 Hunger Strikes.

C811 THE LOOSE BOX [poem]
SOMETHING TO PROTECT [essay]
Parnassus, vol. 25 [February], 2001: 275–277; 308–321.
'Something to Protect' is a review of Nikolay Zabolotsky's *Selected Poems*.
'The Loose Box' was collected with revisions in *Electric Light*.

C812 THE HEART OF A VANISHED WORLD [essay]
Guardian, 24 February 2001: Saturday Review, 1–2.
Excerpt from Seamus Heaney's introduction to *The*

People of the Sea: Celtic Tales of the Seal Folk by David Thomson.

C813 THE BLACKBIRD OF BELFAST LOUGH [poem/translation]
Garm Lu: A Canadian Celtic Arts Journal, Earrach (spring) 2001: 7.

C814 POSTSCRIPT TO ST. LUCIA [poem]
Poetry Review, spring 2001: 41–43.

C815 SALLY ROD [prose poem]
TREA [prose poem]
A PRESENT FROM MR PAUSE [prose poem]
NO HARM [prose poem]
NATURA NATURANS [prose poem]
BROTHER STALK [prose poem]
Dublin Review, spring 2001: 40–45.
The poems appear under the heading: '*from* Private Excursions'.

C816 THE BOILING HOUSE [poem]
The Shop, spring 2001: 10.
Published at Skeagh Schull, Co. Cork.

C817 CASTILIAN SPRING [poem]
DESFINA: AN CHAILLEACH [poem]
The Kenyon Review (spring 2001) and *Stand* (March 2001): 48, 48–49.
This combined issue: The Centennial Celebration of the Nobel Prizes.

C818 TEN GLOSSES: 1. THE MARCHING SEASON; 2. THE CATECHISM; 3. THE BRIDGE; 4. A SUIT; 5. THE PARTY; 6. W.H. AUDEN; 7. THE LESSON; 8. MOLING'S GLOSS; 9. COLLY; 10. A NORMAN SIMILE [poem]
SEEING THE SICK [poem]
Guardian, 24 March 2001: Saturday Review, 12.

C819 TURPIN SONG [poem]
THE GAELTACHT [poem]
SEEING THE SICK [poem]
Three Glosses: A Suit; The Party; The Lesson [poem]
London Magazine, April/May 2001: 31–34.

C820 SONNETS FROM HELLAS: 1. INTO ARCADIA; 2. CONKERS; 3. PYLOS; 4. THE AUGEAN STABLES; 5. CASTALIAN SPRING; 6. DESFINA [poem]
Guardian, 7 April 2001: Saturday Review, 8.

C821 LUX PERPETUA [essay]
Poetry Book Society Bulletin, summer 2001: 5–6.
Seamus Heaney discusses *Electric Light*.

C822 R. S. THOMAS MEMORIAL [memorial tribute]
Poetry Ireland Review, summer 2001: 11–14.
The memorial was delivered by Seamus Heaney at Westminster Abbey, 28 March 2001.

C823 BOOKS FROM IRELAND [poem]
Honest Ulsterman, summer 2001: 34.
Collected with revisions as 'The Bookcase' in *Electric Light*.

C824 LUX PERPETUA [essay]
Guardian, 16 June 2001: Review, 9.
'This article was written for *The Poetry Book Society Bulletin*.'

C825 RHAPSODY AND REBUKE [essay]
Irish Times, 29 June 2001: Arts, 12.
'Seamus Heaney celebrates Czeslaw Milosz, a poet of "simplicity costing not less than everything" – and a fellow Nobel Laureate in literature – who turns 90 tomorrow.'

C826 HERBERT MCCABE, O.P., II [memorial tribute]
Religious Life Review, July/August 2001: 250–252.

C827 THE POET AT NINETY [essay]
Los Angeles Times, 1 July 2001: Book Review, 8.
Seamus Heaney is one of several writers recognising Czeslaw Milosz's 90th birthday in this feature article.

C828 THE GIFT OF TONGUES [review]
Los Angeles Times, 19 August 2001: Book Review, 3.
Seamus Heaney reviews *A Way of Life, Like Any Other* by Darcy O'Brien.

C829 POETRY'S POWER AGAINST INTOLERANCE [essay]
New York Times, 26 August 2001: Week in Review, 13.
Seamus Heaney's comments mark 'the opening this week of the UN's special conference on racism in Durban, South Africa.'

C830 ACTIONS SPEAK LOUDER THAN WORDS IN WAR AGAINST RACISM [essay]
Irish Times, 27 August 2001: 14.
Seamus Heaney's comments mark 'the opening this week of the UN's special conference on racism in Durban, South Africa.'

C831 ARE YOU DOING ANY POETRY WITH THEM? [essay]
American Scholar, autumn 2001: 160.
Seamus Heaney's essay appears in the table of contents as 'The Podium'. The essay is an excerpt from the Inaugural Darcy O'Brien Memorial Lecture, University of Tulsa, 25 April 2001.

C832 TIME AND AGAIN: POETRY AND THE MILLENNIUM [essay]
European English Messenger, autumn 2001: 19–23.
'This is an abbreviated version of a Millennium Lecture delivered at the University of Liverpool, March 22, 2000.'

C833 THE SNOWBALL [poem]
Metre, autumn 2001: 95–96.

C834 FOR ALMA MATER [poem]
Irish News, 9 November 2001: 3.

C835 HORACE AND THUNDER [poem/translation]
Irish Times, 17 November 2001: Weekend, 10.
Seamus Heaney's translation of Horace, *Odes*, 1, 34. Collected with revisions as 'Anything Can Happen' in *District and Circle*.

C836 A DREAM OF SOLSTICE [poem]
Kenyon Review, winter 2001: 1–2.
This is a different version from that of (C771).

C837 THE REAL NAMES [poem]
VITRUVIANA [poems]
Reader, no. 8, 2000: 5–10.
Both poems collected with revisions in *Electric Light*. This issue also contains an interview with Seamus Heaney.

C838 A PRESENT FROM OLD ARDBOE [poem]
Cork Literary Review, vol. 8, 2001: 1.

C839 THE TWO MICE [poem/translation]
Agni, no. 54, 2001: 191–197.
Seamus Heaney's translation from the Scottish of Robert Henryson.

2002

C840 HORACE AND THUNDER [poem/translation]
Times Literary Supplement, 18 January 2002: 40.
Seamus Heaney's translation of Horace, *Odes*, 1, 34.
Collected with revisions in *District and Circle*. This is a different version of the collected poem from that of (C838).

C841 REALITY AND JUSTICE: ON TRANSLATING HORACE, ODES 1, 34 [essay]
HORACE AND THUNDER [poem/translation]
Translation Ireland, spring 2002: 8–11.
'Horace and the Thunder' was collected with revisions as 'Anything Can Happen' in *District and Circle*. This is the same version as (C835).

C842 THE WHOLE THING: ON THE GOOD OF POETRY [essay]
Recorder, spring 2002: 5–20.
'This is a transcript of Seamus Heaney's address at the Annual Distinguished Lecture, Department of International Health and Tropical Medicine, The Royal College of Surgeons in Ireland, 5 November 2001.'

C843 TESTIMONY [poem]
Irish Times, 16 March 2002: 9.
Collected with revisions as 'Anahorish 1944' in *District and Circle*.

C844 SWEET AIRS THAT DELIGHT [essay]
Guardian, 13 April 2002: Saturday Review 4.
'This is an edited extract from Seamus Heaney's *Finders Keepers*.'

C845 ON THOMAS FLANAGAN (1923–2002) [memorial tribute]
New York Review of Books, 25 April 2002: 9.

C846 THE LIFT [poem]
Poetry Ireland Review, summer 2002: 74–75.
This is a different version of 'The Lift' (C851) and (AA72).

C847 THE STRUGA ADDRESS [essay]
A KEEN FOR THE COINS [poem]
SANTIAGO DE COMPOSTELA [poem]
Irish Pages, summer 2002: 114–116.

C848 SIXTH SENSE, SEVENTH HEAVEN [essay]
Dublin Review, autumn 2002: 115–126.

C849 REALITY AND JUSTICE: ON TRANSLATING HORACE, ODES, 1, 34 [essay]
HORACE AND THE THUNDER, AFTER HORACE, ODES, 1, 34 [poem/translation]
THE LIFT [poem]
NONCE WORDS [poem]
Irish Pages, autumn/winter 2002/2003: 50–57.
'Reality and Justice: On Translating Horace Odes, 1, 34' is a reprint of (C841). This is a different version of 'Horace and the Thunder' from that of (C835), (C840), (C841) or the version collected as 'Anything Can Happen' in *District and Circle*. 'The Lift' (see C846) and 'Nonce Words' collected with revisions in *District and Circle*.

C850 THE TRANCE AND TRANSLATION [essay]
Guardian Review, 30 November 2002: 4, 6.
'This is an edited version of the first Sorley MacLean Memorial Lecture, given by Seamus Heaney at the Edinburgh Festival 2002.'

C851 [BOOKS OF THE YEAR] [selection]
Sunday Tribune, 22 December 2002: Artlife, 8.
Seamus Heaney selected the following books: *Becoming George* by Ann Saddlemyer; *The Vell of Order* by Alfred Brendel; *Troubled Thoughts, Majestic Dreams* by Dennis O'Driscoll; *Moy Sand and Gravel* by Paul Muldoon; *The Face of the Earth* by Medbh McGuckian; and Ciaran Carson's translation of *Dante's Inferno*.

C852 POETIC BALANCE: LITERARY & HISTORICAL [essay]
Literary and Historical Magazine, vol. 3, no. 2, [2002] Journal Edition: 9–11.
As part of the essay the editors have reproduced Seamus Heaney's acceptance speech notes upon becoming an Honorary Fellow of the Literary & Historical Society at University College Dublin.

C853 THE BIG WIPER [prose poem]
The Worcester Review [2002]: 47.

2003

C854 TESTIMONY [poem]
Guardian Review, 15 February 2003: 36.
Collected with revisions as 'Anahorish 1944' in *District and Circle*.

C855 SOPHOCLEAN [poem]
New Yorker, 3 March 2003: 78.

C856 HELMET [poem]
New York Review of Books, 25 September 2003: 52.
Collected with revisions in *District and Circle*.

C857 FILIAL CLOSENESS AT WORK [review]
Financial Times Magazine, 27 September 2003: 26, 28.
Review of *W. B. Yeats: The Arch-Poet, 1915–1939*, by R. F. Foster.

C858 BAGS OF ENLIGHTENMENT [essay]
Guardian, 25 October 2003: 4–6.

C859 SINGING HIGH: JAMES CLARENCE MANGAN [essay]
Poetry Ireland Review, 77: 10–17.
This is an edited version of 'remarks to introduce a reading of Mangan's poem' at the Dublin Writers Museum, 1 May 2003.

C860 PIT STOP NEAR CASTLETOWN [poem]
NONCE WORDS [poem]
LINKED VERSES [poem]
Agni, no. 57, 2003: 4–8.
'Nonce Words' collected with revisions in *District and Circle*; 'Linked Verses' collected with revisions as 'Midnight Anvil' in *District and Circle*.

C861 THE HEALING FOUNTAIN [essay]
Prometheus, no. 3, 2003: 6–11.

D

CONTRIBUTIONS TO EXHIBITION CATALOGUES AND PROGRAMMES

D1 Peter Street at Bankside [poem]
Programme for the laying of the Foundation Stone of the Lyric Players Theatre, 12 June 1965.
A short note by Seamus Heaney is also printed here. The poem is collected in *a needle's eye*, The Lyric Players Theatre, Belfast 1979 (Belfast: Lyric Players Theatre, 1979): 45.

D2 The outlaw [poem]
Programme for Cheltenham Festival of Literature, 3–8 October 1966: 43.
'The Outlaw' was one of five poems chosen from 429 entries for the Cheltenham Festival Guinness Poetry Competition. It was read by Seamus Heaney at the Festival on 8 October 1966.
The poem was collected with revisions in *Death of a Naturalist*.

D3 Requiem for the Croppies [poem]
Programme for *Poets' Offering*, The Abbey Theatre, Dublin, Sunday, 25 August 1968: [4].
'Poets' Offering' was 'a poetry reading in aid of the measures being taken by the Missionary Sisters of Our Lady of the Holy Rosary, Killeshandra, to alleviate the suffering caused by the Nigeria–Biafra conflict.' The other participants were: Austin Clarke, Pearse Hutchinson, Thomas Kinsella and Mairtin O'Direain.
The poem was collected with revisions in *Door into the Dark*.

D4 Victorian Guitar [poem]
Programme for *Poets Loused with Song*: 'an entertainment for the cultural edification of the Citizens and the financial edification of the Derry Itinerant Settlement Committee', at the City Hotel, Londonderry, 12 December 1969: [2]. The other participants were: David Hammond, Michael Longley and Derek Mahon.

D5 Introduction [essay]
Exhibition catalogue for *Poetry in Manuscript*, A Queen's University Belfast exhibition of poets' work sheets, 9–28 February 1970, Queen's Art Gallery [1].

The exhibition included an early version and two final drafts of Seamus Heaney's poem 'The Diviner'.

D6 Wedding Day [poem]
Programme for *An Evening of Poetry & Music*, presented by Claddagh Records at the Peacock Theatre, Dublin, 5 July 1970: [4].

D7 Navvy [poem]
First Calf [poem]
Programme for Capella 4, published by Tara Telephone, Dublin Arts Festival, Poetry 1970: 26–27.
Both poems collected with revisions in *Wintering Out*.

D8 T. P. Flanagan [essay]
Programme for *The Irish Imagination 1959–1971*, Municipal Gallery of Modern Art, Dublin, 23 October–31 December 1971: 58.

D9 Where I was born [essay]
Programme for BBC Radio, *Today and Yesterday in Northern Ireland*, summer 1973: 9–12.
The programme's theme was 'Where I was born'. Three black-and-white photographs accompany the text.

D10 T. P. Flanagan [note]
Exhibition catalogue for *T. P. Flanagan, Paintings 1967–1977*, An Arts Council of Northern Ireland exhibition, 13 October–5 November 1977: [3]–[4].

D11 Encounter on Station Island [poem]
Programme for *Tom Delaney Memorial Concert*, Ulster Museum, Botanic Gardens, Belfast, 7 December 1979: [2]–[3].
Collected with revisions as 'Station Island' VIII in *Station Island*.

D12 After the Irish [poem/translation]
Field Day Theatre Company Programme for *Translations* by Brian Friel, 1980: [5].
The original Irish and Seamus Heaney's translation appear side by side. The poem's two sections, 'The small

bird . . .'; 'Look far. Cast . . .'. 'The small bird . . .' was published with revisions in 2001 (C816).

D13 Chekhov on Sakhalin [poem]
Field Day Theatre Company Programme for Brian Friel's translation of *Three Sisters* by Anton Chekhov, 1981: [1].
The programme also includes on the same page a note by Seamus Heaney on the poem.

D14 Introduction and commentary [essay]
Exhibition catalogue for *A Personal Selection: Seamus Heaney*, 20 August–24 October 1982, Ulster Museum: [5]–[6] et al.
In addition to the 'Introduction', Seamus Heaney briefly comments on his favourite works in the Ulster Museum. There are paragraph-long comments by Seamus Heaney spread through the book.

D15 Going Back [poem]
Field Day Theatre Company Programme for *The Communication Cord* by Brian Friel [September 1982]: [4].
Collected with revisions as 'Station Island' X in *Station Island.*

D16 A Schooling [essay]
Programme for *St. Thomas's 25th Silver Jubilee*, 1957–82: 11.
Seamus Heaney writes about his year of teaching at St. Thomas in 1962–1963.

D17 Barrie Cooke [essay]
Exhibition catalogue for *Six Artists from Ireland: An Aspect of Irish Painting*, Department of Foreign Affairs, Government of Ireland [November] 1983: 29–33.
This catalogue was published by the Department of Foreign Affairs for an exhibition in Athens, Greece.
'Barrie Cooke' was reprinted in *Barrie Cooke* by Aidan Dunne (Dublin: The Douglas Hyde Gallery; Belfast: Arts Council of Northern Ireland, 1986).

D18 Heaney on Brodsky [essay]
Programme for *Seamus Heaney and Joseph Brodsky: Gate Theatre Readings*, 6 October 1985: [3].

D19 Ross Wilson: Long Works [note]
Exhibition catalogue, *Ross Wilson: Long Works*, Arts Council of Northern Ireland Exhibition, Belfast, 1986: [1].

D20 I thought of walking round and round a space [poem]
A marked absence, a noted silence, tree [note]
Exhibition programme for *Seamus Heaney–Felim Egan: Towards a Collaboration*, October 1986; Ardhowen, The Theatre by the Lakes, Enniskillen, Co. Fermanagh: [3]–[4].

D21 From the Republic of Conscience [poem]
From the Republic of Conscience, UCG Amnesty Group [Galway], 1987: 2.
See also (AA24).

D22 O Riada's Bounty [essay]
In Memoriam Sean O Riada [poem]
Programme for *O Riada Retrospective*, National Concert Hall, Dublin, 24, 25 and 26 April 1987: [23], [25], [27].
Three concerts in memory of the Irish composer Sean O Riada.

D23 The Schoolbag [poem]
Exhibition catalogue for *A Poet's Pictures: A Selection Of Works Of Art Collected By John Hewitt (1907–1987)*, The Shambles Art Gallery, Hillsborough, Co. Down, October 1987: [4].
The poem is in memory of John Hewitt. 'The Schoolbag' was collected with revisions in *Seeing Things*.

D24 Bourke's Mark [note]
Exhibition catalogue for *Brian Bourke: Paintings and Sculpture 1963–1988*, at the Galway Arts Festival, July 1988: 3.

D25 Henry Pearson: In the middle of the field [note]
Exhibition catalogue for *Henry Pearson:* Columbia Museum of Art Southern Heritiage Series, October 1988–January 1989: [inserted sheet].
There are six variations of the note's design.

D26 [Where does the spirit live? Inside or outside . . .] [poem]
Programme for *Yeats: A Fifty Year Salute*, A Lecture on W. B. Yeats by Seamus Heaney. A Field Day Lecture, Guildhall, Derry City, 28 January 1989: [3].
The poem appears here without a title. It was first published in *The Times Literary Supplement*, 27 January 1989 (C508), where it appeared under the title 'A Small Fantasia for W. B.' and was collected with revisions as 'Squarings' xxii in *Seeing Things*.

D27 The Schoolbag [poem]
The Ash Plant [poem]
The Pitchfork [poem]
Programme for *An Upstairs Outlook: An Evening of Poetry by Seamus Heaney and Michael Longley*, Thursday, 4 May 1989 at the Elmwood Hall, University Road, Belfast: [3]–[5].
Commemorative programme published in aid of the Linen Hall Library Development Campaign. An untitled statement by Seamus Heaney is printed on the back flap. 'The Schoolbag' and 'The Ashplant' collected with revisions in *Seeing Things*. This version of 'The Schoolbag' is different from that of (D23).

D28 Fosterling [poem]
Programme for *50/60*, a reading presented by Poetry Ireland to mark the sixtieth birthday of John Montague and the fiftieth birthday of Seamus Heaney, at the Gate Theatre, Dublin, 11 June 1989: [3].

D29 The Latch [poem]
Programme for Irish Literature Festival, Poetry Center of the 92nd Street Y, New York, NY, 14 May 1990: [single leaf insert].

John Montague and Nuala Ní Dhomhnaill also participated in the reading. Collected with revisions as 'Squarings' xxix in *Seeing Things*.

D30 The Cure at Troy [note]
Field Day Theatre Company programme for *The Cure at Troy*, October/December 1990: [3].

D31 Louis Le Brocquy [note]
Exhibition catalogue for *Louis Le Broquy: Paintings 1940–1990*, Hibernia Fine Art, Kerlin Gallery, January 1991: [1].

D32 Digging Deeper [essay]
Programme for University College Dublin's performance of *Volunteers* by Brian Friel, 14–18 January 1991.

D33 Carolyn Mulholland [note]
Exhibition catalogue for *Carolyn Mulholland*, Adam Gallery, 17 October 1991: 2.

D34 T. P. Flanagan [note]
Exhibition catalogue for *T. P. Flanagan*, RHA, PPRUA, 'A European Journey' and other paintings, Taylor Galleries, Dublin, 26 March–11 April 1992: [1].

D35 Barry Flanagan [note]
The Names of the Hare [poem]
Exhibition catalogue for *The Names of the Hare: Large Bronzes by Barry Flanagan, 1983–1990* with poetry and prose written and selected by Seamus Heaney, Yorkshire Sculpture Park 18 June–31 August 1992: 5; 10–17.

D36 The Cure at Troy [note]
Programme for *The Cure at Troy*, Double Edge Drama, Eton College, for The Edinburgh Fringe Festival, 17–29 August 1992: [3].
Seamus Heaney's 'note' was written especially for this production.

D37 Carolyn Mulholland [note]
Shifting Angles [poem]

Exhibition catalogue for *Carolyn Mulholland and Breon O'Casey*, Narrow Water Gallery, Warrenpoint, Co. Down, 24 September–21 October 1992: [1], [3].
The note is a reprint of (D33); 'Shifting Angles' was collected with revisions as 'Poet's Chair' in *The Spirit Level*. This is the first appearance of the poem.

D38 Felim Egan [note]
Exhibition catalogue for *Felim Egan: Recent Works*. 5–27 November 1992, The Fenderesky Gallery at Queen's Unviversity Belfast: [1]–[2].

D39 An Angler's Crouch [note]
Exhibition catalogue for *Claoclo: Barrie Cooke*, The Haags Gemeentemuseum, The Hague Municipal Museum, 1992: 11–13.

D40 Pamela Hardesty [note]
Exhibition catalogue for *Pamela Hardesty: The Paradiso*, January 1993: [2].
Seamus Heaney briefly discusses *The Divine Comedy*.

D41 To a Dutch Potter in Ireland [poem]
A Sofa in the Forties [poem]
Keeping Going [poem]
Diptych [poem]
Programme for *Poetry International, Poetry on the Road*, Rotterdam, 19 and 20 June 1993: 2–15.
'To a Dutch Potter in Ireland', 'A Sofa in the Forties', and 'Keeping Going', collected with revisions in *The Spirit Level*. 'Diptych' collected as 'St. Kevin and the Blackbird' in *The Spirit Level*.

D42 Postscript [poem]
Admission Catalogue for *Burren College of Art, 1993*: 15.

D43 A Call [poem]
Programme for 25: To celebrate its first twenty-five years, the Gallery Press, in association with the National Theatre Society, presents a Poetry Reading, the Abbey Theatre, Dublin, 2 July 1995: 16.

D44 Birthday rhymes of Dimitri [poem]
Exhibition catalogue for *Dimitri Hadzi: Sculpture, Monotypes, and Paintings 1985–1995*, Kouros Gallery, New York, 2–26 November 1995: 3.

D45 T. P. Flanagan [essay]
Exhibition Catalogue for *T. P. Flanagan*, Ulster Museum, Belfast, 1995: 96.

D46 Bronze heads [note]
Exhibition catalogue for *Bronze Voices*, Belfast, 1995: [3].
Published to coincide with the exhibition *Bronze Voices*. A bronze head of Heaney by the Belfast sculptor Philip Flanagan was included in the exhibition.

D47 Squarings [note]
Programme for *West Cork Chamber Music Festival 1996*, Bantry House, Bantry County Cork, 23–29 June 1996: 20.

D48 Introduction [essay]
Programme produced by the Dublin Arts Council for *Ireland and Its Diaspora Festival*, Frankfurt Book Fair [October] 1996: [5].

D49 The Rain Stick [poem]
Programme for *Seamus Heaney* presented by the Academy of American Poets and the Pierpont Morgan Library, 13 November 1996: [3].
Paul Muldoon introduced Seamus Heaney at this reading at the Pierpont Morgan Library, New York.

D50 Introduction [essay]
Exhibition catalogue for *Conor Fallon*, Kinsale: Gandon Editions, 1997: 7.

D51 Canopy [poem]
Exhibition catalogue for *Canopy 1 David Ward, A Work for Voice and Light in Harvard Yard*, Harvard University Art Museums, 1997: [12]–[13].

D52 Sweet talk and miracles: Notes on *The Cure at Troy* [essay]
Programme for *American Repertory Theatre*, Instititute

for Advanced Theatre Training At Harvard University, March 1997: [2]–[3].

D53 Where is the Head of the Table [essay]
Programme for *Forum:* Creativity toward the 21st Century, Japan, March 1998: 17–19 (with the Japanese text).
Seamus Heaney gave one of the 'Literature Forum' keynote addresses at Yamaguchi Prefectural University in Yamaguchi during the Forum which took place in November 1997. The programme also includes a discussion between Seamus Heaney and Kenzaburo Oe.

D54 Into Arcadia [poem]
Catalogue for *University College Dublin, International Summer School 50th Anniversary*, July 1998: [8].
Seamus Heaney gave a reading at the summer school. The programme includes four drawings of him by Paul Funge.

D55 Vitruviana [poem]
Exhibition catalogue for *Felim Egan*, S. M. A. *Cashiers*, no. 18, 1999: [7].
Seamus Heaney's poem appears in the catalogue for Felim Egan's exhibition at Stedelijk Musem, Amsterdam.

D56 The Bastion [poem]
Exhibition catalogue for *Three Stanzas: Miroslaw Balka, Robert Gober and Seamus Heaney*, an exhibition organised by the Institute of Contemporary Art, University of Pennsylvania, Philadelphia, 16 January–7 March 1999: [6]–[7].

D57 Day One [note]
Programme for *St. Columb's College: The Opening of St. Columb's College* [Derry] *for the New Millennium*, Friday, 7 May 1999: 20.

D58 Untitled [note]
Programme for *Friel Festival*, April/August 1999, published Ferndale Theatre Productions, Dublin, 1999: [22]–[23].
Seamus Heaney comments on Brian Friel's place in 'the roll-book of world drama'.

D59 The Road to Derry (Air: The boys of Mullaghbawn) [poem]
Programme for *Carthaginians* by Frank McGuinness, Lyric Theatre, Belfast, 24 August–18 September 1999: 9.

D60 A Gate Left Open [essay]
Joint programme for *Jane Eyre* and *Diary of One Who Vanished* (Eircom Dublin Theatre Festival '99), 4–16 October 1999.

D61 Threshing Day [poem]
Open Door: Linen Hall Library Millennium Festival, 16–24 September 2000: cover.
The poem is described as: 'from The Loose Box'.
Reprinted in *Images & Reflections: Photographers and Writers Seeing Our Century* (Belfast: Linen Hall Library, 2000): 26. Collected with revisions in *Electric Light*.

D62 Beowulf [poem/translation]
Exhibition catalogue for *Chapter and Verse: 1000 Years of English Literature*, British Library exhibition catalogue, London, 2000: 46–[47].
The catalogue contains a revised typescript page on page 47 showing Seamus Heaney's abandoned first attempt to translate the opening lines of *Beowulf*.

D63 Le Brocquy's *Tain* [poem]
Exhibition catalogue for *Louis Le Brocquy's 'Aubusson Tapestries'*, 2–29 May 2001: Agnew's, Bond Street, London: [5].
This is a collection of six tankas.

D64 A McGlinchey Summer School Launch [essay]
Programme for the *McGlinchey Summer School: Emigration from Ireland to America and Britain since the Famine*; Friday 29 June until Sunday 1 July 2001; Clonmany Inishowen, Co. Donegal: 3–5.
Seamus Heaney launched the summer school on 6 June 2001 at the Abbey Theatre.

D65 The Poet and the Piper [note]
Programme for *The Poet and the Piper*, Waterfront Hall,

Belfast, 10 November 2001: 1.
Seamus Heaney contributes brief notes on his collaboration with Liam O'Flynn and on Liam O'Flynn's playing.

D66 Anne Donnelly: Recent works [note]
Exhibition catalogue for 5–25 June 2002, Peppercanister Gallery, Dublin: [5].

D67 The Blackbird of Belfast Lough [poem/translation]
Programme for the dedication of *The Seamus Heaney Centre for Poetry*, Queen's University Belfast, 2003: [3].
Seamus Heaney's translation from the ninth-century Irish appears on the inside of the back page of the folder (folded card). This is a different version of the poem than that of (D12) or (C813).

E

TRANSLATIONS OF THE WORKS OF SEAMUS HEANEY

ALBANIAN

E1 Seamus Heaney, Muzë Grykore, Përktheu nga origjinali Gentian Çoçoli, Afërdita, Albania, 1999: 124 pp. (Poems selected from Seamus Heaney's publications up to 1996.)

BENGALI

E2 Seamus Heaney, Nobelabijayi Airish kabi Seemaas Hinir Kabita, anubad o prakasana Tapanjyoti Baruya, Dhaka, Desh Prakasana, Bengladesh, 1997: 47 pp. (*Crediting Poetry*, 1995.)

CATALAN

E3 Seamus Heaney, La Llanterna de l'arç, Trilingual edition, Versió catalana de Francesc Parcerisas, Versión castellana de D. Pujol Morillo, Edicions 62, Barcelona, Spain, 1992: 175 pp. (*The Haw Lantern*, 1987.)

CHINESE

E4 Seamus Heaney, *A Collected Combination Edition of Seamus Heaney's Poems and Essays*, Chinese Literature Press/The Writers Publishing House, Beijing 2000: 464 pp. (This edition includes a brief note in holograph by Seamus Heaney addressed to Chinese readers of his work.)

CZECH

E5 Seamus Heaney, Přezimování pod širým nebem; [výběr z veršů], z angl. Přeložil a doslov napsal Zdeněk Hron, Odeon, Čechoslovakia, Odeon, 1985 : 110 pp. (Poems selected from Seamus Heaney's publications up to 1975.)

E6 Seamus Heaney, Jasanová hůl, přeložili Ivana Bozděchová a Ewald Osers, Volvox Globator, Praha, Česká republika, 1998: 115 pp. (*Seeing Things*, 1991 and *The Spirit Level*, 1996.)

E7 Seamus Heaney, Přezimování pod širým nebem: výběr z poezie, přeložil Zdeněk Hron, Mladá Fronta, Praha, Česká republika, 1999: 153 pp. (Selections from Seamus Heaney's publications up to 1996.)

E8 Seamus Heaney, Přezimování pod širým nebem, přeložil Zdeněk Hron, Praha, Česká republika: 2002: 156 pp. (Not seen.)

DANISH

E9 Seamus Heaney, Fra samvittighedens republik, Digte udvalgt og oversat af Uffe Harder, Gyldendal, København, Denmark, 1989: 73 pp. (Selections from *Death of a Naturalist*, 1966; *Door into the Dark*, 1969; *Wintering Out*, 1972; *North*, 1975; *The Haw Lantern*, 1987.)

E10 Seamus Heaney, Markarbejde, På dansk ved Uffe Harder og Annette Mester, Gyldendal, København, Denmark, 1996: 126 pp. (Poems selected from Seamus Heaney's publications up to 1991.)

E11 Seamus Heaney, Fornemmelsen for stedet, På dansk ved Annette Mester, Gyldendal, København, Denmark, 1998: 262 pp. (Selections from: *Preoccupations: Selected Prose 1968–78*, 1980; *The Government of the Tongue*, 1988; *The Redress of Poetry: Oxford Lectures*, 1995; *Crediting Poetry*, 1995.)

E12 Seamus Heaney, *New and Selected Poems 1966–1987*, Gyldendal, København, Denmark. (Not seen.)

DUTCH

E13 Seamus Heaney, De rugwaartse blik, Limited edition, Vertaald door Peter Nijmeijer, Kwadraat, Vianen, Nederland, 1981: 8 pp. (Poems selected from *Wintering Out*, 1972 and *North*, 1975.)

E14 Seamus Heaney, Mistroostig en thuis, Vertaald door Peter Nijmeijer, Kwadraat, Utrecht, Nederland, 1987: 88 pp.

(Poems selected from Seamus Heaney's publications up to 1987.)

E15 Seamus Heaney, Vereffeningen, Vertaling en nawoord Peter Nijmeijer, Meulenhoff, Amsterdam, Nederland, 1991: 71 pp. ('Squarings' from *Seeing Things*, 1991.)

E16 Seamus Heaney, Sweeney's Waanzin, Vertaald door Jan Eijkelboom, Meulenhoff, Stedelijk Museum, Amsterdam, Nederland, 1994: 79 pp. (*Sweeney Astray*, 1983.)

E17 Seamus Heaney, De Genoegdoening van poëzie, Vertaald door Jan Eijkelboom, Meulenhoff Editie, Amsterdam, Nederland, 1996: 233 pp. (*The Redress of Poetry*, 1995.)

E18 Seamus Heaney, Het eerste koninkrijk: Een keuze uit de gedichten (1966–1996), Samenstelling en vertaling Peter Nijmeijer, Meulenhoff Editie, Amsterdam, Nederland, 1996: 118 pp. (Poems selected from Seamus Heaney's publications up to 1996.)

FINNISH

E19 Seamus Heaney, Ojanpiennarten kuningas, Valikoinut ja suomentanut Jyrki Vainonen, Werner Söderström Osakeyhtiö, Helsinki, Finland, 1995: 128 pp. (Poems selected from Seamus Heaney's publications up to 1996, some of which are later collected in *The Spirit Level*.)

E20 Seamus Heaney, Ukkosvaloa, Valikoinut ja suomentanut Jyrki Vainonen, Werner Söderström Osakeyhtiö, Helsinki, Finland,1997: 104 pp. (Poems selected from Seamus Heaney's publications up to 1996.)

FRENCH

E21 Seamus Heaney, Poèms 1966–1984, Traduit de l'anglais par Anne Bernard Kearney et Florence Lafon, Gallimard, Paris, France, 1988: 176 pp. (Poems selected from Seamus Heaney's publications up to 1984.)

E22 Seamus Heaney, Les Errances de Sweeney, Traduit de l'anglais par Bernard Hoepffner, Le Passeur, Nantes, France, 1994: 123 pp. (*Sweeney Astray*, 1983.)

E23 Seamus Heaney, La Lanterne de l'aubépine, Traduit de l'anglais par Gérard Cartier, Le Temps Des Cerises, Pantin, France, 1996: 94 pp. (*The Haw Lantern*, 1987.)

GALICIAN

E24 Seamus Heaney, Traballo de campo, Bilingual edition, Traducción de Vicente Araguas, Xerais, Madrid, Spain, 1996: 134 pp. (*Field Work*, 1979.)

E25 Seamus Heaney, A cura en Troia: Versión do Filoctetes de Sófacles, Traducción Stephanie Jennings [and] Manuel Outeriño, Edicións Xerais de Galicia, Madrid, Spain, 1998: 91 pp. (*The Cure at Troy*, 1990.)

GERMAN

E26 Seamus Heaney, Ausgewählte Gedichte 1965–1975, Bilingual edition, Übertragung von Henriette Beese, Klett-Cotta, Stuttgart, Germany, 1984: 255 pp. (*Selected Poems 1965–1975*, 1980.)

E27 Seamus Heaney, Norden, Bilingual edition, übertragen von Richard Pietraß, Verlag Philipp Reclam jun., Leipzig, Germany, 1987: 128 pp. (*North*, 1975.)

E28 Seamus Heaney, Die Hagebuttenlaterne, Bilingual edition, aus dem Englischen von Giovanni Bandini und Ditte König, Carl Hanser Verlag, München, Germany, 1990: 112 pp. (*The Haw Lantern*, 1989.)

E29 Seamus Heaney, Die Herrschaft der Sprache: Essays und Vorlesungen, aus dem Englischen von Alexander Schmitz, Carl Hanser Verlag, München, Germany, 1992: 236 pp. (Selections from: *Preoccupations, Selected Prose 1968–1978*, 1980; *The Government of the Tongue, The T.S. Eliot Memorial Lectures and Other Critical Writings*, 1988.)

E30 Seamus Heaney, Ausgewählte Gedichte, deutsch von Giovanni Bandini und Ditte König, Carl Hanser Verlag, München, 1995: 159 pp. (Poems selected from Seamus Heaney's publications up to 1994.)

E31 Seamus Heaney, Verteidigung der Poesie: Oxforder Vorlesungen, deutsch von Giovanni Bandini und Ditte König, Carl Hanser Verlag, München, 1996: 294 pp. (*The Redress of Poetry*, 1995.)

E32 Seamus Heaney, Norden, Bilingual edition, aus dem Englischen von Richard Pietraß, Carl Hanser Verlag, München, Germany, 1996: 127 pp. (*North*, 1975; reissue of E27–1987.)

E33 Seamus Heaney, Ausgewählte Gedichte, aus dem Englischen von Giovanni Bandini und Ditte König, Rheda-Wiedenbruck, Bertelsmann-Club, Wien, Austria, 1996: 159 pp. (Book club edition of E30 1995 – Poems selected from Seamus Heaney's publications up to 1991, in addition four poems collected in *The Spirit Level*, 1996 and a selection from *The Cure at Troy*.)

E34 Seamus Heaney, Die Poesie würdigen (Nobelpreis-Rede 1995) und ein Gespräch mit dem Literatur-Nobelpreisträger, Die Rede von Seamus Heaney wurde aus dem Englischen übersetzt von Jürgen Schneider. Das Interview führten Gabriel Rosenstock und Hans-Christian Oeser, übersetzt aus dem Englischen von Hans-Christian Oeser, Häusser, Darmstadt, Germany, 1996: 32 pp. (*Crediting Poetry*, 1995 and an interview.)

E35 Seamus Heaney, Nobelpreis fur Literatur 1995: 'Das Verdienst der Dichtkunst'; Tod eines Naturforschers, Bilingual edition, aus dem Englischen von Uli Aumuller; übertragen von Richard Pietraß, Coron Verlag, Lachen am Zürichsee, Switzerland, 1996: 317 pp. (*Crediting Poetry*, 1995; and *Death of a Naturalist*, 1966.)

E36 Seamus Heaney, Die Wasserwaage, Bilingual edition, aus dem Englischen von Giovanni und Ditte Bandini, Carl

Hanser Verlag, München, Germany, 1998: 139 pp. (*The Spirit Level*, 1996.)

E37 Seamus Heaney, Gedichte, ausgewählt von Raoul Schrott aus dem Englischen von Giovanni und Ditte Bandani und Richard Pietraß, Carl Hanser Verlag, München, Germany, 1999: 47 pp. (Poems selected by Raoul Schrott.)

E38 Seamus Heaney, Dank an die Poesie: Nobelpreisrede, übertragen von Richard Pietraß, Ulrich Keicher, Leonberg, 1999: 26 pp. (Not seen; *Crediting Poetry*, 1995.)

E39 Seamus Heaney, Elektrisches Licht, Bilingual edition, deutsch von Giovanni und Ditte Bandini, Carl Hanser Verlag, München, 2002: 172 pp. (*Electric Light*, 2001.)

GREEK

E40 Seamus Heaney, *Selected Poems 1965–1975*, Hermes.

E41 Seamus Heaney, *The Spirit Level*, Hermes.

E42 Seamus Heaney, *Miscellaneous Selected Poems*, Kastaniotis.

E43 Seamus Heaney, Alphabets, Limited edition, translated into Greek by Stratis Haviaris and Manolis Savidis, Greece, 2000: 88 pp. ('The Fragment'; 'Limbo'; 'What ever you say say nothing'; Glanmore Sonnet II; from '*Helas into Arcadia*'.)

HUNGARIAN

E44 Seamus Heaney, Versei, Válogatta, fordította és az utószót írta Tandori Dezső, Európa Könyvkiadó, Budapest, Hungary, 1980: 77pp. (Poems selected from *Door into the Dark*, 1969; *Wintering Out*, 1972; *North*, 1975.)

E45 Seamus Heaney, Különös gyumolcs, Fordította Fodor András, Géher István, Gerevich András, Imreh András, Mesterházi Monika, Poós Zoltán, Tandori Dezso, Orpheusz Konyvek, Hungary, 1996: 164 pp. (Poems selected from Seamus Heaney's publication up to 1991.)

IRISH

E46 Seamus Heaney, Conlán, aistrithe ag Gabriel Rosenstock, Coiscéim, Baile Átha Cliath 4, 1989: 38. (Selections from: Poems selected from Seamus Heaney's publications through to 1987.)

ITALIAN

E47 Seamus Heaney, Scavando, Poesie scelte (1966–1990), Bilingual Edition, a cura di Franco Buffoni, Fondazione Piazzolla, Roma, Italy, 1991: 139 pp. (Poems selected from Seamus Heaney's publications through to 1990.)

E48 Seamus Heaney, Station Island, Bilingual edition, tradusioni di Gabriella Morisco e Anthony Oldcorn, Arnoldo Mondadori Editore, Milano, Italy, 1992: 166 pp. (*Station Island*, 1984.)

E49 Seamus Heaney, Diptych, Bilingual edition, con una incisione di Guido Strazza, traduzione di Anthony Oldcorn. Di questa cartelletta con una puntasecca su zinco di Guido Strazza, stampa da Antonio Sannino, sono stati tirati da Giogio Lucini, venticinque esemplari numerati da 1 a 25, piu dieci numerati I a X. Milano, 13 settembre 1993. (All'insegna del Pesce d'Oro, Milano 1993). (This is a limited edition of what was collected as 'St. Kevin and the Blackbird' in *The Spirit Level*, 1996.)

E50 Seamus Heaney, In forma di parole, Radure, Bilingual Edition, a cura di Gabriella Morisco, Marcos y Marcos, Milano, Italy, 1995: 55 pp. (Limited edition of the 'Clearances' sequence in *The Haw Lantern*, 1987.)

E51 Seamus Heaney, Attraversamenti, Bilingual edition, a cura di Athony Oldcorn, Libri Scheiwiller, Milano,1995: 117 pp. ('Crossings' from *Seeing Things* and 'Diptych' collected in *The Spirit Level* as 'St. Kevin and the Blackbird'.)

E52 Seamus Heaney, Una porta sul buio. Bilingual edition, Traduzione di Roberto Mussapi. Ugo Guanda Editore, Parma, Italy, 1996: 94 pp. (*Door Into the Dark*, 1969.)

E53 Seamus Heaney, Poesie scelte, Bilingual edition, Traduzioni di Roberto Sanesi, Gilberto Sacerdoti, Nadia Fusini e Francesca Romana Paci, Marcos y Marcos, Milano, Italy, 1996: 244 pp. (Selections from Death of a *Naturalist*, 1966, *Door into the Dark*, 1969, *Wintering Out*, 1972, *Stations*, 1975, *North*, 1975, *Field Work*, 1979, *Selected Poems 1965–1975*, 1980, *The Haw Lantern*, 1987.)

E54 Seamus Heaney, Attenzioni (Preoccupations – prose scelte 1968–1978), Traduzione di Piero Vaglioni, Fazi Editore, Roma, Italy, 1996: 215pp. (*Preoccupations – Selected Prose 1968–1978*, 1980.)

E55 Seamus Heaney, Veder cose, a cura di Gilberto Sacerdoti, Mondadori, Milano, Italy, 1997: 237 pp. *Seeing Things*, 1991.)

E56 Seamus Heaney, Sia dato credito alla poesia, a cura di Marco Sonzogni, Archinto, Milano, 1997: 71 pp. (*Crediting Poetry*, 1995.)

E57 Seamus Heaney, Il governo della lingua: Prose scelte 1978–1987, a cura di Massimo Bacigalupo, Fazi Editore, Roma, Italy, 1998: 227 pp. (*The Government of the Tongue: Selected Prose 1978–1987.*)

E58 Seamus Heaney, *North*, Bilingual edition, a cura di Roberto Mussapi, Mondadori, Milano, Italy, 1998: 140 pp. (*North*, 1975.)

E59 Seamus Heaney, La lanterna di biancospino, Biligual edition, A cura di Francesca Romana Paci, Ugo Guanda Editore, Parma, Italy, 1999: 139 pp. (*The Haw Lantern*, 1987.)

E60 Seamus Heaney, La riparazione della poesia: Lezioni di Oxford, a cura di Massimo Bacigalupo, Fazi Editore, Roma, Italy, 1999: 262 pp. (*The Redress of Poetry*, 1995.)

E61 Seamus Heaney, *The Spirit Level*, Bilingual Edition, a cura di Roberto Mussapi, Mondadori, Milano, Italy 2000: 174 pp. (*The Spirit Level*, 1996.)

E62 Seamus Heaney, *Beowulf*, Trilingual edition, a cura di Massimo Bacigalupo, Fazi Editore, Roma, Italy, 2002: 320 pp. (*Beowulf*, 2000.)

JAPANESE

E63 Seamus Heaney, *Collected Poems: 1966–1991* (in Japanese), translator not listed here, Kokubunsha Publishers, Tokyo, Japan, 1995: 916 pp. (Poems selected from Seamus Heaney's publications up to 1991.)

E64 Seamus Heaney, The Government of the Tongue, Kokubunsha Publishers, Tokyo, Japan, 1997: 371 pp. (*Government of the Tongue*, 1988.)

E65 Seamus Heaney, Collected Poems, translated into Japanese by Tatsuo Murata, Yoshiharu Sakamoto, Toru Sugino, and Koichi Yakushigawa, Kokubunsha Publishers, Japan, 1994. (The eight complete collected trade editions up to 1991.)

E66 Seamus Heaney, *The Spirit Level*, translated into Japanese by Tatsuo Murata, Yoshiharu Sakamoto, Toru Sugino, and Koichi Yakushigawa, Kokubunsha Publishers, Japan, 1999: 170 pp.

E67 Seamus Heaney, *The Place of Writing*, translated into Japanese by Toshi Furomoto and Yoko Sato, Kokubunsha Publishers, Japan 2001: 176 pp.

LITHUANIAN

E68 Seamus Heaney, Kasanti plunksna: eilėraščių rinktinė/ *The Digging Quill: selected poems 1966–1991*, Bilingual edition, Iš anglų kalbos vertė Kornelijus Platelis, Lietuvos rašytojų sajungos leidykla, 2002: 249 pp. (Poems selected from Seamus Heaney's publications up to 1991.)

NORWEGIAN

E69 Seamus Heaney, Tonen Som Kom, Dikt i utval ved Alf Saltveit, Solum Forlag, Oslo, Norway, 1991: 84pp. (Poems selected from Seamus Heaney's publications up to 1987.)

E70 Seamus Heaney, Sansen for Plassen og andre essays, Til norsk ved Grethe Fosse og Jon Fosse, Solum Forlag, Oslo, Norway, 1996: 232 pp. (Selections from *Preoccupations: Selected Prose 1968–1978*, 1980; *The Government of the Tongue*, 1988; *The Redress of Poetry*, 1995 and *Crediting Poetry*, 1995.)

POLISH

E71 Seamus Heaney, 44 Wiersze. Bilingual edition, Biblioteczka Poetów Języka Angielskiego, pod redakcją Stanisław Barańczak. Wydawnictwo Znak, Kraków, Poland, 1994: 171 pp. (Poems selected from Seamus Heaney's publications up to 1991.)

E72 Seamus Heaney, Ciągnąć Dalej: nowe wiersze, przełożył Stanisław Barańczak, Wydawnictwo Znak, Kraków, Poland, 1996: 63 pp. (*The Spirit Level*, 1996.)

E73 Seamus Heaney, Zawierzyć poezji, przekład Stanisław Barańczak, Magda Heydel, Jerzy Jarniewicz, Piotr Sommer, Adam Szostkiewicz, Andrzej Szuba, Wydawnictwo Znak, Kraków, Poland, 1996. 302 pp. (Selections from *Preoccupations: Selected Prose 1968–1978*, 1980, *The Government of the Tongue*, 1988, and *The Redress of Poetry*, 1995.)

E74 Seamus Heaney, Kolejowe Dzieci: Wiersze I Prozy, Wybrał, przełożył, opracował i posłowiem opatrzył Piotr Sommer, Fort legnica '98, Poland, 1998: 105pp. (Poems selected from Seamus Heaney's publications up to 1991 and prose selections from *Preoccupations*.)

E75 Seamus Heaney, Ciągnąc Dalej: nowe wiersze 1991–1996, przełożył Stanisław Barańczak, Wydawnictwo ZNAK,

Kraków, Poland, 1996: 63 pp. (*The Spirit Level*, 1996 and 'Audenesque' collected in *Electric Light*.)

E76 Seamus Heaney, *From the Back of the North Wind, Three Poems*, Bilingual edition, Trzy wiersze, translated by Stanisław Barańczak, Book Art at the Museum, Łódź/ British Council Poland, 2000: 12 pp. ('A Hyperbean'; 'Squarings' vii, 'The annals say . . .'; 'Postscript.')

PORTUGUESE

E77 Seamus Heaney, Da Terra a Luz: Poemas 1966–1987, Bilingual edition, Traducão Rui Carvalho Homen, relogio d'agua, Lisbon, Portugal, 1997: 420 pp. (*New Selected Poems 1966–1987*, 1990.)

E78 Seamus Heaney, Antologia Poética, Bilingual edition, Tradução de Vasco Graça Moura, Campo Das Letras, Porto, Portugal, 1998: 151 pp. (Poems selected from Seamus Heaney's publications through to 1991, and 'The Fragment' revised version collected in *Electric Light*, 2001.)

E79 Seamus Heaney, Miscellaneous Selected Poems, relogio d' agua (world ex Latin America).

PROVENÇAL

E80 Seamus Heaney, Poemas causits, revirade, introduccion e notas de Maria-Cristina Coste-Rixte, Toulouse, Lagarrigue, Droma, France, 1996: 93 pp. (Not seen; poems selected from Seamus Heaney's publications up to 1975.)

ROMANIAN

E81 Seamus Heaney, Knnyebbedsek: [versuri], traducere IN limba maghiară de Tandori Dezsa, Targu Mures, 1999: 18 pp. Not seen.

E82 Seamus Heaney, Lumina eletrică, Cosana Nicolae, Cluj-Napoca, Bucureşti, România, 2001: 119 pp. (Not seen; *Electric Light*, 2001.)

E83 Seamus Heaney, Oracol Şi Alte Poeme, Tălmăciri de Dumitru M. Ion şi Carolina Ilica, Editura Academiei

Internationale Orient-Occident, Bucureşti, România, 2002: 104 pp. (Poems selected from Seamus Heaney publications up to 2001.)

RUSSIAN

E84 Seamus Heaney, Miscellaneous Selected Poems, Molodaya Gvardiya.

SERBIAN

E85 Seamus Heaney, (Šejmas Hini), Nove izabrane pesme, 1966–1987. i Videnje stvari. Gornji Milonovac: Dečje novine, 1996: 170pp. (*New Selected Poems, 1966–1987* and *Seeing Things*, 1996.)

E86 Seamus Heaney, (Šejmas Hini) Mocvarna zemlja: izabrane pesme, Srba Mitrovic, Rad, Belgrade, Serbia, 2000.

SLOVAKIAN

E87 Seamus Heaney, Na okraji vôd (Výber z poézie), Preložila Jana Kantorová-Báliková, STUDŇA, Bratislava, Slovakia, 2000: 93 pp. (Poems selected from Seamus Heaney's publications up to 1996 – excluding *Seeing Things*.)

SLOVENIAN

E88 Seamus Heaney, Močvirna dežela: izbrane pesmi. Translated by Boris A. Novak and Irena Zorko Novak. Didakta, Radovljica [Ljubljana], Slovenia, 1997: 75pp. (Poems selected from Seamus Heaney's publication up to 1996.)

SPANISH

E89 Seamus Heaney, Isla de las Estaciones, Traducción de pura Lopez-Colome, Ediciones Toledo,Tlalpan, Mexico, 1991: 138 pp. (*Station Island*, 1984.)

E90 Seamus Heaney, Norte, Bilingual Edition, Traducción de Margarita Ardanaz, Hiperión, Madrid, Spain, 1992: 152 pp. (*North*, 1975.)

E91 Seamus Heaney, Antología poética, Bilingual edition, traducción de Brian Hughes y Esteban Pujals Gesali, Instituto de Cultura Juan Gil-Albert, Spain, 1993: 207 pp. (Poems selected from Seamus Heaney's publications up to 1991.)

E92 Seamus Heaney, La Linterna del espino, Bilingual edition, Versión de Dídac Pujol Morillo, Ediciones Península, Barcelona, Spain, 1995: 120 pp. (*The Haw Lantern*, 1987.)

E93 Seamus Heaney, Muerte de un naturalista, Bilingual edition, Traducción de Margarita Ardanaz, Hiperión, Madrid, Spain, 1996: 105 pp. (*Death of a Naturalist*, 1966.)

E94 Seamus Heaney, De la emoción a las palabras, Traducción y edición a cargo de Francesc Parcerisas, Editorial Anagrama, Barcelona, Spain, 1996: 307 pp. (Selections from *Preoccupations: Selected Prose 1968–1978, 1980, The Government of the Tongue*, 1988, *The T.S. Eliot Memorial Lectures and Other Critical Writings*, 1988, *The Redress of Poetry*: Oxford Lectures, 1995.)

E95 Seamus Heaney, Antología, Bilingual edition, Versiones en castellano de Joe Broderick, Editorial El Labrador, Santafé de Bogotá, Colombia, 1997: 168 pp. (Selections from: *North*, 1975; *Field Work*, 1979; *Station Island*, 1984; *Haw Lantern*, 1987, *Seeing Things*, 1991; *Crediting Poetry* only in Spanish.)

E96 Seamus Heaney, Viendo Visiones, Versión y presentación, Pura López-Colomé, Cien Del Mundo, Xoco, Mexico, 1998: 115 pp. (*Seeing Things*, 1991.)

E97 Seamus Heaney, El Nivel, Bilingual edition, Versión y prólogo de Pura López-Colomé, Trilce Editions, México, D.F., 2000: 177 pp. (*The Spirit Level*, 1996.)

E98 Seamus Heaney, Tres Ensayos, Traducción Pura López-Colomé, Conaculta, Xoco, Mexico, D.F., 1999: 67 pp. (Three essays: *Crediting Poetry*, 1995; 'The Impact of Translation'; 'Dylan the Durable?')

E99 Seamus Heaney, Luz Eléctrica/Electric Light, Traducción de Dámaso López García, Visor, Madrid, Spain, 2003. (*Electric Light*, 2001.)

SWEDISH

E100 Seamus Heaney, Fältarbete, Dikter tolkade av Roy Isaksson, Fripress, Bokforlag, Bromma, Sweden, 1986: 69 pp. (*Fieldwork*, 1979.)

E101 Seamus Heaney, Hagtornslyktan, dikter tolkade från engelska av Roy Isaksson, Fripress, Bokförlag, Bromma, Sweden, 1988: 63 pp. (*The Haw Lantern*, 1987.)

E102 Seamus Heaney, Grönt Ljus, Tolkningar av Roy Isaksson, Finn Printz-Påhlson, Lars-Håkan Svensson, Lasse Söderberg och Jan Östergren, Fripress Bokförlag, Bromma, Sweden, 1989: 61 pp. (Poems selected from *Death of a Naturalist*, 1966; *Door into the Dark*, 1969; *Wintering Out*, 1972; *North*, 1975; *Station Island*, 1984.)

E103 Seamus Heaney, På Väg, Tolkningar av Roy Isaksson, Finn Printz-Påhlson, Göran Printz-Påhlson, Lars-Håkan Svensson, Lasse Söderberg och Jan Östergren, Natur och Kultur, Stockholm, Sweden, 1994: 208 pp. (Selections from Seamus Heaney's publications up to 1991.)

E104 Seamus Heaney, I syner, Tolkning av Lars Gustafsson, Natur och Kultur, Stockholm, Sweden, 1996: 118 pp. (*Seeing Things*, 1991.)

E105 Seamus Heaney, Dit man hör, översattning Leif Janzon, Natur och Kultur, Stockholm, Sweden, 1996: 306 pp. (Selections from *Preoccupations: Selected Prose 1968–1978*, 1980; *The Government of the Tongue*, 1988; The *Redress of Poetry*, 1995 and *Crediting Poetry*, 1995.)

E106 Seamus Heaney, Vattenpasset, översattning av Ole Hessler, Natur och Kulture, Stockholm, 2002: 175 pp. (Not seen; selection of poems from *The Spirit Level*, 1996 and *Electric Light*, 2001.)

F

INTERVIEWS WITH SEAMUS HEANEY

F1 In a window
Ray Rosenfield, *Books and Bookmen and John O'London's Books of the Month*, November 1966: 106.
The interview material is included in a review of *Death of a Naturalist.*

F2 Turkeys made him a poet
Ray Rosenfield, *Ulster Tatler*, Winter 1966: [36].

F3 Seamus Heaney on poetry
Anonymous, *Fresh Water*, November 1969: no page numbers.
Fresh Water: a publication of St Mary's Teacher Training College, Belfast/St Joseph's Teacher Training College, Belfast.

F4 Poets on poetry: Seamus Heaney
Patrick Garland, *Listener*, 8 November 1973: 629.
Excerpts from Garland's interviews for the BBC1 Further Education Series.

F5 Harriet Cooke talked to the poet Seamus Heaney
Harriet Cooke, *Irish Times*, 28 December 1973: 8.

F6 Caroline Walsh talks to Seamus Heaney
Caroline Walsh, *Irish Times*, The Saturday Interview, 6 December 1975: 5.

F7 The North: silent awareness with Seamus Heaney
Monie Begley, *Rambles in Ireland* (Old Greenwich: Devin-Adair, 1977): 159–170.

F8 [Untitled interview]
Edward Broadbridge, ed., *Seamus Heaney* (København: Skoleradioen, 1977): 5–16. (See B28.)

F9 Meeting Seamus Heaney
John Haffenden, *London Magazine*, 19 (June), 1979: 5–28.
Reprinted with some amendments in *Viewpoints* (London: Faber and Faber, 1981): 57–75. (See C297.)

F10 In the mid-course of his life
Dennis O'Driscoll, *Hibernia*, 11 October 1979: 13.
Reprinted in *Helix* (Australia), February/August 1980.

F11 Seamus Deane talks with Seamus Heaney
Seamus Deane, *New York Times Book Review*, 2 December 1979: 47–48.

F12 Unhappy and at home
Seamus Deane, *Crane Bag*, 1977: 61–67.
Reprinted in *The Crane Bag Book of Irish Studies, 1977–1981* (Dublin: Blackwater Press, 1981): pp. 66–72.

F13 An interview with Seamus Heaney
James Randall, *Ploughshares*, vol. 5, no. 3, 1979: 7–22. (See C303.)

F14 A raindrop on a thorn
Robert Druce, *Dutch Quarterly Review*, vol. 9, no. 1, 1979: 24–37. (See C312.)

F15 An interview with Seamus Heaney
Vivian Steir, *Advocate*, 1979: 4–9.

F16 An interview with Seamus Heaney
Desmond McCabe, *Rake*, 1979/80: 33–44.
Rake was a publication of the University College Dublin English Literary Society.

F17 Interview with Seamus Heaney
Georgina Mills, *Strawberry Fare*, 5 February 1980: 14–18. (See C326.)

F18 Two Irish voices
Anonymous, *Publishers Weekly*, 1980: 84.
Interviews with Seamus Heaney and Jack Holland.

F19 Poet aims verse at Irish War
Paul McEnroe, *Minneapolis Star*, 9 March 1981: 1B, 3B.
The interview is part of an article on Seamus Heaney.

F20 Interview with Seamus Heaney
Helen O'Shea, *Quadrant*, September 1981: 12–17.
Quadrant: published in Sydney, Australia.

F21 Seamus Heaney
David McCullough, *People, Books and Book People* (New York: Harmony Books, 1981): 78–80.

F22 The quiet voice
Pat Mackle, *Arrows*, 1981–1982: 20–26.
Arrows was a publication of Sheffield University.

F23 Artists on art: an interview with Seamus Heaney
Frank Kinahan, *Critical Inquiry*, spring 1982: 405–414.

F24 Seamus Heaney: recognizable poet
Anonymous, *Weekend Northwestern*, 16–17 October 1982: B3.
The interview material is part of a profile of Seamus Heaney.
Weekend Northwestern is published in Oshkosh, Wisconsin.

F25 Seamus Heaney – Bard of the Bogs
Stewart McBride, *Christian Science Monitor*, 22–28 October 1983: 2, 16.
Article with interview material.

F26 An interview with Seamus Heaney
Ruth Frehner, *Anglistenkurier*, 24 November 1983: 4–9.
Anglistenkurier: a publication of the University of Zurich.

F27 Interview . . . Seamus Heaney
Wanda Taylor, *Scrivener*, winter 1983: 7–9.
Scrivener: a publication of McGill University.

F28 An interview with Seamus Heaney
Bryce Milligan, *Pax*, vol. 1, no. 1, 1983: 41–47.

F29 Interview with Seamus Heaney
Thomas O'Donnell, *Cottonwood* 30, 1983: 63–74.
Cottonwood was published by the University of Kansas.

F30 Comfortable image belies serious poet
Deaglan de Breadun, *Irish Times*, 13 September 1984: 13.

F31 A pilgrim's progress
Fintan O'Toole, *Inside Tribune*, 30 September 1984: 1–3, 6.

F32 Poet, pilgrim, fugitive . . .
Bel Mooney, *Times*, 11 October 1984: 8.

F33 Seamus Heaney
Anonymous, *Central Review*, 1984–1985: 13–15.
Central Review: a publication of Trinity College Dublin.

F34 The Bard from the Bogland – Seamus Heaney and his passion for peace
David Remnick, *Washington Post*, 3 May 1985: C1.
This interview was included in the United States *Congressional Record: Senate*, 7 May 1985: SS5564–SS5565. It was submitted by Edward M. Kennedy.

F35 An interview with Seamus Heaney
Patricia McGovern King, *An Gael*, summer 1985: 2–4.

F36 Interview with Seamus Heaney
Anonymous, *gown Literary Supplement*, vol. 31, no.4, 1985: 3–4.

F37 Seamus Heaney at Harvard
Fabienne Marsh, *Poetry Review*, February 1986: 27–28.
Marsh quotes Seamus Heaney as he teaches a creative writing class at Harvard.

F38 Seamus Heaney – a poet of his people
Kate O'Callaghan, *Irish America*, May 1986: 24–30.

F39 A conversation with Seamus Heaney
Michael Toner, *Irish Edition*, June 1986: 1, 8.
Published in Philadelphia.

F40 An interview with Seamus Heaney
June Beisch, *Literary Review*, winter 1986: 161–169.

F41 Seamus Heaney
Anonymous, *Education and the Art*s, Trinity College Dublin: The Educational Autobiographies of Contemporary Irish Poets, Novelists, Dramatists, Musicians, Painters and Sculptors (Dublin: School of Education), 1987: 62–70.

F42 Seamus Heaney: an interview
Rand Brandes, *Salmagundi*, fall 1988: 4–21.

F43 Eliot in another pattern
David Wheatley, *Icarus*, Michaelmas Term, 1988: 5–7.

F44 The home Forum
Michael Huey, *Christian Science Monitor*, 9 January 1989: 16–17.

F45 Heaney discusses Irish Literary tradition
Jack Stewart, *Voice*, 15 February 1989: 10.
Voice: a publication of Emory University, Atlanta, Georgia.

F46 Vertical lift-off at the half century
Richard Pine, *Sunday Independent* (Dublin), 9 April 1989: 18.

F47 Stirring the cultural pot with a wooden spoon
Eileen Battersby, *Irish Times*, 5 June 1989: 5.

F48 Heaney talks to Barry White: what is wrong with life in the north, whatever side you are on
Barry White, *Belfast Telegraph*, 29 June 1989: 9.

F49 Calling the tune
Tom Adair, *Linen Hall Review*, autumn 1989: 5–8.

F50 Celtic spotlight
Anonymous, *Listener*, 7 December 1989: 17.
Interview material from 'Ceremony and Innocence' (BBC Radio 3).

F51 'All the World's a stage'
Mary McCollum, *Irish News*, 22 September 1990: 7.

F52 A dramatic conversation
John Keyes, *Fortnight*, 25 October 1990: 25.

F53 Finding solid ground
Deirdre Purcell, *Sunday Tribune*, 4 November 1990: 25.

F54 The line in the sand
Anonymous, *Babele: Esperimenti Creativi in Linmgue Diverse*, Vol. 1, 1990: 10–12.
Babele: published in Italy.

F55 A conversation with Seamus Heaney
Peter Costa, *Harvard Gazette*, 26 April 1991: 5–6.

F56 Seamus famous: time to be dazzled
Blake Morrison, *Independent on Sunday*, 19 May 1991: 26–27.

F57 Ulster dog gnaws at Ireland's shadows
Ian Hargreaves, *Financial Times*, 1 June 1991: Weekend, XXII.

F58 Poetry: a soul on the washing line
Anonymous, *Economist*, 22 June 1991: 98–102.

F59 'Hearing things'
Anonymous, *Kintullagh*, September 1991: 39.
Kintullagh: a publication of St Louis Grammar School, Ballymena, Northern Ireland.

F60 'Seeing Things', John Breslin interviews Seamus Heaney
John Breslin, *Critic*, winter 1991: 26–35.

F61 Seamus Heaney
David Montenegro, ed., *Points of Departure: International Writers on Writing and Politics* (Ann Arbor: University of Michigan Press, 1991): 180–197.

F62 A conversation with Seamus Heaney
Peter Costa, *Q & A: Conversations with Harvard Scholars* (Cambridge, Massachusetts: Harvard University, Office of News and Public Affairs, 1991): 256–262.

F63 Features . . .
Caron Rohsler, *Alternative*, 23 January 1992: 6.
Alternative: a publication of Magdalen College.

F64 Seamus Heaney recalls boyhood memories
Ivor Howe, *Northern Constitution*, 8 August 1992: 20.

F65 Seamus Heaney: the words worth saying
Steven Ratiner, *Christian Science Monitor*, 7 October 1992: 16–17.

F66 Seamus Heaney
Pedro Sorela, *Babelia*, 19 December 1992: 14–15.

F67 Interview with Seamus Heaney
Nancy Gish, *Hugh MacDiarmid, Man and Poet* (Edinburgh: Edinburgh UP, and U. of Maine: National Poetry Foundation, 1992): 63–70.

F68 Desde la republica de la conciencia
Anonymous, *El Europeo*, January 1993: 60–63.

F69 Seamus Heaney: between north and south: poetic detours
Richard Kearney, ed., *Visions of Europe: Conversations on the Legacy and Future of Europe* (Dublin: Wolfhound Press, 1993): 82–89.

F70 Seamus Heaney
Clive Wilmer, ed., *Poets Talking: The 'Poet of the Month' Interviews from BBC Radio 3* (London: Carcanet, 1994): 77–82.

F71 Seamus Heaney
Seamus Hosey, *Speaking Volumes* (Dublin: Blackwater Press, 1995): 35–39.

F72 Nobel sentiments
Donal O'Donoghue, *RTE Guide*, 12 April 1996: 10–11.

F73 Heaney: an interview
Patricia Harty, *Irish American Magazine*, May/June 1996: 26–28, 30.

F74 Interview with Seamus Heaney
Michael Glover, *Poetry Life*, 1996: 8–12, 15–18.

F75 Seamus Heaney: the art of poetry lxxv
Henri Cole, *Paris Review*, fall 1997: 88–138.
The interview includes a facsimile of the poem 'The Haw Lantern' with revisions in the author's hand.

F76 The making of a poet
Jamie McKendrick, *W Magazine*, autumn 1998: 11–17.
A profile of and interview with Seamus Heaney.
W Magazine is a publication of Waterstone's bookshop.

F77 Interview with Seamus Heaney
George Morgan, *Cynos*, vol. 15, no. 2, 1998: 227–235.

F78 A wandering voice in the storm
Cole Moreton, *Independent on Sunday*, 4 April 1999: Culture, 11.
By Cole Moreton 'about the enduring power of an old Irish tune . . . Port na bPúcaí' the Fairies' Lament'.

F79 Son of the soil
Nicholas Wroe, *Guardian*, 9 October 1999: Saturday Review, 6–7.

F80 The art of rhyme and reason
Michael Ross, *Sunday Times*, 24 October 1999: 4–5.

F81 One voice, two places
Fintan O'Toole, *Irish Times*, 30 October 1999: Weekend Review, 10

F82 A glittering prize at the end of every line
Cosmo Landesman, *Sunday Times*, 30 January 2000: News Review, 5.

F83 The conversation
Karl Miller, *Seamus Heaney in Conversation with Karl Miller* (London: Between the Lines, 2000): 17–60.

F84 Seamus Heaney
Mike Murphy, *Reading the Future: Irish writers in conversation with Mike Murphy*, edited by Clíodhna Ní Anluain (Dublin: Lilliput Press, 2000): 81–[97].

F85 Still finding himself in his poetry
Vincent Browne, *Irish Times*, 31 March 2001: 10.

F86 Seamus famous
Nigel Farndale, *Sunday Telegraph*, 1 April 2001: Magazine, 20, 23, 25.

F87 The poet, his father, the provos and the glittering prizes
Nigel Farndale, *Irish Independent*, 21 April 2001: Weekend, 8, 9, 10.

F88 The railway children
Journeys, National Poetry Day, Thursday, 4 October 2001: 7.
The interview appears in the programme for National Poetry Day.

F89 Interview with Seamus Heaney
Nick Gammage, *Thumbscrew*, autumn 2001: 2–11.

F90 Soul-mark: *The Reader* meets Seamus Heaney
Sarah Coley, *The Reader*, no. 8 [2001]: 11–17.

F91 Seamus Heaney
Stephen Faller, Nathan Ligo, et al., *Talking With Poets*, ed. Harry Thomas (New York: Handsel Books, 2002): 42–69.
Faller, Ligo, and nine other students from Harry Thomas's class 'The Art of Poetry', interview Seamus Heaney.

F92 The Words Worth saying
Steven Ratiner, ed., *Giving Their Words: Conversations with Contemporary Poets* (Amherst: University of Massachusetts Press, 2002): 95–107.

F93 Hokusai, Basho, Zen, and More – Japanese influences on Irish Poets
Mitsuko Ohno, *Journal of Irish Studies* (IASIL–Japan), vol. 17, 2002: 20–21.
In addition to Seamus Heaney, Eavan Boland, Ciaran Carson, Michael Longley, Medbh McGuckian, Paula Meehan, Paul Muldoon, Nuala Ni Dhomhnaill, Cathal O Searcaigh and Joseph Woods, responding in writing to five questions regarding Japanese influences on their work.

F94 Seamus Heaney
John Brown, ed., *In the Chair: Interviews with Poets from the North of Ireland* (Salmon Publishing, Clare: 2002): 75–85.

G
COMMERCIAL AUDIO RECORDINGS

G1 *The Northern Muse, Seamus Heaney and John Montague reading their poetry*
Recorded by LLoyd's International, Belfast for Claddagh Records Ltd, Dublin, 1968.
One 12 in. 331/3 r.p.m. disc.

Contents: Personal Helicon—The Diviner—The Barn—Follower—Requiem for the Croppies—The Wife's Tale—Mother—Elegy for a Still-born Child—Bogland—A Lough Neagh Sequence.

There is an untitled note by Seamus Heaney on the back of the record sleeve. The record also contains 11 poems by John Montague.

G2 *A Concert for Tom Delaney*
Recorded live at the Ulster Museum, Belfast, on 7 December 1979; published by Audio Arts editions, London, 1980.
One audio cassette.

Contents: 'Introduction' and 'Encounter on Station Island' by Seamus Heaney.

The recording was issued in an edition of 300 copies, signed by all of the participants.

G3 *Seamus Heaney and Tom Paulin*
A Faber Poetry Cassette, 1983.
One audio cassette; Seamus Heaney, side one; duration: 30 minutes.

Contents: Death of a Naturalist—Anahorish—Gifts of Rain—The Tollund Man—Bone Dreams—Funeral Rites—Exposure—The Otter.

A booklet containing the poems read by both poets is included with the cassette.

G4 *For Frances Horovitz – A Celebration of Poetry*
TalkTapes 13, London, 1985.
One audio cassette; Seamus Heaney et al., side two; duration: approx. 47 minutes.

Contents: The Underground—Sloe Gin—The Birthplace—The Railway Children—In Illo Tempore—A Kite for Michael and Christopher—Station Island VI (stanzas i and iii)—Station Island XI (St. John of the Cross, translation).

G5 *Seamus Heaney at Harvard: Heaney reads his own poems and poems of Dunbar, Wyatt, Raleigh, Shakespeare, Marvell, Blake, Wordsworth, Hardy and Yeats*
Produced by Poetry Room, Harvard College Library, 1990.
Two audio cassette tapes: sides 1 and 2 recorded 18 November 1987; total duration for all 4 sides: 113 minutes.

Contents: Side 1: Death of a Naturalist—Personal Helicon—Bogland—Tollund Man—Anahorish—Mossbawn: Sunlight—Bone Dreams—Funeral Rites—Exposure. Side 2: Casualty—The Singer's House—The Otter—The Skunk—Station Island, Section VII—Station Island, Section XII—The Scribes—Alphabets. Side 3 and 4: Seamus Heaney reads poems by poets listed in title.

G6 *The Poet Speaks: A Twentieth-Century Anthology Read by the Poets*
Argo/Polygram Records, 1995.
Two audio cassette tapes: Heaney, side 3.

Contents: Follower—Poor Women in the City Church—Poem for Marie—St. Francis and the Birds—Death of a Naturalist.

Other poets reading include: Eliot, Auden, Betjeman, Graves, Spender, Larkin, Hughes, et al.

G7 *Stepping Stones*
Published by Penguin Audiobooks, 1995.
One audio cassette; duration 72 minutes.

Contents: Side one: Mossbawn: Sunlight—Personal Helicon—Bogland—The Tollund Man—Punishment—Strange Fruit—Exposure—Oysters—Casualty—Glanmore

Sonnets: 2, 3, 7, 10—Station Island: VII—Ugolino. Side two: Alphabets—From the Republic of Conscience—Clearances: Prologue, 2, 3, 5, 8—The Wishing Tree—Fosterling—Lightenings: i, ii, vi, vii, viii—Crossings: xxvii, xxxii, xxxiii, xxxiv—Tollund—St. Kevin and the Blackbird—Mint—At the Wellhead.

G8 *The Spirit Level*
Published by Penguin Audiobooks, 1996.
One audio cassette; duration 75 minutes.

Contents: All of the poems in *The Spirit Level.*

G9 *Station Island*
Published by Penguin Audiobooks, 1997.
One audio cassette; duration 75 minutes.

Contents: All of the poems in *Station Island.*

G10 *Beowulf*
Published by Faber–Penguin Audiobooks, 1999.
Two audio cassettes, duration approximately 135 minutes.

Contents: Seamus Heaney's translation of *Beowulf.*

Also issued on CD by Faber–Penguin Audiobooks, 1999 and on cassette and CD by HighBridge Company, *Beowulf: The Original BBC Recording*, 2000.

G11 *Electric Light*
Published by Faber–Penguin Audiobooks, 2001
Two audio cassettes, duration approximately 90 minutes.

Contents: All of the poems in *Electric Light.*

G12 *The Poet and The Piper*
Published by Claddagh Records, 2003.
CD, duration 58 minutes 23 seconds.

Contents: The Given Note—Digging—Bogland—At the Wellhead—The Otter—The Yellow Bittern (An Bonná Buí)—The Glamoured (Gile na Gile)—The Tollund

Man—Midterm Break—Clearances III—Clearances V—A Call—Seeing Things iii—St. Kevin and the Blackbird—The Annals Say—Postscript.

Seamus Heaney performs with Liam O'Flynn on uilleann pipes.

H
EPHEMERA

H1 *Lovers on Aran* [setting]
'Lovers on Aran' set to music by Sean O Riada, published 1972; 25 copies printed and published by Woodtown Music Publications Ltd, Dublin.
This poem was first printed in *Vogue*, 1 September 1965; collected in *Eleven Poems*.

H2 *Internment* [signatory]
Hibernia, 9 August 1974: Supplement '71–Internment–74', 1.
Seamus Heaney was one of 50 signatories to a statement calling for the 'immediate release of all internees in Northern Ireland'.

H3 *Feidhlim Tonn Ri's Castle* [sleeve comment]
Feidhlim Tonn Ri's Castle, Or, The King Of Ireland's Son told by Seamus Ennis with music played on the uilleann pipes and tin whistle. Dublin: Claddagh Records, 1977.

H4 *The Singer's House.* Record [sleeve comment]
The Singer's House. David Hammond with Donald Lunney. Dublin: Sruthan Muligan, 1978.
The poem 'The Singer's House' appears on the record sleeve; collected with revisions in *Contemporary Irish Poetry*.

H5 *The Hunt by Night* [statement]
The Hunt by Night, by Derek Mahon, Oxford University Press, 1982.
The back cover has a statement by Seamus Heaney.

H6 *Poems and Versions* [statement]
Poems and Versions, by Padraic Fallon, Carcanet New Press, Manchester/Raven Arts Press, Dublin, 1983.
The back cover has a statement by Heaney.

H7 *The Grave of William Carleton* [signatory]
Irish Times, 5 May 1984: 19.

H8 *The Dolphin's Way* [CD sleeve]
The Dolphin's Way by Michael O'Suilleabhain, Virgin Music, London, 1985. The sleeve contains an excerpt from 'Station Island XII'. The excerpt provides the title for the CD.

H9 *The Last of the Name* [statement]
The Last of the Name, by Charles McGlinchey, Belfast: Blackstaff Press, 1986.
Paperback back cover and front flap of cloth issue have a statement by Heaney.

H10 *Selected Poems 1968–1986* [statement]
Selected Poems 1968–1986 by Paul Muldoon, Ecco Press, 1987.
Cloth; dust-jacket has a statement by Seamus Heaney.

H11 *Fifty Fables of La Fontaine* [statement]
Fifty Fables of La Fontaine, Translated by Norman R. Shapiro, University of Illinois Press, 1988.
The front flap of the dust-jacket has a statement by Heaney.

H12 [*Letter in Support of Salman Rushdie*] [signatory]
Irish Times, 2 March 1989: 1, 13.

H13 [*Letter in Support of Salman Rushdie*] [signatory]
Guardian, 2 March 1989: 1,13.

H14 *Statement by the International Committee for the Defence of Salman Rushdie and His Publishers* [signatory]
Independent (London), 12 February 1990.

H15 *The Nelson Mandela Irish Reception Committee* [signatory]
Irish Times, 14 February 1990: 9.

H16 *Blood, Earth and Medicine* [statement]
Blood, Earth and Medicine by James Crowden, Parret Press, Somerset, UK, 1991.
Back wrapper has a statement by Seamus Heaney.

H17 *Ulster Trust for Nature Conservation:* Peatlands [poster]
The poster includes an excerpt from Seamus Heaney's poem 'Bogland'. Published by Ulster Trust for Nature Conservation, 1991.
T. P. Flanagan's painting *Where Sheep Have Passed* appears on the poster.

H18 *Ulster Trust for Nature Conservation:* Wetlands [poster]
The poster includes an excerpt from Seamus Heaney's poem 'The Peninsula'. Published by Ulster Trust for Nature Conservation, 1991.
T. P. Flanagan's painting *In Fermanagh* appears on the poster.

H19 *Ulster Trust for Nature Conservation:* Woodlands [poster]
The poster contains an excerpt from Seamus Heaney's poem 'Exposure'. Published by Ulster Trust for Nature Conservation, 1991.
T. P. Flanagan's painting *Lagan Twilight, Barnett's Park, Belfast* appears on the poster.

H20 *Ulster Trust for Nature Conservation:* Meadowlands [poster]
The poster contains an excerpt from Seamus Heaney's poem 'Fieldwork'. Published by Ulster Trust for Nature Conservation, 1991.
T. P. Flanagan's painting *A Summer Meadow, Castle Caulfield*, appears on the poster.

H21 *Mullaghmore Appeal* [signatory]
Irish Times, 19 September 1992: 7.
'We call for the relocation of the proposed Mullaghmore Visitors Center . . .'.

H22 *The Cure at Troy 'Chorus'* [poem/translation]
Programme for *The Cure at Troy* directed by Derek Walcott, Poetry Center of the 92nd Street YMCA, New York, NY, 15 March 1993: [single leaf insert].
The excerpt begins: 'Human beings suffer . . .'

H23 *Markings* [poem]
Programme for *Peile na hÉireann, All-Ireland Football Final*, Dublin, 19 September 1993: 17.

H24 *Petition Urges Northern Ireland Peace Deal* [signatory]
Irish Times, 2 December 1993: 11.
Seamus Heaney is one of 500 signatories. 'We the undersigned believe that there currently exists a real desire for a permanent solution in Ireland. We therefore urge the Irish and British governments to seize any opportunity for peace presented by the Humes–Adams initiative.'

H25 *from The Inferno Canto* 1 [poster]
'from *The Inferno* Canto 1', by Seamus Heaney, MTA (Metropolitan Transit Authority, New York, NY) in cooperation with the Poetry Society of America, Poetry in Motion, 1993.

H26 *Song* [postcard]
'Song', by Seamus Heaney, Poemcard no. 1, 1994, Cathcards: 24 The Heath, Cypress Downs, Dublin 6W. Reprinted from *Field Work*.

H27 *Airy Plumeflights* [statement]
Airy Plumeflights: A Beginner's Guide to Celtic Script & Design, by Timothy O'Neill, Dublin: Lilliput Press, 1994. The back cover has a statement by Heaney.

H28 *On the Eve of President Clinton's Visit* [signatory]
Irish Times, 28 November 1995: 5.
'On the eve of President Clinton's visit we the undersigned are deeply concerned that the opportunity presented by the cease-fire is fast diminishing. . . .'

H29 *The Given Note* [CD sleeve comment]
The Given Note by Liam O'Flynn, Tara Music Company, Dublin, 1995.
The CD sleeve has a statement by Seamus Heaney.

H30 *The Wreck of the Archangel* [statement]
The Wreck of the Archangel by George Mackay Brown, John Murray, Dublin, 1995.
Back cover has a statement by Seamus Heaney.

H31 *Anahorish* [poem]
Programme for *Seamus Heaney–Derek Walcott*, a joint poetry reading at DIA Center for the Arts, New York, 12 April 1996: [3].

H32 *The Harvest Bow* [card]
'The Harvest Bow', by Seamus Heaney, Mill Cottage, Corncraft, Richhill, Co. Armagh, 1996.
Card with harvest bow attached.

H33 *Requiem for the Croppies* [card]
'Requiem for the Croppies', by Seamus Heaney, Mill Cottage, Corncraft, Richhill, Co. Armagh, 1996.

H34 *'Singing Schools'* [linen scrolls]
'Tractors', 'Bogland', 'Thatcher', 'The Tollund Man', 'In Memoriam Francis Ledwidge', 'The First Flight', 'from *Station Island II*', 'Fosterling', 'from *The Cure at Troy*', 'The Errand'; Queens University, Belfast, 1996.
The poems are printed on linen scrolls.

H35 *Standing with Soyinka* [signatory]
New York Review of Books, 24 April 1997: 6.
The letter was signed by seven other Nobel Laureates: Bellow, Gordimer, Morrison, Szymborska, Milosz, Oe and Walcott.

H36 *Reading in the Dark* [statement]
Reading in the Dark by Seamus Deane, Jonathan Cape/Alfred Knopf, 1997.
Cape edition has a statement by Seamus Heaney on back of the dust-jacket; Knopf edition has the same statement by Seamus Heaney on the front flap of the dust-jacket.

H37 *Impediments* [statement]
Impediments by Adrian Rice, Abbey Press, Belfast, 1997 (paperback); 1998 (cloth).
Both paperback and cloth have the same statement by Seamus Heaney on flap of front wrapper/dust-jacket.

H38 *As the Poet Said . . .* [statement]
As the Poet Said . . ., edited by Tony Curtis, Poetry Ireland/Eigse Eireann, Dublin, 1997.

Paperback back cover has a statement by Seamus Heaney.
The book reprints several statements by Seamus Heaney taken from various media sources. One significant source is the section in *Poetry Ireland Review*, 'As the Poet Said' (latterly called 'Pickings & Choosings') compiled by Dennis O'Driscoll. See numbers: 21, 24, 25, 27, 30, 31, 33, 40, 41, 45, 46, 48, 49, 50, 60, 74, 75.

H39 *Medbh McGuckian: Selected Poems* [statement]
Medbh McGuckian: Selected Poems, Winston–Salem, NC: Wake Forest University Press, 1997.
The dust-jacket has a statement by Heaney.

H40 *On the Assassination of Galina Starovoitova* [signatory]
New York Review of Books, 14 January 1999: 65.
The letter was signed by Seamus Heaney and others and sent to the speaker of the Russian Duma on 28 September 1998.

H41 *From Wood to Ridge* [statement]
From Wood to Ridge by Sorley MacLean
Manchester/Edinburgh: Carcanet/Birlinn, 1999 [corrected edition] first published 1989.
The back cover has a statement by Heaney.

H42 *Readings* [statement]
Readings by Sven Birkets, Saint Paul, Minnesota, Graywolf Press, 1999.
Back cover has a statement by Seamus Heaney.

H43 *Elegy for a Departure and Other Poems* [statement]
Elegy for a Departure and Other Poems by Zbigniew Herbert, Ecco Press, New York, 1999.
Dust-jacket has a statement by Seamus Heaney.

H44 *John Clare's Copyright* [signatory]
Times Literary Supplement, 14 July 2000: 15.
Letter protesting copyright restrictions.

TITLE INDEX

Titles are listed alphabetically. Section items are listed in order of appearance in the public domain. Cross-references are cited within the text.

GENERAL INDEX

For each entry section items are listed in order of appearance in the public domain.